Smart Aid for
African
Development

Smart Aid for
African
Development

edited by
Richard Joseph
Alexandra Gillies

LYNNE
RIENNER
PUBLISHERS

BOULDER
LONDON

Published in the United States of America in 2009 by
Lynne Rienner Publishers, Inc.
1800 30th Street, Boulder, Colorado 80301
www.rienner.com

and in the United Kingdom by
Lynne Rienner Publishers, Inc.
3 Henrietta Street, Covent Garden, London WC2E 8LU

Library of Congress Cataloging-in-Publication Data
Smart aid for African development / ed. Richard Joseph
    and Alexandra Gillies.
        p.   cm.
    Includes bibliographical references.
    ISBN 978-1-58826-606-4 (hardcover : alk. paper)
    ISBN 978-1-58826-632-3 (pbk. : alk. paper)
    1. Economic assistance—Africa, Sub-Saharan. 2. Poverty—Africa,
Sub-Saharan. 3. Africa, Sub-Saharan—Economic policy. I. Joseph, Richard A.
II. Gillies, Alexandra, 1978–
HC800.S58   2008
338.910967—dc22

                                                            2008021831

British Cataloguing in Publication Data
A Cataloguing in Publication record for this book
is available from the British Library.

Printed and bound in the United States of America

    5   4   3   2   1

CONTENTS

FOREWORD

Larry Diamond

THIS TIMELY AND COMPELLING BOOK rises from the wreckage of five decades of development failure in Africa, which has also been a failure of analysis and political will on the part of the international community. To the idealism and generosity of spirit that partially motivates aid flows, this volume adds tough-mindedness. The authors—most of whom bring to their chapters several decades of experience in studying Africa and trying to advance its political and economic development—are united in their conviction that aid must be reinvented if Africa is to be lifted out of its persistent poverty and stagnation. Reinventing aid, they make clear, must not only—or even primarily—mean increasing aid. After several decades of large international aid flows to Africa, approaching or exceeding an estimated 1 trillion dollars in total, simply "more" is clearly not the answer. Swimming partially against the tide of global political and moral sympathy that has called for doubling (in effect, unconditionally) aid to Africa, the contributors here appeal for aid to be smartened and made more effective in a number of ways. In the final analysis, "smart aid" is not necessarily inconsistent with more aid, but it is the only way that any amount of aid will be effective.

For at least two decades now, international donors have known that the old practice of unconditional transfers to African governments, however venal and abusive, was not working—that it was failing to lift countries out of poverty, and even doing harm by subsidizing and reinforcing bad governance. But in the midst of the Cold War, Western donors found it hard to cut off or sanction governments whose support they wanted in the competition with the Soviet bloc. With the collapse of the communist bloc (and with it, the Afro-Marxist option) in the late 1980s and early 1990s, a new approach became possible, and since 1990 roughly a score of African countries have made transitions to democracy. Some of these transitions came as Western donors began to pressure or cut off the most hopeless African autocracies. There followed tough and promising talk about the need for better governance to deliver development. "Conditionality" began to shift from economic policy (following the neoliberal "Washington consensus") at least partly to political considerations of open and purposeful governance. However, many of the regimes that would benefit in the 1990s and early 2000s from increasing aid flows were not democracies, but rather—as in Ethiopia and Uganda—autocracies whose leaders had managed to "talk the talk" of governance. A decade and a half later, as each of those countries slips into deepening corruption and authoritarianism under long-serving rulers (Meles Zenawi and Yoweri Museveni, respectively), the need for genuine democracy and not just "good leadership" is increasingly apparent. After all, it was not so long ago that Robert Mugabe was hailed as a progressive leader of a "relatively" democratic system in Zimbabwe. But after almost thirty years in power, that country is nearing collapse under brutal dictatorship, and we are once again reminded of the potentially staggering costs of a system that lacks firm institutionalized means for the constraint and rotation of leaders.

One clear thrust of this book is thus the need for a democratic political context in order for aid to be effective. Without the core institutions of democracy—individual rights, a free press, an open civil society, and free and fair elections to determine who will rule at different levels of government—it is virtually impossible for Africans to monitor what government does and ensure that public resources (including the large proportion of them that derive from international aid flows) will be spent to advance the public good. Yet, "democracy" alone is not enough; about half of the forty-eight states of sub-Saharan Africa now meet at least the minimal test of electoral democracy (as judged by Freedom House), and even most of these are not putting aid to work effectively for development.

Democracy, as Richard Joseph and most of his colleagues in this volume stress, is a necessary but not sufficient condition for aid to be "smart." To make sustained, effective use of aid, African states must wed democracy to good governance. This requires a broader institutional architecture to achieve not only vertical but horizontal accountability. To secure this deeper quality of democratic governance, the key institutions of regulation and oversight must have the legal and operational independence, the financial resources, and the vigorous leadership to hold the executive branch of government accountable, scrutinize one another, and expose and punish corruption and abuse of power. As Peter Anyang' Nyong'o stresses in his eloquent assessment of the long-running tragedy of his country, Kenya, without strong institutions and committed, capable leadership, there is no chance of containing the cancer that corruption has become.

This raises a question that may seem intemperate even for this bold volume: If democracy with serious institutions of accountability is necessary for aid effectiveness, then why give any aid at all, other than urgent humanitarian and health assistance, to states that lack these basic structures? In the absence of strong political mechanisms to ensure that African governments will be accountable to their own peoples, don't large aid flows merely widen the gulf between state and society, reinforcing predatory behavior? Some readers may wish to take the arguments in this book a logical step further and suggest that most *development* assistance (and most of all, general budgetary support) should be conditioned on credible institutional arrangements for democratic and accountable governance: free, fair, neutrally administered and independently monitored elections; a free press; freedom of speech and association; freedom of access to information; budgetary transparency; a parliament with meaningful independent powers; an independent judiciary; serious and autonomous institutions to monitor and prosecute corruption and abuse of power; and perhaps even some devolution of power to elected local government. Similar types of governance standards, I would argue, should be applied to debt relief as well. What is the point of relieving the crippling debts of poor countries if unaccountable, predatory rulers will use the breathing space to continue looting the country while piling up new national debt? Smart debt relief would suspend debt service payments and write down the debt at some steady increment for every year that the country adheres to basic standards of accountable governance. Instead, dumb debt relief has cancelled the debts of the highly indebted poor countries in one fell swoop, while typically securing little in the way of transformed governance in return. Thus, Thomas Callaghy concludes that Nigeria "was given major debt relief too soon" (though he puts the reform emphasis on tough selectivity for economic policy commitment rather than on democratic accountability).

The cry will go out that this is all inappropriate ("neocolonial") interference in the internal affairs of other countries. But when international aid supports 40 or 50 percent of the recurrent budget of a corrupt and repressive authoritarian regime that then delivers little of it to the people in schooling, health care, roads, and other public goods, what is that—neutrality? Or when aid agencies insist on micromanaging the uses of aid both to governments and civil societies, but fail, as the authors of this book note, to focus on the big structural questions of whether any of these actors are democratically accountable, what kind of intervention is that? Broadly, the chapters in this volume suggest that a far smarter approach would be to set certain basic standards or expectations for the structure and quality of governance, monitor those carefully—not unilaterally, but as a partnership among domestic, regional, and international actors (taking seriously the promise in New Partnership for African Development)—and then give countries the freedom to set their own developmental priorities, so long as this is done in the spirit of genuine dialogue between government and citizens.

Such an approach would move away from the old ex ante conditionality: the donor sets certain economic and policy conditions for aid and the recipient promises to meet them, then fails, then renegotiates, then fails again, in an endless cycle of mutual deceit known as the "dance of conditionality." As Joel Barkan explains in his chapter, Kenya under Daniel arap Moi was the poster child for this absurdity, but many other African countries also played the system in this way. The new conditionality is ex post and therefore better understood as "selectivity": standards are set in advance for what is necessary institutionally and in terms of policy performance to qualify for development aid. Those countries that meet the standards get the aid, and the others do not (or do not to anywhere near the same degree). This is the basic operational principle of the Millennium Challenge Account (MCA)—a deliberate attempt to engineer a new vehicle of "smart aid"—but it is not clear that the Millennium Challenge Corporation has been sufficiently tough and independent in the application of the criteria and sufficiently expeditious in negotiating country compacts to make a big difference. And in any case, it is so far just one aid vehicle of just one donor, with a relatively small total budget. Were the "selectivity" approach, focused around democratic and accountable governance, to be applied much more broadly and by the bulk of international aid donors to Africa, one might expect a much more transformative impact. This would especially be so if the criteria were focused more heavily around "governing justly" (which is now just one of three broad categories of conditions applied by the MCA), and if the donors were willing to make the sizeable investments in building institutional capacity that are necessary to help countries put in place serious instruments of democratic governance, such as independent courts, parliaments, electoral management bodies, supreme audit agencies, and counter-corruption commissions.

As many of the chapters in this book make clear, it is not only at the level of Africa's national governments that change must come. Endemic corruption is strongly facilitated by a mass political culture that is accepting of it and that, as the Afrobarometer data presented by Michael Bratton and Carolyn Logan show, generates relatively weak demands from below for accountable government. Accountability involves relationships, not only among government institutions that monitor one another and that hold each other in check, but ultimately between citizens and the state. If ordinary Africans do not look for and demand better governance from their rulers and representatives—if they do not, in the words of Bratton and Logan, become real citizens—then the quest for good governance and broad-based development will lack the national ownership that can elevate it above mere international pressure and give it enduring legitimacy. If the structures of horizontal accountability lack the civic commitment and informed support of a vigilant society, they will gradually be suborned and subverted by die-hard neopatrimonial elements. The battle against neopatrimonialism—the corrupt "big man" syndrome—cannot only be top-down, or it will not be sustainable. But neither can it be only bottom-up, or a mobilized civil society will be able to record few real victories. Fighting the corruption that saps development is not some isolated governance task. It requires a comprehensive, total strategy, an alliance of four types of actors: from below (in civil society), from within the state itself (among civil servants who will execute their duties lawfully and responsibly if given a chance and the right incentives), from above (leaders who envision or reconfigure their interests along good-governance lines), and from outside, in the international community. The task is not simply "reform" of government; it is to change the entire way a political and social system has worked for decades. That can only be done with a sustained, comprehensive approach—and very powerful incentives.

As many of the chapters that follow make clear, the aid agencies and donor governments must themselves change. Currently, their efforts toward reform of aid are too partial and fragmented to bring about the revolution in governance that is needed. The more that donors realign their aid allocations around common, robust standards of good governance with clear expectations for institution building and reform, and the more that they can coordinate their interactions so that weak African states are not left having to comply with literally dozens of different donor agencies and policies, the better the chance for transformative leverage. However difficult this will be for bilateral donors, it will be still more so for the World Bank and other global and regional multilateral donors, which are in theory forbidden to take politics into account and whose effectiveness is undermined by perverse incentives of their own that (as Barkan stresses) put a premium on shoving money out the door.

At the same time, donors need to do a better job of listening to African societies (and empowering them so they can speak). The sad story told by Darren Kew of US aid prescribing specific aid projects in Nigeria while "implementing partners" micromanage the programs over the heads of recipient organizations is all too common in Africa (and beyond). Donors need to do a much better job of responding to what African states and societies see as the specific priorities for generating development and democracy. The key considerations for donors should be that those priorities pursue or observe the principles of good, democratic governance; that they be arrived at through transparent and open dialogue; and that they gradually produce results in terms of development and poverty reduction. As Chapters 8 and 9 on Liberia make clear, the priorities and paths will not be the same in all African countries, and postconflict countries present special needs and vulnerabilities. Inevitably, the country context structures what is necessary and possible and how the broad principles of democratic good governance will be translated into specific institutional realities, requiring what Paolo de Renzio calls here "tailored interventions." This is one reason why Carol Lancaster, with her years of experience in helping to manage the US Agency for International Development, stresses flexibility as a key principle of aid management.

As this book makes clear, we are at a critical juncture. In recent years, moral concerns about Africa's plight have motivated an extraordinary outpouring of engagement and commitment, with significant increases in private and public flows of aid to Africa, as well as much more extravagant official commitments that will not in the near term be met. But rigorous analysis, like that in this book, is showing that the traditional aid approaches have not worked, and that strong institutions and powerful and coordinated incentives are needed to change—no, to transform—embedded patterns of rotten governance. This book offers serious glimmers of hope that we may be arriving at an understanding of what is necessary to bring about that transformation. It will require sweeping change in the content, structure, and underlying assumptions of international aid to generate diffuse norms and potent institutions of accountability. Yet, among societies on both sides of the aid relationship, there is a growing understanding of the need for such sweeping change—to "get smart" in the aid relationship. If international aid donors can gradually refashion their disparate aid programs around these smarter principles and strategies, Africans may someday be able to say of the donor community what Winston Churchill once famously remarked about the United States, that it "will always do the right thing, after exhausting all other possibilities."

ACKNOWLEDGMENTS

THIS BOOK IS THE RESULT of close to five years of planning, thinking, discussion, writing, and revision. We are grateful to the policymakers, scholars, and activists who have been part of this process, several of whom contributed chapters to the book. Their enthusiasm, depth of analysis, and continuing commitment have made for a very rewarding experience. We further express appreciation to the sponsors of several programs at Northwestern University whose support made this project possible: the Ministry of Foreign Affairs of the Netherlands, the John D. and Catherine T. MacArthur Foundation, the Bill and Melinda Gates Foundation, and the UK Consulate General in Chicago.

Our ideas on the topic of aid to Africa and related democracy and governance concerns benefited greatly from interactions with member institutions of the Consortium for Development Partnerships (CDP) funded by the Dutch Ministry of Foreign Affairs. These interactions prompted new thoughts on the important issues in Africa and also on the promise and challenges of international partnerships. The member institutions of CDP are the African Studies Centre–Leiden, Bayero University–Kano, the Centre for Democracy and Development, the Centre for Democratic Development, the Centre for Law and Social Action, Centre pour la Gouvernance Démocratique, the Council for the Development of Social Science Research in Africa (CODESRIA), L'Institut des Sciences Humaines, the Ministry of Foreign Affairs of the Netherlands, the Nigerian Economic Summit Group, Northwestern University, Point Sud, the Royal Tropical Institute, and the University of Ibadan.

Our thanks also go out to members of the staff, past and present, of the Program of African Studies (PAS) at Northwestern University who provided invaluable assistance as the work on this book progressed: Coura Badiane, Kristine Barker, Virginia DeLancey, Nkem Dike, Trina Gunn, Linda Judon, Carmelita Rocha, and Rebecca Shereikis. We also thank Ogechukwu Ezeokoli and Beatrice Nguthu for their research assistance.

We give special thanks to a member of the PAS staff, Kate Dargis, who devoted enormous time and energy to this project. She kept it moving forward whenever progress slowed, and she was a constant source of ideas for its improvement. We cannot imagine the completion of the book without her wonderful assistance.

Widespread poverty persists in sub-Saharan Africa in a world that is experiencing unprecedented growth. Although external aid to Africa has now reached several trillion dollars, there is no sign that a sure path to growth and development has been identified. We hope that this book will improve understanding of this fundamental dilemma and contribute to the formulation of better policies. Ultimately, of course, the answers must be found in Africa. We therefore also hope that the ideas presented in *Smart Aid* will be made readily available to the citizens of Africa and that they will have the opportunity to carry this project forward in a new way.

Richard Joseph dedicates his work on this book to his parents, George Francis and Pearl Theresa.

—*Richard Joseph,*
Alexandra Gillies

1

Smart Aid:
The Search for
Transformative Strategies

Alexandra Gillies and Richard Joseph

IN 2005 UNPRECEDENTED ATTENTION focused on how the global community should address the persistent poverty that characterized sub-Saharan Africa and set it apart from much of the rest of the world. During that "Year of Africa," Prime Minister Tony Blair used the forum afforded him by the UK presidency of the European Union (EU) and G8 to rally a diverse set of constituents and advocates to this cause, who sought to make the year a historical turning point for Africa.

Alongside publicity events and fundraising campaigns, an international Commission for Africa of high-level experts was charged with devising a strategy to launch this transition. Two principal ideas from the resulting report reflect the prevailing wisdom about development assistance. First, much more aid and debt relief for Africa were needed to stimulate economic growth and reduce poverty. Second, the impact of these resources and economic progress generally depended on the emergence of effective and accountable governance.

These two arguments—more aid and better governance—are now at the center of policy debates and action regarding Africa. For instance, the US Millennium Challenge Corporation, created in 2004, has made large grants to countries that show evidence of being well-governed. Poverty Reduction Strategy Papers (PRSPs), which today set the framework for World Bank country assistance, tie the provision of financial resources to improvements in governance and the strengthening of institutions. Similarly, the African Union and the New Partnership for Africa's Development (NEPAD) have advocated a massive influx of external funds and mutual accountability for improved governance among African states.

Will the consensus on these two conclusions produce results that have evaded development assistance efforts for decades? At the peak of the enthusiasm in 2005, and with the pivotal Gleneagles G8 meeting just weeks away, the Program of African Studies of Northwestern University hosted a conference to address this question. Its participants, who included scholars and policymakers from the United States, Europe, and Africa, welcomed the increased attention being devoted to the continent. However, during the ensuing discussions, the need for much more critical thinking about aid and development became apparent. Speakers, drawing on wide experiences across Africa, examined the implications of the current thinking. In particular, they identified the challenges and hazards of massively increasing aid without paying corresponding attention to governance, institutions, and absorptive capacities.

Despite the daunting challenges, conference participants never strayed into the territory of aid-pessimism. They maintained that the donor community *can* play a key role in invigorating development processes in Africa and that some donor initiatives *do* make a difference. The wide-ranging analyses presented at the conference demonstrated that the positive impact of aid depends on the design and implementation of nuanced strategies, an appreciation of the limitations of external actors, and the adoption of a transformative (rather than palliative) mission. To this endeavor, we gave the name *Smart Aid*.

Two years later, although the euphoria of 2005 has subsided, the clear challenges facing Africa have not. Better understandings of what makes aid effective are still needed. Many of the once ubiquitous "make poverty history" bracelets now reside in bottom drawers and perhaps the Live 8 throngs are rocking at a new season of well-intentioned fests. More significantly, the lofty promises of increasing aid levels have fallen short, along with the inevitable slippage in popular attention. The G8 leaders pledged at Gleneagles to double aid to Africa by 2010. However, G8 assistance to the continent in 2006 increased by just 2 percent when the one-time debt relief for Nigeria is excluded (OECD 2007).

Although optimism has abated, 2005 showed that the international community is ready to engage with Africa in a more serious way. The new focus on governance and a willingness to increase aid flows must also be accompanied by realistic and results-oriented strategies. This book emerged from the desire to influence such thinking. In this introductory chapter, we identify several priority concerns, review the volume's contents, and suggest several distinguishing features of smart aid.

The Heart of the Issue:
Incentives and Accountability in Recipient Countries

Several themes from the conference presentations are prominent in the chapters that follow. All participants recognized an essential link between governance and development: without capable and well-led states, sustainable economic advances would remain elusive. They identified a paradox of sequencing. Higher levels of aid would precede the governance environment that is supposedly required to make them effective. Increasing the flow of aid without developing ways to improve probity, transparency, and accountability can reinforce dysfunctional systems. It was also emphasized that African governments encompass a wide range of systems—from failed entities, lacking in legitimacy and capacity, to increasingly consolidated democracies committed to reducing poverty. International engagement must therefore be calibrated to the real nature of African governance and provide incentives to build state capacity, strengthen systems of accountability and inclusion, and facilitate the emergence of robust civil societies.

The shortcomings of aid administration and delivery featured prominently in our deliberations. Aid agencies were seen by conference participants as slow to change their practices. Issues such as the over-reliance on external experts, the creation of parallel structures in recipient countries, the lack of coordination and tied aid were identified as problems many years ago. Yet they persist.

In the conference discussions and in the chapters of this book, issues of incentives and accountability have come to the forefront. Observers of African politics have long noted the concentration of power and resources in the hands of a small elite (Ake 2000; van de Walle 2001; Clapham 1996; Olukoshi 1999). In many countries, such actors benefit greatly from the status quo. To promote positive change, widespread popular demand for development is crucial. Equally challenging, however, is the motivation and behavior of elites since they can accelerate, constrain, or reverse progress.

Incentives can determine whether individuals and collectives find it in their best interests to act in ways that facilitate rather than undermine national development. Economic incentives can influence whether a successful businessperson invests her profits in domestic industry, thereby creating jobs, or instead sequesters them away in foreign accounts. Political incentives can encourage a minister to push for civil service reform, thereby cutting costs and improving performance, rather than just allocating positions among cronies. Mick Moore suggests that governments that rely heavily on domestic tax revenues have a strong interest in boosting the prosperity of their population (Moore 2004). Governments largely dependent on aid or resource rents, however, may lack such motivation (Leonard and Straus 2003; Collier 2007). Institutions and the overall policy environment must therefore be designed to reward pro-development behaviors.

If incentives encourage good behavior, it is also the case that accountability can constrain the bad. When vertical accountability mechanisms exist, such as honest elections, citizens can demand that their government act in ways that advance their interests. In such contexts, the failure to maximize the benefits from a country's resources would not be allowed to continue. Leaders who advance their own interests at the expense of societies would not remain in power long. Institutions such as legislatures, the judiciary, opposition parties, and auditors can enforce horizontal accountability. Parliament can reject ill-conceived budgets, and superior courts can block executive attempts to manipulate public institutions. These mechanisms, and their capacity to elicit responses from those in power, comprise the ingredients of strong domestic accountability. In most of Africa, however, such mechanisms are still weak or absent.

Identifying and building the incentives and accountability systems that underpin development are difficult and complex tasks. Systems that demand and protect good governance depend on myriad relations that tie a society together, particularly between those who enjoy power and those who do not. And these objectives cannot be separated from the wider development context: a healthy and well-educated population is better able to make demands of its government. Moreover, there is much skepticism about how much external actors can meaningfully affect these dynamics (Easterly 2001a, 2006). Consequently, donors have tended to focus their attention and resources on supply-side issues, that is, specific external inputs in the form of loans, grants, equipment, food, medicine, expertise, and policies.

In recent years, external donors, African governments, and citizens worldwide have engaged in multiple assessments of the generally disappointing results of these transfers. There is a growing recognition that externally constructed and supplied "solutions" usually do not work. The weak record of conditionality provides a compelling example (see, for instance, Easterly 2001a; van de Walle 2005), as do the fleeting impact of decades of training programs for public sector personnel.

In recognition of these shortcomings, donors are devoting greater attention to issues of governance and ownership in the hope of influencing the accountability and incentive landscape in recipient countries. The first section of the book focuses on the activities of the donors themselves and how they shape the impact of aid. In the second section, recent donor strategies are evaluated through the prism of pursuit of accountability and incentives. Finally, the third section addresses democracy and governance, international efforts to improve them, and the generally middling outcomes achieved so far.

Donor Limitations: Accountability Dilemmas, Politics, and the International Context

The book begins with chapters on the policies and behaviors of countries and international organizations that provide development assistance. Many of these actors have been involved in Africa for decades and have gained valuable lessons. Examples of learning include the shift of World Bank and International Monetary Fund (IMF) policy away from insisting on the drastic reduction of public sector employment and the imposition of similar conditionalities. However, as will be argued throughout the book, donors still engage in many behaviors that inhibit the effectiveness of aid. Furthermore, donor reform strategies, such as sharp increases in aid and the shift to budget support, can introduce new challenges and risks.

In Chapter 2, Paolo de Renzio reviews challenges that arise from the development community's key priorities of increasing aid and promoting good governance. He shows the interrelationship of these two concerns: donors regard improvements in governance as helping safeguard their increased investments. As aid flows increase, international actors seek to improve local administrative systems, especially by strengthening public finance management. Budget support is another aid modality adopted by donors. It provides donors a way in which aid can be increased without requiring an enlargement of their own administrative operations. Recipient governments enjoy greater latitude in deciding how aid is used. Yet, according to de Renzio, budget support poses macroeconomic and institutional risks that its proponents have not adequately addressed.

De Renzio discusses issues of accountability and the impact of recipient country politics on how aid is actually utilized, themes that feature prominently throughout the book. In aid-dependent countries, donors can hurt domestic accountability if they become the main audience to which governments respond. In a related argument, de Renzio and other authors identify local politics as a frequent donor blind spot. Development partners often focus on formalized statements and rhetorical commitments made by governments, usually crafted to please them. This emphasis on the official comes at the expense of recognizing the political realities of decisionmaking and government behavior.

The issues of accountability, budget support, and aid absorption discussed by de Renzio are prompted by the contemporary emphasis on simultaneously increasing aid and improving governance. Other obstacles that impair donor effectiveness have been around longer and continue to influence outcomes. Carol Lancaster's chapter on US policy identifies factors that have limited the developmental impact of US aid over many years (see Chapter 3). She also suggests why they are likely to endure in the future. Drawing on her extensive research and direct experiences as a USAID administrator, Lancaster suggests three characteristics of smart aid: flexibility, coherence, and coordination. She also identifies factors that inhibit their achievement, such as the congressional earmarking system and the overlapping development mandates of various government agencies. Lancaster discusses the motivations used to justify overseas aid, especially national security interests and humanitarian concerns. She further shows how aspects of the US political system, such as the division of powers, often mitigate against the formulation of clear and consistent policies.

Despite, or perhaps in light of, these shortcomings, donors have tried to enhance the quality of their assistance to Africa and improve relationships with African governments. In Chapter 4 Vivian Lowery Derryck examines the creation of international commissions as a mechanism by which donors can incorporate lessons learned and improve future practices. She gives a generally positive assessment of the UK Commission for Africa and praises its multisectoral approach, its consonance with other initiatives such as the Millennium Development Goals and NEPAD, the raising of public awareness, and its encouragement of partnerships with African governments. Yet Derryck believes the commission was constrained by factors that have traditionally hampered development assistance: competing international priorities, the tendency for Africa to recede from the foreign policy radar, lack of donor coordination, and the difficulty of nurturing long-term public constituencies for international development. While noting the commission's achievements, she also identifies key topics that deserved greater attention: education, gender, and food security.

Evaluating and Learning from Donor Strategies to Improve Aid

The Commission for Africa's activities reflect the upsurge in attention to economic development and poverty alleviation following the decline in aid flows in the 1990s. Along with the mounting frustration with weak development outcomes, this rise can be attributed to several factors.

• The major powers began to perceive failed and lawless states as potential national security threats and liabilities in the escalating war on terror. Frequently citing the example of Taliban-era Afghanistan, several high-level US policy documents place development assistance within this security context, therefore affording it more priority (White House 2002; USAID 2002).

• The widespread optimism that surrounded the end of the Cold War, and the accompanying spread of the third wave of democracy to Africa, abated because of the uneven record of democracy on the continent. Clearly, the sailing was not as easy as anticipated during the heady days of the early 1990s.

• New challenges provoked new responses. Chief among these developments was the HIV/AIDS crisis, which has taken a huge toll on Africa. Its rapid spread prompted new actors to take notice and the donor community to mobilize in new ways. Wars also provoked more urgent responses, such as those in Liberia, Sierra Leone, and southern Sudan, and the rush of donors to assist postconflict Mozambique. More powerfully, the Rwandan genocide illustrated the high cost of noninvolvement.

• The issues outlined above attracted new constituencies that have bolstered the ranks of persons seriously concerned about African development and eager to become directly involved. Prominent among them is the Christian Right in the United States, a newly important advocate for Africa that enjoyed significant political influence during the Bush administration.

• In the 1990s, the contrast between Africa and the rest of the developing world grew more dramatic. As several Asian countries graduated to middle-income status or even higher, the marginalization of Africa within the global economy became more starkly apparent. At the same time, the language and stated aims of African leaders, civil society, and donors converged, creating more common ground. African leaders were more willing to discuss internal political and governance issues and increasingly embraced neoliberal economic strategies. Donors stepped away from the draconian structural adjustment programs of the 1980s and early 1990s, began to recognize the need to "bring the state back in," and prioritized "partnerships" with aid-recipient countries. This commonality of purpose has engendered a less adversarial context than in previous eras.

• A wave of new engagements has drawn greater attention to Africa. The involvement of China, India, and other fast-growing countries has increased, driven in part by efforts to secure access to African energy resources and other mineral wealth. These developments accompany a US effort to diversify its oil import portfolio while a major boom is taking place in commodity prices. New dynamics of foreign involvement in Africa's economies have thus ensued, with potentially significant consequences for governance and development.

In this changing terrain, the donor community has introduced new priorities and strategies. In particular, it has sought to integrate governance and ownership concerns into politically feasible programs that also produce measurable results. In the second section of this book, "Evaluating Strategies for Aid and Debt Relief," several of the more prominent efforts are discussed, including budget support, debt relief, Poverty Reduction Strategy Papers (PRSPs), the Paris Declaration on Aid Effectiveness, and special programs to assist fragile and postconflict states.

Joel Barkan takes up the issue of budget support in Chapter 5. He traces the emergence of this approach within aid policy circles and the motivations driving its application. As part of the current "search for partnership," budget support provides ways of increasing country ownership and reducing transaction costs. Country politics, however, are often poorly incorporated into donor decisions on budget support. The latter's effectiveness is also hampered by the insufficient assessment of noneconomic risks. Echoing another central theme of smart aid, Barkan finds the application of budget support too "supply-side oriented" and not reflecting the "totality of the relationship between the rulers and the ruled." Using the examples of Tanzania and Uganda, he argues that the real incentives driving political behavior in these two countries can undermine the effectiveness of budget support in ways unanticipated by donors. In some contexts, Barkan contends, the prospect of receiving budget support will not, by itself, create sufficient incentives for better governance.

The influence of another kind of external incentive, namely debt relief, is the focus of Chapter 6 by Thomas M. Callaghy. He traces the path of the debt relief movement, from the highly indebted poor country initiatives to Iraqi debt relief, and then details the successful campaign by Nigeria to reduce its large external debt. In 2005, this campaign led to a historic deal in which Nigeria paid off $30 billion of its Paris Club debt for only $12 billion, essentially a 60 percent write-off. Callaghy's account of the negotiations and networking that led to this decision provides a fascinating glimpse of the multiplicity of actors who influence aid and debt policies, such as technocrats, think-tank experts, and development agency officials.

Like Barkan, Callaghy argues that whether debt relief is effective depends on the structure of incentives and recipient country politics. He is concerned that the potentially positive effects of debt relief on policymaking in Nigeria may have already worn off and the reform movement may have lost momentum and direction. Debt relief and budget support can result in sharp increases in the financial resources available to country governments to tackle their development needs. Whether these aims are achieved, however, depends on domestic political and incentive issues that donors often do not have the time or training to understand well.

Drawing on his extensive experiences as a development practitioner, Ian Hopwood offers an evaluation of Senegal's experience with two major donor initiatives in Chapter 7. Like budget support, Poverty Reduction Strategy Papers resulted from a desire to increase country ownership over development planning and to improve donor coordination. Hopwood praises their more explicit focus on reducing poverty, their participatory approach, and the attention paid to harmonization. However, he believes that the gains in practice are still modest. Hopwood's critiques coincide with the concerns about accountability and incentives raised throughout the book and also consider technical obstacles in budgeting and donor staffing. The PRSPs still do not rely sufficiently, he argues, on the "users" of government services and other demand-side groups. Instead, they are conducted in parallel with the country's political process. And they are not well integrated with other national agendas and the work of key ministries.

Hopwood also reviews the mixed record in Senegal of the Paris Declaration on Aid Effectiveness. In 2005, donor community representatives came together in a high-level forum in Paris to discuss issues of ownership, alignment, and harmonization. The resulting declaration spells out the steps they would take to achieve these goals and a monitoring system to track their progress. Even though it is too early to judge the impact of these commitments, Hopwood identifies challenges to be overcome. Such international pronouncements often do not take account of serious obstacles on the ground. Organizational practice and individual incentive issues within donor agencies could produce resistance to harmonization and alignment. These practical concerns reflect one of Hopwood's cardinal points: the effectiveness of aid policies depends not just on their design but also on their implementation by imperfect institutions operating in diverse country contexts.

Recent years have seen the design of new strategies to deal with weak, failing and postconflict states, such as the Organization for Economic Cooperation and Development Fragile States Group, the Commission on Weak States and US National Security, the United Nations Peace Building Commission, and an effort by the European Union to devise a common policy on fragile states. Motivations for this increase include the link between failing states and national security mentioned above, and the persistence of violent conflicts in such countries as Democratic Republic of Congo, Uganda, and Somalia. These environments present daunting challenges for international actors as well as for country governments as they must contend with staggering short-term and long-term needs. In Liberia, for example, the Ellen Johnson-Sirleaf administration inherited a country in which GDP per capita had fallen by as much as 80 percent; where publicly supplied water and electricity had stopped for fifteen years; where, from 2000 to 2005, government spending averaged a paltry $85 million annually for a population of 2.5 million; and where an entire generation of children grew up largely uneducated (Sayeh 2007).

In Chapter 8, John Ohiorhenuan identifies the areas in Liberia that deserve priority attention in order to rebuild an environment that has been thoroughly destroyed. Enhancing security requires programs such as disarmament, demobilization and rehabilitation; civil service reform; and the rapid creation of more jobs. Macroeconomic policy must balance the urgent need to scale up services and connect them to longer-term policies on inflation and debt sustainability. Not to be overlooked are the reasons that prompted the outbreak of violent conflict in the first place. Their elimination may require decentralizing the government, strengthening the rule of law, and initiating truth and reconciliation proceedings. In addition, oversight mechanisms are needed to facilitate the emergence of responsible and accountable economic management.

Ohiorhenuan devotes significant space to the last point, which also is relevant to other chapters in the book. How can transitional or new peacetime governments that often contain former combatants be motivated to act in the long-term interests of their countries? In Liberia, donors introduced a new strategy, the Governance and Economic Management Assistance Programme (GEMAP), to encourage good economic governance. Yet this mechanism also constrains the sovereign autonomy of the Liberian government. Ohiorhenuan raises concerns about GEMAP's strategy of embedding donor representatives in the decisionmaking processes in key ministries. How does such a practice conform to public sector capacity building? Does it create an unsustainable form of external intervention? Do such arrangements improve the short-term political horizons and reduce the systemic corruption that plagued previous government? Arriving at an appropriate mix of political incentives is at the heart of ensuring that postconflict governments have a stake in economic reform.

Good Governance, Democracy, and the Influence of Donors

Along with the measures described above, a significant portion of recent donor activity in Africa has been directed toward advancing democracy and good governance. Since the political openings that followed the end of the Cold War, international and African actors have gained wide experience in promoting such transitions. So far, most African countries have shown highly uneven progress, with states superficially acting in ways that encourage development, and a number of political systems that remain staunchly authoritarian or fall into the category of virtual or pseudo-democracies (Zakaria 1997; Young 1996; Ottaway 2003; Joseph 1998; Diamond 1996). Since the emergence of good governance and democracy depends fundamentally on the evolving relationship between government and the governed, a persistent question concerns how external actors can have a positive impact in this arena.

The chapters in the section on governance and democracy examine donor activities from different perspectives. Taken as a whole, the authors emphasize the importance of effective incentive and accountability systems. They demonstrate that even though external actors can play a positive role, they can also have a negative impact on local governance and democratic dynamics.

Chapters 9 and 10 address corruption, a problem that has spawned much criticism of African governments and their external sponsors. Prominent contributions to the literature on African politics emphasize the embedded nature of corrupt practices in the clientelistic logic that dominates the politics of many African countries (Joseph 1987; Bayart 1993; Olivier de Sardan 1999; Clapham 1996). The chapters by Will Reno and Anyang' Nyong'o follow, to differing degrees, this line of thought as they emphasize the country-specific organization of corruption, its historical roots, and the need for locally driven responses. The variation between their cases, war-torn Liberia (Chapter 9 by Will Reno) and the relatively stable Kenya (Chapter 10 by Peter Anyang' Nyong'o), illustrates how pervasive corruption continues to complicate donor-recipient country relations.

Reno's chapter complements Ohiorhenuan's on Liberia. In this beleaguered country, criminality has triumphed over the rule of law for many years. He reviews how the relationship between corruption and the exercise of political power has evolved during Liberia's postcolonial history. Drawing on comparative examples from East Asia, he offers a provocative analysis of how corruption can sometimes *contribute* to the coherence and effectiveness of the state. Reno's analysis poses challenging options for international actors. He contends that since corruption is an integral part of the political economy of many African countries, overcoming the former will require reinventing the latter. Such a task exceeds what most donors are willing to undertake or could accomplish. This paradox obliges them to consider alternative strategies, such as GEMAP. Reno advances alternatives for how donor involvement might be made more effective. Donors are confronted by difficult choices between promoting reform and advancing national security, as reforms can destabilize local arrangements of power and social relations. One policy option is for the government to work with, rather than dismantle, wartime networks such as youth associations. These networks, unlike donors or even politicians, have links to communities that have disengaged from the formal structures of the state. Some readers are likely to inquire whether such practices would enhance integrity and trust in state operations. Nevertheless, Reno's arguments suggest that corruption cannot be tackled with formal and centralized institutional safeguards like GEMAP alone.

Anyang' Nyong'o's chapter provides a forthright examination of corruption in postcolonial Kenya. The author, a parliamentarian and prominent academic, delivered an earlier version of the chapter to a large audience at the University of Nairobi. It therefore reflects the original aim of reaching a domestic audience. Nyong'o emphasizes the limited effectiveness of international actors in combating corruption as well as their minimal interest in doing so in the past. His contextualized discussion of corruption sheds light on why this problem has been resistant to externally driven counterstrategies.

Despite its close focus on the Kenyan setting, Anyang' Nyong'o's analysis holds instructive lessons for donors: (1) the critical importance of democracy in fighting corruption, (2) the striking gap between government rhetoric and practice, and (3) the urgent need for local answers and local champions to combat corruption. The crafting of domestic political incentives to weaken corruption features prominently in his chapter. By demonstrating the persistence of elite-driven corrupt practices in Kenya, the chapter provides insights that should inform donor strategies and expectations. His recommendations echo Bratton and Logan's insistence on democracy and access to information as key to improving governance and reducing corruption.

In Chapter 11, Michael Bratton and Carolyn Logan use multicountry Afrobarometer survey data to challenge the assumption that voting in elections necessarily endows individuals with ownership of their political systems and the will to control their leaders. Accountable governance, they argue, requires more than just votes. In Africa, the demand for governmental accountability from the electorate remains low, and elected leaders and the various arms of government often enjoy wide latitude to do as they wish. The authors then identify country characteristics, such as political history and elapsed time since decolonization, that influence whether populations *effectively* claim their democratic rights.

The arguments of Bratton and Logan hold important lessons for donor policymaking. The fundamental challenge is to help make government more accountable to citizens rather than donors. The authors propose strategies that can be used to strengthen vertical accountability, such as administrative decentralization, budget transparency, the involvement of electoral representatives in their constituencies, civic education, and others. The Afrobarometer data presented in their chapter and online enable policymakers to learn more about how Africans view their governments. Afrobarometer findings can increase understanding of local contexts upon which aid decisions are made.

Bratton and Logan contend that donors can, inadvertently, weaken domestic accountability through the overuse of conditionalities. Darren Kew takes up similar issues in Chapter 12, on donor–civil society relations in Nigeria. Donors are often drawn to civil society actors as an alternative or supplement to their relations with country governments. Kew describes the evolution of this practice and the patterns that often characterize these interactions. Problematic elements include donor ambivalence about capacity building and the forming of partnerships, and the growth of civil society opportunism as reflected in the emergence of myriad nongovernmental organizations.

Kew's chapter contributes important insights on the role of civil society in fostering a democratic culture. He suggests that civil society groups can advance democracy in two important ways. First, they can provide relevant analysis, oversight, and advocacy. Second, they can serve as "classrooms of democracy" in which individuals learn to engage in citizenship behaviors shown by Bratton and Logan to be deficient. Drawing on two Nigerian case studies, Kew argues that the nature of the relationship between donors and civil society has an impact on the effectiveness of this learning process. Democratically structured relationships bolster democratic learning, but undemocratic interactions can reinforce neopatrimonial tendencies. Kew's case studies demonstrate how administrative decisions that may appear expedient in Western capitals can have negative consequences in Africa.

In Chapter 13, Richard Joseph takes up the link between misrule and underdevelopment and brainstorms about how international actors can contribute to its reversal. The donor community, and actors within Africa, have neither significantly improved governance systems nor created the kinds of agile and predictable institutional environments required for progress in a globalized economy. In response to these shortcomings, Joseph advocates forms of international cooperation that increase institutional capacities and foster norms and behaviors of good governance. The constant drain of skilled workers and professionals from the continent adds urgency to this agenda.

Capacity-building bridges include collaborative programs to improve higher education, innovative international incentives for good governance, greater engagement of the new African diasporas, and creative public-private partnerships. Such interactions should facilitate learning, involve new actors, and provide alternatives to the usually cyclical and unsustainable practices of donors seeking to replenish the drain of African financial and human capital with their own.

The Delivery of Smart Aid

The debate on the future of international development assistance has tended to become oversimplified into two warring camps: aid-optimists, who believe that drastic increases must be made in international development assistance to fill the investment gaps that inhibit growth in Africa; and aid-pessimists, who contend that such massive increases will exacerbate economic underperformance and weak and autocratic governance on the continent. This edited volume is not intended to speak for either camp. Rather, its authors recognize the critical and strategic role that aid can play in strengthening public and private institutions so they can better serve the interests of Africa's people. Assuming a more modest perspective, the authors acknowledge the limited but real potential benefits of foreign assistance to accelerate growth and development. They offer no easy and glib solutions. Instead, the chapters detail the nuanced local understandings and clarity of purpose that are required if smarter use is to be made of aid resources.

Understandably, there are points of disagreement and differences in emphasis among the authors. What is remarkable is the wide area of consensus achieved despite the complexity of the issues discussed and the diverse experiences on which the authors draw. There are certain recurring themes. The achievement of locally determined development goals, and their sustainability, depends ultimately on the nature and interplay of domestic forces, especially local sociopolitical dynamics. These can neither be created nor replaced by foreign actors. If aid is to foster sustainable development, it must facilitate the emergence of enterprising private and public sectors as well as stronger systems of accountability to protect them. Appropriate incentives and transparency are central to the achievement of this mission. Operationalizing these ideas, we recognize, is difficult. However, the tone of this volume remains constructive throughout. Although we recognize the necessity of high levels of aid, we believe more attention should be paid to how it can be a transformative rather than permanent aspect of African governance.

PART 1

Donors and the Delivery of Aid

2

More Aid or Smarter Aid?
Donors, Governance,
and Accountability

Paolo de Renzio

A T THE G8 SUMMIT in Gleneagles in 2005, rich countries pledged to drastically increase development assistance in the wake of reports by the Commission for Africa (2005) and the UN Millennium Project (2005). A few years down the line, however, figures show little sign of aid being "scaled up." In fact, excluding debt relief for Nigeria, aid to sub-Saharan Africa in 2006 increased by only 2 percent in the context of a global decline because other large debt relief operations, including Iraq, ended (see Figure 2.1). Moreover, new aid commitments are mostly linked to specifically targeted initiatives, such as funding for HIV/AIDS programs, education, or climate change.

Many rightly blame donor countries for not living up to their promises, but there are some tensions underlying this debate that deserve to be highlighted. Apart from the domestic political difficulties faced by donor governments in justifying massive increases in foreign aid against competing budget pressures, two factors have shaped the reluctance of donors to provide large additional amounts of aid: worries over aid effectiveness and absorptive capacity, and a perceived lack of progress on the governance agenda that was meant to represent Africa's side of the Gleneagles deal. Just as an example, the Africa Peer Review Mechanism led by the New Partnership for Africa's Development (NEPAD) is making slow progress, whereas the cases of Zimbabwe and Sudan have shown the limited capacity of regional bodies to address difficult governance situations. That could be partly linked to the growing role of China as an alternative source of assistance to African governments.[1]

In this chapter I discuss these underlying tensions, highlighting how the current aid debate does not sufficiently recognize the contradictory role

Figure 2.1   ODA from DAC members, 1990–2006, and Projections to 2010

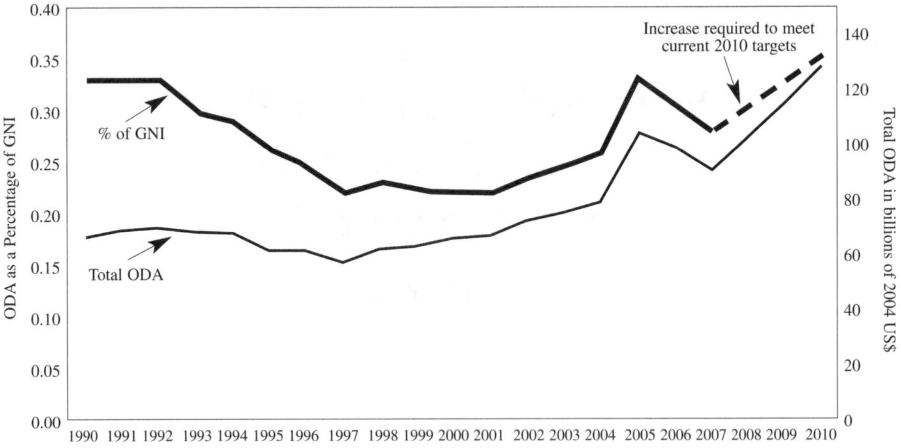

Source: OECD, Development Assistance Committee, 2008, http://www.oecd.org/dac/stats.

that donors play in promoting governance reforms and achieving development outcomes in recipient countries. In order to illustrate the main argument, the case of new aid instruments such as general budget support (GBS, see also Chapter 5 in this volume) will be considered, along with other donor efforts directed at strengthening public financial management (PFM systems) and domestic accountability institutions. These tensions should represent the core of any discussions on how to make aid smarter and therefore more effective.

Aid Effectiveness and Absorptive Capacity

The possibility of large increases in aid flows has sparked a lively debate on aid effectiveness and the issue of "absorptive capacity" (de Renzio 2005b). Given existing doubts on the effectiveness of past aid flows in promoting economic growth and reducing poverty, how can aid increases be managed in order to ensure their effective use?[2] Two issues have emerged in recent academic and policy debates about different aspects of absorptive capacity. The first one relates to the macroeconomic impact of large aid increases (see Heller 2005; Foster and Killick 2006; Birdsall 2007; Gupta et al. 2005), whereas the second one is concerned with the potential political and institutional effects of increasing levels of aid dependency (see van de Walle 2005; Moore 2004; Moss, Pettersson, and van de Walle 2006).

In a recent International Monetary Fund (IMF) paper titled "Pity the Finance Minister," Heller describes the complex issues in macroeconomic management facing recipient governments should aid double in size. First, large inflows of foreign currency could trigger "Dutch disease" effects and reduce the competitiveness of the country's exports. "Thus, while foreign assistance may enable a resource transfer to an aid-recipient country—providing vital commodities and financing the provision of critical social services as well as investments—the downside effect might be a weakening of a country's capacity to grow itself out of poverty and aid dependency" (Heller 2005, p. 5).

Second, financing a higher portion of government expenditure through a source such as aid, which is highly volatile and unpredictable, can be quite risky for monetary and fiscal policy. Donor conditionalities and bureaucratic procedures often mean that aid resources are not fully disbursed or made available without considerable delays. This preempts the recipient government's capacity to adequately plan and implement a number of activities, especially those that require the hiring of personnel and the delivery of services to the population.

Turning to the political and institutional implications of scaling up, Todd Moss, G. Pettersson, and Nicolas van de Walle talk about the existence of an "aid-institutions paradox": although one of the primary purposes of aid is to "build effective indigenous public institutions" (2006, p. 4), one of its unintended consequences may be to undermine that same objective. Just as with oil, there can be an "aid curse" that might create "perverse incentives and lead to anti-developmental outcomes" (p. 5). Because they relax resource constraints and therefore perpetuate government inefficiency, high (and increasing) aid flows can allow governments to postpone much-needed public sector reforms. As Joel Barkan also contends in Chapter 5 of this volume, by financing incumbent governments, donors may be preventing healthy domestic accountability mechanisms from developing, potentially propping up antidevelopment regimes (see Lockwood 2005, p. 68).

There are also clear institutional and technical constraints at play. In low-income countries, more capacity is needed to generate credible strategies, policies, and programs to transform higher aid levels into positive development outcomes. Planning and budgeting systems, along with service delivery mechanisms, may not be adequate to absorb large increases in available resources without increasing wastage or fueling leakage and corruption. Human capital shortages may prevent a quick scale-up of service delivery, especially in health and education, where qualified doctors, nurses, and teachers are key.

Donors, Governance, and General Budget Support

The response to these challenges by aid advocates, which inevitably includes most donor agencies, is that a good part of the solution lies in the use of new modalities that promote a different dynamic between donor agencies and recipient governments, moving beyond old-style conditionality and addressing issues of proliferation and fragmentation of donor interventions. The general argument claims that some of the main determinants of aid effectiveness are *government ownership* of development policies and better *donor coordination* to reduce the transaction costs generated by aid management. Channeling resources through the recipient country's budget is a way of addressing both concerns at the same time. In those countries with a good performance record and stronger institutions, providing direct support for the implementation of sectoral policies, or more generally to the national budget, has therefore come to be seen as a way of addressing issues of absorptive capacity, while at the same time strengthening domestic accountability mechanisms. This conclusion has been reflected in donor programming in a number of countries—but notably not in the United States—where aid flows are increasingly being channeled through budget support programs. Surveys carried out for the Strategic Partnership with Africa (SPA) showed that GBS amounted to 25.7 percent of the total aid from SPA donors to a sample of African recipients in 2004, going up to 27.8 percent in 2005 (SPA 2006).

Despite this trend, however, available evidence presents contradictory views on the effectiveness of budget support as an aid modality. The first evaluation of GBS carried out in Tanzania (Lawson et al. 2005) shows that it has been associated with a major expansion in health and education services. However, a number of shortcomings were also noted: (1) there were few signs of improved efficiency of public spending or of long-term obstacles to service quality being addressed; (2) the role of parliament in the budget process has remained weak, mainly for political but also for more technical reasons; and (3) the expected improvements in intragovernment incentives and democratic accountability are not yet apparent.[3] Although outcomes have improved remarkably in respect of macroeconomic stability, investment, and growth, at the same time poverty impacts remain uncertain. In summary, budget support in Tanzania has not generated many of the positive effects expected of it, some of which are necessarily long-term. But the gains that have been made are important and, most likely, would not have been achieved by any other aid modality.

The more comprehensive cross-country evaluation of GBS programs highlights the diversity of reasons that led to the adoption of budget support as an aid modality in different countries, and the arrangements that were put in place to manage it.[4] Changes in the nature of dialogue and conditionality, considered inherent in budget support programs, have "tended to be gradual, to be present as an intention before [they are] realised in practice, and to be more significant in the eyes of the donors than in those of partner governments" (IDD and Associates 2006, p. S3). Moreover, the vulnerability of budget support to political risk is seen as the result of inadequate analysis carried out before channeling funds through local budget systems. Nevertheless, the evaluation found that GBS has supported increases in pro-poor expenditure, in allocative and operational efficiency, and in government discretion. It has also contributed to strengthening budget processes, in particular by "requiring sector ministries to engage directly in the national budget process," and improving public finance management, despite the need "for more systematic collaboration to support coherent national PFM capacity building strategies" (p. S5). To the extent that budget support has had "greater penetration (by virtue of its duration, relative importance . . . and the sophistication of dialogue arrangements it supports and uses)" (p. S6), it has also been more efficient in strengthening incentives for policy reform within government.

There are, however, a number of caveats the study highlights. First, "the continuation of parallel off-budget modalities undermines progress." Despite the fact that budget support can be seen as only one of a range of modalities donors can use, its coexistence with a large number of fragmented projects can significantly limit its positive effects.[5] Second, the evaluation finds that "technical solutions are not effective or durable without political commitment" and that budget support "does not transform underlying political realities." Although that might sound like an obvious statement, its implications can be quite substantial, as is argued below.[6] Third, "donors need to be careful that their accountability demands do not overshadow those of national institutions" and "need to be sensitive about becoming too intrusive" (IDD and Associates 2006, p. S6). The last issue will also be addressed in more detail in a later section.

A more critical view of budget support is presented by Tim Unwin, who claims that "budget support, as the preferred means of delivering the economic growth and liberal democracy agenda, is much more problematic than many working in donor agencies are willing publicly to acknowledge" (2004, p. 1512). Among the reasons for this are (1) the lack of predictability that comes from existing governance and the fiduciary risks to which budget support is subject; (2) the incapacity of donors to recognize that African political systems are often incompatible with the sort of participatory processes and transparent administrative practices that form the basis for budget support; and (3) the fact that donors use budget support as a way of "pushing money out the door" as their budgets increase while staff numbers are reduced.

These contradictions have been picked up by a number of authors who support the view that an "aid-institutions paradox" indeed exists (see also Chapter 5 in this volume). With different degrees of criticism of current trends in the aid system, they question the role that donors are playing in supporting poverty reduction efforts in aid-dependent countries. Nicolas van de Walle (2005), for example, claims that the root causes of poverty in many poor countries lie in the entrenched clientelist nature of their political systems. Aid, he argues, can play a positive role, but only if donors come to grips with the politics and incentives that currently prevail in many poor countries. That has not happened so far. By pursuing contradictory objectives and policies, donors have promoted what he calls "*ventriloquism,* in which the donors make clear what their policy expectations are, and governments understand what they need to say and do in order to get the foreign assistance" (van de Walle 2005, p. 67; emphasis in original). Underlying all this are political systems in which formal democratic rules are often just a respectable façade for well-established networks of patronage that see the state not as a developmental agent, but as a source of the rents that keep the cogs of the clientelist machine spinning. In such systems, budget systems and processes are manipulated to serve this purpose.

Some of these arguments are reflected in a study of the budget process in Malawi (Rakner et al. 2004), where the "theater" of respecting formal rules and procedures is coupled with the predominance of informal practices that determine the way in which budget resources are actually distributed and reflect the clientelistic nature of the country's political system. In such an environment, donors exerted little influence over budget policies or reform efforts, since a high level of mistrust between the government and donors created vicious circles of budget-support suspensions and reform reversals (see also the analysis in Booth et al. 2006).

A slightly different argument is presented by Graham Harrison, who examines the cases of Uganda and Tanzania and discusses "post-conditionality" politics in these two countries. In selected better performing countries, Harrison argues, the relationship between donors (especially the World Bank) and governments has moved beyond the arm's-length conditionality approach typical of structural adjustment programs to a "post-conditionality" approach where donors are much more closely involved in policymaking. We see this, for example, in the support they give to administrative reforms (including budget reforms) in central ministries, and in the arrangements related to GBS operations. "Within post-conditionality regimes, it becomes far less insightful to make distinctions between external and internal interests. . . . [Donor intervention] is not exercised solely through conditionality and adjustment, but to a significant degree through a *closer* involvement in state institutions and the employment of incentive finance" (2004 p. 77).

This new type of arrangement brings about a sort of mutual dependence between donors and state elites, whereby governments dependent on high levels of donor funding do their best to comply, at least formally, with the reform agenda being promoted by donors, and donors get to use these countries as "success stories" in international arenas. All that, however, takes place at the expense of a more genuine and transparent debate over reform agendas (for the case of Mozambique, see Hodges and Tibana 2004; de Renzio and Hanlon 2007).

According to these views, a complex picture emerges of donor roles in promoting the effective management of aid resources through national budgets. Although donor agencies recognize, at least informally, many of these issues and contradictions, much of their effort has focused on finding ways to bypass them rather than confront them directly. Examples are the promotion of budget reforms aimed at increasing government leadership and control and strengthening formal systems and support for domestic accountability institutions such as parliaments, auditors, and civil society to foster environments more conducive to government transparency and responsiveness. In practice, however, these efforts often boil down to experiments in the social and political reengineering of African societies that donor agencies are not well suited to undertake.[7]

Can Donors Promote Budget Reforms and Domestic Accountability?

Existing evidence from budget reform processes to some extent corresponds to the mixed picture described above for budget support, highlighting the difficulties faced by countries undergoing budget reforms and by the donor agencies that support them. William Dorotinsky and Robert Floyd (2004) have summarized some findings for heavily indebted poor countries (HIPCs) since the mid-1990s. They conclude that, even though budget formulation has improved in a number of countries, budget execution and accountability are still very weak in the majority. Thus, fewer than a third of the twenty countries surveyed adhered closely to the budget as adopted, and 90 percent of the African countries surveyed failed to produce final audited accounts within twelve months of the end of the fiscal year, rendering meaningful parliamentary oversight impossible. A more recent review of progress in twenty-six HIPCs (IDA and IMF, 2005), based on sixteen different indicators of the quality of budget systems, found that their performance showed a slight improvement overall between 2001 and 2004, though the extent of progress was mixed across countries and indicators. These mixed results happened despite substantial donor support, with an average of seven donor agencies involved in supporting budget reforms in each country.[8]

A recent World Bank evaluation, *Capacity Building in Africa* (World Bank 2005a, pp. 28–29), concludes that "while there have been successes, Bank support for capacity building has encountered considerable difficulty in the area of public financial management." The report criticizes the frequent focus on reorganizing government units and introducing sweeping, unfamiliar techniques such as performance budgeting that have been "transplanted from outside the country" and "depend on consultants for implementation." (p. xv) The authors point out that capacity-building efforts can be undermined by difficult "governance issues," including the nonimplementation of agreed-upon reforms, particularly in sensitive areas such as procurement and parliamentary oversight.

Donors have also supported domestic accountability mechanisms, not only as part of the democratization process but also as a necessary condition for improving the effectiveness of aid resources channeled through national budget systems.

Parliaments

Parliaments can play an important role in keeping the executive arm of government accountable for the use of public resources. Parliaments approve budget legislation, authorizing governments to raise revenues and spend them on maintaining their apparatus and delivering services, and analyze audited accounts, verifying whether governments have in fact delivered on budget promises. In reality, however, their effectiveness in Africa varies, depending on institutional, political, and capacity factors.

Among the factors shaping the role of parliaments are: (1) *budget calendars,* which determine how much time parliamentary committees are given to analyze budget proposals before approving them; (2) the constitutional definition of *amendment powers,* which state the extent to which parliaments have the right to reject or amend budget proposals and reports submitted by the executive; (3) the availability of and access to *technical advice* (such as the existence of a parliamentary budget office) to support parliamentary analysis and decisionmaking on budget proposals and reports; and (4) the characteristics of *political regimes,* such as their presidential or parliamentary nature, the number of political parties in parliament, the dominance of the party in power in terms of majority votes in parliament, and so on (see Wehner 2004). These various characteristics will determine the degree and significance of parliamentary intervention in the budget process, both at the approval and at the oversight stages.

A study carried out on patterns of accountability in Tanzania (Lawson and Rakner 2005), found that parliament's role in holding the executive accountable is currently not very effective. The formal measures to enforce accountability may be in place, but often the spirit of their intent is lost in the mechanistic way they are applied. Legislators need the right incentives in order to play a more meaningful role, both in terms of encouragement by their political parties and having the necessary information and resources. Similar findings exist for Ghana (Killick 2005). In a review of Latin American legislatures, Carlos Santiso argues that "capacity constraints and information asymmetries tend to explain why parliaments do not exercise their budgetary powers effectively, while governance constraints and the nature of executive-legislative relations tend to explain why they sometimes do not exercise them responsibly" (2004, p. 70). This is an important point.

Even if some of the systemic weaknesses that undermine the role of parliaments as a domestic accountability check on national budgets were tackled, it would not automatically lead to improved budget processes and outcomes, or to budgets that better reflect rational policymaking or a poverty focus. As Allen Schick warns, "one scenario is for the legislature to reinforce fiscal discipline . . . another is for it to undermine discipline by bombarding the budget submitted by the government with legislative amendments that trim revenues and boost expenditures" (2002, p. 15).

In a review of the role of parliaments in four African countries, Barkan and his colleagues (2005, p. 252) note that "the extent of a legislature's authority is largely a function of the evolving incentive structure confronting individual members of the legislature" and that the incentive structure is heavily influenced by the structure of African societies, characterized by clientelistic politics and weak political parties. Thus legislators spend much time worrying about patronage politics and looking after their own constituencies rather than focusing on their policymaking and legislating function or on executive oversight through the work of the parliamentary committees. Donor support for parliaments has been limited to a small number of agencies focusing on technical support and has been seen as a complex area, also because of the potential negative effects of electoral processes and shifts in institutional leadership. Nick Manning and Rick Stapenhurst (2002) claim that some factors for the success of parliamentary support activities include linking legislative assistance to broader reform processes and ensuring domestic political support for strengthening the legislature's role.

Supreme Audit Institutions

Supreme audit institutions (SAIs) are another important type of budget oversight institution. They take different forms in different institutional settings (auditors-general, *cours des comptes,* administrative tribunals, etc.), reporting to either parliament, the supreme court or an audit board, with the role of checking government accounts through audits in order to ensure the proper and effective use of public funds, compliance with laws and regulations, and transparency through the publication of audit reports (DFID 2005).

A review of the functioning of SAIs in Malawi, Tanzania, and Uganda (Wang and Rakner 2005) suggests that the institutional capabilities of the supreme audit institutions are limited in all three countries. Limitations belong to four categories: (1) *mandate,* as in some cases when SAIs do not report directly to parliament, or the scope of their audit is limited to certain categories of spending or by the existence of off-budget funding; (2) *capacity,* in terms of both financial and human resources; (3) *autonomy,* as the effectiveness of SAIs is often limited by appointment and dismissal procedures or by the need to lobby government or donors for the necessary resources; and (4) *relational resources,* in particular with parliamentary committees and with the media and civil society, to ensure adequate follow-up to audit findings.

Rick Stapenhurst and Jack Titsworth (2001) highlight similar challenges but add the need for a supportive institutional environment for SAIs to function effectively, including a good relationship with the ministry of finance, both in terms of supplying information and following up on recommendations, and the importance of linking into international audit knowledge networks and harmonizing with international standards. Limited donor coordination and off-budget donor funding also remain a concern in ensuring the effectiveness of the audit function within budget processes.

Civil Society

Civil society involvement in budget policies and processes is a relatively new phenomenon, stemming from an emerging international consensus on the need for more transparent and inclusive budgeting processes and for more civil society participation in development policy in general. Civil society budget work takes a number of forms, including linking applied research and advocacy campaigns to the production of timely and accessible information on government budgets, training grassroots groups, and monitoring budget implementation (International Budget Project 2001). Although civil society budget monitoring is more common in middle-income countries, independent budget groups are now active in a number of low-income countries as well. This trend has become more apparent as donor countries have started providing specific support for civil society organizations to monitor the use of resources freed up by debt relief programs and provided as budget support.[9]

The Uganda Debt Network, for example, has been quite successful in putting pressure on the government to improve budget implementation in some key service delivery areas such as health and education, by training local monitors who check the implementation of government-funded contracts and by reporting the results of such monitoring both in policy forums at the national level and through the media (Azeem, de Renzio, and Rankumar 2006). In Tanzania, however, Lawson and Rakner (2005) found that civil society is rather weak as a source of "societal accountability" and plays a limited role as a democratic check on executive power.

The capacity of civil society groups to influence government policies depends on a number of factors:

1. The nature and characteristics of the *political environment* and the existence of institutionalized channels for civil society involvement and

participation in the budget process. Such opportunities may be created by processes of political transition, such as in the case of South Africa (de Renzio 2005b). Alternatively, they may depend on government initiatives, similar to the ones taken by the Brazilian Workers Party (Partido dos Trabalhadores) in Porto Alegre and other municipal councils, where part of the investment budget was allocated on the basis of participatory budgeting processes that relied on civil society participation.[10]

2. The degree of *transparency* and *access* to budget information, which determines the degree to which civil society organizations can analyze and assess the government's budget policies and proposals. In a review of thirty-six countries (Gomez, Friedman, and Shapiro 2005), the International Budget Project found that two-thirds of countries regularly make available some of the key budget documents but fail to release other essential information, and even then, access is limited and sometimes only granted upon request. Moreover, scores for the "facilitating public discourse and understanding" category are much lower, revealing the reluctance of governments actively to promote more openness in the budget process.[11]

3. Internal *capacity* constraints, relating both to the technical skills necessary for budget analysis, which may be in short supply outside the public sector, and to the necessary linking of such analysis to wider advocacy work, including building networks with other civil society organizations and with key officials within government and other institutions.

4. In many cases, the existence of *donor funding,* which represents one of the few available sources of financing for civil society organizations to carry out budget monitoring and advocacy activities. The associated risk, however, is that of undermining the independence and credibility of the analysis, either because the authors may not want to be seen to criticize donor behavior, or because they may be domestically accused of being on the donors' payroll.

This brief review of the evidence suggests that the role of donors in promoting budget reforms and strengthening domestic accountability institutions is not a straightforward one, in the sense that large interventions in the form of technical support and capacity building are likely to yield immediate benefits, as Ian Hopwood demonstrates in Chapter 7 of this volume. Rather than being based on abstract notions of technical fixes and global "best practices," donor support should recognize the limitations posed by political and institutional factors, which shape the environment in which institutional reform takes place. Donors should tailor interventions to each specific arena, mindful of the contradictions highlighted in previous sections.

Conclusion

Recent aid debates, linked to commitments by the G8 countries to substantially scale up their development assistance programs, have focused on ways of addressing some of the perceived underlying causes of low aid effectiveness. Donors have responded by introducing programmatic support modalities, such as sectoral and general budget support, aimed at increasing country ownership of development policies and programs; reforming and strengthening planning and budgeting institutions; and correcting for distortions in accountability stemming from aid dependence. The available evidence to date, however, only partially supports the arguments made in favor of such shifts.

The role that donors can play in strengthening government ownership, budget systems, and domestic accountability is more complex than many are willing to admit. Different actors and interests play different roles in shaping government policies and priorities. In aid-dependent countries, accountability mechanisms are shaped both by external factors, such as the influence of donors on budget choices, and by domestic factors, including clientelist practices and the role played by parliamentary committees and civil society organizations. Formal processes and procedures can be in contradiction with informal forces, and institutional incentives defined by existing rules and regulations may not be mirrored by individual ones driven by personal interest and patronage.

The key question, then, is what can be done to ensure that aid (whether it increases or not) is channeled in ways that address absorptive capacity constraints, maximize its effectiveness, and promote better governance. These three issues are heavily intertwined, as stronger country institutions will be better able to use aid effectively, but aid itself, as we have seen, can undermine institutional strengthening. No ready-made solutions are available, but the least that donors can and should do is recognize the existence and the potential implications of the aid-institutions paradox and look for ways to address it. Doing so might imply reconsidering the rationale behind the "scaling up" of aid; giving more emphasis to the quality of aid flows and of the relationship between donor agencies and recipient governments; and putting politics, governance, and accountability concerns at the center of the aid effectiveness debate.

Notes

This chapter draws heavily on two previous articles, de Renzio 2007 and 2006.

1. In an interview with the *Financial Times* on February 6, 2007, Meles Zenawi, Ethiopian prime minister, was quoted as saying, "Good governance can only come

from inside; it cannot be imposed from outside. That was always an illusion. . . . What the Chinese have done is explode that illusion."

2. See, for example, the sweeping critique contained in Easterly 2006.

3. In particular, the study notes that "there appears little evidence of parliament's scrutiny of public finances improving significantly since the expansion of discretionary funding in the budget" and also that "doubts remain over the depth of [Tanzanian NGOs' capacity] to challenge decisions over resource allocation. In summary, the evaluation did not find clear evidence of improving accountability to domestic stakeholders" (Lawson et al. 2005, p. S6).

4. The evaluation covered seven countries (Burkina Faso, Malawi, Mozambique, Nicaragua, Rwanda, Uganda, and Vietnam) and was coordinated by the Development Assistance Committee of the OECD. See IDD and Associates 2006.

5. This point is also made in the case of Ghana by Quartey (2005), and is an important one in the sense that it further undermines the scope for enhancing domestic accountability, which is almost by definition limited to on-budget funds.

6. Williamson (2006, p. 147) argues that in the cases of Uganda and Tanzania, high-level political support for PFM reform preceded the onset of GBS as an aid modality, highlighting how "the role of GBS in upgrading PFM systems was secondary to these [internal] factors."

7. See, for example, some of the discussion on the role of donors in Chapter 11 in this volume.

8. The total spending of donor agencies on public sector financial management jumped from $6 million in 1990 to $150 million in 1995 and $800 million in 2001 (OECD, Creditor Reporting System database, www.oecd.org/dac/stats/idsonline; in 2002 prices).

9. Interestingly, however, a recent study carried out by CARE and ActionAid International (2006) points out how the shift to GBS has excluded NGOs from forums where crucial issues such as conditionalities, budget allocations, and spending limits are discussed between donors and governments.

10. For more information on participatory budgeting, see De Souza (2001). In other towns across Brazil, however, where local governments were less open and responsive, civil society found it much more difficult to engage with the budget process (de Renzio 2005b). This contradiction, and some of the factors shaping the success of participation and pro-poor budgeting, are further discussed in Brautigam (2004).

11. In some cases, despite a general lack of budget transparency, civil society organizations have been able to put pressure on governments to improve service delivery. For the example of Mazdoor Kisan Shakti Sangathan in India, see Jenkins and Goetz (1999).

3

How Smart Are Aid Donors? The Case of the United States

Carol Lancaster

TO PROVIDE SMART AID—aid that is effective in promoting economic and social progress in recipient countries—you need smart aid donors, as well as capable and committed recipient governments. Considerations of smart aid typically focus on capacity: the capacity of aid donors to understand and deliver effective aid, as well as the capacity of recipient governments to use it well. But there is also an important discourse on the willingness of recipient governments—especially those in Africa—to use aid well for development. Corruption, disorganization, patronage politics, and political repression can all impede the impact of what would otherwise be smart aid.

Another part of the smart aid discourse that is often neglected is the willingness on the part of donor governments to provide smart aid. Here the problem is often less one of capacity or corruption than of domestic politics. And those politics are very evident in US aid programs where the allocation and use of aid are heavily constrained by the influence of domestic interest groups and congressional earmarks as well as by the diplomatic imperatives of the administration. This chapter explores the impediments to smart aid emanating from these sources on US aid to Africa. It begins by considering what smart aid is and is not from the point of view of the aid-giving government and examines the constraints on smart aid based on domestic politics. It goes on to examine the deep determinants of those constraints and concludes with a look into the future of smart US aid.

Is US Aid to Africa Smart?

First, what is smart aid? It is easy to identify but difficult to define. It is aid that works to achieve the goals of the donor and recipient. In terms of development (another word with contested meanings), it usually means aid that supports economic growth and poverty reduction, social inclusion, and democracy and good governance in recipient countries. Aid for controlling river blindness is an example of smart aid—well planned and implemented, adequately funded and effective. Aid that helps expand quality education for girls is smart aid. Aid that supports needed currency adjustments that can be sustained is usually smart. Aid that enables free and fair first elections to take place is typically smart too. Aid that fails to achieve its goals because it is poorly planned, badly implemented, inappropriate to local needs and conditions, and underfunded is clearly dumb aid.

Aid that is provided for purposes other than development is not necessarily dumb aid; but its smartness should not be judged on the basis of its contribution to development. In the case of the United States, foreign aid has always had multiple goals, of which promoting development and furthering US national security interests have predominated. A rough estimate is that approximately half of US economic assistance is shaped by national security concerns, and that has been the case for a considerable time.[1] The political imperatives of allocating substantial amounts of aid to countries whose governments are weak, corrupt, repressive, and uncommitted to the betterment of their peoples' lives led to large amounts of assistance being provided to the former governments of Democratic Republic of Congo, Somalia, Sudan, and others. That was not smart aid from a development point of view. In some cases, this aid may have even undercut development progress by prolonging poor governments in power. Whether it was smart aid from the point of view of US diplomacy can also be questioned.[2]

Although we may know smart aid for development when we see it (though often considerable time must pass before we can make a firm judgment), it is harder to define in advance whether a particular aid-funded activity is smart. Whether aid works depends on the capacity of the donor to understand the problems it is attempting to address, the donor's ability to shape its aid to help resolve those problems, the willingness of the recipient to collaborate with the donor in resolving those problems and the capacity to do so, and—usually outside the control of aid donors—a context of aid giving over time that facilitates success. And for us to know whether aid has been smart, we need to be able to identify the results of aid interventions, including being able to attribute results to the intervention when typically there are myriads of intervening variables.

Clearly, this process is not simple. Donors often fail to understand the complex problems of African development, whether they are planning projects, program support for policy reforms, or support for ministerial budgets. And the most complex and difficult problems are those at the heart of the development process in Africa—the functioning (or nonfunctioning) of African institutions, involving both states and markets. We know that they are extremely important. But we often do not know why they function poorly (there is no widely accepted theory of institutional functioning); and we seldom know what to do about their poor functioning. Indeed, donors often exacerbate institutional weakness with their multiple and diverse advice and aid interventions. One could apply a common saying to aid and state institutions in Africa: what doesn't kill them (through transaction and other costs) may (through capacity development) make them stronger. But there is no guarantee.

The other major problem with defining smart aid is that it may turn out to be smart (i.e., effective) or not depending on circumstances that are not under the control of either donor or recipient and are often unforeseeable. A spillover of conflict from one state to another can destabilize the latter and undercut all the good that aid intervention could have accomplished. A major economic disruption, for example, a collapse in export prices or a surge in the price of energy and food imports, can undercut aid effectiveness by making it difficult for a government to buy from abroad what the country needs to produce and consume. And where aid fails, it is not always easy to ascertain whether it was planned and implemented poorly or whether the political or economic context undercut its effectiveness. We are pretty sure the $1.6 billion in aid the United States has provided Democratic Republic of Congo (DRC) since 1960 has failed to produce lasting positive development results, mainly because of the political context of corruption, incapacity, and conflict. But what about the nearly $2 billion in US aid to Kenya over the same time period? How much was smart and how much was not and why?

The main purpose of this chapter is to explore one element in the capacity of the United States to provide smart aid: that is, the role of domestic politics of aid giving in the United States. My central argument is that because of domestic politics, the capacity of the United States to provide smart aid is seriously constrained, and these constraints are not likely to disappear anytime soon.

Impediments to Smartness in US Foreign Aid

What explains the mixed purposes of US aid that has limited its smartness from a development point of view? Two important elements to be considered in answering these questions are the fundamental ideas shaping US aid and the political institutions within the United States that have influenced the politics of aid giving.

Ideas

The major ideas shaping US aid reflect a fundamental tension in US history and society between classical liberals (and libertarians), who prefer limited government, and humanitarians, who regard the state more expansively as a vehicle for redistributive policies at home and abroad. In no other aid-giving country has the debate on foreign aid between these two traditions been as clearly defined and enduring. It commenced in the US Congress in 1794 and surfaced again in Congress during the Irish potato famine. In both cases the libertarians won, arguing that the use of US public funds to provide benefits to foreigners was inappropriate and prohibited by the Constitution. However, the acceptance of the use of public resources for relief abroad gradually increased through the nineteenth century, and by the end of World War I it was unquestioned (see Lancaster 2006, chap. 3).

But the libertarian argument still had considerable currency. It resurfaced in the aftermath of World War II in response to the proposal to create an aid program for stabilization and development abroad—a much more ambitious set of goals than aid for relief. For example, in his 1960 book, *The Conscience of a Conservative,* Barry Goldwater declared,

> The American government does not have the right, much less the obligation, to try to promote the economic and social welfare of foreign peoples. Of course, all of us are interested in combating poverty and disease wherever it exists. *But the Constitution does not empower our government to undertake that job in foreign countries,* no matter how worthwhile it might be. Therefore, except as it can be shown to promote America's national interest, the Foreign Aid program is unconstitutional. (Goldwater 1960; emphasis in original)

Since Goldwater's day, the arguments about foreign aid have been more about the effectiveness of aid in furthering economic and social progress in poor countries. Initially, those opposing aid argued that because it strengthened the states receiving it, it was bound to be ineffective and also have deleterious side effects. In any case, according to crititcs, it seldom reached those who really needed it. Aid's advocates, the humanitarians, arguing often from the left of the political spectrum, claimed that adequate quantities of aid fostered the preconditions for development (infrastructure, education, and health services). It also could be used to leverage reforms in poor countries to support economic growth and poverty reduction and, when targeted to the poor, could help improve livelihoods. Aid should therefore be provided generously. Since the 1990s, arguments that aid has been ineffective have been based more on empirical findings, especially with regard to sub-Saharan Africa.[3] The argument continues today between those, like Jeffrey Sachs, who urge major increases in aid, especially for African countries, and others, like William Easterly, who argue that such aid would be wasted or worse given the problems of weak institutions and limited absorptive capacity.

The prolonged debate in the United States on foreign aid appears to have had a few adverse consequences: dampening public support for aid, reinforcing the views of the skeptics, and raising doubts about aid's efficacy among those without strong opinions. A variety of public opinion polls has shown that just over half of the public tend to favor foreign aid.[4] A study of public opinion regarding foreign aid in Development Assistance Committee (DAC) countries, published by the United Nations Development Programme (UNDP), showed that support in the United States was the lowest of all DAC member states, both in 1983 and 1995—at 50 percent and 45 percent, respectively—well below the DAC averages of 78 percent and 80 percent for those years (Stern 1998, p. 15). It seems likely that public debate over aid in the United States has also led the public to assume that US foreign aid was much larger than it really is, further dampening public support.

The limited and usually tepid support in the United States for aid for development made it imperative to produce rationales if aid giving were to be sustained over time. During the Cold War, the rationale cast the United States in the role of a great power and leader of the Western alliance against the socialist bloc and its allies. The political leadership in the United States in the years after World War II regarded an expansion of Soviet influence as a threat to US security that must be resisted. Public concessional transfers to help the recovery and stabilization of friendly governments, in the face of this challenge, became a key element of the policy to contain communism.

It soon became apparent that a sizable program of aid driven entirely by national security considerations would not survive long in the cauldron of Washington politics. It looked too much like "walking around money" to critics on the left (and at times on the right)—a form of international payoff to gain political support from foreign governments for US policies. There was one particular problem with the effectiveness of aid purely for diplomatic purposes. It had been justified as a means of containing Soviet influence, but as mentioned earlier, the continuation of the Cold War and its spread to less developed countries in the 1950s undercut that argument. There needed to be an additional rationale to justify the prolonged aid giving that would appeal to realists—many of whom were on the political right but a few on the left as well—and to idealists on the left and among the general public. Promotion of development in poor countries as a means of Cold War containment, in addition to being an end in itself, blended the realist and idealist rationales. Both ideas, involving national interest and national values, were important for sustaining US foreign aid throughout the twentieth century and provided the intellectual and normative basis for its constituencies inside and outside government. This dualism in purpose is still very much in evidence today, with aid for development often paired with aid for the global war on terror.

Institutions

It is not only the varied ideologies that have made US aid different from that of other major aid-giving countries, but also the nature of its political institutions. The United States has a presidential system. The major elements of government are politically autonomous of one another, with the president and members of Congress (both the Senate and House of Representatives) standing for election independently—in contrast to parliamentary systems, in which the prime minister is elected by the parliament. Further, elections are based on a winner-take-all system, discouraging the creation of third parties that could (as many do in the European parliamentary systems) promote niche issues like foreign aid. Political candidates are chosen in local primary elections, making members of Congress more beholden to their constituents than to their parties, thus tending to weaken party discipline.

Finally, both the executive and legislative branches of government contribute to shaping policies and determining federal expenditures. The executive proposes annual levels of expenditures that must then be appropriated by Congress. These expenditures can be cut, increased, amended, or ignored. As a result, Congress (including members and their often powerful staffs) plays an active and pervasive role in deciding the size as well as the use of those expenditures as well as oversees the programs they fund. Congress has a practice of directing federal government expenditures to specific activities favored by members and their constituents. This tendency has been particularly evident in foreign aid legislation, involving numerous earmarks and directives that are often regarded as the price for garnering votes from members who fear they will be penalized by their constituents for voting for an unpopular program.

The role and influence of Congress expands access to the political process not only for members of the House of Representatives and Senate but for many private groups and individuals who have ties to individual members. This fragmentation in political power makes US aid both more rigid in what it can do and more diffuse in what it does than the aid programs of other countries. Interest groups seeking to influence the direction of aid include population and family planning organizations, environmental lobbies, women's empowerment organizations, universities, the labor movement, ethnic and affinity groups, faith-based organizations, and many others. Their influence is visible in the earmarks and initiatives that shape US foreign aid.

These characteristics also make the US political system one of the most adversarial of any in the developed world, and this characteristic has influenced US foreign aid. The separation of powers and the weak party discipline typical of US politics enable members of Congress to act relatively independent of their parties, from the executive, and from one another (but with an eye always on the preferences of their constituents). Except in times of humanitarian crisis abroad, citizens supporting aid are typically less vocal than those opposing it. Indeed, many members of Congress have not hesitated to attack aid and support cutting it, even when their party controls the White House.

The characteristics of US aid giving that make smart aid difficult therefore derive in significant measure from fundamental norms and institutions within American society. These deep determinants explain the mix of purposes—essential for domestic political reasons—and the many restrictions on US aid that may seem irrational to the casual observer. Further, these deep determinants will not change easily. Therefore, indicating that the United States will most likely never provide the kind of assistance desired by strong advocates of development aid. Aid will always be a second-best instrument for promoting development in Africa and elsewhere.

Constraints on US Aid Policies

To have the best chance of being smart, aid donors—singly and together—need to be flexible, coherent, and coordinated in their policies and implementation. That is especially true in Africa, where obstacles to smart aid may be most challenging and complex. Flexibility, coherence, and coordination are constrained in most aid programs. Among all major aid-giving governments, they are probably most limited in the US aid program. Let us examine these problems and see why they exist.

Flexibility

One of the key elements of a smart aid program must be flexibility—the flexibility to adapt aid to diverse conditions in developing countries as well as the flexibility to make changes when those conditions shift or with the learning that should come from aid interventions. While no aid donor can offer assistance in the absence of a broad policy framework, the tighter that framework becomes, the less flexibility the donor will have to shape aid to local needs, preferences, and opportunities.

US bilateral aid in general is the least flexible of any from major donor countries. The aid is delivered in a broad policy framework that aims to promote economic growth, poverty reduction, and democracy in poor countries, to fight HIV/AIDS, and to provide humanitarian relief for natural and man-made disasters. Within that framework, different administrations and leadership teams emphasize different goals. In the case of the United States at present, there are twenty-one presidential initiatives (see Figure 3.1) funded with bilateral assistance. They do not constitute a coherent policy and create a number of demands on the use of aid.

Most of these initiatives are surely worthy. Many are broad in scope and can be interpreted as such by aid planners. Together, however, they serve to constrain the flexibility of US foreign aid.

The largest of these initiatives—the President's Emergency Plan for AIDS Relief (PEPFAR)—was announced in 2003 with the aim of providing

---

Figure 3.1 US Foreign Aid, 2006: Presidential Initiatives

Afghanistan Road
Africa Education Initiative
Centers for Excellence in Teacher Training
Central American Free Trade Agreement
Clean Energy Initiative
Congo Basin Forest Partnership
Digital Freedom Initiative
Faith-based and Community Initiatives
Global Fund to Fight AIDS, Tuberculosis, and Malaria
Initiative to End Hunger in Africa
Trade for African Development and Enterprise
Volunteers for Prosperity
Water for the Poor Initiative
Global Climate Change
Middle East Partnership Initiative
Millennium Challenge Account
President's Emergency Plan For AIDS Relief (PEPFAR)
President's Initiative Against Illegal Logging
Trafficking In Persons
Women's Justice and Empowerment in Africa
Accelerating the Fight Against Malaria

Source: USAID, "Presidential Initiatives," http://www.usaid.gov/about_usaid/presidential_initiative/.

$15 billion over five years to fight HIV/AIDS. The funding was concentrated in fifteen key countries, most of which are in sub-Saharan Africa. In 2007, President George W. Bush announced a doubling of aid for PEPFAR for the coming five years to $30 billion. This aid would provide for prevention, treatment, and care for many of the victims of this modern-day scourge that has especially devastated Africa. But every good deed has its problems, and PEPFAR is no exception. It threatens to inject an additional degree of inflexibility into US aid giving by committing such large amounts to fighting a single disease in particular countries. And the inflexibility of PEPFAR monies is greater than that of other US aid programs. Once the United States begins to fund antiretroviral drugs to save the lives of the victims of this disease (many of whom are poor people in poor countries), it is committed for the duration of their lives (unless they and their governments can find alternative sources of financing for the drugs). Withdrawing the aid, because of budgetary shortages or the rise of other needs and priorities or any other reason, will make the United States complicit in the certain death of those benefiting from the drugs—a morally repugnant position. Further, this aid is set to become so large a portion of total US bilateral aid to PEPFAR recipients that it will (and judging from some evidence, already has) draw resources from other activities in recipient countries' health systems and may exert a gravitational pull on all US aid toward funding activities associated with making PEPFAR a success (for example, nutritional supplements). The figure (Figure 3.2) demonstrates the extraordinary size of PEP-FAR monies relative to other US bilateral aid in several African countries.

Over the past several years, these initiatives have been further complicated by the organizational reforms implemented by the secretary of state, which reclassified countries into categories related to their political and economic characteristics. It is the explicit policy that aid will be tailored to the particular needs of these countries with the implicit idea (or hope) that, with the right policies and enough aid, countries will move from being underdeveloped and poor to graduating from US aid. This approach has a certain attractive logic. However, there is no evidence-based theory behind this "stages of growth" approach to aid giving and no reason to think that countries fit easily into one category or another. This reform is part of a broader set of changes in US aid giving that is part of the administration's "transformational diplomacy." But the aid reforms, which were very controversial among the administration, Congress, and external aid-giving groups, have stalled since the sudden departure in April 2007 of Ambassador Randall Tobias, who was initially in charge of their implementation.

Administration policies and presidential initiatives are not the tightest constraints on US aid giving. Congress imposes legislative earmarks (carrying the force of law) and "directives" (carrying the force of politics since they typically reflect the priorities of important members of Congress and their staffs and constituents) on major bilateral foreign aid programs each

Figure 3.2 US Aid for Fighting HIV/AIDS in Kenya, Tanzania, and Zambia, and Total US Bilateral Aid, 2008

Kenya   Tanzania   Zambia

Source: USAID, *International Affairs Budget, 2008,* country aid charts, www.usaid.gov/policy/budget/cbj2008/fy2008cbj_highlights.pdf.

Note: The white slice of pie represents aid for fighting HIV/AIDS; the dark area is the remainder of US bilateral aid planned for 2008 in these countries.

year in its appropriations bills. The major US bilateral aid programs are Child Survival/Global Health and Development Assistance (totaling $3.4 billion), managed and implemented by the US Agency for International Development (USAID), and the Economic Support Fund (ESF, totaling $3 billion). Other programs in 2008 include Food Aid (also known as PL480 from the 1954 law authorizing it), amounting to $1.3 billion; aid for Eastern Europe and the newly independent states of the former Soviet Union, amounting to $700 million; aid in the Millennium Challenge Account (managed by the Millennium Challenge Corporation, or MCC), amounting to $1.5 billion; $4.7 billion in PEPFAR; and $1.5 billion in multilateral aid. (These figures do not include a number of smaller aid programs located in independent US government agencies or in twenty-four government departments.) An examination of the legislation appropriating aid under the Child Survival/Global Health and Development Assistance accounts shows that in past years the total aid earmarked exceeded the total aid appropriated. (Aid managers know how to double count to make this apparent absurdity work.) The monies in the Economic Support Fund are also heavily earmarked—in this case for particular countries rather than for particular uses, as in the other two accounts (see Lancaster 2006, pp. 88–89).

The aid programs above are among the oldest in US bilateral aid giving. Other programs are less earmarked, but nevertheless most carry some restrictions. For example, food aid carries requirements on where it must be purchased (mainly in the United States) and how it is shipped (mainly on US ships), making the aid considerably less flexible in responding to emergencies in distant places and more expensive because US shipping charges are well above world rates. Aid from the MCC has not yet been earmarked. Multilateral aid is difficult to earmark, given the nature of international organizations. There is a clear tendency in the US Congress to earmark any aid that can be earmarked. And these earmarks accumulate over time.

The impact of earmarks and directives on aid management flexibility is significant. It means that only certain kinds of aid—for example, funding for family planning—is available in particular countries regardless of whether family planning is a high priority of the government or society. During my years working in USAID, we would typically ask the mission directors (based in recipient countries and managing aid programs) what their needs and budget proposals were for the coming fiscal year. We would then go through a prolonged review process of budget proposals in Washington, D.C., and then send an overall budget to the White House and later to Congress for approval. When the appropriations finally came back, we had to return to mission directors to tell them that, regardless of their preferences, they had to provide aid based on the categories decided in Washington, and not in the countries where they were located. The earmarks, in effect, distorted the budget process and undermined any pretense of providing aid according to recipient needs and preferences rather than those of the US administration and Congress. I do not mean to suggest here that the aid provided was not useful; it often was. But it was usually not allocated according to what was most needed or wanted in particular countries. In effect, US aid was and is primarily "donor-driven," raising questions about its smartness vis-à-vis the development needs and aspirations of recipients and their potential "ownership" of the activities aid financed.

Coherence

There are several factors that undermine the coherence of US aid. One is that there are now two main aid agencies—the MCC and USAID—and one large aid program (PEPFAR). The division of labor between these agencies is still being determined, as we shall see below. Meanwhile, the Department of Defense (DOD) has begun to provide aid to help "stabilize" fragile states with "ungoverned spaces" (in which terrorists might operate). This aid is provided to governments and communities in the Sahel and the Horn of Africa. DOD appears set to expand this non-combat-related aid and become potentially another significant source of economic assistance in Africa and elsewhere.

It is increasingly uncertain where control over USAID will be located in view of the organizational reforms proposed in 2006 by Secretary of State Condoleezza Rice. Before the establishment of the MCC, USAID was the major bilateral aid agency in the US government. It was primarily responsible for policy and implementation of three aid programs: Child Survival, Development Assistance, and Food Aid. It also managed ESF, aid to Eastern Europe, and aid to the newly independent states of the former Soviet Union. It also oversaw the implementation of aid-funded programs addressing global issues like infectious diseases, including HIV/AIDS. USAID undertook programs in all types of developing countries—"good performers," states with mediocre governments and policies, weak and failing states, and states recovering from conflict.

The MCC was created in 2004 as a separate US government corporation with a board of directors drawn from government agencies and a few outside organizations engaged in development work. It was made separate from USAID and the Department of State (the then secretary of state, Colin Powell, reportedly wanted it located at the State Department) because its mission and modus operandi were different from those agencies. The purpose of the MCC was to foster development in low-income countries that were good performers according to some sixteen criteria, including degree of political freedom, market openness, lack of corruption, and government expenditures on social services. Further, MCC assistance was intended to be large enough to make a measurable impact on development and also create incentives for other governments to want to meet the eligibility criteria. Finally, MCC aid was intended to be "recipient-driven"—to reflect the preferences and priorities of the governments receiving the aid rather than the policies and directives of Washington.

In its goals and objectives, the MCC had much to recommend it. However, the emphasis on good performers left USAID uncertain which countries and development objectives it should focus on. Should it operate in the same countries as the MCC (many of which had established USAID field missions) or should it refocus its work in countries that were not good performers? To what extent would the MCC utilize USAID's staff and missions to plan and implement its programs, given that the number of MCC staff was initially intended to be no more than 100 persons and (initially at least) many of them would lack development experience? Which of these aid agencies would lead US development assistance in a given country, and who should other donor agencies or recipients talk to when they wanted to get a sense of the direction of US foreign aid policies generally?

Five years after the establishment of the MCC, those issues are still not fully resolved. USAID has increased its focus—at least at the rhetorical level—on failing and failed states. In 2005, the agency issued its "Fragile States Strategy" and created an Office of Conflict Mitigation and Management to deal with issues of state failure (USAID 2005b). With the aid reforms underway, that focus seems set to strengthen. But USAID continues to deal mostly with good performers. And, after nearly five years, the MCC has finally begun to disburse its funding, which, it appears, will be much less for most recipient countries than originally conceived. The creation of the MCC has exacerbated policy and programmatic incoherence in US foreign aid, already complicated enough because of a variety of bilateral programs located in USAID and the Department of State and multilateral aid programs located in the Treasury. In the case of US aid to Africa, the question of which aid agency will take the lead in recipient countries that qualify for MCC assistance remains unclear. The PEPFAR program adds to this incoherence since it has a very large amount of funds to disburse (and it is disbursing them rapidly), but it is not the only agency funding programs to fight HIV/AIDS. USAID does so too. And as noted previously, to fight HIV/AIDS effectively, aid for more than prevention, treatment, and care is needed. PEPFAR monies cannot fund activities outside these three goals. Will that be the future responsibility of USAID in Africa?

The second major problem involving the coherence of US aid relates to the reforms announced by Secretary Rice in early 2006, in which the administrator of USAID would henceforth also be the director of foreign assistance (DFA) within the US Department of State. This office has now been set up, and the entire budget operation of USAID has moved over to the DFA office in the Department of State. The intent of this reform was to give greater coherence to the aid programs of USAID and the Department of State by having the DFA deciding on their budgets and programming. This decision is part of a broader pattern in which responsibilities traditionally located in USAID have migrated to the State Department, including leadership in HIV/AIDS (the coordinator for the President's Emergency Program on HIV/AIDS is located in the State Department), leadership in democracy promotion and postconflict interventions, and USAID's role in setting its own strategies and priorities. The State Department has a sizable democracy promotion budget of its own and has set up an Office of the Coordinator for Reconstruction and Stabilization. USAID's priorities for individual countries are now set within the broader country planning exercises led by the State Department. These changes may prove to be the first big step toward a gradual incorporation of USAID into the Department of State, in view of the current integration of budget and planning functions of the two agencies.

In the 1990s an attempt was made to bring about such a merger. But would a merger between USAID and the State Department be a good idea? Would such an action provide more coherence to the aid programs of these agencies? The answer to the second question is most likely yes, but for that reason—in the view of this writer—it is *not* a good idea. The mission of the US Department of State has long been primarily to promote US interests with other governments and to manage crises in relations with those governments—all within the context of the US role as a lead state in world politics. This mission has required hard-headed "realist" thinking on the part of policymakers, has focused on relations between governments primarily, and has brought with it an emphasis on the short-term crisis management.

These elements in the modus operandi of the Department of State are quite different from the longer-run horizons of USAID, the need to work with governments and civil society organizations (sometimes those opposed to the government), and the emphasis on promoting economic and social progress in foreign countries. It is highly likely that a merger between USAID—smaller and far less influential than the Department of State—and the latter will result in the mission and operational imperatives of the latter overwhelming those of the former, thereby undermining the development mission of USAID. And such a merger would arguably disadvantage Africa in US aid giving since the diplomatic priorities of the US government are focused elsewhere, even if development priorities remain in Africa.

Coordination

Problems of coordination of aid programs and agencies within the US government are related to problems of coherence in the aid programs themselves. Different aid programs with similar or overlapping goals can—when they approach these goals in different ways—create problems for recipient countries. Programs can be replicated, leading to a waste of resources. Similar programs undercut one another if they use approaches that conflict. Most importantly, multiple aid programs taking different approaches to similar problems can impose excessive transaction costs on recipient governments or organizations for several reasons: (1) the administrative costs of managing different aid-funded programs and projects (the elements of which may not be interchangeable); (2) the long-term budgetary demands of maintaining such projects (demands that are not always considered in the haste on the part of donors and recipients to allocate and receive aid); and (3) the weakening of recipient budget and planning processes when different agencies approach different parts of the government (not always including the ministry of finance or planning, which is supposed to coordinate aid inflows) with aid proposals and their diverse administrative requirements. Some diversity of interventions can be important in furthering beneficial economic, political, and social change in other countries. Different approaches may turn up important lessons on how to achieve goals. But too many diverse interventions with little coordination, either by donors or recipients, can become costly and dysfunctional—a problem long evident in many African countries where governments have had to deal with as many as forty separate aid donor agencies.

The problem of coordination addressed here is *within* the US government. We have mentioned the two principal bilateral aid agencies—USAID and the MCC. But they are far from being the only aid programs sponsored by the United States. It is no exaggeration to say that virtually every federal department and many sub-cabinet-level agencies have their own aid programs. The Department of State's programs have already been mentioned, along with PEPFAR and DOD. The Department of the Treasury runs a technical assistance program on tax and fiscal policy amounting to over $100 million annually and is responsible for US participation in the multilateral development banks like the World Bank and the African Development Bank and Fund. The Department of Labor has a program to address problems of child labor abroad in excess of $100 million annually. It is not possible to say how much foreign aid is administered by these nonaid agencies since they do not have such a category in their budgets. Nor would they want to have it for domestic political reasons, since foreign aid has traditionally been unpopular. Moreover, they may face legal and political problems by appearing to run their own foreign aid programs. In recent years, there has been an effort to improve the data on the amounts of aid provided by non–foreign affairs agencies. The size of this aid is significant, reaching $4 billion in 2003 and exceeding $6 billion in 2004. The agencies involved are listed in Figure 3.3.

At present, there is nowhere in the US government where coordination of these diverse sources of foreign aid takes place. Given the number of powerful departments and agencies engaged in aid giving abroad, and the lack of data on what they are doing, such coordination may in fact be impossible. It may only be US ambassadors in the field who have a sense of the totality of aid expenditures in their countries. By the time they learn them,

**Figure 3.3 US Government Agencies Involved
in Providing Foreign Aid, FY 2006**

African Development Foundation
Department of Agriculture
    Agricultural Research Service (ARS)
    Animal and Plant Health Inspection Service (APHIS)
    Cooperative State Research Education and Extension Service (CSREES)
    Foreign Agricultural Service (FAS)
    Forest Service (FS)
Department of Commerce
    US Patent and Trademark Office (PTO)
    Commercial Law Development Program (CLDP)
    International Trade Administration (ITA)
    National Institute of Standards and Technology (NIST)
    National Oceanic and Atmospheric Administration (NOAA)
Department of Defense
    Defense Security Cooperation Agency (DSCA)
    Defense Threat Reduction Agency (DTRA)
    US Army Corps of Engineers (USACE)
Department of Energy
Department of Health and Human Services
    Centers for Disease Control
    Substance Abuse and Mental Health Services Administration (SAMHSA)
Department of Interior
    Compact of Free Association
    US Fish and Wildlife Service
Department of Justice
Department of Labor
Department of State
Department of Treasury
Environmental Protection Agency
Export-Import Bank
Federal Trade Commission
Inter-American Foundation
Millennium Challenge Corporation
National Endowment for Democracy
Overseas Private Investment Corporation
Peace Corps
US Trade and Development Agency
US Agency for International Development (USAID)

Source: USAID, *US Overseas Grants and Loans* ("the Greenbook"), http://qesdb
.cdie.org/gbk/USG%20Organizations.html.

however, it is often too late to have any influence over their size or policy direction. It is probable that the costs in aid effectiveness from this chaotic situation greatly outweigh the benefits to the US government and to recipient governments of multiple aid sources within a single donor—let alone from multiple donors. The United States is not alone in the fragmentation of its aid programs: the French have long administered aid out of multiple agencies; the Japanese have done the same historically; and there is a tendency for German government agencies to mount their own aid programs. This may be an inevitable consequence of globalization. International problems such as disease transmission, energy use, agricultural production, water use, environmental degradation, finance, and transport are no longer confined by national boundaries. Thus the challenge of coordination *within* the US government, in addition to that among donor governments, further limits smart aid to Africa—and does not offer great promise of being alleviated.

The Way Forward

That said, structural and cognitive constraints on public policies and programs can change. One might ask if there are any signs of change in these elements underlying US foreign aid. It does appear that something fundamental has begun to change in US politics that could affect foreign aid, namely, the appearance of a new "interest group" or perhaps "social movement"—the evangelical movement and the Christian Right—and its increasing engagement in foreign aid giving. As these groups have become more familiar with the problems of poverty, disease, and suffering in the world and more involved in aid giving, they have also become advocates for foreign aid, including aid for activities in sub-Saharan Africa.[5] Should the evangelical movement's engagement in foreign aid continue to expand, it could circumscribe or even undercut the traditional resistance to aid—especially development aid—from US conservatives, expand the consensus supporting aid across the political spectrum, reduce the conflicting purposes so long necessary to sustain political support for foreign aid within the United States, and even lead to an increase in aid to Africa where poverty and other problems of importance to this movement are prominent. This impact is already evident in the strong support from much of the Christian Right, as well as the Left, for money to fight HIV/AIDS—seen by evangelical Christians as an act of good Samaritanship to help innocent women and children afflicted by HIV/AIDS.

Constituencies for government spending programs usually bring their own agendas to those programs, and the evangelicals are no exception. Their socially conservative values are already reflected in aspects of US aid giving. For example, there is now the requirement that a portion of the new funding for the fight against HIV/AIDS be dedicated to emphasizing abstinence from sexual activity as a means of preventing the spread of the disease. However, not all the policy preferences of the evangelicals collide with those of the political left. Both oppose human trafficking, slavery, religious oppression, human rights abuses, corruption, and authoritarian governments. There are broad areas of potential agreement among aid's traditional supporters and the evangelicals. But the differences will have to be managed if this new force in US politics is to expand the constituency for aid rather than divide it. This challenge will be particularly evident in aid to sub-Saharan Africa. The base constituency for aid to that region—African American groups—will need to consider whether and how to collaborate with evangelicals on the size, country distribution, and, above all, objectives of aid to Africa.

What does this essay suggest about the future of US aid, smart or otherwise? First, domestic factors will continue to constrain US aid giving. The recent reforms raise questions about how and whether US aid should be organized to be as smart as it can be to achieve its goals within narrow constraints. Some of the recent reforms are turning out to be bureaucratic disasters, slowing to a halt the functioning of the aid bureaucracy. The next administration has three choices with regard to its aid program. The first would be to merge what is left of USAID into the State Department and make reforms there so that an aid program can be effectively managed. This change would likely politicize even more the allocation and use of US aid and lead to its eventual demise if Congress and the public perceive it to be a political payoff for US allies.

Second, the administration can extract USAID from the State Department and merge it with the MCC and probably PEPFAR to create a new, sub-cabinet-level aid agency. That might give new life to the administration's pursuit of development in US foreign policy and provide an opportunity to rethink the basic goals of aid and how to achieve them. Third, it could merge MCC, USAID, PEPFAR, multilateral aid programs, the Peace Corps, and smaller aid programs elsewhere in the US government into a new, cabinet-level development agency. This option, favored by much of the development community, appears the most costly politically. New legislation would be needed from Congress at a time when the president would have other high-priority issues for which congressional support is needed. One thing is sure: nothing will happen of significance with regard to US aid until the next administration takes over in Washington in January 2009.

In sum, the politics of US aid may soon change fundamentally. These changes may take US aid in directions quite different from past ones—a greater emphasis on development and related issues, the mobilizing of a broader basis of domestic support, and more aid being directed to the neediest countries, especially in Africa.

Notes

1. See my book, *Foreign Aid: Diplomacy, Development, Domestic Politics* (University of Chicago Press, 2006), chap. 3, for the basis of this calculation.

2. There are, to my knowledge, no rigorous efforts thus far to evaluate the diplomatic impact of foreign aid.

3. See, for example, Dollar 1998. His is the most prominent statement about problems of aid effectiveness, especially in countries with poor policy environments, but there are many other studies and still no broad consensus on the degree to which aid has been and can be effective and why.

4. Gallup Poll, p. 1546. The poll was taken in 1958, and 51 percent of those polled were "for" foreign aid. A number of other polls came up with similar percentages. However Steven Kull, polling for PIPA, found in 1995 that over 80 percent of the US population agreed with the statement that "the United States should be willing to share at least a small portion of its wealth with those in the world who are in great need". See Steven Kull, *Americans and Foreign Aid,* PIPA, School of Public Affairs, University of Maryland, 1995, p. 3. Again, the differences in these results undoubtedly reflect the differences in the way the polling questions are asked. Kull's question is framed in strongly ethical terms. Other questions typically include the term "foreign aid," which often elicits a negative reaction based on all the factors we have described.

5. By 2004, the Association of Evangelical Relief and Development Organizations (set up in 1978) had forty-eight members. By the beginning of the twenty-first century, the growing activism of the evangelical movement was being noted in the US media. See, for example, Peter Waldman, "Evangelicals Give US Foreign Policy an Activist Tinge," Associated Press, MSNBC, 2004, http://msnbc.msn.com/id/5068634/. Further, one influential senator, Sam Brownback from Kansas, has begun to take a particular interest in development in Africa. If he and others like him become more engaged with development issues in the region, that could also change the quantity and smartness of US aid to Africa.

4

The Commission for Africa: Assessing the Approach

Vivian Lowery Derryck

FRICA WILL PROVIDE the most important test case of foreign assistance effectiveness for decades to come. The continent has virtually
every development paradox confronting aid workers and donors:
periodic famine, endemic disease, persistent illiteracy, decaying infrastructure, and underperforming economies. They contrast with the potential of
abundant natural resources, reforming governments, and untapped reservoirs of intellectual and social capital.

Assistance takes multiple forms. It ranges from official development assistance (ODA) offered by bilateral donors, to concessional loans from international financial institutions such as the World Bank, to outright grants
from aid agencies such as the US Agency for International Development
(USAID) and the UK Department for International Development (DFID). To
these can be added assistance from nongovernmental organizations (NGOs)
and contributions from philanthropists seeking important and measurable results from their investments.

The smarter use of all these sources of assistance requires intellectual
energy, creative financing, enhanced donor coordination, and motivated
constituencies. One source for sparking new ideas, harnessing resources,
encouraging multilateral cooperation, and motivating constituencies is the
work of international commissions.[1]

Commissions have a long and distinguished history as a way of responding to major global challenges. They are an underappreciated resource
whose members can present broad ideas and stimulate innovative thinking
about key challenges and then find advocates for them and donors to pay for
their implementation.[2] As a recurrent feature of international governance, effective commissions can attract leading thinkers from national governments,

the United Nations, and the Bretton Woods financial institutions, as well as eminent persons worldwide to address urgent issues.

The 1979 Brandt Commission advanced the concept of sustainable development, and the 1983 Brundtland Commission, formally the World Commission on Environment and Development, emphasized the nexus between environment and development. The 1994 Carnegie Commission on Preventing Deadly Conflict brought into sharper focus threats to world peace from intergroup violence and underscored the need for concrete mechanisms for conflict prevention. These commissions, along with others, generated momentum and fostered new levels of collaboration to address pressing global challenges. They served as forums for sharing knowledge and generating interest in particular causes, although their records of implementation and policy outcomes often fail to meet their lofty expectations.

The Commission for Africa, conceived, motivated, and championed by British prime minister Tony Blair in 2005, illustrates the strengths of commissions as well as the obstacles they face in having a discernible impact. In this chapter I begin with an overview and assessment of the report that emerged from the commission's deliberations. I pay special attention to its most valuable contributions and identify a few areas that deserve greater attention. There is much to compliment in how the initiative was planned and executed. Several obstacles likely to frustrate the commission's agenda are outlined. The aim here is to assess the utility of commissions in addressing such complex international challenges as accelerating economic development in Africa.

The Blair Commission and Its Findings

The Commission for Africa, often referred to as the Blair Commission, was the latest major effort to address Africa's enduring development needs and mobilize the required financial resources. The commission of seventeen eminent persons called for a new compact between African states and the international community. It acknowledged the weak capacity of African states, the need for a new level of accountability among African countries, and a commitment from industrialized nations to help strengthen African capacity. The commission proposed a comprehensive agenda of good governance, peace and security, expanded investments in human capacity building, poverty reduction and growth, and increased trade. These advances would be funded by increases of $25 billion per year in development assistance to Africa until 2010, with an additional $25 billion per year provided by 2015 if warranted by the outcomes of the first period (Commission for Africa 2005, p. 16).

The Blair Commission began as a noble idea in February 2004, in anticipation of the UK chairing of the G8 in 2005. At the beginning of his second term, Prime Minister Blair identified two priorities—Africa and the environment—and regretted that he had not pursued them during his first term. Blair used the G8 presidency to focus attention on Africa's mounting needs and the potential to address them, especially poverty reduction, through increased help from the international community.

It is a testament to this commitment that, with competing priorities such as the war in Iraq, the prime minister followed through on his promise. He provided constant leadership for the effort, ensuring that Africans comprised the majority of the commission, personally chairing meetings, and challenging his government and the British public to respond to the commission's recommendations. Timed to take advantage of the G8 presidency and to highlight the UN Millennium Development Goals (MDGs) adopted in 2000, the commission provided an impetus—the big push—to a worldwide campaign to reduce African poverty.

For the commission, Blair gathered a group of eminent women and men, including Ethiopian head of state Meles Zenawi, South African finance minister Trevor Manuel, UN chief economist for Africa K. Y. Amoako, and former US senator Nancy Kassebaum, as well as representatives of the private sector. Each commission member served in his or her personal capacity. The commission's mandate was to identify Africa's key challenges and provide concrete recommendations on how they should be confronted.

The project was based on certain fundamental assumptions, beginning with the recognition of a global common interest in responding to Africa's distress as a moral imperative. At the beginning of *Our Common Future: The Report of the Commission for Africa,* the commission boldly stated: "African poverty and stagnation is the greatest tragedy of our time. Poverty on such a scale demands a forceful response" (Commission for Africa 2005, p. 13). In addition, the commissioners assumed that the Millennium Development Goals and the post–September 11 understanding of the link between poverty and national security should facilitate the mobilization of increased financial resources for Africa. Another assumption was that industrialized nations possessed sufficient resources to provide an additional $25 billion in annual aid for Africa by 2010 (and a further $25 billion per year by 2015).

The project was intended to establish a compact between Africans, who would acknowledge their share of responsibility for the problems of the continent and accept enhanced accountability, and their partners, who would fund a new push specifically to support major capacity-building initiatives (p. 14). The viability of this arrangement rested on the assumption that both sides would live up to their part of the agreement: African governments would strengthen democratic institutions, the rule of law, and transparency, and the international community would provide the financial inputs required to accelerate development.

In pursuit of these aims, the Commission for Africa drew on several strengths. First, the majority of the commissioners were African, so their views reflected firsthand experience. Second, the commission took a multi-sectoral and integrated approach in its report, noting, for example, the relationships among good governance, conflict resolution, and security. Third, the report emphasized the need to strengthen transcontinental institutions such as the African Union (AU) and the New Partnership for Africa's Development (NEPAD). Fourth, the report placed responsibility for Africa's shortcomings on both Africans and the donors.

The report identified five priorities: governance and capacity building, peace and security, investments in people by improving social infrastructure, growth and poverty reduction, and increased trade. Most presentations and roundtable discussions of the report have focused on three priorities—good governance, peace and security, and trade.[3] However, I will reverse the order and take up peace and security first. Without peace, so fundamental for development, efforts to advance governance and economic prosperity in Africa will languish.

Peace and Security

Africa has experienced more conflicts in recent years than any other region, with the genocide in Darfur, the Somalian civil war, and the devastation of Zimbabwe. The commission's report uses the example of Democratic Republic of Congo to show the high mortality rates and negative impact of violent conflict on sustainable development (p. 39).

The report cites several contributors to large and small conflicts, including the high demand for such commodities as oil, diamonds, and timber and the proliferation of small arms. It notes the deplorable conduct of some foreign businesses, which deliberately fuel conflict by supplying weapons, arming security forces, and supporting dictatorial regimes.

The commission called for greater support for anticorruption protocols and the strengthening of the early warning and conflict resolution mechanisms of the UN and African regional organizations (p. 41). One recommendation, for a UN Peace Building Commission, has since become a reality. In addition, peace and security required closer coordination between the relevant UN agencies and the Peace and Security Council of the African Union, one of the institutions the commission pledged to support and strengthen.

Unfortunately, the report does not address food security in the context of peace and security. Most African countries have not yet tackled the linkages among environmental degradation, population growth, and food security. An estimated 186 million Africans currently suffer from undernourishment and malnutrition. In a vicious cycle, food insecurity contributes to conflict, and conflict exacerbates food insecurity, as displaced populations are unable to plant and harvest crops. A discussion of food security could have increased awareness of the multisectoral nature of Africa's challenges.

Food security is a first priority for a healthy population, and healthy people have a lower disease burden. Thus, increasing food security promotes a healthier workforce and higher labor force participation. Food security also correlates with increased school attendance, and a healthy population would be more receptive to messages of good governance.

Good Governance

As a key priority, the commission asserts that an effective state—namely, one that protects its citizens, delivers services, and supports economic growth—is the fulcrum of development, and that Africa's weak states lie at the heart of its predicament (p. 28). The report proposes strengthening the state by investing in capacity building, increasing accountability and transparency, reducing corruption, and improving information systems and the quality of data.

The first recommendation, investing in capacity building, suggests the need to strengthen the AU and its regional mechanisms such as the African Peer Review Mechanism (APRM). The fact that twenty-three African nations have already signed on to be reviewed is an indication of African verbal commitment to the mechanism. Nevertheless, the APRM cannot be legitimized until the AU develops the tools and authority to deal forthrightly with such situations as the devastation of Zimbabwe during the years of President Robert Mugabe's misrule and intransigence.

The report makes a timely call for investment in capacity building for African professionals and the strengthening of key institutions such as parliaments. Dominant executives and weak parliaments have been the bane of African states for decades. Empowered and capable parliaments can provide needed checks and balances on the executive. Building legislative capacity by pairing African legislators with their counterparts in other countries or on other continents or by arranging legislative exchanges is an excellent way to build relationships among African legislatures as well as between African and developed country legislators. An added benefit is the possibility of introducing new vitality to sluggish national parliaments.

The report also discusses the need for improving financial transparency in government and business. It calls for increased donor support for the Extractive Industries Transparency Initiative (EITI) and strongly encourages more African countries to join the protocol. Corruption and anticorruption measures are discussed in a separate section from accountability and transparency, indicating the importance that the commissioners attached to these issues. The report underscores that corruption is a two-way process and recommends using existing agencies, such as national export credit agencies, to address corruption (p. 156) rather than proposing bold actions such as the launching of national anticorruption campaigns.

The governance section links the capable state to economic growth and contends:

> All the evidence shows that reductions in poverty do not come without economic growth. . . . Economically, since growth is driven principally by the private sector, that requires governments to provide a climate in which ordinary people—whether they be small farmers or managers of large firms—can get on with their tasks untroubled, and feel that it is worthwhile investing in their future. (p. 28)

Trade

The third major priority highlighted in various discussions and presentations in the report was trade. Acknowledging an unstable investment climate, weaknesses in infrastructure, and unskilled workforces that combine to produce a substantial competitive disadvantage, the report calls for African nations to produce more high-quality goods and to reduce intra-African barriers to trade. At the same time, it encourages developed nations to eliminate subsidies and lower tariffs and to increase their efforts to complete the Doha Round of trade negotiations.

The report highlights several trade policy initiatives that African governments could implement and identifies the economic benefits that would accrue to their countries (p. 261). Implementing these recommendations will, however, be difficult. Many of the suggested steps rely on the willingness of African governments to remove barriers to trade at their borders, which often serve as valuable sources of tax revenues. Major movements on this front seem unlikely. Going beyond the current trade protocols of regional organizations such as the Common Market for Eastern and Southern Africa (COMESA) and the Economic Community of West African States (ECOWAS) and reducing other intraregional barriers, do not appear to be priorities for most African countries.

The commission's call for developed countries to reduce tariffs has been reflected in the 2000 US African Growth and Opportunity Act (AGOA). This initiative provides greater access to US markets for thirty-eight eligible sub-Saharan African countries, allowing more than 6,500 products to enter the United States free of tariffs. Because the emphasis was on textiles until 2007, most of the potential advantages of AGOA have not been fully explored. Nevertheless, the AGOA model is viewed by some development specialists as a model to be adopted by the European Union (EU) to foster its trade with the continent.

There are two other impediments to quick gains in trade. First, in Africa the overwhelming bulk of trade is in primary products so African economies are highly vulnerable to commodity price fluctuations. The second impediment is Western unwillingness to make major changes in their trade regimes.

On the one hand, some countries such as the United States provide training to strengthen African capacities in trade negotiations for the Doha Round. On the other hand, there seems to be little commitment to reduce or eliminate farm subsidies in Europe or to greatly modify the EU's common agricultural policy for this round. In the United States, the sugar and cotton lobbies are so strong that there is virtually no chance of removing subsidies on those items in the near term. Clearly, implementing the trade recommendations will face major hurdles that risk impeding any meaningful movement on this crucial aspect of the commission's agenda.

Underemphasized Opportunities

In addition to food security, there are other issues mentioned in the report that did not receive the amount of attention they deserve. The report would have benefited from a discussion of education, not only in the context of enhancing national capacity but also as a building block for sustainable development. Education is critical to fighting poverty and increasing the capacity of citizens to hold the state accountable. Education is not only the linchpin for building a capable state but also expands the continent's intellectual capital, so necessary for faster integration into the global economy. Information technologies (IT) can help stimulate the development and dissemination of intellectual capital. Even though the report calls for greater investments in science and technology, it did not make the link between IT and formal education. New technologies represent a potent learning tool, from primary education through universities, and provide one of the best opportunities for rapidly improving Africa's access to global intellectual resources.

Education featured prominently in British efforts to publicize the commission and its goals. The commission developed a large set of curricular materials and videos to introduce children to its work and key recommendations. It is unfortunate that the report did not emphasize the essential contribution of education to sustainable development and highlight the theme of education as a basic human right.

The second area that could have been given further emphasis in the report was gender. The commission missed the opportunity to discuss the unique potential contributions of African women in meeting the challenges of building state capacity and accountability. Many studies have confirmed that women are critical to designing and implementing sustainable development initiatives. Countries that do not invest in women have higher rates of poverty, weaker governance, and are generally less stable.[4]

Nobel Laureate Wangari Maathai, during a 2005 visit to Washington, D.C., noted that rural women listed the following as priorities: energy (especially wood for producing charcoal); water (they estimate spending two or

more hours a day obtaining potable water); food (they worry about the inadequate daily nutritional intake of their children); and income (they embrace microfinance and other strategies for raising rural incomes). All four
of the women's priorities are mentioned in the report, but there is no discussion of strategies for incorporating the particular needs of women into the
implementation of various programs. One way to highlight gender would be
for further reports of the commission's recommendations to follow the
model of the African Union, in which heads of state are required by AU
statute to report at each annual summit on their country's progress in achieving gender parity.

Commission Ideas and the Push for Implementation

Decades of experience with commissions indicate that certain criteria appear to determine the differing degrees of success. With regard to these criteria, the Blair Commission did almost everything right, at least in respect
to elements within the control of its organizers. Participants in a successful
commission should represent government and the private sector, reflect a
gender and ethnic balance, and come from both the global South and global
North. The Blair Commission passed all these tests. Moreover, the majority
of commissioners were Africans, and all are respected in their fields.

Another criterion looks at the intellectual bases for a commission's
work. The Blair Commission had a clear premise, also reflected in two recent African initiatives, the African Union and NEPAD. Based on African
input, the commission articulated five priority areas and recommended concrete actions. The commission also coordinated its activities with those of
the United Nations, including specialized agencies with an African focus,
such as the UN Economic Commission for Africa, and with the Millennium
Development Goals.

Successful commissions are chaired by leaders of international reputation and compelling moral authority (Thakur, Cooper, and English 2005, p.
10). Tony Blair's strong intellect and long-standing commitment to Africa
are well known. The fact that he chaired the commission's meetings, delivered several national lectures on Africa, and personally discussed the work
of the commission with other heads of state spurred others to take the issue
more seriously.

The most important criterion for a successful commission is a strategy
for building a constituency. Without acquiring the momentum to attract
greater numbers of advocates, the best ideas and proposals will perish. The
commission orchestrated the rollout of the report at the G8 Summit in Gleneagles, preceded by the Live 8 concerts and the launch of Business Action
for Africa. It succeeded in drawing greater attention to Africa than at any
other time in recent memory.

Along with efforts to engage the wider public, Blair engaged his government in constituency-building activities. All departments and ministries were required to respond to specific sections of the commission's report and to state the concrete actions they would undertake to help implement its recommendations. Prime Minister Blair appealed to the wider British public as well. Schoolchildren could learn about the work of the commission online. The Royal African Society hosted discussions with the commissioners. The Live 8 concerts made use of pop culture to publicize the cause. The prime minister traveled overseas to publicize the work of the commission, and British Foreign Service officers were detailed to the United States to raise awareness there. Major fundraising efforts engaged the private sector. Chancellor of the Exchequer Gordon Brown introduced an initiative through the International Finance Facility to forward fund a large increase in British aid to Africa. Post-Gleneagles advocacy in the UK has continued. Since the commission's Report, the UK has made a major commitment to primary and secondary education. It has also reached out to civil society with "Red Nose Days" in which people wear red clown noses while raising money for developing countries. The effort has so far raised considerable sums for this purpose.

Successful commissions must have good timing (Thakur, Cooper, and English 2005, p. 8). It is hard to overestimate the importance of timing: commissions can become hostage to other international developments or crises. In this instance, Tony Blair was singularly unlucky. He planned to announce the commission's key finding with great fanfare on the second night of the July 2005 G8 meeting. Unfortunately, that same day, multiple bombs exploded during the rush hour on London underground trains and on a bus, killing fifty-two and injuring hundreds. The prime minister was obliged to return to London, leaving the announcement of the G8's decisions to another official who was not as intimately familiar with the initiative and therefore lacked Blair's passion and conviction about its potential. Moreover, media attention was suddenly diverted from the deliberations at Gleneagles to the postbombing carnage and confusion.

Commissions with successful outcomes must have an effective strategy for the dissemination of their main ideas and recommendations. Here the commission initially faltered. It was intended that the commissioners would serve as advocates for the report's recommendations, but they did not have the initial resources to press its ideas. Within a year, however, an Africa Progress Panel chaired by Kofi Annan was established to monitor the annual progress of the G8's commitments to Africa. The panel, formed at the midway point of the Millennium Development Goals timeline of 2015, is charged with influencing country leaders and policymakers to work toward concrete achievements. In the months leading up to the G8 Summit in Heiligendamm, Germany, panel members worked closely with German chancellor Angela Merkel and Prime Minister Tony Blair. They encouraged a focus on the delivery of Gleneagles commitments and criticized the G8 leaders for their failure to meet them. The same is true of the G8 meeting in Hokkaido, Japan, in July 2008. Funded by Bill Gates and including luminaries such as musician Bob Geldorf and Olusegun Obasanjo, former president of Nigeria, the panel will help ensure that issues of African development remain an annual focus of G8 meetings. However, even such well-respected leaders cannot guarantee that funding levels will match the pledges and lofty rhetoric. It is now clear that the big push to boost foreign aid by 2010 will not meet its target, which also puts in doubt the further commitments for 2015.

Obstacles to Delivering on Promises Made

Though the Commission for Africa was well intentioned and ably executed, the successful implementation of its recommendations face many hurdles. Some of these obstacles, described below, represent a complex of factors that widen the gap between intention and practice, thereby impeding the impact of a commission on its chosen subject.

Crowded International Agendas

The Commission for Africa aimed to focus international attention on Africa in 2005 during Blair's G8 presidency. The commissioners probably knew that they could not sustain attention to Africa for more than a few years. However, they hoped to maintain enough momentum to ensure that serious consideration of Africa would take place at the two subsequent G8 summits in St. Petersburg, Russia, in 2006, and Heiligendamm, Germany, in 2007. This momentum has carried through to Hokkaido in 2008. Since Gleneagles, exogenous factors intruded to divert the spotlight. As the commission conducted its work, and during the activities leading up to the G8 summit, the December 2004 tsunami disaster struck in Asia, thereby diverting the attention of many development and humanitarian actors. Other catastrophes followed, such as the October 2005 earthquake in Pakistan and the May 2008 cyclone and flooding in Myanmar. Sharp increases in oil and food prices, while having a global impact, have again called attention to the special vulnerabilities of Africa.

New players have also entered the equation. In particular, China has become a major investor in and lender to Africa. To date, China has not shown an interest in accompanying this involvement with efforts to address governance and development issues. Finally, the use of the G8 as the commission's primary platform poses some difficulties because its member countries vary widely in their concern for African development. When Russia chaired the G8 in 2006, President Vladimir Putin did not share the commission's priorities of building capacity and strengthening accountability in Africa. Indeed, he initially planned to focus on poverty in the former Soviet republics of Central Asia until he was reminded that Africa had been discussed at the last six G8 summits. Prior to the 2007 G8 meeting at Heiligendamm, German chancellor Angela Merkel was also not known for making major commitments to Africa or to poverty alleviation. However, German NGOs, Tony Blair, and others ensured that sufficient attention was paid to Africa on that occasion. Significantly, at the German summit's conclusion, Chancellor Merkel stressed the summit's two key priorities of Africa and the environment. Japan's prime minister, Yasuo Fakuda, placed aid commitments to Africa squarely on the G8 agenda at Hokkaido, alongside climate change and food security. However, apart from re-affirming unmet promises to scale up aid made at Gleneagles, most of the attention devoted to Africa was consumed by the Zimbabwean catastrophe.

Absorptive Capacity and Donor Coordination

The commission report called for an increase in ODA to Africa by an additional $25 billion per year by 2010, with a further $25 billion per year after 2010 if warranted by the progress made. Concerns have been raised about whether Africa can absorb so much assistance in such a short time. The questions of aid effectiveness and absorptive capacity are perennially debated, and recommendations abound. In *Overcoming Stagnation in Aid-Dependent Countries* (2005), Nicolas van de Walle called for performance-based aid, locally driven rather than government-led interventions, and targeted conditionalities. Nancy Birdsall, president of the Center for Global Development, has suggested that donors and development specialists should shift their focus from specific aid amounts and examine the importance of establishing a strong African middle class. Such analyses represent a widely held belief that the kind and quality of aid matters more than its amount. The report rightly says that increasing assistance will require enhanced coordination among donors and between donors and recipient countries. The famous case of more than seventy different reports required for one project in Tanzania remains a cautionary tale. The report correctly identifies the need to build accountable budget and management systems in recipient countries so that they can effectively absorb donor funds and track financial transactions. Accountable, transparent budgets are also essential to allay the qualms of skeptical publics in some donor countries.

Donors should identify the sectors in which they have comparative advantages. For instance, the United States has acquired substantial expertise in girls' education. It should be persuaded to devote more resources to this area while Great Britain and its Department for International Development (DFID) target more resources to transparency and anticorruption activities.

The report also recommends greater support for the AU and NEPAD. Before complying and increasing financial support, donors will want to see safeguards for transparency, enhanced monitoring and evaluation systems, and progress in strengthening the APRM.

Recruiting Private Sector Involvement

In view of the general recognition of the private sector as an essential contributor to sustainable development, the next question is: can the private sector be enlisted to participate fully and productively in the ambitious program proposed by the commission? In view of the report's emphasis on building infrastructure, the participation of private companies will be essential. Successful infrastructure construction and upgrading generally requires effective and efficient procurement systems to ensure that firms operate transparently and develop safeguards against corruption. Along with addressing these governance issues, countries would benefit from the creation of new opportunities for public-private partnerships that involve governments, businesses, and civil society organizations and facilitate new understanding among the parties of each other's long-term perspectives.

Sustaining Constituency Support

The Commission for Africa built a strong initial public constituency in the UK through children's programs, public meetings, the Live 8 concerts, and wide dissemination of the report to diverse audiences. However, this broad approach to constituency building was not replicated in other countries, nor has it proven durable in the UK. The failure to generate continuing public pressure will hamper the pursuit of several of the commission's aims, particularly those that run contrary to the interests of donor governments or other, more politically powerful interest groups. For instance, a sustained constituency is needed to pressure the European Union and the United States on World Trade Organization negotiations, especially concerning agricultural subsidies. In addition, such a constituency could counteract public opinion skeptical of the importance of debt relief in the pursuit of poverty alleviation and long-term growth. "Compassion fatigue" also poses a risk. The commission proposes an increase of foreign assistance of $25 billion per year by 2010 and a possible doubling to $50 billion per year by 2015. Will Western publics support such high outlays and the goal of 0.7 percent of gross domestic product contribution to ODA? Since aid to Africa actually fell in 2006, and the pledges of some donors, including the Italians, French, and Germans, were not fulfilled, there is a strong likelihood that the 2010 financial goal will not be reached.

Following the initial burst of activities in 2005, the commission's efforts at constituency building in donor countries, as well as in Africa, have fallen short. Ideally, to develop these constituencies, an enduring commission institutional structure should have been created. An untapped resource is the African diaspora, which has considerable resources and influence worldwide. Although no continuing secretariat exists, perhaps the Africa Progress Panel can gather the will and resources to assume such a constituency-building role as part of its efforts to advance implementation of commission findings.

Country-Level Implementation

Recent efforts to reshape the delivery of US foreign assistance illustrate the domestic institutional and political factors that adversely affect the implementation of internationally conceived agendas. Post-9/11 articulations of US foreign policy cast foreign aid as essential to reducing poverty and thereby building the capacity of vulnerable states to reduce their susceptibility to terrorist ideologies. Appreciation for the pivotal role of foreign assistance has also been reinforced by the Iraq War and the acceptance of nation building as a foreign policy objective. In this new context, US policymakers have concluded that US foreign assistance was fragmented and ineffective. The resulting reorganization seeks to improve US coordination of reconstruction and stabilization activities in postconflict countries and at-risk states, with the secretary of state serving as the lead actor in coordinating other agency activities.[5]

Reflecting this new dispensation, an Office of the Coordinator for Reconstruction and Stabilization was established in the State Department to plan and organize civilian agencies' responses to overseas crises in 2004. The position of a second deputy secretary of state was created in 2006, with the holder serving as director of foreign assistance and administrator of USAID. This official has direct responsibility for all USAID and Department of State foreign assistance funding and is expected to provide oversight for all other foreign assistance programs, including the multibillion-dollar programs of the Millennium Challenge Corporation and the Office of the US Global AIDS Coordinator. At the same time, the Department of Defense has assumed a larger role in foreign policy coordination and stabilization efforts in postconflict countries.[6] These directives for the Departments of State and Defense signal their rising power over development assistance and program implementation, leaving the role of USAID, the traditional lead agency charting foreign assistance direction, diminished and unclear. These major changes are particularly significant for Africa, the region that receives the largest share of US official development assistance, and they directly affect the US ability to make timely strategic decisions about aid priorities and to support the agenda identified by the Commission for Africa. Whether these changes will improve or inhibit this support remains to be seen. Either way, this restructuring demonstrates how domestic imperatives and events regularly trump international directives such as the commission agenda in determining donor methods and priorities.

Conclusion

The shifting context described above has prompted the United States to convene the HELP Commission to examine the future of US foreign assistance. Along with participating in international commissions, the United States has a long history of convening commissions and study groups at the national level to address broad policy issues. The 1985 Committee on African Development Strategies, sponsored by the Council on Foreign Relations and the Overseas Development Council and co-chaired by Lawrence Eagleburger, a future secretary of state, and Don McHenry, a former US permanent representative to the UN, greatly influenced US policy toward Africa. Its recommendations, aimed at the US Congress and the UN General Assembly, led to the creation of the US Development Fund for Africa, which guided US strategies and funding for Africa from 1986 to 1998. At the multilateral level, the committee's report, released at a 1985 Special Session of the UN General Assembly, focused international attention on Africa and was instrumental in later UN structural reforms.

Two decades later, the HELP Commission, chartered by Congress in 2006 in response to the 2003 HELP Commission Act, is reviewing US foreign assistance with the goal of delivering policy proposals to the executive and congress. The commission focuses on poverty reduction and promotes economic self-sufficiency in developing countries. Its members include high-profile economic and finance experts such as economist Jeffrey Sachs and Mary Bush. Although it is a national commission, the HELP Commission continues the Blair commission legacy as a vehicle to explore ideas. However, a certain level of redundancy with the latter commission indicate the risk of commissions becoming repetitive events whose reports are never translated into transformative results. This latest commission effort may build on the work done by the Commission for Africa, or it may result in duplicative or even contradictory analyses and findings.

Despite these hesitations, the Commission for Africa still gives us reasons to be optimistic about the impact of the exercise itself, about the future of commissions, and about Africa's future. One positive consequence of the Blair Commission has been the realization that without a follow-through mechanism, its recommendations will lose traction. The Africa Progress Panel, formed in response to this observation, is a monitoring mechanism that future commissions should incorporate into their initial plans. The Africa Progress Panel can provide a continuous policy voice by advocating sustained attention to track the pursuit of the commission's recommendations.

Moreover, by capitalizing on the stature and influence of its members, the panel members could also help build a constituency for Africa.

The Blair Commission demonstrated that commissions can still engage eminent personalities to discuss critical issues, mobilize financial support, and motivate constituencies. The Africa Progress Panel could demonstrate the importance of a follow-on mechanism for policy commissions. The Blair commission catalyzed commitments of leaders from the global North and global South to the continent's sustainable development. More importantly, it helped instigate and publicize a commitment from African leaders to accept responsibility for the role they must play in overcoming the development challenges facing the continent. The commission provided a forum to build a consensus among global businesses, multilateral financial institutions, development specialists, and civil societies about the high financial, security, and human consequences of Africa's success or failure. These groups will reinforce the need for donors and the international financial community to stay involved in this effort.

The enduring lesson learned from the Commission for Africa is this: a global campaign led by influential champions can help identify the priority issues, inspire constituencies, and mobilize resources. The Blair Commission may or may not achieve its desired targets of increasing development assistance to Africa, but it has succeeded in provoking constructive and critical thinking on African development and poverty reduction. One outcome of the campaign is, of course, the collaboration of an international group of scholars and policy practitioners that has explored what is required to make aid to Africa not just bigger but much smarter.

Notes

1. National commissions, often convened to discuss major domestic issues, will be discussed later in the chapter.

2. Gareth Evans makes a compelling case for international commissions in Thakur, Cooper, and English (2005, pp. x–xii).

3. Comments by Ambassador Miles Wickstead and Sir Nicholas Stern, senior professional staff to the Commission, at the Chicago Council on Foreign Relations.

4. Gender and development has attracted considerable policy research and action. There are many Internet sites that record this work, such as www.worldbank.org/gender/, www.bridge.ids.ac.uk/, and www.cedpa.org.

5. DOD determined that it now has a dual mission: (1) fighting and winning wars and (2) stabilizing countries after armed conflicts. Directive 3000.05 states that "stability operations are a core U.S. military mission that the Department of Defense shall be prepared to conduct and support." It continued: "They shall be given priority comparable to combat operations and be explicitly addressed and integrated across all Pentagon activities." The directive makes a distinction between immediate and long-term goals, noting, "The long-term goal is to help develop indigenous capacity for securing essential services, a viable market economy, rule of

law, democratic institutions and a robust civil society." "President Issues Directive to Improve the United States' Capacity to Manage Reconstruction and Stabilization Efforts," US Department of State, Fact Sheet, Office of the Spokesman, Washington, DC, December 14, 2005. http://www.state.gov/r/pa/prs/ps/2005/58067.htm.

6. Department of Defense Directive 3000.05, 4.1 and 4.2. Issued November 28, 2005. For access to the classified document, refer to document control number OSD 75774-04.

PART 2

Evaluating Strategies for Aid and Debt Relief

5

Rethinking Budget Support for Africa: A Political Economy Perspective

Joel Barkan

SINCE THE END OF THE 1990s, budget support—the policy of making direct monetary transfers to the treasuries of poor countries to support their development—has become a preferred instrument of the international donor community for providing development assistance. As such, budget support represents an increasingly larger component of total development assistance, especially to the lowest-income countries, which are disproportionately African. For the World Bank, budget support accounted for roughly 13 percent of all International Development Association (IDA) lending in 2001.[1] By 2004, the share attributed to budget support had jumped to 43 percent and by 2005 to 50 percent. Over the same period, commitments to budget support rose from 22 to 55 percent of IDA.

Budget support via the mechanism known as the Poverty Reduction Strategy Credit (PRSC) now accounts for 49 percent of all Bank lending to Africa. Conversely, 62 percent of all PRSC lending worldwide goes to Africa. The share of each "country portfolio" attributable to budget support, however, varies greatly, as indicated in Table 5.1. That said, between a quarter and a half of Bank lending to individual African countries is provided in the form of budget support.

Major bilateral donors, with the notable exception of the United States, likewise favor budget support over other forms of aid. Roughly a quarter of all British aid is now provided in the form of budget support. The Netherlands and the Scandinavian countries provide a quarter or more of their aid to Africa in the form of budget support. One could also argue that even the United States has tilted modestly toward budget support through the establishment of the Millennium Challenge Corporation (MCC) and its objective of making unrestricted grants to "good performers," a qualified form of budget support.

Table 5.1 Share of World Bank "Country Portfolio" Attributable to Budget Support, 2005

Country	Percentage
Cape Verde	62
Madagascar	49
Rwanda	48
Burkina Faso	47
Uganda	45
Benin	42
Ghana	38
Senegal	37
Mozambique	35
Ethiopia	35
Tanzania	27

Source: World Bank, Operations and Country Services Unit, 2005.

Budget support, narrowly defined, is not new. The International Monetary Fund (IMF), and to a lesser extent the World Bank as well as various bilateral donors, have long made cash transfers to support stabilization programs and programs of structural adjustments. These transfers, also known as nonproject assistance (NPA), were popular during the 1980s and 1990s to facilitate and cushion the impact of macroeconomic reforms in the short term, usually from one to three years. The current embrace of budget support, however, is for the primary purpose of financing long-term development, including, as necessary, the day-to-day operations of government.

Budget support represents a very different way of providing aid compared to traditional development assistance, in which donors provide grants or loans to pay for commodities or technical assistance or both on a project-by-project basis. Budget support is preferred over traditional aid for at least three reasons. First, and most important, it is viewed as the vehicle for shifting from conditionality-based lending to the establishment of harmonious "partnerships" between donor and recipient countries. Second, budget support is viewed as the mechanism for achieving more efficient lending by reducing the transaction costs associated with international aid. Third, when administered selectively, budget support rewards "good" performers while denying or reducing aid to "poor" ones, but without formally resorting to aid conditionality.

The Failure of Conditionality

By the end of the 1990s, it was clear that the practice of conditioning aid on the performance of recipient countries was not an effective approach. During the 1980s, when structural adjustment programs (SAPs) were initiated to address Africa's economic crisis of zero growth and declining per capita incomes, aid was conditioned on the promise by recipient countries to implement five basic macroeconomic reforms: (1) the progressive reduction of government deficits to balance the budget over time; (2) the deregulation of the economy to reduce rent seeking and free up internal markets for entrepreneurs and investors; (3) the end of price controls for basic commodities, including food, and the gradual elimination of consumer subsidies for these products to stimulate production; (4) the privatization of state-owned enterprises (SOEs); and (5) the shift from fixed to market-determined rates for foreign exchange.

This package of reforms was often resisted by African leaders because it could make them unpopular and undermine their power. What made "good sense" to macroeconomists sitting in Washington, D.C., or London was not viewed so positively in Abuja, Douala, Nairobi, or Dar es Salaam. Balancing budgets could eliminate inflation, but it would also reduce social services and put many civil servants out of work. The deregulation of markets might stimulate investment by local and foreign entrepreneurs, but it would reduce opportunities for rent seeking by underpaid civil servants. The end of price controls and the elimination of consumer subsidies for basic commodities might stimulate food production and improve the lives of rural dwellers, but prices paid by urban consumers for these products would rise sharply. Privatization of SOEs would help balance state budgets and, in a few cases, transform these money-losing businesses into productive and profitable firms, but it would also throw many out of work. And although the end of fixed exchange rates would stimulate the production of exports and reduce chronic current account deficits, it would make imports dearer and raise the cost of living for the middle class and urban dwellers.

The consequence is that major donors such as the World Bank and IMF negotiated agreements with African governments in which the former agreed to loan the latter substantial amounts of money—often between $200 million and $1 billion annually—in return for implementing the desired reforms. Yet, as William Easterly has noted in his illuminating book, *The Elusive Quest for Growth* (2001), most of these agreements failed. Little growth occurred because there was little commitment on the part of African leaders to undertake genuine reform. Moreover, most donor agencies, and especially the World Bank, did not enforce their own conditionalities for aid but simply rolled over the loans. They were not, in a word, "serious" about their own programs.

The result was an "SAP cycle" of broken promises and suspended and resumed aid. Following a formal agreement between the Bank and the IMF on the one side and the recipient country on the other, the international financial institutions (IFIs) would lend, but the recipient would only "pretend to adjust" (Easterly 2001a, p. 110). The agreement would then be suspended or terminated entirely, and the flow of aid would stop. The country would then slip back into crisis. Following a series of visits by officials from the IMF and the Bank to the pretending country, a new agreement would be negotiated (or the old one renegotiated), and the dance between donor and client would begin again.

It was a seemingly endless dance. As Easterly notes, the Bank and the IMF gave Kenya nineteen adjustment loans between 1979 and 1996 (Easterly 2001a, p. 107); Pakistan received twenty-two adjustment loans between 1970 and 1997 (Easterly 2001a, p. 109); Haiti, twenty-two; Liberia, eighteen; Ecuador, sixteen; and Argentina, fifteen—a veritable "merry-go-round of crisis–IMF bailout–crisis–IMF bailout, and so on ad infinitum" (Easterly, 2001a, p. 115) *with no meaningful economic growth or poverty reduction.*

Conditional aid also drove a wedge between the donors and developing countries, including most African countries. Relations between donors and clients had become adversarial and increasingly "noisy"—the former frustrated with the small number of success stories (e.g., Benin, Ghana, Uganda, and later Tanzania), the latter increasingly angry and pushing back. What had been intended as a virtuous cycle of reform and renewed economic growth had degenerated instead into a vicious cycle of stagnation and standoff.

The standoff was compounded by a growing list of conditions that the recipient countries were expected to meet. By the middle of the 1990s, basic macroeconomic reforms were not enough. In addition, recipient countries were expected to be making progress toward good governance, which was defined in different ways by different donors. For the bilateral aid agencies, especially the US Agency for International Development (USAID), the Netherlands, and the Scandinavian countries, good governance meant significant progress toward democratization, especially the holding of free and fair multiparty elections, the end of human rights abuses, and greater freedom for civil society groups. For multilateral agencies such as the World Bank and selected bilaterals such as the UK Department for International Development (DFID), good governance meant the absence or significant reduction of corruption. In any case, these additional "governance" criteria required that recipient governments change the ways they did business vis-à-vis their own citizens. Environmental standards and standards for gender equity and poverty reduction were often added. Recipient countries felt that the goalpost were constantly being moved; that they were being asked to do more and more in return for aid. Not surprisingly, they began to resist, deeming the entire relationship between donor and recipient as asymmetrical and inherently unfair. They demanded rethinking and adjustment by the donor community itself.

Aid recipients also demanded movement on debt relief, an idea first raised at the beginning of the 1990s but that gained little traction from the perspective of the donors on the grounds that nonreformers should not be rewarded by canceling their debts. Indeed, such cancellation was viewed as a disincentive for countries willing to reform. Recipient countries countered that until the burden of debt service was lifted through debt cancellation, or a substantial restructuring of existing loans, no amount of reform would lead to renewed economic growth and poverty reduction.

The Search for Partnership

The response by the donor community to break the standoff was the search for partnerships via the PRSC—the Poverty Reduction Strategy Credit offered by the World Bank and the IMF as a mechanism to address the problems of the heavily indebted poor countries (HIPC). In return for the reduction or cancellation of sovereign (but not private) debt, HIPC countries were expected to devise their own strategic plans for poverty reduction and reform. Such plans were to be articulated in the Poverty Reduction Strategy Paper (PRSP), in which recipient countries would state how the monies saved from debt relief and increased concessional aid would be invested in programs to reduce poverty. By asking recipient countries to devise their own plans and reforms, rather than being pressured to implement a list of donor conditions, donors sought to respond to the demands for "ownership" of the reform programs and increased aid. Once the PRSP was completed and accepted by the IFIs, the PRSC (i.e., the actual cash transfer) would be made. As noted above, PRSC lending, which takes the form of budget support, accounts for 49 percent of all Bank lending to Africa.

The PRSP/PRSC process was also intended to be a process of consultation between the governments of recipient countries and their citizens and between donors and recipients. In short, a partnership rather than a *diktat*. But partnership also had its limits in that the donors, particularly the World Bank, specified that the funds received from the PRSC, or saved from debt relief, must be channeled into social welfare expenditures.[2] Moreover, not all countries would receive debt relief.

The search for partnership in Africa was also nurtured in 2000–2001 by an initiative mounted by African leaders: the New Economic Partnership for Africa's Development (NEPAD). The brainchild of four African presidents—Abdelaziz Bouteflika (Algeria), Thabo Mbeki (South Africa), Olusegun Obasanjo (Nigeria), and Abdoulaye Wade (Senegal)—NEPAD sought to put an African stamp on the concept of partnership in two important ways: first, by demonstrating that Africans were as serious about economic and political reform as the donors; and second, by establishing an organizational structure and a process through which Africans would set reform standards for themselves and then use those standards to evaluate each other's performance. NEPAD would thus identify the countries that were worthy of donor support and those that were not.

The key to NEPAD's ultimate success will be the process of peer review. Under this procedure, known as the African Peer Review Mechanism (APRM), African governments submit themselves to being judged and rated by other Africans through a formal assessment conducted by the NEPAD secretariat. The procedures and personnel needed to implement the APRM were established in 2005. It is too early to judge whether the process is credible or if it will become another exercise in equivocation by African organizations and countries. The long-held principle, "Do not interfere in the business of your neighbor, or your neighbor will interfere in yours," remains well entrenched among African leaders, as has been tragically demostrated in the Zimbabwean crisis. Nevertheless, NEPAD holds out the prospect for serious peer review, a process that could have great impact if it is truly implemented.[3]

Budget Support as a Vehicle for Partnership

The provision of budget support is a logical response to demands by African leaders for partnership and ownership regarding aid for development. It requires no rigid conditionalities and is, in a fundamental sense, an expression of trust by members of the donor community in the anticipated performance of recipient governments and, by extension, their leaders. Budget support starts with the premise that the relationship between donor and recipient will be productive and harmonious and not adversarial.

The provision of budget support is also viewed as a mechanism that will substantially reduce the transaction costs of giving and receiving aid. For the donor, budget support holds out the prospect of disbursing substantial sums of money with reduced overhead costs. The staff requirements associated with the management and implementation of conventional aid projects are either no longer necessary or substantially reduced. For bilateral donors, the procurement regulations associated with conventional projects are also simplified, thus lowering the extent to which commodities and technical assistance must be sourced from the donor country. Donor procurement also requires putting such sourcing out for competitive bid, evaluating bids, writing contracts, and so on, all of which involves massive amounts of time and personnel. Although a shift to budget support still requires donors to monitor the overall performance of recipient countries, this monitoring can be confined mainly to the content and implementation of the macroeconomic policies of the recipient government. Monitoring will also continue, albeit with less emphasis, of the extent of poverty reduction, the capacity of the civil service to deliver vital social services, political stability, the extent of democratization, and reductions in the level of corruption.

Budget support also facilitates the harmonization and coordination of donor assistance among the donors themselves. Freed (or partially freed) from providing assistance on a project-by-project basis, donors can devote less time to ensuring complementarities across their different projects, and especially across projects aimed at a single sector or subsector (e.g., primary or higher education as part of a country's overall strategy for educational development, agricultural research, etc.).

At a time when the G8 countries led by the United Kingdom have committed themselves to increased aid for Africa, while the smaller bilateral donors such as Ireland, the Netherlands, and the Scandinavian countries seek to maintain or raise their levels of assistance, the opportunities for lowering the transaction costs of aid via budget support are very attractive.[4] The agencies charged with providing aid for developing countries are small in terms of personnel, and budget support enables these agencies to disburse large amounts of money without expanding their staffs.

Budget support is similarly attractive at the World Bank, where "moving the money" has long been the basis for successful careers. The pressure on Bank staff "to meet our lending targets" is relentless and no doubt a major reason for the succession of failed loans cited by Easterly in his critique of Bank practice.[5] Although the World Bank is the largest development agency, it is a bank in the conventional sense that its operations depend financially on lending its available capital to potential clients.[6] Bank staff are rewarded for "bringing the agreement to the Board," that is, for succeeding in negotiating a new loan agreement with a recipient country and having it approved by the Bank's board of directors. The Bank's emphasis on budget support is thus partly driven by an institutional dynamic and culture that has little to do with the needs or conditions of the recipient countries.

Lastly, budget support is appealing to officials of both the bilateral donor agencies and the Bank for a reason rarely mentioned in the halls of these institutions—that it reduces the fiduciary responsibility on the part of any one donor for making loans that do not result in significant poverty reduction. When aid from multiple donors is comingled and delinked from a series of specific projects, the progress of which can be monitored and periodically evaluated in the field, no one official or donor agency can be held accountable for poor outcomes in the recipient country. The extent to which this "silent" consideration drives budget support, however, is difficult to assess.

Budget support is likewise welcomed by recipient countries. For recipients, budget support holds out the prospect of more predictable aid flows from one year to the next. It reduces the transaction costs for recipient countries for the same reason that it reduces such costs for donors. Recipients have fewer individual projects for which they must conform to the regulations and reporting requirements of different donors, and donor coordination issues are reduced. Budget support also gives recipients a large measure of flexibility to move funds around to different areas of need, though recipient governments must follow agreed-upon guidelines regarding major areas of expenditure. These include minimum targets for expenditures on social service delivery and poverty reduction and limits on expenditures in the security sector.

Though important, such guidelines are not rigidly enforced. Moreover, where recipient governments are not totally transparent in their budgetary process, such guidelines are circumvented. For example, in cases in which a significant portion of the budget is allocated to the office of the president and is not subject to the normal public audit, large sums can be channeled to the security services or used for political patronage.

Such expenditures are obviously inconsistent with the principal objective of budget support, which is poverty alleviation. Indeed, it is precisely because money is fungible and budget support is not tied to any one project that it is subject to being misused. That is especially true in countries where donors provide between 30 and 50 percent of all government revenues, such as in Tanzania and Uganda. In these situations, "partnership" means that within broad limits, namely the maintenance of sound macroeconomic policy and some general understandings regarding the emphases of government policy, recipient governments can pretty much do as they choose.

Why Budget Support Is No Panacea for Donors or Recipients

Budget support is predicated on the assumption that a combination of "getting the macro policy right" and "partnership" via this type of aid will result in faster development and poverty reduction than project-based lending. Although the logic is sound, the actual record of budget support suggests that the reality varies quite a bit from country to country. That is to say, budget support is appropriate and fosters productive partnerships in some, but not all, countries.

This reasoning that budget support will succeed where conditionality-based assistance failed is flawed in at least three respects. First, it focuses exclusively on the potential benefits to be derived from budget support, as discussed in the previous section, without *any* systematic consideration of the potential or actual downside risks. Second, the argument for budget support rests on a highly selective and distorted understanding of the concept of governance by the leading providers of this form of assistance. Third, the argument is, to some extent, driven by the institutional imperatives of these organizations and, to a lesser extent, those of the leading bilateral advocates of budget support.

With respect to the first problem—that Bank staff and the staff of other donors do not consider the downside—the argument for budget support is excessively "economistic" in perspective. The argument rests mainly on the near universal experience of developing countries since independence, namely, that without sound macroeconomic policies, economic growth and poverty reduction cannot be achieved. The evidence is especially persuasive in sub-Saharan Africa, where the crisis of economic stagnation of the 1970s and 1980s was associated with chronic overspending on social welfare services and unsustainable subsidies for state-owned enterprises and urban consumers. The result was stagflation—rising prices, declining production, and declining per capita income for rural dwellers. Yet, as the experience of the 1990s and the first half-decade of the twenty-first century has demonstrated, "getting the macro right" is a necessary *but insufficient* requirement for poverty alleviation.

The same may be said about the economic benefits to be derived from budget support. For the reasons discussed, budget support does reduce the direct transaction costs of overseas development assistance for both donors and recipients. However, this reduction does not guarantee aid effectiveness. Indeed, as discussed below, the unintended consequences of budget support represent another set of "transaction costs" that outweigh the savings in the reduction of direct transaction costs. Improved macroeconomic policies and the reduction of aid transaction costs, though important, are not the only variables determining aid effectiveness.

It is no surprise that the principal institutions advocating budget support are those such as the Bank, which are largely staffed by economists rather than by practitioners of other disciplines. It is another classic example of what one does not look for, or ask questions about, one does not find. The result is that, until recently, other variables that are not overtly "economic" in nature but highly relevant for aid effectiveness have been largely ignored. These variables fall under two general headings: societal context and governance, especially its *political* component.

With respect to the first, it is not an overstatement to say that context—especially the historical, sociological, and cultural context within which aid programs are implemented—greatly affects the outcomes of these programs. It makes a big difference whether a country is a plural society prone to fracture along sociocultural lines, or whether it is a relatively homogeneous and stable society free of these cleavages. Context matters especially for budget support. Because budget support takes the form of cash transfers to the treasuries of recipient states, it cannot be fine-tuned to local conditions as conventional aid projects can. In fact, the opposite is the case: budget support is usually hostage to the local context.

With respect to the second, the Bank's understanding of the concept of governance is flawed because it is an interpretation largely devoid of politics. Both the Bank and the IMF define governance in terms of whether a recipient country engages in good *economic* governance. They ask first, whether the government of a recipient country pursues a sound macroeconomic policy and, second, whether its state apparatus, particularly the ministry of finance and related agencies such as the revenue bureau and the auditor general's office, manages macroeconomic policy and the budget process well. This definition of good governance also assumes an absence or tolerable levels of corruption, because corruption should be limited where government is an effective manager of the economy. It would also include an efficient civil service capable of implementing social service delivery, a key to poverty alleviation. This definition of governance focuses almost exclusively on the bureaucratic or "supply side" of the concept.

The standard meaning of governance, however, includes much more than what the Bank and the IMF consider when making arguments for budget support. In its most basic and broadest sense, governance is "a system of governing." In other words, it encompasses the totality of relationships between the rulers and the ruled, between those who control the state and citizens. Governance includes much more than what the state does to or for society—the administrative and supply-side dimension of governance. It also includes the "demand side" of the relationship—how citizens and organized interests are able to make claims on the state via intermediary institutions. They include interest groups, political parties, legislatures, and the judiciary, as well as informal structures such as patron-client networks. In short, governance also includes the institutional arenas that constitute a country's *politics*.

The Bank and the IMF, however, pay little attention to the demand side of governance, with the occasional exception of the judicial process. Politics is usually regarded as the proverbial elephant in the room, the phenomenon that one pretends does not exist but knows one cannot ignore. The reason cited most often by Bank staff for not giving the elephant its due are the bylaws of their organization that explicitly forbid the consideration of a recipient country's politics when determining the level of development assistance. But the main constraint, as suggested above, is the dominant and pervasive economistic perspective of Bank staff. Most simply do not inquire about the impact of politics on the supply side of governance, or on economic development itself, because such queries are not on their cognitive agenda. "We don't do politics," or "We should know more about politics, but we have few people who understand politics," is the typical lament.

The result is that some directors of Bank country programs in Africa misread or ignore elements of the political process that undermine the viability of their programs. The Bank's programs of budget support in Ethiopia and Uganda are two of the most egregious examples. In each case, the Bank has continued to lend, though some modest cuts to or reallocations away from budget support were announced for both countries in 2006.[7] In Ethiopia, the Bank continued budget support as part of a program disbursing over $1 billion a year, despite declining agricultural production and a continuing military standoff with Eritrea (and now Somalia). Not until after a patently fraudulent election, followed by the repression of protests in Addis Ababa in 2005, did the Bank's country team acknowledge that there was a governance problem and temporarily suspend and then reconfigure budget support. Budget support has also continued in Uganda, despite an alarming rise in the level of corruption and rising levels of poverty and HIV/AIDS. Presidential elections held in February 2006 also fell well short of "free and fair standards."

The downside of budget support is particularly evident in respect to the informal structures of African politics. Because most African countries are agrarian, plural societies, clientelist politics and clientelist political organizations dominate political life. One result is that political parties are weak and are often parties in name only. Rather than mobilizing the electorate on the basis of their policy positions or ideology, parties are fluid coalitions of ethnoregional leaders and their respective clienteles who mobilize the electorate on the basis of their local identities, such as the community within which one resides, the ethnic group to which one belongs. In this context, the people who can provide large amounts of patronage in the form of jobs or cash to their retinue and constituents are the winners. But jobs and cash are in short supply, which is why budget support is so appreciated by government leaders.

Because money is fungible, budget support is a significant provider of political finance, although that is not intended by lending agencies. Similarly, budget support is the unintended funder of corruption because the principal impetus for corruption, especially on a large scale, is the need for political finance. Thus the diversion of large amounts of funds into unaudited accounts, or to accounts for which audits are not disclosed to the public, enables a portion of budget support to be used to maintain patronage machines.

The problem of ignoring the elephant is not as acute among the leading bilateral aid organizations, especially those that maintain active programs of democracy promotion. The United States, the United Kingdom, the Netherlands, and the Scandinavian countries all fall within this category and have a more holistic view of governance. All except the United States are significant contributors to budget support. It is perhaps for this reason that several of these bilateral aid agencies, in marked contrast to the World Bank, have periodically retreated from budget support by shifting a portion of such funds to conventional project assistance (e.g., the United Kingdom and the Netherlands in Uganda in 2005). The British are increasingly sensitive to the challenge they face in balancing their objective to scale up the proportion of UK bilateral aid provided via budget support with the need to maintain "good political governance" (DFID 2004b).

The point is that notwithstanding the attractive aspects of budget support, it is no panacea for development. It works best where the political context is supportive, that is, where there is political stability, transparency, and accountability by government to the governed. In other words, where there is democracy, good governance in the political and demand-side dimensions of the term matters as much as good governance in the economic management sense. Both are necessary if budget support is to realize its potential for reducing poverty across Africa.

A Tale of Two Countries: The Tortoise and the Hare

Tanzania and Uganda are both aid-dependent countries that receive a substantial portion of foreign assistance via budget support. While aid provides roughly half the annual government budget for each country, their respective revenue authorities collect only 12 to 13 percent of gross domestic product (GDP) in taxes. The extent of their dependence on aid is clear when one compares the situation in these two countries with neighboring Kenya where the role of aid has declined in recent years. Aid presently accounts for less than 5 percent of Kenya's current budget. The country receives no budget support, and the Kenya Revenue Authority collects between 22 and 24 percent of GDP—a figure that has risen steadily in recent years. Prior to the 2007 elections, Kenya was emerging as the most democratic country in East Africa. Its annual rate of economic growth had risen in recent years to 6 percent, the same as Tanzania's and higher than Uganda's. This development in turn suggests that budget support per se does not determine economic growth. Rather, it is the combination of sound macroeconomic policy and good governance *broadly* defined (i.e., the quality of both supply-side and demand-side aspects of the relationship between the rulers and the ruled).

A comparison of the three countries, but especially Tanzania and Uganda, illustrates the uses and misuses of budget support. It also shows why this form of aid must be accompanied by both macroeconomic *and* political reform. Here we have the proverbial tale of the tortoise and the hare. In this comparison, Uganda is the sprinter and the hare, the country that moved first and fastest with macroeconomic reform, but whose reforms eventually slowed and have proved shallow because they have been largely limited to the economic dimensions of good governance. Tanzania is the tortoise, the plodder that started slowly but is now well on its way to completing the entire course because it has made significant political as well as economic reforms. The result is that Tanzania's rate of economic growth currently exceeds Uganda's and is rising. By contrast, Uganda appears to have entered a period of slow but steady decline, notwithstanding large, continuing inflows of budget support from the World Bank, the United Kingdom, the Netherlands, and Denmark that provide budget support under the Uganda Joint Assistance Strategy. An overview of the comparative performance of the two countries, as well as their respective commitments to both economic and political reform, is presented in Table 5.2.

Table 5.2 The Tortoise and the Hare

	Uganda (the "Hare")	Tanzania (the "Tortoise")
"Pace" of reforms, 1985–2005	"fast" then "slow"	"slow" then "fast"
Political elite committed to sustaining macroeconomic reforms?	Yes	Yes
Ruling political elite committed to democratic reforms?	Limited	Genuine
Senior civil service committed to civil service reform?	Unclear	Yes
Mobilization of the electorate on the basis of ethnic identities?	Yes	Infrequent
Clientelist politics?	Yes	Yes
Clientelist politics has degenerated into neopatrimonial rule?	Yes	No
Term limits enforced?	No	Yes
Civil service reform includes serious pay reform?	No	Yes
Privatization of state-owned enterprises completed honestly?	No	Yes
Rate of economic growth 1990–1995		
1996–2000	5	6
2001–2005	7	5.6
Percentage living in poverty 1990–1995	38.6	56
1996–2000		33.4
2001–2005	36	37.7

During the course of the 1990s, both Uganda and Tanzania put their macroeconomic houses in order. Uganda had begun to do so even earlier, between 1987 and 1989. Upon taking power by armed struggle at the end of 1986, President Yoweri Museveni and his National Resistance Army (NRA) assumed responsibility for a failed state and a once prosperous economy that had dwindled into near subsistence following two decades of authoritarian rule, civil war, and poor economic policies. The economy had collapsed and its rejuvenation was essential for the rebuilding of the Ugandan state. Although initially skeptical of the IFI prescription for economic stabilization and adjustment, Museveni soon accepted the terms of the donors to secure massive infusions of aid. The economy responded quickly. By 1991 a functioning market economy had been reestablished across the southern two-thirds of Uganda. Between 1991 and 1995, growth averaged 8 percent a year, one of the highest in Africa.

Museveni also moved swiftly to reconstitute the Ugandan state. The president and the leadership of the NRA transformed the army into the National Resistance Movement (NRM), a big tent to which all Ugandans would nominally belong. A national legislature was indirectly elected through NRM structures, and in 1994 a constitutional review commission and a constitutional assembly were established, which together wrote a new constitution.

The hallmark of the new constitution was the Movement System of governance, a system that initially resembled nonpartisan, elected, municipal government in the United States. Under this system, political parties were allowed to exist but could not nominate candidates for office or campaign on their behalf. Instead, all candidates competed for office—at the local and district level, for the National Assembly, and for the presidency—on the basis of their "individual merit." Competitive elections were reintroduced in 1996 for all levels of government. They were judged among the best in Africa, well administered and "free and fair." Museveni, who was genuinely popular for having rebuilt the Ugandan state and rejuvenated the economy, was elected to his first five-year term as president by winning more than 80 percent of the vote. Civil society enjoyed the freedom to function. The Ugandan press was also allowed considerable latitude in its reporting. In light of its recent past and the turnaround Museveni had engineered, Uganda was judged an African "success." Museveni himself was hailed as one of the "new leaders of Africa," a reformer who had rescued his country from the abyss. Donor money arrived in ever-increasing amounts, ultimately in the form of budget support.

For Tanzania, the pace was much slower. During the early 1980s, when Julius Nyerere was still president, Tanzania refused to adopt the five basic macroeconomic reforms reviewed at the beginning of this chapter. The donor community responded by suspending aid. Not surprisingly, the economy declined. By the late 1980s, Nyerere grudgingly accepted reforms, but the embrace was limited and began with small steps. For example, Tanzania introduced a policy of floating exchange rates over an extended period that lasted well into the 1990s. It also took Tanzania the entire decade of the 1990s to close down its money-losing public enterprises that had initially numbered more than four hundred.

Though he resisted economic reforms as dictated by the IFIs, Nyerere embraced political reform by stepping down from the presidency in 1985 and appointing a constitutional review commission that led to the return of multiparty politics in 1992. He also instituted the principle of term limits by restricting the tenure of all future Tanzanian presidents to two five-year terms. Nyerere's successor was Ali Hassan Mwinyi in 1985, who was in turn succeeded by Benjamin Mkapa in 1995 and then Jakaya Kikwete in 2005. Tanzania's continued adherence to presidential term limits since Nyerere's death in 1999 has firmly established the norm that institutions count more than incumbents and that power should not be concentrated in the hands of one individual for too long.[8] Although Tanzania remains a one-party-dominant state—the ruling party, Chama cha Mapinduzi (CCM), has won every multi-party election since 1995 with at least 70 percent of the vote—decisions within the central committee of CCM and within the cabinet are collective decisions that often follow intense debates.

In marked contrast, Uganda has evolved into a one-party-dominant system in which all major decisions are made by Museveni. Politics has degenerated into a system of neopatrimonial rule reminiscent of Africa prior to the 1990s (Barkan 2005; USAID 2005a; World Bank 2005c). Once hailed as one of the new leaders of Africa, Museveni governs Uganda as Daniel arap Moi and Mobutu Sese Seko governed Kenya and Zaire at the height of their power: through a combination of patronage and kleptocracy. There is, however, one important difference. Whereas Moi and Mobutu paid no heed to the laws of economics and resisted macroeconomic reform, Museveni has continued to embrace them to ensure continued inflows of donor assistance, especially budget support.

Space does not permit a detailed analysis of Uganda's gradual decline, but two important aspects should be mentioned. The first is the single-minded commitment, on the part of Yoweri Museveni, to retaining power. The second is the need to secure a steady infusion of finance for his regime, especially budget support, by adhering to the macroeconomic policies that have endeared him to the donor community since 1987.

Museveni has steadily rolled back key provisions of the 1995 constitution that laid the foundation for democracy in Uganda. In the run-up to the 2001 elections, the president and his government harassed the principal opposition candidate, Kizza Besigye, by ordering the police to deny him permits to hold public rallies or by canceling permits already issued. Opposition party meetings were sometimes broken up by hired thugs. Civil society groups were harassed, and the press came under increasing pressure from the government. The irony is that Museveni would have been elected easily without resorting to such tactics. Following the 2001 election, and faced with a constitutional limit of two elected terms, he maneuvered Uganda's National Assembly into passing constitutional amendments in 2005 that repealed the ban on a third elected term. The amendments also changed Uganda from the "Movement" system to a conventional multiparty system. The NRM thereby became the ruling party and a vehicle for personal rule similar to African parties of the one-party era.

In the run-up to the presidential elections in February 2006, Museveni was again challenged by Besigye, who returned from four years of exile in South Africa to campaign for the presidency. In addition to facing the same harassments as in 2001, the challenger was detained for a month and charged with rape and treason, the first to be tried by a civilian court and the second by a military tribunal. Although he was eventually released, he was required to appear in court weekly, thus depriving him of opportunities to campaign. Not surprisingly, Museveni won the election, but this time by a narrower margin of 59 to 37 percent.

The Museveni regime maintains itself in power through an extensive network of patronage, family ties, and kleptocracy, of which a major pillar is the Uganda People's Defence Force (UPDF), including its 10,000-man praetorian guard, the Presidential Guard Brigade (PGB). The PGB is commanded by Museveni's son, who is married to the daughter of the current minister of foreign affairs. That minister, who had extensive business dealings with the president's brother, was previously censored by the National Assembly and dropped from the cabinet for corrupt practices. The brother, who was once head of the UPDF when it looted gold and coltan in Democratic Republic of Congo, and who was co-owner of a company that provided all ground services (freight transfers, ticketing, baggage transfers) at Entebbe International Airport, is currently minister for internal affairs. It is also alleged that individuals and senior officers in the army in northern Uganda have profited from the twenty-year war against the Lords Resistance Army by looting the payroll of the UPDF and violating procurement procedures for military equipment.[9]

Notwithstanding the adherence to sound macroeconomic policy, the politics of the past half-decade in Uganda, in combination with the war in northern Uganda, have taken their toll.[10] Once hailed as a model in the fight against HIV/AIDS, the prevalence rate of the virus is again on the rise. Although it would be wrong to blame budget support for Uganda's declining performance, the lavish assistance by the donor community has propped up the economy and the regime and thus financed "bad governance" in the form of neopatrimonial or prebendal rule (Joseph 1987).

By adhering to term limits and by governing collectively, Tanzania's leaders have slowly but firmly instituted a series of structural reforms that have laid the basis for sustained economic growth. The proof can be seen in the economic statistics that have been improving steadily since the late 1990s and especially 2003. Under Mkapa, Tanzania embarked on what is arguably the most comprehensive set of government reforms in Africa. Supported by the World Bank, the government vastly improved its financial systems. It also embarked on a difficult restructuring of the civil service, including pay reform and performance-based budgeting. Another item on the agenda is an ambitious policy of local government reform and the renewal of the judicial system. Although the latter two programs will take years to complete, they should make vital contributions to the country's development.

The bottom line, as indicated in Table 5.2, is that Tanzania's reforms have involved much more than sound macroeconomic policy. It has also involved a partial restructuring of the country's political system and eventually the Tanzanian state. On the supply side, and albeit to a lesser extent on the demand side, governance in Tanzania has changed greatly since the one-party era ended in 1992. Tanzania, like Uganda, remains a one-party-dominant system in terms of the percentage of votes garnered by the ruling party. But it is a very different system regarding who holds power, for how long, and for what purpose. Uganda is a pseudo-democracy, whereas Tanzania is an aspiring if not yet liberal democracy. In politics *and* in economics, the tortoise is trumping the hare. The difference would be even greater had the donor community not lavished budget support on the recidivist rabbit.[11]

Smart Versus Dumb Budget Support

Four lessons are already apparent regarding budget support to Africa:

• Like most previous "solutions" to the conundrum of Africa's under-development, budget support alone is not a panacea, despite its many attractions. Simply pumping more money into African countries with few strings attached ensures neither development nor the reform of critical state institutions, without which sustained development will not occur.

• Budget support, when combined with sound macroeconomic policy alone, can finance and sustain bad governance, especially the reemergence of neopatrimonial rule, corrupt practices, and a retreat from democratic reform.

• Context, and especially the political context, matters. If sustainable development is contingent on state institutions that are accountable, transparent, and relatively free of corruption, then budget support should only be provided to countries in which there is a serious commitment to both sound macroeconomic policy *and* democratic and administrative reform. Even though budget support is intended to facilitate partnerships with African governments and to avoid the resentments associated with aid conditionality, some measure of "conditionality," including political reform, is unavoidable. The existence of "the elephant in the room" cannot be denied.[12]

• Large-scale budget support, even when matched with countries that can make effective use of this type of assistance, such as Tanzania, perpetuates aid dependency. When donors provide between one-third and one-half of the annual budget, and do so with few requirements, there is little incentive for recipient governments to develop other revenue sources. Although such donors may intend to free up money for the private sector, it is not fair to poor countries such as Kenya that do not receive budget support yet generate substantial tax revenues on their own.

In conclusion, "smart budget support" represents *a qualified opportunity* for major donor agencies, such as the World Bank and DFID, to disburse substantial sums with lowered transaction costs for donors and recipients. Because it is not contingent on explicit conditionalities or micromanagement by donor agencies, it is also user-friendly aid that nurtures partnerships. Whether budget support actually supports sustainable development and poverty reduction in Africa, however, depends on the quality of governance in recipient countries. Budget support can thus be smart or dumb. It can nurture the development of countries that have made genuine commitments to both political and economic reform, such as Benin, Ghana, and Tanzania. Or, it can perpetuate bad governance, as in the cases of Ethiopia, Rwanda, and Uganda, where authoritarian rulers have succeeded in manipulating the donor community. Providers of budget support need to be more realistic and broaden their perspective and understanding when promoting this new approach to African aid and development.

Notes

The views expressed by the author in this essay are his alone and should not be construed as reflecting any official position of the World Bank.

1. IDA (International Development Association) is the World Bank's long-term concessional window for the poorest countries, via which it provides loans at zero interest, but that charges a 0.75 percent annual service fee. Loans are to be paid back over a forty-year period, beginning with an initial grace period of ten years. Approximately 50 percent of all IDA lending goes to Africa. The Bank disburses roughly $9 billion annually via IDA. The Bank employs two additional mechanisms for providing assistance to developing countries: its standard loans from the International Bank for Reconstruction and Development (IBRD) and its loans for commercial ventures through the International Finance Corporation (IFC). Both IBRD and IFC loans are made at low market rates, for the purpose of making capital available for projects and programs that commercial banks would ordinarily not fund or would fund at higher rates of interest.

2. The Bank took this position to counter the prevailing view that SAPs had reduced the delivery of key social services to reforming countries, especially to rural dwellers. Some recipient countries, however, considered it an unwarranted constraint, especially the requirement to invest in social service delivery over critically needed infrastructure such as roads and energy.

3. At the time this chapter was written, only four countries—Ghana, Kenya, Uganda, and South Africa—had been assessed by the APRM, and only one, South Africa, had had its report released. It is noteworthy that the assessment was critical about the high levels of crime and poverty in that country.

4. It should be remembered that in 2006, only the Netherlands, Luxembourg, Denmark, Norway, and Sweden met the G8 goal of devoting 0.7 percent of GDP to overseas development assistance—all small countries with a limited capacity to disburse this amount of funds to their "development partners."

5. This exhortation was typical of Calisto Madavo, during his tenure as vice president for the Africa region at the Bank from 2000 to 2005. In bimonthly emails to staff, including this author, Madavo regularly urged Bank personnel to meet lending targets "while maintaining quality." Unfortunately, the two goals were often at

odds with each other (that is, the greater the volume of money lent, the lower the quality of the loans), but it is a common situation in commercial banking.

6. Although it is a multilateral development agency, the World Bank functions more like a conventional bank than most observers outside the institution are aware. This is particularly true with respect to its IBRD window. Funds deposited at the Bank by its principal donor members are not directly passed on to borrowers but are used to leverage even more funds for prospective clients by serving as guarantees for bonds that the Bank sells on international capital markets. The funds from the sale of these bonds are then lent to various recipient countries. Although loans made via the IDA consist of funds deposited for that purpose and are used directly for lending to the world's poorest countries, a portion of IDA loans are made from repayments and interest obtained from conventional IBRD loans as well as from repayments of earlier IDA loans.

7. These cuts or reallocations in budget support were in large part triggered by the Bank's bilateral partners in budget support. Put simply, the bilateral aid agencies have been far more sensitive to the problems of political governance in Ethiopia and Uganda than the Bank, though the Bank's country teams eventually woke up to the obvious.

8. One indication of the commitment to the principal of term limits is that in the run-up to the most recent presidential election, held in October 2005, the ruling party, Chama cha Mapinduzi, completed its nomination process of Mkapa's successor in April, a full six months before the election. Moreover, neither Mkapa nor Mwinyi before him ever broached the possibility of amending the constitution to permit a third term.

9. The scams were the subject of two government commissions of inquiry into army operations in the Congo (Uganda 2002a) and in the north (Uganda 2003) as well as a government white paper (Uganda 2002b).

10. One indicator of Uganda's macroeconomic policy is the rise in the value of the Ugandan shilling against the US dollar.

11. By 2005 and in 2006, the donor community slowly woke up to its predicament in Uganda and reduced the portion of aid allocated to budget support. The World Bank reduced its program of budget support by $135 million, or roughly 10 percent. The British, the Irish, and the Dutch also reduced their commitments to budget support, though not to their total levels of assistance to Uganda.

12. It is noteworthy that for perhaps the first time, the Bank's Independent Evaluation Group has identified "the political economy of reforms" as a critical variable in whether poor countries perform. "The evaluation finds that anticorruption campaigns and related reform programs have been less effective when they have not taken enough account of the local political circumstances" (World Bank 2006).

6

The Search for Smart Debt Relief: Questions of When and How Much

Thomas M. Callaghy

IN MANY WAYS, debt relief has been the wedge that led to recent proposals to give considerably more aid to Africa, coming from a new constituency that did not exist fifteen years ago. This story has a lot to say about the prospects for "smarter" debt relief and aid generally. The basic fact is a political one: the definition of smarter debt relief varies greatly, depending on how key actors define their core interests and how those interests change over time.

The Evolution of Debt Relief

Although important, the Group of Eight (G8) governments, including the United States, have not been the driving force of change in the debt regime.[1] It is necessary to look also at other actors to explain the nature of this evolution, especially advocacy and development nongovernmental organizations (NGOs).

At the core of the evolution of the debt regime is the broadening of the processes of international economic governance, especially the role of new actors and ideas and the institutional contexts that support them. The rise of the heavily indebted poor country (HIPC) debt initiative in 1996 brought important but ultimately limited change to the debt regime for a designated group of countries. The striking innovations included the systematic treatment of multilateral debt based on the notion of debt sustainability, focusing debt relief on poverty reduction after the revision of the program in 1999 under NGO pressure. In the process, the center of gravity of the debt regime shifted from the Paris Club of sovereign (bilateral) creditors to the

International Monetary Fund (IMF) and the World Bank, institutions that are now more open and accountable than in the past. As we shall see, the emergence of the Multilateral Debt Relief Initiative (MDRI) in 2005 was another major step in the attempt to make debt relief smarter.

These changes in the debt regime were brought about by a confluence of factors: (1) slow and uneven learning by bilateral and multilateral creditors about the existence of a group of states that were not benefiting much from structural adjustment while greatly increasing their debt loads; (2) the growing pressure, influence, and effectiveness of a new set of actors in international economic governance—networks of NGOs that believed the existing situation was unjust and untenable and had new ideas and proposals of their own, plus a social movement that supported them; (3) the influence of a group of economists, both inside and outside creditor institutions, who provided knowledge, advice, and technical understanding on this issue; (4) leadership by a group of small creditor states and eventually several members of the G8, especially Britain; (5) a World Bank leadership that was more open to new ideas; and, (6) eventually, tough negotiations between all major creditor countries, the IMF, the World Bank, and, to a lesser extent, some of the major NGOs. This outcome was not inevitable: a change in one or two factors, such as different G8 governments, leadership at the Bank, or the absence of NGO pressure, could have led to a quite different outcome.

The major path in the evolution of sovereign debt has been from debt collection to debt rescheduling, to aid and structural adjustment, to debt "sustainability," to small-scale forgiveness and poverty reduction, and finally, to major debt cancellation for a set of poor countries. One official has called it the slippery slope of debt. The original aim of the HIPC initiative was to provide debt sustainability that would help remove a major constraint to investment and growth and spur further adjustment, in part by galvanizing increased private external investment. It is not at all clear that this happened. By the time the revised or "enhanced" HIPC initiative emerged in 1999, the focus had shifted markedly to poverty reduction. By 2005 the emphasis was on nearly complete cancellation of debt owed to the IMF, the World Bank, and the African Development Bank (AfDB). On the donor side, it was hoped that this expanding debt relief process would strengthen the legitimacy and country "ownership" of structural adjustment programs. It soon became clear that it would be difficult to accomplish. The Poverty Reduction Strategy Paper (PRSP) process that emerged out of the enhanced HIPC process might be viewed, in its grandest form, as a meager attempt by creditor countries to extend their own "compromise of embedded liberalism" to the poorest countries of the world, based on a relatively small pot of funds.[2] The long-term question remains how this partial, if not outright feeble, extension of embedded liberalism might be financed and implemented effectively and what its effect on the debtors might be. The political fact is that the NGOs have won the battle over HIPC debt savings: they are to be devoted exclusively to "poverty reduction."

The HIPC initiative has not been a magic bullet. It has been important for a number of countries, but very far from turning Africa and other poor countries around. In this context, it is not clear that an exclusive focus on poverty is the correct one. By the time of the enhanced HIPC initiative in 1999, there was a sense that the process had acquired multiple objectives but still had only one instrument. The objectives included debt sustainability, regularization of relations with creditors, poverty reduction, and growth. There was also an increasing perception that debt relief was just one part of a much larger picture, one that needed to be dealt with for real debt sustainability to be achieved. But an even larger question remained: Was it possible, as the new Bush administration came to power in 2001, and especially after the tragedy of September 11, to go beyond the HIPC initiative?

From HIPC to MDRI: The Geopolitics of Debt Relief

The administration of George W. Bush came to power with a policy of "drop the debt and stop the debt." It was not enthralled by the debt relief process and spent much of its first three years pursuing two policy tracks simultaneously: (1) containing the cost of HIPC debt relief as well as any new incremental policy innovation—its version of "drop the debt"; and (2) pushing a proposal to significantly increase the ratio of grants to loans—the "stop the debt" part. The first track eventually encountered serious geostrategic hurdles and intense G8 politics over a concept that the Bush administration had openly scorned—"odious debt."

NGO coalitions were working to achieve much more dramatic changes in the strategic relationship between Africa and powerful external actors. With great consistency, they maintained their demand for full debt cancellation and an end to structural adjustment while arguing for substantial increases in aid, especially grants, to meet the Millennium Development Goals. They linked these issues to AIDS, the larger African health crisis, increased war and violent conflicts, declining state services and infrastructure, and unfair trade practices by the industrial democracies. In regard to trade, Oxfam charged that the G8 was content to have debt remain the focus of debate in order to draw attention away from major trade reform. September 11 and its aftermath stalled efforts for greater debt relief, but by early 2004 major pressure for additional debt relief had been resumed because the HIPC process was scheduled to end on December 31 of that year. This pressure came from the NGOs and African governments, as well as a number of smaller European governments, but also from some parts of the World Bank and a few major states. Gordon Brown, the British chancellor of the exchequer, announced in

April 2004 that "there is now a window of opportunity to make progress on this issue, and I'm hopeful that when we meet at the annual meetings we'll have made the most of this opportunity" (Swann and Crooks 2004; see also Elliott 2004). Brown believed this opportunity existed because the Bush administration, in its efforts to get major debt relief for Iraq, appeared to be softening its position on HIPC reform. Others were less optimistic.

Not long after the US invasion of Iraq, the Bush administration realized that, despite having the world's second-largest oil reserves, Iraq needed major relief on its external debt of roughly $120 billion. The administration argued that Iraq deserved a 90–95 percent reduction of its $40 billion Paris Club debt, relief for which it was not qualified under existing Paris Club rules, despite earlier rule-breaking deals for Poland, Egypt, and Russia. Former secretary of the Treasury and secretary of state James A. Baker became a special envoy whose task was to travel the world persuading countries to join the financial "coalition of the willing." The United States, which held a relatively small proportion of Iraq's debt, was now ready to characterize Saddam Hussein's borrowings as "odious debt."

Canada supported the US demand for 90–95 percent debt relief, as did Britain, but major G8 opposition emerged from France, Germany, Japan, and Russia. President Jacques Chirac of France asserted that Iraq should not get a better deal than the world's heavily indebted poor countries, making it clear that little progress would be made on Iraq until more was done for these countries. He declared that Iraq should get no more than a 50 percent reduction, a position supported by much of the rest of the G8. At the G8 meeting in Sea Island, Georgia, in June 2004, the United States presented a stunning proposal to cancel all the multilateral debt that HIPC countries owed to the IMF, the World Bank, and the African Development Bank. The tacit quid pro quo would be support for the US position on Iraqi debt. This proposal was presented as an example of "compassionate conservatism" in the larger context of the Millennium Development Goals. John Taylor, then undersecretary of the Treasury for international affairs, said, "We need to complete the 'drop and stop the debt' vision put forth by President Bush at the start of his administration."[3] Treasury Secretary John Snow put it in the context of the administration's larger approach to development and international financial institutions: "I believe the Bretton Woods Institutions have a responsibility to continue their own reform, for example by doing more to reinforce debt sustainability in poor countries. . . . Employing both grants and debt relief together would give the poorest countries a chance to reach their international development goals of the Millennium Declaration without adding to debt burdens."[4]

The British had a similar proposal that Gordon Brown had formulated prior to the 2004 G8 meeting. They took the additionality issue (debt relief should not come out of existing aid resources) very seriously by offering to cover 10 percent ($180 million) of the cost to the World Bank and the AfDB, while insisting that the IMF portion be financed with its gold reserves. The United States rejected these positions and remained silent about how to finance its own debt relief proposal. Any decision was put off until the annual IMF/World Bank meetings in Washington, D.C., in early October.

At those meetings, the HIPC process was extended for the third time, to the end of 2006, to allow eleven more African HIPC countries, all with serious conflict or arrears problems, to join the process. The Bush administration was eager to get a deal on Iraqi debt, but it wanted to do it on the cheap while swallowing its often-voiced concerns about moral hazards—the worry that debt relief will only encourage more borrowing in the belief that more debt relief will be forthcoming. Facing an enormous budget deficit and the huge cost of the Iraq War, the United States, unlike the British, wanted the Bank and the IMF to finance this major debt relief from their own resources.

Many observers viewed the US proposal as a geopolitical ploy. As one European diplomat put it: "When the United States asked us for so much debt relief for Iraq, we said the answer was to also relieve the debt of the poorest nations. Now the Americans are trying to come along with debt relief for the poor but we are afraid they will dry up the money . . . that these poor countries deserve" (Becker 2004). Intense discussions at the IMF/Bank meetings failed to reach an agreement, bogging down in quarrels about how to finance any new multilateral debt relief. It was only agreed that the G8 would report on its discussions by the end of 2004.

The British were scheduled to take over the presidency of the G8 in 2005, and Gordon Brown was committed to having Britain lead the G8 into major new debt relief by the July summit in Gleneagles, Scotland. Some NGOs supported the US position and wanted the Bush administration to formally commit to this major new step and resolve the cost and additionality issues later. A senior Jubilee USA official supported the US position as follows: "We laud Brown for his commitment to 100% debt cancellation, but his call to finance debt cancellation through G7 government appropriations threatens to scuttle a deal. Brown's commitment, though generous, is unnecessary considering the international financial institutions' vast resources."[5] Others viewed the British proposal as more responsible and remained critical of the US position. Many of these NGOs supported major debt relief for Iraq because of the obvious "odious debt" precedent it would set. The UN joined the chorus, with various agencies calling for full multilateral debt relief for poor countries—the Office of the Secretary-General, United Nations Conference for Trade and Development, and UN-AIDS, among others.

After President Bush was reelected in November 2004, the United States redoubled its efforts to get major debt relief for Iraq while remaining silent on its surprising and unexpected June 2004 Sea Island debt cancellation proposal. A compromise Paris Club deal was reached on November 21 that would cancel 80 percent of Iraq's debt in three stages over four years if Iraq met certain conditions. A number of NGOs noted the rapid movement on debt relief for Iraq and the slow movement toward more debt reduction for African and other poor countries. Germany and France wanted some reconciliation with the reelected Bush administration after their sharp disagreement with the United States over the invasion of Iraq. Russia, however, was the last holdout, and it took all-night negotiations to reach a Paris Club deal for Iraq. The Russians subsequently made it clear that its support was linked to a "mutual understanding" about the handling of Russia's own debt to the Paris Club and better treatment for its companies in Iraq. NGOs, which had previously met with Paris Club officials to argue for an immediate moratorium on Iraqi debt service, did not believe the Paris Club agreement went far enough, some calling it scandalous. In an early December report, Oxfam warned that the "war on terrorism" threatened to bring back an era when assistance was determined by "security considerations rather than developmental need." Max Lawson, its chief policy adviser, noted that "debt relief for Iraq shows that rich countries can find the resources for foreign aid if they need to" (Balls 2004). As we will see with Nigeria, geopolitical factors were indeed preeminent.

The Iraq Paris Club deal left the US position on debt relief for Africa up in the air. The Bush administration remained silent on the issue as it approached the end of its G8 presidency in 2004, leaving the issue to the British instead. Britain was very anxious for major movement on poor country debt and development assistance generally, while it led the G8 in 2005. In a speech to the Council on Foreign Relations in New York, Brown finally made the details of his proposal public. He identified the countries that would be eligible—the fifteen HIPC countries that have completed the full HIPC process, twelve of them African, and six other low-income countries—Albania, Armenia, Mongolia, Nepal, Sri Lanka, and Vietnam. As usual, however, the devil really was in the details, especially over financing. The British proposal was billed as a core part of a new Marshall Plan meant to support the Millennium Development Goals.

Most of the major NGOs supported the British plan, albeit with some modifications, and spent considerable energy campaigning for it prior to the G8 summit in Gleneagles. Major pressure was aimed at the Bush administration to honor its 2004 Sea Island pledge now that it had achieved a Paris Club deal for Iraq, but it was made all the harder by the administration's stubborn unilateralism in foreign affairs. The United States agreed to the creation of MDRI, but only after getting most of its way about financing it. In the end, the Bush administration had to put up very little money.

The Multilateral Debt Relief Initiative is separate from the HIPC initiative but is linked to it operationally. Under the MDRI, the World Bank's International Development Association (IDA), the IMF, and the AfDB's African

Development Fund will provide 100 percent debt relief on eligible debts to countries that reach the HIPC completion point. Although the MDRI is an initiative of the three international financial institutions, the decision to grant debt relief was ultimately the separate responsibility of each institution, and their approach to coverage and implementation has varied. In deciding to implement the original G8 MDRI proposal, the IMF modified the use of its resources so as to be consistent with its principle of uniformity of treatment. Thus, it was agreed that all countries with per capita income of $380 a year or less (whether HIPCs or not) would receive MDRI debt relief financed by the IMF's own resources through the MDRI-I Trust. HIPCs with per capita income above that threshold would receive MDRI relief from bilateral contributions administered by the IMF through the MDRI-II Trust. The MDRI-I Trust draws on resources from the 1999–2000 off-market sales of the IMF's gold, and the MDRI-II on transfers of contributions originally provided to fund concessional lending to low-income countries under the Poverty Reduction and Growth Facility. The MDRI funding for the World Bank is far more complicated and much more dependent on future donor contributions.

NGOs criticized the MDRI for applying only to HIPC countries, plus a few non-HIPC countries, rather than all poor countries, and for covering debt only up to the end of 2004 for the IMF and to the end of 2003 for the Bank. Unlike the HIPC Initiative, MDRI is not comprehensive in its creditor coverage (see Figure 6.1). It does not involve participation of Paris Club (bilateral) donors, commercial creditors, or multilateral institutions other than the three mentioned above. In early September 2006, for example, Malawi reached its HIPC completion point, receiving $1.1 billion in debt relief from its Paris Club creditors, the IMF, and the Bank, and an additional $1.4 billion in MDRI debt relief from the IMF, the Bank, and the ADF. Assuming no additional debt accumulation, Malawi now has a much more sustainable debt service burden of about $5 million a year between 2006 and 2025.[6]

Nigeria and the Return of Geopolitical Debt Relief to Africa

Although Nigeria was on an early list of potential HIPC countries, in the end it was not eligible for HIPC debt relief, much to its dismay.[7] After the return to democratic rule in 1999, Nigeria received a modest Paris Club rescheduling (its fourth) as part of a "democratic dividend" at the end of the Clinton administration. Because it was not what is called an "IDA (International Development Association) only" country at the World Bank, it was not eligible for more generous "Naples terms" (up to a two-thirds write-off) from the Paris Club, which would have retired considerable debt. Columbia University economist Jeffrey Sachs and the NGOs insisted that Nigeria become a HIPC country, but it remained a "blend" country, able to borrow from both

**Figure 6.1 Debt Burdens in Eighteen Completion-Point HIPCs
Before and After HIPC and MDRI Debt Relief**

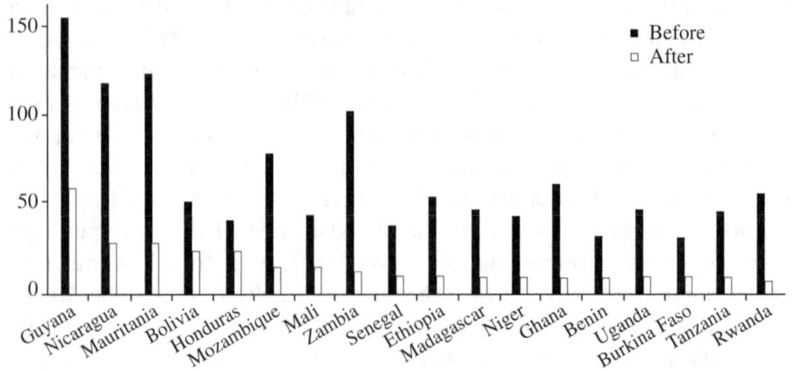

Source: World Bank, *Global Development Finance 2006* (Washington, DC: World Bank, 2006), p. 94.

the International Bank for Reconstruction and Development (the original core of the World Bank) and IDA. When Iraq received its stunning Paris Club deal in November 2004, many NGOs and Nigerians asked why Nigeria, also a member of the Organization of Petroleum Exporting Countries, should not receive similar treatment. The Nigerian government certainly believed that it was owed such a deal despite the fact that oil was over $60 a barrel in late 2004. It had been working without success to get one since its 2000 Paris Club rescheduling. On top of the technical hurdle of not being IDA-only, it was widely perceived that Nigeria's economic management was weak. In short, most bilateral and multilateral creditors did not believe that major debt relief for Nigeria was a smart move. Yet, less than a year later, Nigeria had signed a major Paris Club debt reduction deal, which was fully implemented by May 2006 when oil was over $70 a barrel. How was that feasible, and was it a smart thing to do? In the end, this extraordinary debt deal was made possible by an interesting blend of geopolitics, better performance by Nigeria, creative work by a Washington think tank, and help from the NGOs, although the latter did not think the final deal was generous enough. One might call it a "blend" debt deal.

During President Olusegun Obasanjo's first term, economic performance remained poor, and Nigeria's reputation for corruption persisted. After his re-election in April 2003, Obasanjo put together an impressive, high-quality, technocratic, economic team consisting of Ngozi Okonjo-Iweala as finance minister, Mansur Muhtar as director-general of Nigeria's Debt Management Office and, after April 2004, Charles Soludo as governor of the Bank of Nigeria. All three have doctoral degrees in economics and extensive overseas ties: Okonjo-Iweala as a World Bank vice president; Muhtar as a senior economist in the Bank's Africa region; and Soludo as a consultant for the IMF, World Bank, and various UN agencies. In May 2001, as consultants to the government, they organized an international conference in Abuja funded by the UK Department for International Development. It was an incipient effort to devise a debt relief strategy for Nigeria. A book was eventually produced in 2003, *The Debt Trap in Nigeria: Towards a Sustainable Debt Strategy,* but a clear strategy remained elusive. By this time, the government had produced a National Economic Empowerment Development Strategy as part of a declared intention to significantly improve economic performance. Initial external reaction was highly skeptical of the country's ability to implement such reforms in a sustained way. But other obstacles also existed.

At Davos in January 2004, Okonjo-Iweala had an unplanned discussion about Nigeria's debt problems with Nancy Birdsall, president of the Center for Global Development (CGD) in Washington, D.C., who agreed to see how her center could help. The first focus of attention was a technical hurdle the creditors were using—Nigeria's "blend" status and the need for "IDA-only" status to qualify for Paris Club debt relief. At the time President Bush announced his debt reduction proposal at the June 2004 G8 meeting in Sea Island, CGD began circulating a draft working paper in Washington: "Double Standards, Debt Treatment, and World Bank Country Classification: The Case of Nigeria" (Moss, Standley, and Birdsall 2004).[8] CGD held a seminar on the topic in early October. The paper was subsequently revised and formally released in early November, just before the US elections. After President Bush won reelection and a Paris Club deal was quickly reached for Iraq, President Obasanjo came to Washington and met with President Bush. Debt relief was on the agenda, along with oil, terrorism, security, and other important international and African issues. By this time, Nigerian foreign exchange reserves had reached $17 billion; the windfall was being saved rather than wasted, as it had been during previous oil price booms.

In January 2005 Britain took over the chair of the G8, and Gordon Brown declared 2005 the "Year of Africa." By this time, Nigeria's external debt had reached $36 billion. The same month, CGD staff met with Okonjo-Iweala and Muhtar to discuss next steps. In late February, CGD facilitated high-level contacts between Okonjo-Iweala, the IMF, and the US Treasury, which allowed her to make Nigeria's new case for major Paris Club relief. In early March the center circulated a CGD brief based on the "Double Standards" paper to all World Bank executive directors and senior treasury officials in the United States and Britain. Among the G8 members, Britain was the most interested in a debt deal for Nigeria, and it held the largest amount of Nigeria's Paris Club debt, 25.5 percent.

The campaign to give Nigeria IDA-only status continued throughout the spring of 2005. Even assuming that it might eventually be successful, another major issue remained: What kind of debt deal might Nigeria get from the Paris Club? Significant Paris Club skepticism remained, especially in France, Germany, and Japan, which held 20.4, 16.7, and 15.3 percent of Nigerian debt, respectively, with the United States holding only 3.3 percent of the debt. Todd Moss, a CGD research fellow, developed the notion of a deal involving a discounted buyback along with a sizable upfront payment, rather than rescheduling payments over a number of years. In early April, the center issued a short note, "Resolving Nigeria's Debt Through a Discounted Buyback," that laid out the proposal.[9] It included a suggested fair discount rate of between 20 and 33 percent, roughly in the range of Naples terms and the final settlement of Argentina's dramatic December 2001 bond default. CGD suggested that such a deal might create pressure for a similar debt reduction arrangement from Nigeria's commercial and multilateral creditors.

The stated rationale for this type of deal, which would essentially mean an exit from the Paris Club and Nigeria's bilateral debt, was that it would support the ongoing economic reforms in Nigeria—tip the balance in favor of the reform triumvirate, help consolidate Nigeria's fragile democracy, dampen opposition to any debt deal short of total and immediate write-off, provide payback support for Obasanjo's regional conflict resolution efforts, and generally support Nigeria's overall stability while encouraging its engagement on major international issues on oil, terrorism, and security. In late April 2005, CGD staff met in Washington, D.C., with a delegation from the Nigerian Senate to brief them on the deal and the creditor politics surrounding it. Finally, in June the World Bank quietly, with no formal announcement, reclassified Nigeria as IDA-only. Then on June 11, the G8 finance ministers announced a deal on what was to become MDRI for countries completing the HIPC process. Although Nigeria was not included in this major expansion of sovereign debt relief, the ministers welcomed Nigeria's progress on economic reform, noted its move to IDA-only status, encouraged continued reforms, and stated that they were prepared to provide a fair and sustainable solution to Nigeria's debt problems in 2005 within the Paris Club.

One last major obstacle remained. Any Paris Club deal requires the debtor country to have an ongoing and on-track economic reform program with the IMF. IMF programs have been extremely controversial in Nigeria for decades. Both politicians and the public have strongly opposed them at every turn. For its 2000 Paris Club agreement, Nigeria signed a one-year agreement without any intention of drawing from the authorized funds. This fig leaf allowed Nigeria to meet the technical requirements of the Paris Club. In April 2005, with Nigeria in mind, G8 finance ministers agreed that the IMF should create a formal monitoring arrangement for countries not receiving financial assistance, to be called the policy support instrument (PSI).

With these key elements in place, the Paris Club met on June 29, 2005, and stated its willingness to enter into negotiations with Nigeria for an "exceptional" phased and comprehensive treatment of its Paris Club debt, once the PSI was created. On October 5, 2005, the IMF approved the creation of the PSI for low-income countries in order to "signal" its endorsement of a country's polices via periodic surveillance of economic performance. Two days later, Nigeria formally applied for a two-year PSI, which was approved on October 17. The Paris Club then met October 18–20 and, after some very tough bargaining between the creditors and Nigeria and among the creditors themselves (Germany, Japan, and the Netherlands had the strongest objections), approved a comprehensive "exit" treatment of Nigeria's debt, based on economic reforms since 2003 as validated by the PSI. It was to take effect in two phases, in which Nigeria would first pay the Paris Club $6.1 billion in arrears in November and then make a second payment of $6.1 billion after the first PSI review (scheduled for March 2006) was completed. That would amount to a "buyback," or debt write-off, of the remaining $18 billion of Nigeria's Paris Club debt. The end result, after the arrears were paid off, would amount to a debt cancellation of roughly 67 percent, comparable to Naples terms. The first PSI review was completed on April 17, 2006, and Nigeria made its second and final payment on April 21, successfully completing the deal and Nigeria's long struggle for Paris Club debt relief. It left Nigeria with about $5 billion in external debt, mostly to London Club (private) creditors.

The prime mover behind Nigeria's debt relief success was Finance Minister Okonjo-Iweala. She provided the necessary vision, connections, toughness, and perseverance, while CGD provided key elements of the strategy that eventually meshed well enough with the reevaluated interests of major creditors. This is not to say that it was a sure thing. It was, after all, very political. But was it also an example of smart debt relief? Or was it just another example of what I have called the ritual dances of the debt game, in which an African ruler uses a well-connected technocratic team and temporary reform to lull creditors into a major deal? The answer is not clear.

In a totally unexpected move, President Obasanjo removed Okonjo-Iweala as finance minister on June 21, 2006, and named her foreign minister while leaving her as the head of the economic reform team. She resigned as foreign minister, however, on August 3, following her sudden removal as head of Nigeria's Economic Intelligence team by President Obasanjo. In May his efforts to change the constitution to allow him to run for a third term, which had cost the country a good deal of money, were blocked by the Nigerian National Assembly. If the debt agreement with Nigeria was smart because it helped bolster economic reforms and reformers in Nigeria and consolidate its democracy, from this perspective it seems to have failed. In the end, was this extraordinary debt deal a mistake? From a development point of view, the answer may well be yes, as it has not dramatically changed the view of external investors about the wisdom of putting resources into Nigeria, nor is it likely to lead to significant poverty reduction. From a geostrategic point of view, many key actors still believe that it was a smart move. The CGD still feels that, given what was known at the time, it was a smart, if risky move. Among other things, the Nigerian story reinforces the point that Africa's main problem is not that it is poor. It lacks the kind of political incentives required for sustained economic reform, whether the country is rich or poor, while being hindered by low levels of state capacity. One of the main tragedies of Nigeria is that it has more wealth and capacity than most African countries, yet it continues to squander both.

Reflections on the "Hows" of Smarter Debt Relief

We are witnessing a big push for expanded debt relief and for much larger aid flows for Africa—the One Campaign of Bono and others, the UK-hosted G8 summit, the Commission for Africa, Jeffrey Sachs's UN Report and his 2005 book, *The End of Poverty,* and so on. In combination with the campaign for more debt relief, a debate has restarted about whether expanded aid flows to Africa are a good idea. The two major ends of this debate can be seen in recent exchanges between Sachs and William Easterly—the former saying we must do more and that it can have a positive impact, whereas the latter says the opposite in his 2006 book, *The White Man's Burden.* This debate points to a major dilemma. More money will not guarantee solutions to many of Africa's problems, but less money will certainly make them worse, with serious consequences for millions of Africans and the rest of the world. Nigerian debt relief and the subsequent actions by the government seem to demonstrate this point.

A much more balanced, honest, and informed position is that taken by Nicolas van de Walle in his book, *Overcoming Stagnation in Aid-Dependent Countries* (2005, p. 81–83). Van de Walle asks when there should be conditionality for new aid resources. He points to the "odd combination of NGO and academic critics . . . and development community insiders" that opposes conditionality. "Some form of performance-based allocation of aid resources," van de Walle believes, "is a sine qua non of reform." He recommends both selectivity and conditionality. He also notes that such an approach will not be easy: there are no magic bullets. There does not exist, he believes, "a powerful constituency for change in both the West and the developing world." However, I have long argued that a constituency made up of international NGOs and some donor countries does exist. The question is whether it has the right answers and can achieve its objectives.

Beyond geopolitics, the ultimate dilemma of debt relief for Africa is a larger political one. Since debt is one part of a much larger development context, growth is central to the effort to achieve debt sustainability. For their part, the NGOs do not have any viable counterfactual about how total debt write-off, and an end to externally imposed structural adjustment programs, would actually bring about the poverty reduction and sustainable development they advocate. Despite a great deal of fancy rhetoric, they have never been able to square this circle. For their part, many African governments simply want full debt cancellation, an end to structural adjustment, and the ability to borrow more.

On the international side, the key to growth in developing countries is to give them access to markets in countries in the Organization for Economic Cooperation and Development (OECD). The NGOs clearly realized the importance of this issue and began to work on it. They succeeded in their debt campaign by bringing it into the domestic political arenas of the OECD industrial democracies, a process quite different from the one that led to the failure of the new international economic order endeavor of the late 1970s and early 1980s. However, they are finding it much harder to get the same results with trade reform. The lack of progress in the Doha Round of the World Trade Organization talks does not give much hope on this front.

On the African side, incentives are absolutely central, and conditionality, for all its faults, is crucial. In my view, Nigeria was given major debt relief too soon; it has never been able to sustain serious economic reform. Van de Walle recommends forms of conditionality that do less "micromanaging," arguing instead for basic macroeconomic targets and, above all, political conditionality. He notes that reform has come in very few places in Africa, usually in places with "visionary leadership." He would rather use conditionality to build new democratic institutions that will foster reform. More specifically, he contends, "military governments should not receive a penny of donor assistance," and "donors should withdraw from countries in which the constitution does not provide for term limits or in which the leader has been in power longer than, say, 12 years." By these criteria, neither Ghana under Jerry Rawlings nor Uganda under Yoweri Museveni would have deserved assistance, despite the significant amount of economic changes these two "visionary leaders" introduced. Uganda has shown that debt relief can be used as a tool to increase transparency and accountability, whether it is fully democratic or not.

My own view is that support should be given to governments that actually engage in real, sustained economic reform, whether they are democratic or not. Van de Walle's point about leadership is correct; it is what the weak record of reform in Africa shows. But he undermines it by focusing on political conditionality of a specific type. Democracies with leadership that rejects or neglects economic reform will do no better than semi- or undemocratic states with leaders that embrace reform. So, donors should support those who actually walk the walk, democratic or not. This means selectivity and sticking to it. By van de Walle's criteria, Nigeria should have gotten major debt relief in 2005; by my criteria it is much less of a smart move. But

Nigeria also reminds us of one of the key lessons learned—that debt relief, and aid more generally, are very political processes.

I support expanded debt relief for additional but carefully selected African countries, along the lines of an expanded HIPC process with a larger multilateral debt reduction component. It would include continued use of relatively detailed conditionality in an effort to achieve more development-oriented outcomes. Debt relief can, and should be, part of smart aid for Africa. It is highly questionable, however, whether the return of geo-political debt relief to countries such as Nigeria, which have not engaged in serious and sustained economic reform, constitutes smart aid. Interestingly, my views are more congruent with those of an earlier work of van de Walle's Center for Global Development colleagues: *Delivering on Debt Relief* by Nancy Birdsall and John Williamson. Whether the major powers and the NGOs can achieve such an outcome remains very open to question. It is, after all, very political and is affected by widely varying interests and values.

An additional element of progress has emerged from the HIPC/MDRI process since the late 1990s—the rise of a more sophisticated concept of debt sustainability. Debt in and of itself is not bad, but how it is used and whether it is kept within bounds matter quite a bit. The IMF and the Bank created very useful debt sustainability notions and indicators (IDA and IMF 2006), which produced a very productive debate among the creditors, the international financial institutions they control, NGOs, and academics about debt sustainability.[10] As Figure 6.1 shows, changes in the debt regime have brought major debt relief to fifteen African countries since 1996.[11] Ten other African countries have received some HIPC debt relief but have not yet been approved for MDRI debt reduction, and seven HIPC countries had not yet entered either process. The Paris Club has continued to provide debt relief for non-HIPC countries such as Nigeria, Kenya, and Gabon.

The hope for additional progress on debt and trade raises the concerns of those who worry about the political underpinnings of globalization: Will the major industrial democracies be able to adjust their own domestic politics so that larger and smarter changes in the debt and trade regimes can be made? Given past track records and current events, serious doubt exists. If debt relief is to mean anything, growth and trade on one side, and African incentives and capacity on the other, must be tackled simultaneously. Necessities, however, do not often become realities. Getting HIPC and MDRI was hard enough, and it was a very political process. Achieving major additional and productive debt relief for more African countries will be the same. Globalization worriers have a right to be concerned—the political underpinnings of international economic governance are central to Africa's future, and they may not be up to the task.

Notes

I want to thank Megan Davidow for her wonderful research help on this chapter.

1. For a more detailed version of this tale and its implications, see Callaghy (2004, 2003) and Callaghy, Kassimir, and Latham (2001).

2. See Ruggie (1982). The Paris Club countries have never applied embedded liberalism—using the state to buffer the social and political consequences of needed adjustment. It is what they practice, not what they preach to the debtors.

3. Speech at the Senate "Poverty and Debt Relief Photo Exhibit," October 14, 2005.

4. Speech to the Bretton Woods Committee Twentieth Anniversary Meeting, Washington, DC, September 30, 2004.

5. Marie Clark, Jubilee USA Network Statement, September 30, 2004, Internet.

6. For more on MDRI, see http://www.imf.org/external/np/exr/facts/mdri.htm, http://siteresources.worldbank.org/INTDEBTDEPT/Resources/mdri_eng.pdf, and http://www.afdb.org/pls/portal/docs/PAGE/ADB_ADMIN_PG/DOCUMENTS/ OPERATIONSINFORMATION/(6%20PAGES)%20MDRI%20(ENG).PDF. The fifteen African countries that had received MDRI debt cancellation from the three institutions by August 2006 were Benin, Burkina Faso, Cameroon, Ethiopia, Ghana, Madagascar, Mali, Mauritania, Mozambique, Niger, Rwanda, Senegal, Tanzania, Uganda, and Zambia.

7. This section is based on confidential interviews conducted in Washington, DC from May to August 2006.

8. See http://www.cgdev.org/content/publications/detail/2741/.

9. See http://www.cgdev.org/content/publications/detail/3223/.

10. For contrasting views on debt sustainability, see IMF and World Bank (2004) and Oddone (2005).

11. Malawi obtained MDRI debt reduction in September 2006.

7

Donor Policies in Practice: The Challenges of Poverty Reduction and Aid Effectiveness

Ian Hopwood

TODAY THERE IS an unprecedented degree of consensus on the international development agenda, concentrated principally on the Millennium Development Goals (MDGs) and poverty reduction, with some attention to democratic reform and human rights. The major challenge now is for political leaders and policymakers to determine how to implement that agenda in an Africa still marginalized in the global economy and prone to conflict and natural disasters. The quest has fostered a proliferation of responses that crowd the development marketplace. They include, as the chapters in this book demonstrate, direct budget support, sectorwide programs, poverty reduction strategies, aid effectiveness initiatives (the Paris Declaration), UN reform, former UK prime minister Tony Blair's Commission for Africa, and new funding instruments such as the Global Fund to Fight AIDS, Tuberculosis, and Malaria. As Carol Lancaster shows in Chapter 3, in the case of the United States, outgoing President George W. Bush has created several specialized aid initiatives in addition to the multiplicity of programs already conducted by various agencies of the government.

In this chapter I focus on two major global responses: recent efforts to reduce poverty and the implementation of the Paris Declaration on Aid Effectiveness, adopted at the High Level Forum of donors and recipient countries in 2005. I highlight some country-level factors in the formulation and delivery of aid that usually receive insufficient attention. Much that is written about aid centers on the substance of reform and the criteria for determining levels of financial support. In other words, a focus on the *what* and the *how much*. My analysis pays more attention to *how* aid agencies do their work and the nature of their relationships with the countries concerned. In this latter regard, Phyllis Pomerantz, a former senior World Bank official in

103

southern Africa, argues that a fundamental ingredient of smart aid is the development of trust between the two parties in the aid relationship, a trust based upon the following elements: a degree of shared purpose, commitment, reliability, familiarity with local conditions, transparency, and honest and open communications (Pomerantz 2004, pp. 10, 23).

Much is at stake in an Africa beset with pervasive poverty and disease as well as natural and man-made emergencies that together produce some of the highest levels of malnutrition, illiteracy, and child and maternal mortality in the world. Millions of young children and hundreds of thousands of women die each year from preventable childhood illnesses and complications arising from pregnancy and childbirth. In response to these conditions, the UN Millennium Project, the 2002 UN Conference on Financing for Development in Monterrey, the 2005 Gleneagles G8 meeting, and other forums have called for significantly increased aid flows (UN Millennium Project 2005, pp. 239–257). Meanwhile, aid critics emphasize absorption constraints, poor governance, and aid's generally disappointing results (Easterly 2006). The debate continues between those who affirm that Africa is poor because of bad governance and those who contend that governance is bad because Africa is so poor (Rice 2005).

This debate on African development has often been conducted at high levels of abstraction, focusing on a broad diagnosis of Africa's ills and the prescriptions to be administered by donors and African governments. Unfortunately, the sweeping generalizations and blanket prescriptions tend to obscure the fundamental importance of specific country dynamics in determining aid outcomes. This said, it is still useful to keep in mind some shared contextual features when discussing smart aid for Africa. Most sub-Saharan African countries have fragile economies that are susceptible to shocks and are, to varying degrees, aid-dependent. With a few exceptions, they are weak polities and semidemocratized states in which domestic politics tend to be highly patronage-based, with fragmented party systems and a weak civil society. Many are currently or have recently been greatly affected by violent conflict. In general, policy and program implementation capacity is low, and reliable and timely data are scarce. Apart from abundant natural resources in some countries, an important part of Africa's wealth resides in the "deep reservoirs of nonstate, unofficial social organizational energy, trust and self sacrifice" that have remained difficult to harness for development (Galvin 2004, p. 8). In this context, it is challenging to conceive and implement effective aid interventions aimed at reducing poverty, inducing growth, and enhancing capacity in sustainable ways.

It should further be borne in mind that the effective management and disbursement of aid are not ends in themselves but rather contributions to the achievement of development outcomes. The potential of aid to produce these development results should not be overestimated. For Michael Edwards

(2004, p. 111), "external assistance is never the key factor in promoting internal change, and always a blunt weapon in the fight against poverty and violence. Nevertheless the right sort of help at the right time can be very influential in creating more space for local forces to get things right." Conversely, donors can destabilize and undermine ongoing, but fragile, reform programs (Pomerantz 2004, p. 9).

These observations confirm my experience that what really counts are the ways in which national actors make use of available aid instruments to achieve their policy or program objectives. They need to draw on their own ideas, convictions, and experience to implement their visions and incorporate external aid resources into formulas they think can work for their countries. A key determinant of success is the ability of these local actors to adjust and adapt the formulas over time, in the light of implementation experiences and opportunities. Consistent with this view, the 2003 *Annual Review of Development Effectiveness* used by the Bank to evaluate its support for policy reform found that there is no single "success formula": "Good results have been obtained with very different policies and institutions, supported by different combinations of Bank instruments and thematic/sectoral mixes, with the mix tailored to the country situation and country preferences, and usually evolving over time" (World Bank 2003, p. viii). The importance of the "how" over the "what," of actors over instruments, also holds true at local levels: "It is not a particular set of policies that brings results at the grassroots," according to Michael Edwards, "but the development of people's capacities to advance themselves and work with others on common tasks against a constantly shifting background of opportunities and constraints" (Edwards 2004, p. 74).

For aid agencies, recognizing and coming to terms with these dynamics is of capital importance. Instead of relying on the institutional blueprints and economic models of visiting missions of economists and engineers, emphasis is shifted to the "messy" and contextually embedded perspectives of social scientists and resident development practitioners. More reliance is placed on nationally (and locally) formulated development visions that can then be translated into objectives and strategies. A framework is created for a pragmatic "learning" process of implementation that can evolve over time. In this process, unexpected problems arise, unanticipated opportunities and avenues for action open up, and new partners come on board, especially if the initial results are encouraging. Almost always, the results achieved are not what were originally expected, thus reflecting the uncertainty of the change process and the need for course corrections. Even in cases where an initiative "fails," some learning can take place, and the participating actors can be better prepared to take advantage of future opportunities.

From this perspective, aid should be considered as an "experimental mission," furthering economic, political, and social change amid uncertainty. This understanding calls on aid donors not to avoid risks but rather to be prepared to take "reasonable" risks. Although knowledge about what works continues to improve, especially in technical areas such as health care, the paths to large-scale change are not well understood. There are no causal chains that enable us to predict how technical inputs will translate into outcomes on the ground. The same set of inputs can result in very different outcomes, and different inputs can produce similar outcomes, depending on the country context. The variability in contexts make it difficult to rigidly apply lessons from one country to another. Even among neighboring countries with apparent similarities, there are often different histories and cultural endowments, different social and political conditions, and different capabilities for managing national resources.

Based on the above general observations, I will now review the implementation and initial results of two major instruments currently shaping aid practices: the Poverty Reduction Strategy Paper (PRSP) and the Paris Declaration on Aid Effectiveness.

The Ambitions and Realities of PRSPs

PRSPs have become central to the negotiation of development assistance in over forty African countries.[1] They originated in the late 1990s as part of the arrangements for the enhanced heavily indebted poor countries (HIPC) initiative. In essence, this approach strives to link aid flows with comprehensive poverty reduction strategies developed by recipient countries. Through the HIPC process, debt relief was to be provided in return for a commitment to use the financial resources thus freed up to reduce poverty. The PRSP arose as a mechanism to structure poverty reduction plans. Once adopted as the framework for the HIPC initiative, they came rapidly to be seen by the boards of the International Monetary Fund (IMF) and the World Bank, among others, as having the potential to be the overarching country-level policy document that would guide all concessional aid flows. PRSPs strive to be the following:

- Country-driven, involving broad-based local participation.
- Comprehensive, in recognition that poverty is a multidimensional problem.
- Results-oriented, with emphasis on tangible end results for the poor that can be monitored.
- Partnership-oriented, leading to better donor coordination, under government leadership.
- Long-term, focusing on reforming institutions and building capacity in addition to reaching short-term goals.

PRSPs originally covered a three-year period, but many now have a five-year time span, are aligned with the Millennium Development Goals, and to a lesser degree include strategies for economic growth. The emphasis on national ownership has been driven by the wide recognition that the imposition of policy conditions that accompanied structural adjustment programs had, in most cases, not achieved their goals (Killick 1998; Dollar and Svensson 2000). The PRSPs can therefore be viewed as an attempt to move away from these old ways of doing business in favor of broad-based, nationally owned strategies in which policy commitments are defined by the responsible governments, subject to "endorsement" by the boards of the Bretton Woods institutions (Killick 2004, p. 15).

The PRSP instrument has been subjected to analysis and assessment by bilateral donors, the World Bank, the IMF, international nongovernmental organizations (NGOs), and research institutions such as the Overseas Development Institute in the UK. Comparable published research from African sources is not as easily accessible, suggesting a need to balance the debate through the wider and more systematic dissemination of the knowledge generated and lessons learned by African researchers, policymakers, and development practitioners.

The available literature, confirmed by personal experience, leads to the conclusion that the results of the PRSP have been rather modest so far. On the positive side, reducing poverty has become a more prominent aspect of the policy agenda of governments. There is a more explicit focus on poverty in the official discourse, and the PRSPs have become an important factor in negotiating and allocating aid. National expenditures have increased in some strategic poverty-related areas, notably the provision of basic social services.[2] There is a stronger but often still inadequate link between poverty planning and budgeting, and there is better monitoring of poverty levels. The emphasis on participatory approaches has facilitated civil society mobilization around the poverty issue. It has also opened new spaces for expanding the involvement of citizens and civil society in policy formulation, monitoring, and implementation. The advent of PRSPs has stimulated more international attention to the harmonization of donor assistance and its alignment with national priorities. Harmonization and alignment have also been pursued at country levels, so far with uneven results, as will be discussed later.

What is missing? The increased government focus on poverty needs to be translated into more consistent long-term institutional commitments, with stronger operational dimensions. Ownership of the PRSP among the big "spending" ministries, such as health, education, and agriculture, has often lagged behind. Usually well-supported by external assistance through sectorwide programs or traditional projects, the ministers and officials of these ministries can lack strong incentives to get involved in the national poverty reduction strategy. Especially when the PRSP is largely financed through the government budget and supplemented by general budget support from donors, such ministers may fear a loss of control over sector priorities, targets, and indicators, as well as reduced donor funding if they have to "compete" for their share of funds through ministry of finance arbitration. In the usually centrally driven PRSP process, local government involvement also tends to be limited, resulting in weakened local ownership. In Senegal, for example, it is only with the country's second PRSP (PRSP2), covering 2006–2010, that locally elected leaders have seized the opportunity to establish themselves as essential entry points for PRSP implementation.

There have also been weaknesses in the design of PRSPs. The overall structure is similar in many countries, with its triple pillars of access to basic social services, promotion of employment and wealth creation, and measures to protect the most vulnerable (social safety nets, etc.). Within this framework, the analysis of the causes and determinants of poverty and the corresponding "results chain" needs to be strengthened. At present, there is apparently no consensus on the mix of interventions that will yield maximum poverty reduction effects, which leads to a lack of focus and weak prioritization of interventions.[3] In this regard, the World Bank admitted that it "has yet to specify an operational results chain that effectively links its country level interventions with poverty outcomes and ensures that its assistance is based on measurable poverty results" (World Bank 2004a, p. xiii). Arriving at such a blueprint for poverty reduction is indeed a complex challenge, especially in view of the variety of country contexts.

The approach to planning and budgeting has also posed problems. In assessing how to achieve ambitious poverty targets and MDGs, there have been tensions between planning on the basis of moderately ambitious financing frameworks (drawn largely from the poverty reduction and growth facility frameworks) and planning on the basis of estimates of what it will really cost to reach them. The latter approach, "aspirational financing," has been advocated by Jeffrey Sachs in the context of the pursuit of the Millennium Development Goals (UN Millennium Project 2005). It implies very significant additional resource mobilization, both domestic and external. With regard to budgeting, weakness of linkages within the interrelated triangle of PRSP, annual budgeting, and medium-term expenditure frameworks has resulted in inadequate operational ties between budgets and desired poverty outcomes.

PRSP credibility is weakened when they are based on the expectation of very high growth rates. For example, Senegal's PRSP2 aims for a real annual growth rate of 7 percent to 8 percent per annum. Even though Africa's growth performance has improved in recent years, growth rates of this magnitude have never been sustained over time, except in a few special cases. Globally, less than half the Bank's borrowing countries recorded continuous per capita growth rates during the five years between 2000 and 2005 (World Bank 2006a, p. xii). Moreover, the relationship between economic growth and poverty reduction requires further elucidation. Greater attention must be devoted to the distributional impact of growth and to the concept of pro-poor growth to ensure the best possible poverty reduction effect for any given growth rate, as well as the strategies needed to protect the poor if growth falters.[4] Furthermore, the integration of the social and productive sectors has been weak. If growth should be pro-poor, then investments in health and education should also be more explicitly pro-growth, for example, by tackling problems such as malaria that have direct consequences for productive investment and wealth creation.

Civil society consultation needs to be taken beyond the stage of debate and translated into deeper forms of government accountability to citizens (for similar arguments, see Chapters 11 and 12 in this book). Parliaments, national audit offices, and the media all have important roles in this regard. Accountability for results has been advanced on the supply side, with governments providing more information about and access to spending plans, essentially to reassure donors that the debt relief and subsequent additional financing are being well used. Demand-side accountability from service users such as trade unions and the media is less evident, although there are efforts being made to achieve it in some countries. In Senegal, for example, civil society, including private voluntary organizations, women's associations, the trade unions, and private sector representatives, participated actively in the formulation of PRSP2 and will continue to be involved, both in formal review meetings and in implementation. These actors, including user groups such as the Consumers' Association and Parent-Teacher Associations, are making increasing use of the radio and the press to hold government accountable and to push for improved services.

The goals of the PRSP would be better served through improved donor coordination and genuine alignment and harmonization, two pillars of the 2005 Paris Declaration on Aid Effectiveness. Unfortunately, there is still a wide gap between declaration and practice. Donor activity is proliferating and is still too fragmented at the country level. Globally, the proliferation of special initiatives and new financing instruments (often with tightly focused, globally set priorities, such as the Global Fund to Fight AIDS, Tuberculosis, and Malaria and the Fast Track Initiative for Education) do not facilitate flexible funding for comprehensive and integrated national poverty reduction strategies. The alignment with national priorities and the national ownership of the PRSP can be diluted by "backstage donorship," whereby donors seek to ensure that their favorite projects or particular priorities are included. One potentially positive trend in favor of alignment is the increase in direct budget support, whereby aid flows directly to the ministry of finance to be allocated through national budget mechanisms in support of the country's development objectives (Koeberle, Stavreski, and Wallise 2006). However, a significant proportion of these and other donor resources are still tied to annual disbursement cycles, so "predictability" of aid is not yet assured, thereby inhibiting countries from taking bold initiatives that they may have to halt abruptly if the donor support decreases subsequently.

Another gap has been the lack of attention to the communication aspects of poverty reduction. The PRSP has too often remained an instrument of technocrats, macroeconomists, and secondarily sector development specialists, who are usually neither motivated nor equipped to communicate powerful messages to key actors and to the general public about what is at stake and what needs to be done. In particular, there is a pressing need to communicate evidence on what works to political leaders and also to the media, civil society, and the wider public. Lack of a communication strategy also means that, in many situations, the lower tiers of government remain only vaguely aware of new poverty initiatives emanating from the center of government (Driscoll and Evans 2005, p. 10).

A major conclusion from the PRSP experience so far is that the political aspects of poverty have been generally neglected. Poverty reduction clearly has a significant political dimension because it involves transforming relations of power, patterns of access to state resources, government policy priorities, and legislative frameworks in order to enhance opportunities for the poor to secure livelihoods, enjoy equitable access to state services, and become less vulnerable. To what extent have the PRSPs managed to strengthen the political constituency for poverty reduction? Are poverty issues more meaningfully reflected in the national policy agenda and consistently translated into specific pro-poor policy decisions and budget allocations? The Senegal experience suggests that achieving these fundamental shifts will take time. So far, tangible pro-poor measures have proven easier to introduce in the health sector, thanks mainly to increased government and donor support for specific measures that can help certain vulnerable groups (e.g., free health care for the aged, subsidized bed nets, and malaria treatment prioritizing women and young children) and in the poorer regions (e.g., free caesarean sections and deliveries in health centers and contracting health staff for service in remote areas).

Because political leaders are usually more inclined to commit themselves to programs they think will work in the near term, political will and ownership would be enhanced if there is a body of accessible knowledge and practice showing how short-run gains are possible in the fight to reduce poverty. In reality it is proving difficult to identify effective strategies that can be applied on a large enough scale to make a significant difference within a reasonable time frame. At present, even in countries where poverty is decreasing, the reasons are not always clear and may have more to do with revived growth than with direct antipoverty interventions. At this stage the clear verdict is that the poverty reduction effects of PRSPs have been limited at best, for both the conceptual and operational reasons described above.

A Country-Based Approach to Poverty Reduction Strategies

What can be done, it must be asked, to ensure that the current emphasis on poverty eventually makes a positive difference in the lives of poor people? The preceding analysis suggests a number of ways to ensure more effective responses. PRSPs have most clearly succeeded where they coincided with a preexisting national project for poverty reduction articulated by political leaders and widely shared by citizens.[5] This observation draws attention, first, to the critical role of national leadership and political will. The role of the donor in this regard is limited; leadership and political will cannot be created by external pressures or persuasion. After a visit to Ghana in 2005, the eminent management specialist Henry Mintzberg concluded that "we (external actors) don't develop leaders so much as foster the conditions that bring leadership out. . . . key among these conditions has to be the self-respect that derives from working things out for ourselves, individually and collectively" (Mintzberg 2006, p. 6). In a similar vein, in an analysis of the limited efficacy of conditionality to secure desired policy changes, Tony Killick (2004, p. 17) quotes an IMF paper on conditionality policy issues that asserts the primary role of external agencies "is to identify reformers, not to create them" (IMF 2001, p. 55).

A second factor is the need to base donor decisions regarding aid allocations and implementation strategies on a sound analysis of the policy process, the overall political environment, institutional capacity, and the historical and cultural context in the recipient countries. Accomplishing all that implies understanding and acting upon not only the formal structures but also the underlying, more informal, structures of power and practice that can render the formal structures ineffectual (Evans 2004, p. 34). Stephan Haggard talks about "digging beneath institutional arrangements to the political relationships that create and support them" (2004, p. 75).

A third factor relates to staff quality, their deployment, and their mode of operating. Getting good results depends heavily on the quality of aid agency staff, especially those at the country level. These staff must be prepared to invest time in establishing close working relations with the key partners and understanding their policy agendas in order to seek convergence and a basis for collaboration. Once they have acquired this essential knowledge of the context and the actors, it is important they stay long enough in the country to be effective.

To ensure sustained performance by staff, Pomerantz underlines the need for greater recognition of the significant bureaucratic and psychological

pressures on aid agency staff in the field who undertake difficult and sometimes dangerous work. A fundamental problem lies in the fact that staff feels
responsible, and are held accountable, for programs whose ultimate success
or failure lies outside their grasp. Over time, they may adjust by rationaliz-
ing their position and feeling less responsible. Individual and organizational
accountability then diminishes. If aid effectiveness in Africa is to improve,
staff working in the continent must have a commitment to excellence, but
excellence here does not mean the ability to write the most polished reports
or to be technical experts zipping from country to country. Excellence working in the African context means, above all, staff who are able to blend technical expertise with political, institutional, social, cultural, and environmental knowledge, who possess analytical and people-oriented skills, and have
the ability to integrate specific policies and programs into a broader framework (Pomerantz 2004, pp. 144–146).

There are signs that authority and decisionmaking are being devolved
more often to local donor representatives. The expectation of African government officials is that frequent interaction with these representatives can
lead to greater influence on their donor interlocutors, and bring the locus of
decisionmaking closer to them. It is further expected that decentralization
will improve donor decisionmaking, generally perceived to be slow and
opaque, and permit greater flexibility in the application of policies and procedures. The downside is that the expanded size and number of in-country
offices, as a consequence of decentralization, can result in cumbersome internal management processes and more donor coordination meetings
(Pomerantz 2004, pp. 124–125). It can also mean a reduction in the number
of long-term advisers with a substantive sector-specific role to strengthen
capacity and facilitate implementation. The shift to direct budget support
may also contribute to the reduction in the sector-specific expertise in donor
agencies and lead to more reliance on specialists in cross-cutting areas such
as public finance and performance management. It would be better for PRSP
implementation if agencies maintain a blend of macroeconomic expertise
and substantive knowledge of specific policy sectors.

A fourth factor that can increase aid's chances at success is a commitment to a country-driven approach. Aid agency staff should avoid bringing
preconceived ideas and plans and unveiling them as if they were delivering
the Holy Grail. National actors become understandably frustrated when the
donors insist that their models and solutions represent the only viable approach. It can generate mistrust and suspicion, especially when the same
donor has advanced quite different policies with the same single-minded
zeal in the past.[6] This tendency is evident in the important area of institutional development. Peter Evans criticizes the imposition of uniform institutional blueprints, "institutional monocropping" as he calls it, a practice that
rests on the general premise that effectiveness does not depend on a fit with

the sociocultural environment, and on the more specific premise that ideal-ized versions of Anglo-American institutions are optimal development in-struments (Evans 2004, p. 33). This expectation contradicts the real spirit of the relationship conveyed in the Paris Declaration on Aid Effectiveness, whereby the donor plays more of a facilitator role by helping to provide "space" for genuine national solutions to emerge, almost invariably in a step-by-step manner over time.

This country-driven approach implies pragmatism in the selection of aid instruments. At a time of increased donor pressure to achieve results via budget support and sectorwide programs, it is important to recognize that specific development projects still have a place, even if some project aid can be criticized for high transaction costs, lack of sustainability, and so on. In countries not yet ready for major reforms and policy-based lending, project assistance can play an essential role, helping to develop local capacities, building mutual confidence and trust among key actors, promoting networks and coalitions, and demonstrating possible strategies for change.[7] Killick also points to the need for further evidence concerning transaction costs, ar-guing that where there is a combination of sectoral program aid and direct budget support, the tendency to develop rather elaborate mechanisms for di-aloguing, monitoring, reporting, and evaluating imposes substantial burdens on in-country aid agency staff and their national counterparts.[8]

A fifth factor is that donors should foster a learning environment, both individual and organizational. Unfortunately there are many constraints on learning: prevailing organizational cultures, the pressure to meet disburse-ment targets, lack of appropriate incentives, rapid staff turnover, increasing reliance on temporary staff and consultants, career advancement criteria un-related to performance of past projects, insecurity and a rapid pace of change, and the unequal nature of the aid relationship (OECD/DAC 2001; Ostrom, Gibson, Shivakumar, and Andersson 2001). Evaluation processes can help promote this learning, and a performance management approach can ensure that course corrections and systemic changes are made. For many years, evaluation has fallen short of expectations, illustrated by the fact that the list of lessons learned appended to many project/program evaluations is "almost always banal, uninformative, and so general as to apply anywhere" (Berg 2000, pp. 7–8). Keith Mackay, however, points to welcome improve-ments in evaluation, citing the growing number of countries with strong monitoring and evaluation systems; a more committed set of stakeholders, including government ministers, senior officials, donors, and academics; and the creation of national evaluation societies in sixteen African countries (Mackay 2006, pp. 12, 15).

To accelerate their own learning, aid agencies must seek to make better use of local knowledge and experience available in every country from a di-verse range of sources, including national researchers, program beneficiaries, actors in the national bureaucracies, private voluntary organizations, and other development partners. The key challenges involve how to document and draw lessons for scaling up successful projects and how to learn from the rich contextual knowledge and implementation experience of local actors who are not accorded sufficient "voice" in current processes. Needless errors are made because "there has been a notable lack of learning from the experiences of people and organizations that are part of the process of defining aid policy and its implementation. In contrast, in the business sector, an organization's ability to learn faster than its competitors has long been claimed as a key to success" (Takahashi 2006, p. 39).

A sixth factor is the importance of avoiding the perverse effects of the current emphasis on results-based approaches in the context of the PRSPs and the MDGs.[9] Achieving high-quality development results takes time, but pressure from politicians and other influential actors to show results quickly can divert attention from the quality of the results. The World Bank (2006a, p. xiii) concludes that a judicious combination of long-term objectives and interventions that yield quick and visible results has proved effective, thereby avoiding excessive "short-termism." The focus on results and on the achievement of performance targets as "triggers" for the disbursement of donor funds can lead the donor and the national counterparts to display excessive prudence and adopt more easily achievable targets in order to avoid losing possible funding. This observation also implies that an independent source of reliable performance data is needed to help resist the inevitable pressures to massage and manipulate the record of results.

The challenge is further complicated in many countries by the dearth of up-to-date and disaggregated data on poverty, and differences over the best ways to measure them. The most frequently mentioned indicator for the poverty MDG—the percentage of the population living on less than a dollar per day—reflects a narrow a concept of poverty. A widely used and somewhat broader alternative is the percentage of the population whose incomes fall below a poverty line based on the cost of a minimum basket of essential goods for basic human survival. Unfortunately, too often these indicators are not informed by recent and reliable data and are not used to guide programmatic and budget choices. The "data demand" generated by the current emphasis on poverty is stimulating interest in strengthening the often neglected national statistical systems, and is fueling the demand for large-scale data collection exercises.

Despite the above shortcomings, it is important to persevere and to improve poverty reduction strategies in light of implementation experience and lessons learned. In the case of Senegal, learning from the limited impact of the first PRSP (2003–2005) has resulted in a PRSP2 that is more comprehensive, with a cost-based priority action plan and strengthened implementation mechanisms. The new document covers a period of five years and has integrated the MDGs and the national strategy for accelerated growth. As time passes, PRSPs will certainly have to evolve from the "one size fits all" of the first generation and take increasingly diverse forms, more rooted in country realities and "nationally owned."

The Paris Declaration Agenda in Practice

How far can some of the issues raised above be addressed through the implementation of the 2005 Paris Declaration on Aid Effectiveness? The declaration has been endorsed by more than 100 donor and developing countries and multilateral organizations. Its main elements are

- Ownership: Partner countries exercise effective leadership over their development policies and results-oriented strategies and coordinate development activities.
- Alignment: Donors base their overall support on partner country national development strategies, institutions, and procedures (for example, for financial management and audits).
- Harmonization: Donors actions are more harmonized, transparent, and collectively effective (including simplification of procedures and a better division of labor).

The declaration also emphasizes managing resources and improving decisionmaking for results and mutual accountability (i.e., donors and partner countries are both accountable for development results).

The most significant progress at the Paris forum was the agreement in principle on a set of targets for changes in donor, recipient, and joint behavior that can be monitored. They constitute the core of a new compact on "mutual accountability," binding the participant nations and institutions (Rogerson 2005, p. 531). This compact represents a systematic attempt to tackle perceived inefficiencies and weaknesses in development cooperation that have been repeatedly identified.

Implementation of the declaration as a pilot program will proceed in several countries, including Senegal, where country plans of action will be prepared utilizing twelve specific indicators for reporting progress and drawing on published examples of good practice (OECD/DAC 2007). A major evaluation is planned for 2008–2009, probably comanaged by Denmark and Vietnam. This exercise will provide an opportunity to go beyond the indicators, to analyze the underlying assumptions, and to better articulate the logic of the Paris commitments, including the implied linkages between aid effectiveness and development effectiveness. It is too early to assess the overall impact of the declaration. However, some key challenges have arisen.

In the first place, there is a need to address the "disconnection" between high-level global declarations and organizational practice. Commitments made at a high political level must be translated into reality through strong "signals" to lower bureaucratic levels, both at donor headquarters and inside recipient countries, so that staff behavior is brought into line with the harmonization and alignment objectives. The accomplishment of this goal may require organizational restructuring, the issuance of strong policy guidelines, and the review of procedures and individual incentives (formal and informal).

Inevitably, there are a number of constraints. At a political level, although everyone in principal favors harmonization, in practice politicians are more concerned about visibility, and actors such as private voluntary organizations and UN agencies may be concerned about losing part of their funding. Partner governments may also have mixed feelings because harmonization could reduce their negotiating space when they face an increasingly "monolithic" donor group that functions as a cartel. For many in developing countries, there is a sense that when donors speak of government-led efforts, they often mean recipient governments traveling the path that the donors have chosen, and at the donors' pace (Pomerantz 2004, p. 149).

At an institutional level, there appears to be a gradual decentralization of resources and responsibilities to country levels, although with significant differences in the degree of implementation across agencies. The review and simplification of rules and procedures can be slow. There is an ongoing tension between, on the one hand, the classic bureaucratic culture of the aid agency that emphasizes compliance, control, and careful management of project inputs, and on the other, the need for a new spirit of innovation that "lets go" of time-consuming and fastidious controls in favor of managing by and for results.

Finally, there is insufficient attention paid to individual incentives, a serious oversight as it is widely acknowledged that personalities and individual characteristics are fundamental factors in the success or failure of harmonization and alignment efforts at the country level. Aid agencies need to place more attention on human resource management to ensure that the implications of the Paris agenda are taken into account in recruitment and skills development, and in incentive systems both informal and formal that can shape attitudes and behaviors (de Renzio 2005b; Ostrom, Gibson, Shivakumar, and Andersson 2001). One crucial factor affecting individual incentives is the extent to which promising country-based initiatives, which often call for exceptions to established norms, are vigorously supported by senior managers (Rogerson and De Renzio 2005, p. 3).

Assessing overall progress is not facilitated by the apparent absence of an explicit results framework for the Paris agenda. However, country-level progress indicators with common definitions are being used, in particular for the monitoring of harmonization and alignment efforts. In an effort to generate comparable data, the progress indicators are quite simple, even superficial, proxies for more complex underlying processes. Their simplicity illustrate the problem of finding the right quantitative and qualitative tools to measure progress in complex areas of institutional change, capacity building, and aid governance where the objectives are often diffuse and hard to quantify.

In Senegal, the monitoring process has helped promote reciprocal commitments among donors and a constructive dialogue with the Ministry of Economy and Finance. The first annual monitoring exercise in 2006 revealed significant information gaps and wide divergences of interpretation and appreciation in relation to implementation criteria of the Paris Declaration. These include parallel implementation structures, transparent and monitorable performance assessment frameworks, and estimates of aid allocations.

There is clearly a long way to go to fulfill the promises of the Paris Declaration. There are great disparities in levels of engagement and commitment among aid agencies and partner governments. On the donor side, Chapter 3 in this book draws attention to the complexity and lack of coherence in the aid provided by the United States. An aid agency that takes harmonization seriously must be willing to redefine its objectives and subordinate its own activities and outputs to a commitment to joint outcomes and results, thereby contributing to the *total effectiveness* of the aid effort in a particular country (De Renzio, Booth, Rogerson, and Curran 2005, pp. 4, 7).

From the recipient side, Andrew Rogerson identifies differing responses according to three broad categories of countries: (1) middle-income countries with fewer donors who prefer to manage donor relationships individually; (2) fragile states and low-governance environments where donors are very cautious (outside of humanitarian assistance) and it is unclear whether the Paris Declaration incites them to do more, do less, or try something completely different; and (3) relatively well-performing low-income countries. With its high levels of aid dependence and extensive involvement of multiple donors, this latter group represents the central battleground for the aid effectiveness agenda. Such countries seek a material payoff from the Paris Declaration in terms of more flexible and predictable aid and less conditionality from donors. From their perspective, the declaration could result in less (or less intrusive) upward accountability from recipient governments to the donors (Rogerson 2005, p. 534).

Fragile states and low-governance environments, by contrast, require special attention to help them become eligible for PRSP funding. They are home to more than 500 million people (World Bank 2006a, p. 18), and their constraints require special attention as reforms to aid relationships are being considered. Chapter 8 in this book gives an example of the major challenges posed by postconflict Liberia and the structures created to address them. To the extent that donors are really moving toward aid allocations based on performance criteria, is there a need to avoid excessive concentration of scarce aid resources on the "aid darlings"? The World Bank, for example, advises that "Bank lending, both overall and on a per capita basis, was concentrated on countries that had relatively good policy environments" (World Bank 2004a, p. vii).

Conclusion

Improvements in aid management and effectiveness in line with the Paris agenda will take time and require perseverance to overcome considerable bureaucratic inertia and other political and technical constraints. Moreover, the results flowing from any improvements will still be suboptimal until there is more progress in the restructuring of world trade on a more equitable basis.[10] Progress toward smarter aid will be further inhibited by the fact that, contrary to declared intentions, effectiveness criteria are not always uppermost in donor decisionmaking. Political, strategic, historical, and bureaucratic considerations are still major determinants of aid allocations, as compared with country need (poverty), policies (good and bad), and performance (Rogerson 2005, pp. 539–540; Gunning 2004). Notwithstanding these constraints, experience suggests that when a developing country government shows commitment, leadership, and the will to engage in proactive coordination, its development partners are much more likely to improve their aid performance in line with the Paris agenda of alignment, harmonization, and mutual accountability. Similarly, successful poverty reduction strategies, as well as progress toward the attainment of the MDGs, depend not only on increased and sustained aid flows and well-formulated policies but also, and critically, on the political commitment and national capacity to advance a country-owned development agenda, adjusting and adapting it over time to overcome constraints and incorporate lessons learned.

Notes

The author is UNICEF representative in Senegal, where he has served since 2000. This is written in his personal capacity, and the views and opinions expressed are his own.

1. As of the end of March 2008, more than seventy full PRSPs have been circulated to the Fund Executive Board, as well as about fifty preliminary or "interim" PRSPs. IMF fact sheet. http://www.imf.org/external/np/exr/facts/prsp.htm.

2. This increased funding needs to be accompanied by improved quality and utilization rates in order to enhance health and education outcomes. Killick further argues that the emphasis on the provision of social services risks diverting attention from more fundamental causes of poverty (Killick 2004, pp. 8–10).

3. For example, the Senegal PRSP2 (2006–2010) has 144 objectives and strategies, 505 priority actions, and 113 priority objectives.

4. There is a growing literature on these issues. See, for example, "Achieving Poverty Reducing Growth," World Bank 2006a, pp. 5–19, and World Bank 2004b.

5. The cases of Uganda and Vietnam are cited in Driscoll (2005, p. 19).

6. I sometimes feel that there are too many people in the donor community who have found "the solution" and who are looking for problems to "fit" their solutions.

7. A study of the experience of eight African countries that embarked upon significant health sector reforms in the 1990s highlighted the decisive role of reform-minded national actors, who in several countries came to work together in pursuit of an ambitious shared vision as a result of their earlier involvement in project-level innovation (Hanson 1998).

8. See Killick 2004, pp. 18–25, for a discussion of the evidence relating to transaction costs and the choice of aid modalities that points to the need for more research.

9. For an insightful review of results-based management in development cooperation, see Binnedijk (2000).

10. For example, farm subsidies in the global North amount to $US250 billion (Saith 2006, p. 1190).

8

Economic Reforms and Development Assistance in Postconflict Liberia

John F. E. Ohiorhenuan

RECREATING A VIABLE ECONOMY after prolonged violent conflict remains one of the most serious challenges of development. Yet, until relatively recently, beginning this task was considered to be feasible only after peace has been secured. Now, however, a broad consensus is emerging among conflict analysts and development economists that the economic dimensions of peacemaking are ultimately as important as achieving basic security in war-torn countries.

In this chapter, I review the Liberian experience in an attempt to draw some lessons about the role of the international community in supporting efforts to stimulate economic recovery in the immediate aftermath of conflict when the peace is still fragile. In particular, I ask whether the technical and financial support of the international partners was "smart," in the sense of being tailored to obtain the best possible results in this specific context. The actions of development partners across time and sectors are reviewed in terms of the quality and effectiveness of their assistance. In the case of Liberia, we are able to trace the evolution of policy and recovery and the role of the government and development partners, from the signing of the peace agreement in 2003 through the transitional governance period up until democratic elections in November 2005 and through the first year of the elected government.[1]

Characteristics of the Postconflict Liberian Economy

Since the military coup in 1980, and excluding a three-year period of relative calm from 1998 to 2001, Liberia has experienced intense conflict and, correspondingly, a sustained political, social, and economic disruption. By the time a cease-fire was reached in 2003, the country had experienced economic regression, severely deteriorated infrastructure, social decay, disintegrated institutions, and corroded governance procedures.

Economic Regression

During the three decades of conflict, Liberia's resources were, for the most part, diverted from production to the destruction of assets. Figure 8.1 shows how, following the military coup in 1980, real gross domestic product (GDP) plummeted from over US$700 million to around US$100 million in 1995. Charles Taylor's offensive against Samuel Doe in 1989 marks the beginning of the long-lasting civil war. The economy rebounded slightly after the signing of a peace agreement in 1996 and continued to grow around the time of the 1997 elections, which placed Taylor in office. However, it began to decline again with the sudden deterioration in the security situation in 2001 and the imposition of a UN ban on timber exports in 2003 (IMF 2005b). Real GDP per capita followed a similar path, declining from almost US$1,000 per capita in 1980 to below US$100 in 1995, and hovering just below US$200 since 2001.

Figure 8.1 Real GDP per Capita, 1960–2004 (constant 1995 US dollars)

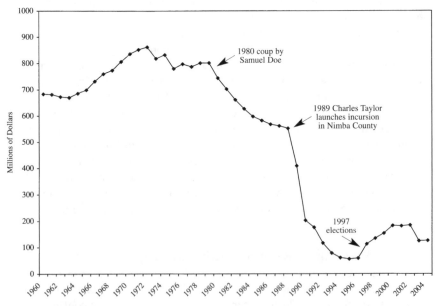

Sources: Government of Liberia, United Nations, World Bank, and International Monetary Fund, *Interim Poverty Reduction Strategy (Final Draft),* Monrovia, January (2006), p. 3; GDP per capita data based on World Bank, *World Development Indicators, 2004.*

Widespread insecurity and asset destruction resulted in a highly disabling environment for legitimate productive activity.[2] Opportunities in the formal business sector were so limited that Liberia suffered from substantial flight of human and financial capital (IMF 2005b). Not surprisingly, therefore, unemployment is very high, and the informal sector, primarily petty trading, absorbs about one-third of the economically active population.[3] With the destruction of legitimate economic activity, parallel illicit economies emerged and served to boost the fortunes of the warlords and provide livelihoods for their constituents.[4] One study charged that in 2000 Charles Taylor profited from approximately US$100 million in timber fraud (Global Witness and International Transport Workers Federation 2001).[5]

A speedy return to economic normalcy was also compromised by the fact that a large proportion of the population resided in camps and was therefore limited in its ability to invest and plan for the long term.[6] Indeed, 490,000 Liberians were estimated to be internally displaced in 2003, and 350,000 were thought to be outside the country as refugees (NTGL, UN and WB 2004, p. 38).

Infrastructure Deterioration

Liberia's infrastructure deteriorated during the conflict, as opposing combatants employed a deliberate strategy of destruction or as basic maintenance ceased. By the end of the conflict in 2003, the road network had not been maintained for three decades, the Monrovia sewage plant had been out of operation for more than ten years, and the rail and port infrastructure that once facilitated the vibrant exports of iron ore and timber had simply collapsed (NTGL, UN, and WB 2004, p. 63). The port of Monrovia and Roberts International Airport were open to limited traffic but restricted by safety hazards and the lack of adequate equipment and international certification.

Social infrastructure was not spared. In 2003 only 10 percent of the population was estimated to have access to health care. Indeed, little of the health infrastructure that existed before the war was functioning, as 242 out of 293 public health facilities had been looted or forced to close because of lack of staff and supplies (NTGL, UN, and WB 2004, p. 51). A similar picture could be painted for education. The Liberia Rapid Assessment of Learning Spaces 2003–2004 found that learning spaces in 31 percent of the 3,840 educational facilities assessed were completely or mostly destroyed, and another 27 percent of the learning spaces were partly destroyed (NTGL, UN, and WB 2005, p. 54).

Social Decay

Social cohesion and trust, the core of society's social capital, were also severely eroded in Liberia. With close to 1 million people having left their homes, communities were fragmented, and community-level networks of social and economic exchange, developed over several decades, were destroyed.

Human capital had also been depleted by "brain drain" and years of neglect of the education system. In-country authorities estimate that between 80 percent and 90 percent of skilled Liberians left Liberia during the conflict years, and the majority have not returned. With the war, education essentially stopped for a decade in Liberia, and, as a consequence, young adults today are less educated than their parents' generation. This lack of skill, together with the war-induced contraction of opportunities, has resulted in staggeringly high unemployment and underemployment. This large mass of unemployed youths constitutes a significant conflict risk—without alternative livelihood opportunities, the youth are relatively easy picking for armed groups seeking to mobilize soldiers.

Disintegration of Institutions and Governance Processes

While the civil war raged in Liberia, national and local institutions were rendered dysfunctional, resulting in very poor governance and widespread corruption (Liberia et al. 2006). The rules of the game necessary for the effective functioning of state institutions had been mostly absent in the years leading up to the conflict. The situation worsened with the civil war—civil servants were not paid, revenue collection procedures were neither transparent nor accountable, and provision of basic services and public goods almost ceased. Under these conditions, impunity and corruption flourished, with state functionaries furthering personal and parochial interests.

In the immediate aftermath of the conflict, the judicial system was massively under-resourced, with only five qualified prosecutors in the country, ten public defense counselors, and circuit courts in only six of the fifteen counties (NTGL, UN, and WB 2005, p. 38). The weakness of the system resulted in a general lack of faith in the police, corrections systems, criminal investigations, and the justice system as a whole, leading to frequent incidents of mob justice (International Crisis Group 2006).

These pathologies paint a picture of an economy with a most severe case of fragmented markets, informational asymmetries, and, like other postconflict economies, extremely high transactions costs.

The Challenges of Liberia's Postconflict Economic Policy

Faced with such systemic weakness, the newly established authorities in Liberia had to seek the simultaneous attainment of several policy objectives. Among the most important of these were creating a secure environment for economic recovery, reestablishing a proper governance oversight system, and reconstituting social and human capital. In this section I focus on these objectives since they have elicited considerable international attention. It is also with regard to these objectives that the interaction between the development partners and the national authorities can be seen most clearly.[7]

The period under review in this section begins with the Comprehensive Peace Agreement (CPA), which was signed in August 2003 following the cease-fire in June of that year.[8] Peace talks resulted from increasing international pressure to end the regional conflict involving not only Liberia, but Sierra Leone, Guinea, and Côte d'Ivoire as well. The International Contact Group on Liberia (ICGL) was formed to provide a high-level forum for coordination and discussion by all parties with an interest in Liberia. It held its first working session on December 19, 2002, in Dakar, Senegal, and its second in New York on February 28, 2003. It comprised representatives of the UN, the European Union, the African Union, the Economic Community of West African States (ECOWAS), France, Morocco, Nigeria, Senegal, the United Kingdom, and the United States (Amnesty International, May 2003,).[9]

The CPA provided for a national transitional government (NTGL), drawn primarily from the former warring parties, and established a timetable for a transition to an elected administration in January 2006.[10] The CPA created a number of independent commissions, including the Governance Reform Commission (GRC) and the Contract and Monopolies Commission (CMC). These two entities were to oversee the implementation of socioeconomic, administrative, and governance issues during the two-year transitional period.

Following the signing of the peace agreement, the reconstruction effort began in earnest in Liberia, supported by a host of development partners.[11] The UN was represented by thirteen agencies: FAO, UNDP, UNEP, UNESCO, UNFPA, UN-HABITAT, UNHCHR, UNHCR, UNICEF, UNIFEM, UNOPS, WFP, and WHO.[12] The World Bank, International Monetary Fund (IMF), and the International Organization for Migration (IOM) were also very active. Among the bilateral partners present in Liberia were China, Denmark, Germany, Ghana, Ireland, Japan, Nigeria, Norway, South Africa, Sweden, the United Kingdom, and the United States (Liberia et al. 2006, p. 89). Of these partners, the United States (for historical reasons) has been by far the largest donor, contributing close to 50 percent of the total official development assistance (ODA).[13] Indeed, as an example of the role of donor financing, the 2006 *Human Development Report for Liberia* estimates that in the early 2000s about 85 percent of activities in the areas of health, education, water purity, and sanitation were donor-funded (UNDP 2006).

Creating a Secure Environment

After more than twenty years of violence, a priority for Liberia was to secure the foundation for development to resume. That meant, in the short term, taking measures to break the dynamics of violence. In the medium to longer term, the challenge would be to strengthen the delivery of justice and citizen security and implement a broad spectrum of social and economic programs targeting "high-risk" groups or potential conflict triggers.

After the United Nations Peacebuilding Support Office closed its doors in July 2003,[14] a multinational force in Liberia was established (UN Security Council 2003b) to support the implementation of the cease-fire agreement and prepare for the longer-term United Nations stabilization force that would support the implementation of the CPA. The parties to the peace agreement had requested an international peacekeeping force to secure the cease-fire, create a zone of separation between the belligerent forces, and provide a safe corridor for free movement of persons (Liberia et al. 2003, Article III). The United Nations Mission in Liberia (UNMIL) force, established in September 2003 (UN Security Council 2003a), while relatively successful at securing the peace in Monrovia encountered challenges outside the capital. In the forests, for example, local officials complained about the control exerted by two rebel groups, the Movement for Democracy in Liberia (MODEL) and Liberians United for Reconciliation and Democracy (LURD) at border crossings. Even in regions where UNMIL was present, looting continued, as peacekeepers, having no mandate to arrest, were not able to engage in policing (UN Security Council 2004a). This continued insecurity hindered the launch of reconstruction efforts.

In an effort to address the underlying dynamics of the violence, the CPA also called for the establishment of an interdisciplinary and interdepartmental National Commission for Disarmament, Demobilization, Rehabilitation, and Reintegration (DDRR) activities (Liberia et al. 2003, Article VI). The intention was to demobilize 53,000 combatants and, over a period of three years (NTGL, UN, and WB 2004, p. 41) assist their reintegration into society though formal schooling, vocational training, and support for sustainable livelihoods.

The DDRR program was supported financially and technically by the UN and other partners and is an example of both how quickly development partners were able to mobilize assistance, and how coordination and planning sometimes suffered as a consequence. Although international partners quickly provided the support that Liberia needed to disarm and demobilize, it turned out that the initial estimate of 53,000 combatants was off by almost 100 percent. By the end of 2004, 103,325 combatants had been demobilized. This gross underestimate put the system under considerable pressure, especially at the reintegration stage.

Part of the reason for the high caseload was that the initial counts underestimated the number of female and child combatants.[15] In-country experts also explained that because of the unconventional nature of the conflict and the uncertainties even after the CPA, it was not feasible to get commanders to bring in their troops in formation. Rather, the modus operandi was for combatants to bring in their weapons and show reasonable familiarity with their use. Not surprisingly, combatants, who often had more than one firearm, shared the weapons among nonfighters so they could present themselves for the DDRR program and benefit from the reintegration allowances and training. With such a high rate of unemployment, the fact that more people could benefit from vocational training can be judged as a good thing, but the vastly elevated numbers put pressure on the program.

A 2006 evaluation of the DDRR process found that the DDRR program in Liberia made possible a much better life for those ex-combatants who completed their program of training, compared to those former fighters who chose not to register but to reintegrate on their own. In almost every sub-facet of the dimensions of reintegration (social, economic, and political), the DDRR program completers were decisively more advanced in their efforts to reintegrate than those combatants who chose self-reintegration, or any other category for that matter (Pugel 2006).

Reports from people working closely with the DDRR program on the ground indicate that some reintegration initiatives were more successful than others, however. Different development partners offered different packages of support, and combatants were largely free to choose between them. The program today is finding that a number of combatants who had opted for "cash for work" models, rather than those focused on livelihood skills, are returning to the program, claiming not to have been successfully reintegrated. The United Nations Development Programme (UNDP) office in Liberia estimated, toward the end of 2007, that over two years since the disarmament process was completed, there were still about 9,000 ex-combatants who had yet to be reintegrated.

Even though disarmament of combatants and deployment of UNMIL would enhance security in the immediate period, the government and international partners also recognized that sustainable recovery required the development of national capacities to provide security. In pursuit of this aim, the armed forces were to be restructured into a unified, cohesive military (NTGL, UN, and WB 2004, p. 40), and an interim police force was to be established—staffed by well-vetted personnel and outfitted with essential equipment and training (including on human rights) (NTGL, UN, and WB 2004, p. 89). Reform of the police began early, and by the end of 2004, 646 police officers had been trained and vetted to provide law and order in Monrovia, and 200 had been deployed to twelve counties (NTGL, UN, and WB 2005, Annex 1). Training and reform for the new Armed Forces of Liberia, however, did not begin until after the elections, but is expected to be completed for the 2,000-strong force by the end of 2008.[16]

A number of initiatives outlined in the transition planning documents and supported by development partners are aimed at the potentially high-risk group of unemployed youth, to provide them with livelihood opportunities to reduce the temptation of violence. These included labor-intensive public works programs, training and credit schemes to support young people's efforts to devise and implement income-generating activities, grants for further education, and job placement assistance. Sports and leisure activities have also been promoted, as a way of building social cohesion and reducing idleness. Despite these efforts, the challenge of youth unemployment remains a high priority. The newly elected government has developed a national youth policy that builds on these initiatives by emphasizing the need for youth to be included institutionally in decisionmaking and for budgetary allocations to specifically target youth in areas such as education, HIV/AIDS, and economic governance (Liberia et al. 2006, p. 66).

Establishing a Governance Oversight Mechanism

Rigorous oversight of the management of public finances and national resources and the establishment of robust systems of public control and oversight of the economy are necessary prerequisites for postconflict economic recovery. In a country like Liberia, where mismanagement of national resources played such a critical role in igniting and propelling the conflict, oversight is especially important as a sign to the population that the state is committed to peace and long-term prosperity.

Indeed, mismanagement of national resources was so extreme in Liberia that in 2001–2006 the country was subjected to a vast array of UN sanctions (see Figure 8.2 for a brief overview of the history of sanctions in Liberia). These sanctions were introduced to ensure security, promote transparency and accountability in all functions of governance, and safeguard natural resources. In practice, however, they proved to be ineffective because the country's devastating capacity constraints made it nearly impossible for the sanctions to be properly implemented and enforced. In 2004 a report of the United Nations Panel of Experts on Liberia revealed that all the Security Council sanctions had for the most part been disregarded. Individuals covered by the travel ban were making flights on a regular basis, illicit diamond mining and trading persisted and posed a serious threat to the credibility of the Kimberley Process, and logging and pit-sawing continued under the control of previously warring factions.[17] Ironically, despite their ineffectiveness, and because the benchmarked reforms were not met, sanctions were continually renewed until 2006.[18]

Issues of economic governance were so important in Liberia that they were included in the Comprehensive Peace Agreement. The CPA mandated that the Governance Reform Commission ensure transparency and accountability in all government institutions and activities, including acting as an ombudsman promoting good governance (Liberia et al. 2003, Article XVI). The Contract and Monopolies Commission was mandated to oversee activities of a contractual nature undertaken by the NTGL (Article XVII). Specific

---

Figure 8.2 History of Sanctions in Liberia

UN Security Council Resolution 1343 (2001) placed a ban on the transportation of arms as well as diamonds and on travel of by key government officials in order to end Liberia's involvement with the conflict in Sierra Leone.

UN resolution 1408 (2002) renewed sanctions on Liberia for another twelve months and established audit regimes to ensure the legitimate usage of revenue from shipping and timber.

Resolution 1478 (2003) extended sanctions to timber.

Resolution 1521 (2003) renewed sanctions on arms, diamonds, and timber and travel by key individuals.

Resolution 1532 (2004) called for the seizure of the assets of Taylor and his associates.

Resolution 1572 (2004) imposed an arms embargo on Côte d'Ivoire, noting Liberia's permeable borders and ethnic ties between various groups along the border between the two countries as having facilitated the exchange of weapons.

UN Security Council Resolution 1579 (2004) renewed measures on arms and travel as well as timber and diamonds that were imposed by Resolution 1521 (2003).

Resolution 1683 (2006) adapted the arms embargo to allow Liberian police and security forces to use weapons.

Resolution 1689 (2006) removed sanctions on Liberian logs, to be reviewed after a period of ninety days.

Resolution 1753 (2007) lifted diamond sanctions.

Source: Report of the United Nations Panel of Experts on Liberia, S/2004/955.

---

proposals were made later in 2003 to strengthen revenue collection, budgeting, and financial management practices; establish a computerized financial management system; build the capacity of the Auditor-General's Office; reform public sector procurement to enhance transparency; and restore a functioning banking system based on clear international prudential regulations (NTGL, UN, and WB 2005, p. 103). All policy actions were to be located within transparent and accountable procedures for budgeting, financial management, procurement, accounting, auditing, and reporting that were in line with current best practices and consistent with the overarching need to reposition the economy for longer-term transformation (NTGL, UN, and WB 2004, p. 66).

Indeed, implementation of policy reforms for improved governance seemed to have gotten off to a good start during the transition period. In March 2004, the IMF Executive Board stated, "In view of Liberia's recent record of cooperation and sound policies and its limited technical capacities and overwhelming reconstruction needs, Directors supported the resumption of Fund technical assistance." However, by the end of 2004, doubts were being raised by the international community about the commitment of the NTGL to reform. Late in 2004, under the Institutional Support Program (ISP),[19] the European Commission (EC) commissioned an in-depth systems' and financial audit of the Central Bank, as well as five other state-owned enterprises.[20] Although the audit was initially intended to review performance under the Taylor regime with a view to providing reform recommendations going forward, a lack of data apparently led the auditors to embark, *without prior agreement with the NTGL,* on an audit of current activities instead. The audit findings revealed extensive NTGL mismanagement and underscored the urgent need for reform. Poor choices in public financial management were delaying reform implementation, and reports of widespread corruption were appearing in the Liberian media. The various factions within the NTGL accused each other of siphoning off state finances for personal gain, increasing fears for the stability of the peace process (UNDPKO and World Bank 2006). The Contracts and Monopolies Commission failed to oversee the award of contracts because it was totally bypassed by government agencies entering into contracts and concessions (World Bank and UNDP 2006, p. 7).

In December 2004, the International Crisis Group had also called for a radical international approach in Liberia, proposing, among other things, that an international group should assume responsibility for public revenue collection (UNDPKO and World Bank 2006).[21] The EC audits were the evidence needed to organize international action along these lines. Discussions were held among the EC, the World Bank, the United States, and the IMF and later ECOWAS, and it was finally concluded that a robust plan was needed to prevent further mismanagement of revenues.

Despite heavy resistance from the NTGL, substantial coordinated donor pressure eventually led to the Governance and Economic Management Assistance Programme (GEMAP). The first key step in the design of GEMAP took place when international partners and the NTGL met for the annual review of Results-Focused Transitional Framework (RFTF) progress in Copenhagen on May 9–10, 2004. With many speakers airing concerns about the extent of corruption and its impact on recovery, the NTGL accepted the need for a stronger international presence in Liberia's financial management. An action plan for economic governance was then elaborated, based on a preliminary plan drafted by the United States, with the IMF and the World Bank further developing its technical aspects and the EC drafting a political framework.

The NTGL and other West African states raised concerns about the infringement on sovereignty that could result from the proposed arrangement. ECOWAS, in its role as arbiter of the CPA, also expressed concerns that such a plan would deflect attention from the CPA timetable and potentially undermine it. ECOWAS acknowledged the severity of corruption but favored dealing with it after the elections. However, agreement for an action plan was finally secured after significant lobbying by New York, Washington, D.C., and

Brussels and other European capitals. UN Secretary-General Kofi Annan also discussed the matter personally with the ECOWAS leadership and with other African leaders who had reservations.

With the international community in agreement, donors increased pressure on the NTGL to accept the plan by threatening to suspend aid. For example, the EC sent a letter stating that continued development funding was contingent on the implementation of GEMAP, and the United States threatened to withhold support for security sector reform. These pressures, coupled with the potential link between Security Council sanctions and the implementation of GEMAP, helped expedite its signing (UNDPKO and World Bank 2006).[22] The final version of GEMAP was presented as a joint solution agreed between the NTGL and its international partners (see Figure 8.3 for details on GEMAP).

Drawn-out negotiations delayed the signing of the GEMAP agreement until September 2005, one month before presidential elections. Consequently, it became a moot question whether it was the right tool to improve transitional governance since there were only a few months overlap. Implementation during these few months was also slow—partly because there was no detailed road map for its implementation. The environment for reform changed markedly after the elections. The new government, led by President Ellen Johnson-Sirleaf, declared war on corruption and stated that it "will use all conceivable legal resources to tackle it forcefully and effectively to recapture state resources for national development" (Liberia et al. 2006, p. 63). Speaking to the US Congress in early 2006, the president declared:

> With few resources beyond the will of our people, I want you to know we have made a strong beginning. During my first few weeks in office, by curbing corruption we have increased government revenue by 21 percent, relative to the same period last year. We have cancelled non-compliant forestry concessions and fraudulent contracts. We have required senior government appointees to declare financial assets; implemented cash management practices to insure fiscal discipline and sharpen efficiency; met the basic requirements for eligibility under the US general system of preferences and initial Exim Bank support.[23] We have restored good relationships with bilateral and multilateral partners; commenced the process leading to an IMF Staff Monitoring Program; accelerated implementation of the Governance Economic Management Plan—the GEMAP; and we have also launched a Truth and Reconciliation Commission to investigate the abuses of war. (Johnson-Sirleaf 2006)

There is evidence that the new government is working hard to manage Liberia's natural resources more effectively. Even though illegal artisan mining of diamonds continues in several parts of the country, the government has made significant progress toward meeting the requirements of accession

---

Figure 8.3　Governance and Economic Management Assistance Program

The Governance and Economic Management Assistance Programme (GEMAP) was established with the primary goal of restoring economic stability to the government of Liberia. GEMAP is a joint venture between the NTGL, the European Union (EU), ECOWAS, the African Union (AU), the United States, IMF, and the World Bank. In conjunction with the international community, GEMAP is dedicated to the implementation of good governance in the Republic of Liberia, through the execution of its six presiding principles: (1) improving financial management and accountability, (2) improving budgeting and expenditure management, (3) improving procurement practices and granting of concessions, (4) establishing effective processes to control corruption, (5) supporting key institutions, and (6) building capacity.

With these six interlocking components, GEMAP expects to revitalize Liberia's economy by reestablishing its economic framework, streamlining its financial institutions, and promoting transparency and accountability among revenue-generating agencies and institutions within the government. GEMAP will implement its six components by including international experts with cosigning authority in key governmental institutions, including the Ministry of Finance (MOF), Central Bank of Liberia (CBL), Bureau of Budget, Ministry of Lands, Mines, and Energy (MLME), National Port Authority (NPA), Roberts International Airport (RIA), Liberia Petroleum Refining Corporation (LPRC), Forestry Development Agency (FDA), Bureau of Maritime Affairs (BMA), and Bureau of Customs and Excise (BCE).

Technical assistance is limited to key revenue-producing governmental institutions, as well as those institutions that manage monetary expenditures. The Economic Governance Steering Committee (EGSC) manages oversight of the GEMAP operation. President Ellen Johnson-Sirleaf chairs EGSC, with a representative of the international community serving as deputy chair. To date, the IMF has placed a chief administrator in the CBL and financial controllers for the state-owned enterprises have been placed through US funding at the NPA, RIA, FDA, and LPRC (the controller for the BMA is on hold awaiting an European Commission [EC] management study investigating the BMA's integration into the MOF). In addition, the EC has replaced a customs operations expert in the BCE, and the United States funded the placement of a concessions expert in the MLME and a port operations specialist in the NPA.

Total funding for GEMAP institutions amounted to $19,647,309 in 2005–2007. That included $4,248,199 in 2006–2007 from the EC; $7,045,532 in 2006–2007 from the United States; $353,578 in 2005–2006 from the UK; and $900,000 in 2006–2007 from the IMF.

Source: Government of Liberia, *Governance and Economic Management Assistance Program (GEMAP) Status Report: Year 1*, 2006.

---

to the Kimberley Process Certification Scheme. In the forestry sector, the Liberian Congress enacted a national forestry reform law in October 2006. Government revenue has also increased due to the implementation of Forestry Development Authority checkpoints throughout Monrovia. Meanwhile, the Forestry Reform Management Monitoring Committee is considering proposals for allocations of forestry concessions. Similarly, a joint government-UNMIL task force has been established to undertake a comprehensive assessment of Liberia's rubber plantations.

Because of the efforts to improve governance, sanctions have been lifted. In 2006 Security Council Resolution 1689 (2006) removed sanctions on Liberian logs. In 2007 the sanctions on diamonds were lifted.

Reconstituting Social and Human Capital

A major constraint on Liberia's recovery process is the critical shortage of capacity at all levels: individual, organizational, and social. Poor public service conditions, salary levels incompatible with reasonable expectations of living standards, the flight of qualified staff to other countries, crisis-related deaths, infrastructure damage, and excessive reliance on donor-funded positions have severely constrained capacity development in Liberia (Liberia and UNDP 2006).

The CPA recognized the urgent need for capacity building in both the security forces and the civil service more generally. The necessary steps to reconstitute key institutions were laid out in a needs assessment document, which called for the appraisal of civil service capacity and systems at the county, district, and town levels; revamping the capacity of the Civil Service Agency, including the provision of required hardware and training; and civil service reform through retraining and the streamlined, transparent recruitment of civil servants (NTGL, UN, and WB 2004, p. 46). Under the NTGL, the security forces did indeed undergo some training, but wider national capacity building for economic governance did not get under way significantly until after the elections.

One objective of GEMAP was to foster proper leadership and management capacities. It initially filled capacity gaps by bringing in international experts whose mandate afforded them significant powers. In particular, these officials had to sign off on many financial and expenditure decisions made in key ministries, including the revenue producing institutions of government. While it recognized that international experts could not be regarded as a long-term, sustainable solution to capacity problems, however, GEMAP's provisions to provide technical assistance and build capacity were vague (GEMAP 2005, p. 15).

This situation has improved somewhat. Plans are underway to create a ten-year human capacity development strategy and action plan (Liberia et al. 2006, p. 68). In addition, the new government, with support from development partners, has launched several programs aimed more directly at fostering national talent by persuading skilled members of the diaspora to return, and by training Liberians for senior and midlevel management positions (Liberia et al. 2006, p. 68).

Two such programs are the Transfer of Knowledge Through Expatriate Nationals and the Liberia Emergency Capacity Building Fund, which are designed to bring qualified Liberian expatriates back home (Liberia et al. 2006, p. 15). The government has also recently initiated another program called the Senior Executive Service (SES). Its aims include injecting top professionals able to spearhead and manage change in the public sector; reforming administrative systems and procedures for effective human resource management with an emphasis on merit, performance, service, and results; and placing SES personnel strategically in line ministries, departments, and agencies. The government hopes to recruit 100 professionals into positions that have been re-profiled for maximum impact in the civil service reform program. In addition, the program will offer training and counseling, job search support, and exit pay for staff whose positions have changed or disappeared. Evaluations will be performance-based, compensating high performers and encouraging low performers to find more suitable positions (in light of Liberia's conflict situation, termination will be considered a last resort). The SES will eventually be folded into the rest of the civil service reform process. The program is estimated to cost $9.7 million in the first three years, and external assistance will be required (Liberia 2007a, Annex).[24]

Reconstituting social capital also represents a great challenge. The conflict "traumatized people and eroded social capital, including trust, traditional norms and customs, social cohesion and networks within communities. Without healing and strong social capital, implementation of national programs and policies in rural Liberia is likely to be thwarted as communities fail to rise to the challenge of exercising collective ownership, initiative and cooperation" (Liberia et al. 2006, p. 13). The Truth and Reconciliation Commission, established in the Comprehensive Peace Agreement (Liberia et al. 2003, Article XIII), but only officially launched in 2006, is an important step forward. The new government has also established the Independent National Commission on Human Rights as a way to "fight a culture of impunity and protect and promote human rights, including economic, social and cultural rights." A Center for Conflict Transformation has also been established at the University of Liberia, and Liberia's civil society is active, with no less than twenty NGOs focusing on "peace building and conflict-sensitive development issues" (Liberia et al. 2006, p. 62).[25]

Some Lessons for Postconflict Economic Policy

Development partners have been very visible in postconflict Liberia—mediating the peace process, working to bring international and national partners together for the assessment and recovery-planning exercise, assisting with provision of security and technical assistance, and providing funds for interventions in a broad array of sectors. In the security sector, even though coordination among development partners could have been stronger in some areas, overall they were relatively effective at improving security from the early stages. In terms of improving overall economic governance, how effective have the development partners been? In this section I consider whether, in hindsight, anything could have been done differently for better results.

The Environment for Reform

During the transition period, the interest of the NTGL authorities in their short-term ability to profit from weak systems seems to have outweighed any incentives they may have had to undertake reforms in the interest of wider economic recovery.[26] Since the elections, the environment has certainly become more conducive to sustainable reform. It is too early to say that the economy is now on a strong path to growth, but the government has been successful in driving some tough governance reforms forward that were aimed at improving transparency and accountability, supported by national capacity-building programs.

That turn of events should surprise no one. The NTGL had to include all the major protagonists in the conflict; and it clearly had a short lifespan before the democratic elections. Most parties within the transitional government understood that they had little chance of being elected and therefore, acting in self-interest, adopted what for them was an optimal strategy—to maintain a system that allowed them to maximize the extraction of rents while they could.[27] A recent review of the GEMAP explains that

> NTGL opposition to a robust anti-corruption strategy was predictable. The GEMAP threatened to interrupt lucrative personal incomes for individuals and threatened many of them with public embarrassment if not judicial investigation. Approaching their final months in power, with no chance of participating in the subsequent government, there was little incentive for senior NTGL leadership to take a different stance. At a very basic level, NTGL assent was always going to be reluctant. (UNDPKO and World Bank 2006, p. 20)

The democratically elected government, however, has a stake in ensuring more transparent and accountable governance and a better-performing economy because therein lies the possibility of longevity in power. The Liberian experience emphasizes the need for a governing authority with a desire to implement reform. Sustainable economic recovery rests on the ability of national actors to properly implement policies. It is especially important that policymakers consider what can be done to engender good governance during transitional periods, when incentives for reform are not necessarily in place.

Smart Interventions?

Operating in an environment that for the most part was not conducive to economic reform, the development partners took several separate measures to try and improve the situation. They promoted the inclusion of economic governance provisions in the CPA, they supported the imposition and renewal of sanctions, and they came together to design and support the introduction of GEMAP. Whether, at the time, those interventions were the smartest is a difficult question. In hindsight, some clear lessons can be drawn to, hopefully, facilitate smarter development assistance in similar circumstances.

Economic Provisions in Peace Agreements

The peace agreement in Liberia provided some space for dialogue on economic governance. The Liberian agreement is not unique in this way, and a recent study of peace agreements finds that they increasingly include provisions for economic governance (see Figure 8.4). That is what we would expect as the economic dimension becomes more prominent in general peacebuilding. However, the weak performance record of the Governance Reform Commission and the Contract and Monopolies Commission, institutions established by the CPA, show that including provisions in the agreement does not necessarily lead to effective implementation.

Figure 8.4 Economic and Institutional Provisions of Peace Agreements

A recent study conducted jointly by the UNDP and the World Bank examined twenty-seven peace agreements concluded between 1990 and 2006 to assess the extent to which provisions are made for different aspects of state building. Provisions are grouped into six categories: security, state administration and governance, justice, socioeconomics, political structures, and special postwar integrative measures (for example, reintegration of ex-combatants and transitional justice).

The study looked at both the scope and depth of inclusion. For example, provisions were judged not only on their frequency of inclusion but also on their specificity, that is, whether there was a general statement of intent, an identification of qualitative benchmarks, or a timetable for implementation.

It was found that peace agreements emphasize issues of security and political power. The most common provisions concerned security sector reform, disarmament and demobilization, and elections. Over time, there has been a tendency to widen the scope but narrow the depth as more sectors are included, but with fewer mechanisms attached to them to verify the progress of implementation. This tendency is especially common in socioeconomic and state administration and governance issues, which are increasingly included but often only as statements of intent.

Source: UNDP and World Bank, *Peace Processes and State-building: Economic and Institutional Provisions of Peace Agreements*, July 2006.

Whether the international community could have done anything to change this outcome is not clear. Acting as mediators and advisers to the peace process, they could perhaps have encouraged more detailed provisions about the role and function of government institutions to be included in the peace agreement. For example, the agreement established commissions, but what they would deliver was left vague. The mandates were general, calling for "transparency and accountability in governance in all government institutions and activities" rather than specifying policy reform milestones. Had milestones been listed, it may have been easier to monitor the NTGL performance and to hold it accountable. The peace agreement also did not thoroughly address the tough questions on the management of national resources.

From a political economy perspective, these apparent gaps are understandable. In Liberia's case, reform of national resource management and the civil service was kept deliberately vague because those issues were potentially explosive and could easily have derailed the talks. The mediators felt that resource management and civil service reform were such contested and difficult areas, and in need of major reform and requiring wider national consensus, that they would be best handled in the context of a democratically elected government.[28] Indeed, it is broadly acknowledged that peace agreements typically carry only "what the traffic can bear" (UNDP and World Bank 2006) and have to leave many of the key issues unresolved in the interest of reaching a compromise to end the war.

It is also questionable whether an agreement with time-bound deliverables, for example, would in practice have proved any more effective. Indeed, many of the provisions made in the peace agreement were addressed in more detail in later recovery plans that were endorsed by the government (for example, the RFTF). But still, delivery was poor. The root cause goes back to the question of effective commitment. If the governing authority has no stake in the future, it is almost impossible to design accountability mechanisms because there is no effective punishment.

Smarter Sanctions?

Sanctions are complex instruments. If effective, they safeguard natural resources, limit conflicts fueled by their revenues, and reduce corruption. At the same time, however, they also withhold from the government valuable revenue that could be directed toward the recovery effort. If ineffective, exploitation and corruption continue. A full analysis of the role and effectiveness of sanctions in Liberia is beyond the scope of this chapter. It seems clear, however, that certainly until 2006, sanctions in Liberia did not yield their full intended results.[29]

However, I do not mean to say that they should have been removed altogether. Doing so before the appropriate checks and balances were in place would have significantly increased the risk of a resurgence of conflict. With the ability to trade freely, the incentive to seize control of resources would have soared. Groups would have been likely to fight for control, using resource revenues to fund armies to defend their positions. The point is that the monitoring mechanisms for sanctions were poor, and the international community could have been more supportive in implementing the sanctions. In addition, recently we have seen that UNMIL's increased presence in certain logging and mining areas has had a positive effect on enforcement. Those forces could have been deployed earlier.

Coordinated Action for Reform in a Hostile Environment

The transitional government's interest in its short-term ability to profit from weak government systems outweighed any incentives it may have had to undertake reforms in the interest of wider sustainable economic recovery. It seems to represent a clear case of an absent constituency for reform: "The biggest difficulty is not that the policy analyst does not know what to do. . . . The real difficulty is finding the political and institutional actors who will fully implement these reforms because it is in their interest to do so. . . . the absence of a constituency for reform has been the primary constraint on positive change in the stagnant low-income states" (van de Walle 2005, p. 79).

Some of the actions that development partners took during the transition period may also have compounded this negative environment for reform. The approach taken in the EC audits in late 2004 was highly antagonistic and damaging of trust. The EC was initially invited by the NTGL to audit the Taylor regime but it instead conducted an audit of NTGL operations without the government's prior consent. This disrespect for state sovereignty became the major issue and a diversion from the rational consideration of the audit results.

Nevertheless, owing to the international consensus that mismanagement was widespread, development partners were eventually successful in pushing through GEMAP. The NTGL made vigorous attempts to alter the GEMAP model, but the strength of the collective international support for GEMAP and the decision by key development partners to use threats of personal punishment to push the NTGL to accept reform proved too powerful:

> In the context of a non-reform minded government, the threat of punitive measures is likely to be more significant than promises of assistance. In the case of the NTGL, two threats appeared to play a deciding role. The first was the US threat to withhold security sector reform assistance: while the EC warned that it would withhold a planned aid package, and the World Bank signaled it might follow the IMF's walk-away, the US threat had particular resonance for Liberia's leadership. The second was the potential

travel ban on Chairman Bryant and his senior officials. NTGL was vocifer-
ously opposed to the link between existing Security Council sanctions and
the GEMAP but the idea, never made explicit, that failure to sign GEMAP
might result in similar travel restrictions being imposed appeared to play a
key role in Bryant's individual calculations. (Liberia 2006a, p. 21)

Without such strong unity of donor purpose, GEMAP may not have gotten off the ground. It is also highly unlikely that it would have been tolerated
for very long by the elected government, given its high level of invasiveness.

GEMAP's Effectiveness as a Tool to Reduce Corruption

GEMAP is today operating in an environment more conducive to reform,
making its original design seem less appropriate. Development partners ap-
plaud Liberia's democratic election process and the manifest commitment
to reform. At the same time, they maintain international technical assistants
in revenue-raising institutions with co-signing authority. It amounts to non-
elected alien staff with veto power being placed in a legitimate elected government's institutions. Liberian leaders are very concerned that it sends a
message that in the eyes of the development partners, Liberia's political and
administrative leadership is still totally corrupt.

Indeed, GEMAP as it currently stands offers little in the way of a tool
for long-term development and can only ever be seen as an emergency response mechanism. A sustainable recovery strategy for a sovereign state requires acquiring as quickly as possible the capabilities critical for sound
economic management and oversight.

Development partners and the government seem to recognize that fact
and have already increased efforts to create a stronger civil service. It is now
critical that those efforts are sustained so that there can be a fairly rapid transfer of ownership from the donor community to the government. It is clearly
time for the government to take full charge.

Conclusion

The conflict in Liberia spanned three decades, during which time resources
were, for the most part, diverted from production to the destruction of
assets. GDP plummeted as widespread insecurity and asset destruction
resulted in a highly disabling environment for legitimate productive activity. Infrastructure deteriorated as opposing combatants employed a deliberate strategy of destruction or as basic maintenance ceased to take place. Social cohesion, trust, and human capital were also severely eroded. National
and local institutions were rendered dysfunctional as corruption became
widespread.

Resuscitating an economy in this state requires that the authorities meet several objectives, including creating a secure environment for economic recovery, instituting an oversight system, and reconstituting social and human capital. In this chapter I have shown, first and foremost, that economics and politics are inextricably linked—one cannot begin to address economic governance reform without an understanding of the political governance structure and the interplay of the interests of the various power brokers.

Although the Liberian case demonstrates that the peace negotiations can provide space for dialogue on the economic dimensions of peacebuilding, it also reveals that there are likely to be limitations on the important issues that can be addressed. Some issues may simply be too potentially divisive and are left out of the peace process for fear that they would derail the process. Moreover, the same or other issues may be so important for the country that the peace negotiators conclude that they should be left for a legitimate and representative government.

Perhaps most fundamentally, the Liberian case suggests that ultimately, the most important factor for economic reform is whether the governing authority has a stake in the future that outweighs incentives to engage in corrupt activities today. Ensuring such a stake is perhaps the smartest action the international community can take. Sanctions and direct interventions are possible options, but as I have shown, they are complex instruments and may not always have the desired effect. The appropriateness of different interventions can also change dramatically with time. The design of the GEMAP seemed to make sense, given the NTGL's reluctance to adhere to good governance, but the protracted negotiations meant that in the end GEMAP came too late to tie the hands of the NTGL. Instead it became a tool to supervise an elected government. Since the elections, the aspirations of the government and the development partners in terms of good governance have become more aligned. GEMAP no longer seems like the most appropriate mechanism.

What constitutes smart development assistance in these challenging environments is an issue that deserves far more attention than it has received to date. At this point, the smartest assistance in Liberia is likely to be that which focuses on transferring the reigns of economic policy and governance over to indigenous authority as quickly as possible. The key to success will lie in the effective execution of reform policies through the engagement and consultation of local, national, regional, and international stakeholders. Most importantly, the bonds of trust must be restored among the international community, the national government, and the people it serves. Fortunately, the new government recognizes this challenge and is eager to engender this trust. It is engaging partners in policy dialogue, building confidence in the prudent use of donor resources, and working hard to address the waste and corruption of the past.

Notes

1. The term "development partners" includes the international financial institutions, the United Nations, and bilateral donors.

2. The impact of the conflict on private legitimate business can be glimpsed from data on business registration. For example, when violence intensified in 2001, business registrations fell to 661, from 963 in 2000 (Liberia, Republic of, 2004, p. 31).

3. Official Liberian government statistics estimate unemployment to range between 75 and 85 percent in the postwar period (data collected by UNDP Country Office 2007, with original source as Central Bank Research Department and Government of Liberia). But even taking into account the big role of remittances from the diaspora, this figure seems unnaturally high. Underemployment may be a better term to describe the labor market, since with no formal social safety net, most people have to engage in some activity (subsistence or petty trading) to live.

4. An interesting exception, the telecommunications sector—the privately managed and financed mobile phone services (which started in 1997)—followed, against all odds, the explosive growth path observed in the region. There are now 50,000 mobile phone customers in Liberia, or five times the number of conventional phone subscribers in 1990 (NTGL/UN/WB 2004, p. 63).

5. To arrive at their estimate, Global Witness took the difference between total trade revenue (US$106 million) and declared revenue by the Central Bank of Liberia (US$6.7 million).

6. The population of Liberia is estimated at 3.5 million in the IPRSP.

7. For a more general overview of these objectives and their associated challenges, see UNDP 2005.

8. See GOL, LURD, MODEL, and Political Parties 2003 (available online at http://www.usip.org/library/pa/liberia/liberia_08182003_cpa.html).

9. Although the World Bank had a representative within the ICGL, economic and governance issues were not prioritized, and indeed the main role of the international community was to mediate between the different parties.

10. The NTGL was an all-inclusive government established to replace the existing government of Liberia. It consisted of three branches: the National Transitional Legislative Assembly (NTLA), the executive, and the judiciary. Through seat allocation the NTLA sought to be inclusive: the government of Liberia received twelve seats; Liberian's United for Reconciliation and Democracy, twelve seats; Movement for Democracy in Liberia, twelve seats; political parties, eighteen seats; civil society and special interests, seven seats; and the counties, fifteen seats.

11. More information on the initiatives planned for recovery can be found in the planning documents prepared by the NTGL, the elected government, and the development partners. Major planning exercises during the transition period included the organization of a Post-Conflict Needs Assessment and the consequent Results-Focused Transitional Framework (RFTF). Following the elections, the new government set to work quickly with a 150-day action plan that focused on regularizing many financial processes in government, delivering services to the population to demonstrate a peace dividend, and laying some of the foundations for a long-term reform program. More recently, an interim poverty reduction strategy paper (I-PRSP) has been adopted that will lead Liberia to 2008, when the intention is to have a PRSP in place.

12. FAO (Food and Agriculture Organization), UNDP (UN Development Programme), UNEP (UN Environment Programme), UNESCO (UN Educational, Scientific, and Cultural Organization), UNFPA (UN Population Fund), UN-HABITAT (UN Human Settlements Programme), UNHCHR (UN Office of the High Commis-

sioner on Human Rights), UNHCR (UN High Commissioner for Refugees), UNICEF (UN Children's Fund), UNIFEM (UN Development Fund for Women), UNOPS (UN Office for Project Services), WFP (World Food Programme), and WHO (World Health Organization).

13. OECD/DAC data shows the US average contribution in 2004–2005 to be $96 million, from total ODA that averaged $225 million over that period. During the same period, other major contributions included EC, $42 million; Sweden, $14 million; UK, $12 million; Norway, $9 million; Netherlands, $8 million; and Germany, $6 million.

14. A deterioration of the security situation in Liberia prompted the need for a stronger presence in Liberia. A letter from the Secretary-General to the president of the Security Council envisaged the appointment of Jacques Paul Klein as special representative for Liberia. Consequently, the mandate of the United Nations Peace-Building Support Office in Liberia "will naturally have to be terminated. The office, including its staff and assets, would be absorbed by the office of my Special Representative" (S/2003/769).

15. The RFTF estimate for the number of combatants was taken from estimates provided in the First Progress Report of the Secretary General on the UN Mission in Liberia (S/2003/1175, para. 22).

16. By December 2006, 106 recruits had completed basic training for the armed forces, and 500 more were due to start in early 2007. Basic training and restructuring for the 2,000-member armed forces is expected to be completed by the end of 2008. As for the police, by January 2006, 2,479 officers had completed training, 577 were under training at the Police Training Academy, and 496 were undergoing field training. Complete restructuring and training of the 3,500-member Liberia National Police is due by 2007 but is likely to be extended due to the decision to add a gendarmerie type unit. Also to date, 358 Special Security Service personnel have been trained. Restructuring of several other security agencies, such as the Ministry of National Security and the Coast Guard, has yet to begin and is contingent on the development of a national security strategy to prevent overlapping goals and functions (IRIN 2007b, p. 3).

17. The Kimberley Process Certification Scheme (KPCS) is an international certification scheme that requires that any shipment of rough diamonds to or from a participating state be accompanied by a Kimberley Process certificate guaranteeing that the rough diamonds are "conflict-free." The diamond industry committed to a system of self-regulation to support the KPCS system, including establishing a code of conduct to prevent trade in conflict diamonds, implementing a system of warranties requiring that all invoices for sales of diamonds warrant in writing that the diamonds are conflict-free, keeping records of warranty invoices and having these audited, and informing company employees of government regulations and industry policies to prevent the trade in conflict diamonds (Amnesty International 2006).

18. For example, in the timber sector, benchmarked reforms included the establishment of a system for depositing all forestry revenues in accounts directed by the Ministry of Finance and the imposition of penalties on companies violating sanctions.

19. The ISP is a joint venture between the EC and Liberia to implement reforms in governance and financial management. Under the ISP, the EC agreed to undertake organizational and financial audits of the Liberia Petroleum Refining Corporation, the Forestry Development Agency, the National Port Authority, the Roberts International Airport, and the Bureau of Maritime Affairs, and at the request of the NTGL, the Central Bank of Liberia as well (European Commission 2006a).

20. The EC commissioned Ernst and Young to do the audits.

21. Their recommendation went as follows: "Convene a working group to pre-

pare the political, technical and administrative modalities of a mechanism to assume responsibility for revenue collection for a projected 15- to 25-year period, including an oversight board with mixed international and Liberian composition but controlled by the former and supported by a team of experts (forensic accountants) and international customs officers" (International Crisis Group).

22. Early drafts of GEMAP called for Security Council endorsement, but that met heavy resistance from the NTGL, who argued that it did not allow for a clear exit strategy.

23. The Export-Import Bank of the United States.

24. UNDP, the World Bank and USAID have so far contributed $1 million each to this program. There remains a funding shortfall of over $6 million.

25. Despite these efforts, renewed conflict over land rights, particularly in Nimba County, is a potential threat to peace and security in the region. Mandingo returnees from camps in Guinea have come home to find their land occupied by the ethnic groups the Gios and the Manos, who claim that the land was stolen from them three generations ago and that the land is rightfully theirs. The new government established a seventeen-member special committee to investigate these land disputes after street riots took place in Ganta in May 2006; however, their findings have not yet been made available (IRIN 2007b).

26. Myopic preferences by the transitional government were evident not just from the continued corruption and efforts to sidestep sanctions, but also from the policy stances they adopted on various macroeconomic issues. In the area of investment, for example, the authorities argued that generous import duty exemptions, and changes to the investment code to give new international investors wide-ranging exemptions, were needed to signal the return of stability to prospective investors. The IMF expressed concern that such reforms could undermine the revenue base, preferring instead that the authorities mobilize higher budgetary revenue and channel it to basic infrastructure, health, and education expenses. It argued that foreign investment was influenced by long-term considerations of a country's stability and social peace, as well as availability and reliability of infrastructure and a skilled and healthy labor force (IMF 2005a [Report Number 05/166], p. 12).

27. The chairman and vice chairman, as well as all principal cabinet ministers within the NTGL, were not able to contest for any elective office during the 2005 elections in Liberia (Liberia et al. 2003).

28. Interview with General Abdulsalami Abubakar, Special Envoy of the Secretary-General to the Gambia, October 6, 2006, New York.

29. That is not to say that sanctions did not have some positive impact. In reference to arms sanctions, for example, a recent paper finds that "the impact was partly symbolic (a political cost) since the Liberian government under Charles Taylor was clearly named and shamed, and partly substantial (economic cost) since the embargo made the purchase of new weapons more difficult and expensive while delivery became more unpredictable" (Wallensteen, Eriksson, and Strandow et al. 2006).

PART 3

The Challenges of Promoting Good Governance and Democracy

9

Rethinking Anticorruption Efforts in Liberia

Will Reno

CONTEMPORARY AID and anticorruption efforts in Liberia have a long genealogy of extensive international oversight. One Liberian historian even used international interventions to address corruption and mismanagement to mark the periods of his country's history. His history of "national finance and some financial difficulties" includes "The Loan of 1870," "The Loan of 1906," "The Loan of 1911" (which some argue is "The Loan of 1912"), and "The Loan of 1926" and their provisions for foreigners to manage the government's revenue collection, and in some instances, directly control government spending (Yancy 1954, pp. 95–113). The Governance and Economic Management Assistance Programme (GEMAP) that followed the May 11, 2005, meeting of major donors in Copenhagen is the most recent in this series and is central to debates about "smart aid." Essentially imposed upon the government of Liberia at that time, GEMAP was the result of donor government and multilateral institution frustration at Liberian official mismanagement and corruption. That was not how donors who had pledged more than $520 million in aid had envisioned Liberia after the end of its war of almost fourteen years in 2003.

In August of that year, warlord-turned-president Charles Taylor was forced into exile and later faced charges for war crimes before an international tribunal. The new interim president, Gyude Bryant, seemed to repeat Liberian history. Chosen because he was politically acceptable to all the major factions in the war, Bryant ruled through distributing patronage and was himself suspected of embezzling government funds. Because of these difficulties, GEMAP was designed to challenge the established rights of sovereign states to run their own affairs and placed non-Liberians at the center of Liberian internal administration. International experts from the

GEMAP consortium—the UN, International Monetary Fund (IMF), World Bank, the European Commission (EC), the United States, and African regional organizations—have countersigning authority in the country's central bank, state-owned enterprises, and the government's accounting office. GEMAP also provides for external auditors and the creation of an anticorruption commission.

The intervention of GEMAP members in internal governance, especially in economic and fiscal affairs, reflects the intractability of corruption in Liberia. A UN Security Council document recognizes that "many Liberian elites profit from the system of corruption and undue influence and have resisted its reform" and that many citizens and ex-combatants in particular still rely on these networks for survival (UN Security Council 2006b, p. 8). This joint intervention takes place against the backdrop of GEMAP members' separate efforts. The UN Mission in Liberia's 15,000-strong peacekeeping force (UNMIL), for example, plays a major role in providing security and will continue to do so up to its scheduled 2008 withdrawal. Thus GEMAP and these other efforts are "smart" in seeking to change how the country is run rather than simply providing short-term remedies to reverse corruption. As the list of loans above suggest, they are not the first such effort. Backers of this plan recognized its lineage when they wrote: "USAID, in particular, was motivated by a sense of déjà-vu. In 1988, it sponsored a Liberian Economic Stabilization Support Project that also put foreign experts with countersigning authority into government agencies" (Dwan and Bailey 2006, p. 8).

The victory of Ellen Johnson-Sirleaf in the November 2005 presidential election, however, distinguishes GEMAP from earlier loan schemes. Johnson-Sirleaf was trained as an economist and worked for Citibank and the World Bank prior to her most recent entry into politics. Upon taking office, she became chair of the Economic Governance Steering Committee (Donald Booth, the US ambassador to Liberia, is the deputy chair), a GEMAP decisionmaking body designed to coordinate the efforts of Liberian government officials and foreign experts. This coordination with GEMAP at the very top of Liberia's government substantially improves the prospects for success of this anticorruption effort, although the new president also faces entrenched groups in government and elsewhere that have a vested interest in the system of patronage politics and personal aggrandizement that she and GEMAP seek to dismantle.

GEMAP's approach reflects an analytical link between Liberia's state administration and corruption, a problem that shaped state decline and the war that followed from 1989 to 2003. It makes sense, therefore, to examine the organization of corruption in Liberia and to assess whether the GEMAP approach is likely to succeed. Will placing foreigners in key positions in the state bureaucracy eradicate corruption among indigenous Liberian officials? Will

GEMAP create a context for smart aid in which a new state administration uses foreign-supplied resources to improve services to the country's citizens? In this chapter, I explore the organization of corruption in Liberia to determine whether imposing discipline on state bureaucratic operations will eliminate or marginalize the key elements of that bureaucracy responsible for corruption. It is an especially difficult task in Liberia, for I argue that the organization of corruption in Liberia reflects basic elements of authority in that country. Authority figures, including many who have no official position in the state as well as those who hold high office, see their personal and community interests aligned with the illicit economy more than with the usual tasks of governance. More important, the 1989–2003 war and the previous decade under the rule of President Samuel K. Doe (1980–1989) saw a marked expansion and decentralization of these parallel structures of authority. By the time the war ended in 2003, relationships of corruption and authority, both inside and outside the state administration, had not only become much more intertwined. They also resembled a network much more than a hierarchy, especially when compared to the pre-1980 period. These developments have significant implications for the performance of foreigners' prescriptions, especially insofar as they focus on reform of the state administration rather than on an effort to reorder these wider social relations.

In the second section I explore this broader political economy of corruption and pay particular attention to the interests of international actors involved in GEMAP. Many of their reports stress "strengthening capacity" and "modernizing administration" and portray official corruption as a technical obstacle to be overcome (see, e.g., IMF 2007, p. 9). Yet some international participants are acutely aware of the nonbureaucratic and nonstate elements of authority in Liberia. They balance their interests in pursuing political stability with the promotion of GEMAP. These two goals may conflict when short-term stability requires catering to the interests of local actors who play key roles in networks of corruption or when the political will of outsiders to pursue controversial measures is weak. I use this section to contrast Liberia's organization of corruption with the organization of corruption in other countries, especially in East Asia. This comparison demonstrates the limits of "best practices" and other analyses that focus on administrative practice and often fail to take into account the underlying structures of the problems that this particularly interventionist form of aid seeks to resolve.

I end the chapter with prescriptions for a smarter version of aid to post-conflict societies. To some extent, GEMAP already reflects the outcome of political compromises and the limits of foreign capacity to fundamentally restructure the exercise of power in Liberia. Moreover, clearer understandings of the networks of corruption beyond the institutional confines of the state offer prospects for improving the future implementation of aid.

The Organization of Corruption in Liberia

Liberia's government has included individuals like Charles Taylor, who are exemplary corrupt officials. While he was the country's president from 1997 to 2003, he operated in both the private and public realms. In 2001 and 2002, Taylor personally controlled an estimated $200 million in annual proceeds from business operations, or between two and three times the entire budget for government operations (UN Security Council 2002, p. 11). These commercial operations were organized around Taylor's official position as head of a sovereign state. Once in office, he skillfully combined that position, and his personal discretion over commercial operations that Liberian laws (and from 2001, the UN) defined as illicit, to assert his authority in Liberia and over rebels in Sierra Leone. It even appeared that Taylor did business with agents of Al-Qaida, probably out of commercial rather than ideological motivation (Farah 2004). This sort of corruption, in which holders of state office participate in far-flung networks of illicit commerce, defined the regime during that period. More important, its practice was central to the president's exercise of authority. Taylor's mode of governance intentionally blurred distinctions between private and public spheres and overshadowed the state's institutional structure.

The administration that replaced Taylor upon his exile in August 2003, after his June indictment for crimes against humanity before the Special Court for Sierra Leone, included many individuals who headed the militias that had appeared after the war started in 1989. Some had fought with Taylor, and others had fought against him. This National Transitional Government of Liberia (NTGL) included George Dweh, the speaker of the National Assembly, a cofounder of the armed group Liberians United for Reconciliation and Democracy (LURD). Dweh was accused of embezzling $92,000 and was relieved of his duties in March 2005. Unhappy with this judgment, he returned to the floor of the legislature with his bodyguards and held members hostage until UNMIL, introduced with the new government in 2003, intervened (Sleh 2005, p. 1). NTGL officials signed numerous concession agreements, including some for timber and diamond mining in violation of Security Council sanctions. In the case of timber, it resulted in the issuing of concession awards covering 2.5 times more timbered territory than the country possessed (UN Security Council 2006b, p. 15). Moreover, outgoing NTGL officials voted to keep their official Jeep Cherokee vehicles, an act that caused US Ambassador Donald Booth to threaten to declare them persona non grata if they tried to travel to the United States. In any event, some were already covered by a UN travel ban (UN Security Council 2006a).

Jacques Klein, the Secretary-General's special representative in Liberia, called for more intensive international intervention when he stated: "It would have been more expedient for the Security Council to have granted the Mission executive mandate" at the NTGL's inception in October 2003, rather than to have left them to tolerate this degree of corruption in the provisional government (Ellis 2006, p. 109). Even without that authority, international actors collected extensive documentation of corruption among the officials of Liberia's government. The UN Panel of Experts enforcing economic sanctions, IMF and World Bank officials who were negotiating debt relief and future loans, and auditors from the Economic Community of West African States (ECOWAS) and European Commission also provided abundant evidence of official corruption.

Liberia's form of corruption is especially damaging to efforts to build government capacity, deliver services, and eliminate security threats to the state, since so many government officials are in fact past members of factions that fought in the war and are implicated in illicit commerce and abuses of state office. But corruption in and of itself is not necessarily damaging to state capacity. Corruption was once thought to be compatible with economic growth and political stability in Africa. In the early 1970s, a Belgian scholar identified the rise in Zaire (now the Democratic Republic of Congo) of what he called "bureaucratic Caesarism." He saw Mobutu Sese Seko as using patronage networks to control a disparate group of local elites and subject them to the dictates of rational economic management. He believed that Mobutu was trying to integrate these informal business-state relations into existing systems of loyalty based on ethnic patron-client ties (Willame 1972, pp. 131–134). Almost two decades later, a US academic labeled it an absolutist regime that recalled seventeenth- and eighteenth-century French kings. He saw networks "organized around a presidential monarch who has adapted a colonial state structure to recentralize power . . . to control a complex and fragmented society and extend the state's limited domain" (Callaghy 1984, p. 5; see also Roth 1968). But by the 1980s, no scholar (that I can find) thought that patronage contributed to state building in Liberia (Liebenow 1987).

Prior to the start of the war in 1989, Liberia's presidents had different personal styles but shared a common method of patronage that left rural strongmen with high degrees of personal control over local politics. That system worked fairly well for William Tubman (president from 1944 to 1971) because the entire political establishment was extremely narrow, limited to a group of people who knew each other on a personal basis and, in many instances, whose sons and daughters intermarried. The hinterland was ruled through a sort of indirect rule copied from British colonial administration and was not fully integrated into the institutions of the rest of the country until 1963. Those from the interior who did join the educated elite and became government officials had to deport themselves in the fashion of the coastal elite and integrate as best they could into this small group (Brown 1982). So long as this patronage network included these close personal connections, it was relatively easy to control. The president had numerous means of sanctioning the disobedient beyond simply using the power of the state against them. Tubman even took it upon himself to manage the marital affairs of his associates and socialize with them at church services, at Masonic Temple rites, and in other shared settings. Conducted in this way, corruption functioned as patronage to knit together a constellation of local strongmen under the dictates of the leader of the state. The 1950s saw the capital-based elite facilitate the integration of hinterland politicians into Liberia's system of national politics. New revenues, which were turned into private fortunes, financed a far-flung patronage network under the eye of President Tubman (see Wreh 1976). This arrangement bore some resemblance to the bureaucratic Caesarism identified in Congo, a particularly inefficient sort of machine politics that, in a more open and competitive way, characterized many US cities through the first half of the twentieth century.

The arrival of Firestone Tire and Rubber Corporation, which was responsible for over 60 percent of state revenues from 1950 to 1970, reinforced the hierarchical organization of patronage-based corruption centered on the person of the president. Although starting from a very low base, Liberia became the world's second-fastest-growing economy (after Japan) during the 1950s, with annual growth of over 8 percent and a tenfold expansion of government revenues (Clower et al. 1966, p. 23). This additional income gave Tubman money to distribute at his personal discretion, so he had less need to worry about building strong revenue collection agencies or taxing wealthy people (many of whom were his political clients and even family members). These resources also gave him autonomy from the country's legislature since he did not need official appropriations or require financial contributions from strongmen from the hinterland. Insofar as Tubman and his successor, William Tolbert (1971–1980), could keep personal control over their clients, this patronage system was relatively stable. In fact, it was among the world's most stable. Until its overthrow in 1980, Liberia had the fourth most durable regime in the world, founded in 1847 upon Liberia's independence.[1] Tubman's and Tolbert's True Whig Party ruled continuously from 1878 to 1980, surviving more years than the Communist Party of the Soviet Union.

A decisive shift occurred with the 1980 overthrow of Tolbert's government and the installation of Sergeant Samuel K. Doe as president. This challenge came after Tolbert responded to growing pressures to liberalize his regime and distribute patronage resources more widely. Those events disrupted the tight enforcement of the centralized patronage network, which was based upon the dense social connections and personal knowledge that presidents shared with their political clients. Doe was politically vulnerable and had to rely upon people with whom he did not share the kinds of personal ties and insider knowledge that had benefited previous presidents. It left him less able to control their personal interests and strategic positions in his patronage network. Some of Doe's associates also could take advantage of their own local ties to begin to exploit their positions in the patronage network without effective oversight. It was much harder for Doe to maintain surveillance and levy sanctions upon individuals who had their own power bases and whose daily activities were less visible to him. All that severely affected the stability of the political system that he inherited.

Had an arrangement like GEMAP, or more intense versions of the various loan regimes in earlier decades, been applied to Tubman's or Tolbert's centralized, hierarchical organizations of patronage, it is conceivable that some corrupt subordinates could have been removed from their positions. Although that would have raised risks of political instability when they opposed such measures, the centrality of the state bureaucracy as a vehicle for patronage would have offered a feeble but still institutional basis for building a state administration. Rapid extension of services in an environment in which the state already provided a fairly high degree of security might have mitigated the capacity of disgruntled former clients to organize opposition. The key point here is that a network of corruption had not yet superseded the state, and the state administration itself was still central to providing and ultimately shutting off resources to political clients. But once clients integrated themselves into a network of corruption in which they had more control over their immediate environment, as during the Doe regime, the effectiveness of simply removing corrupt officials and tinkering with oversight mechanisms was radically reduced. The focus of smart aid thereafter must extend beyond reforming state institutions and replacing officials. It must directly interfere with the connection between local authority and a highly decentralized system of illicit commerce. In doing so, it risks upsetting what postconflict stability exists in Liberia and testing the political will of outsiders who support GEMAP, the UN mission, and other elements of intervention.

Doe built his authority in precisely this kind of networked and decentralized way. His associates in government included some of the capital-based elite who already had their own deep roots in the politics of patronage in the country. Some newcomers rose by virtue of their positions in the military. Thomas Quiwonkpa, a key army supporter of Doe's during and right after the coup, was appointed to head the army and used this position to carve out his own power base and promote his own supporters. They included his aide-de-camp, Prince Yormi Johnson, who later became a commander in the National Patriotic Front of Liberia (NPFL) for future wartime commander and President Charles Taylor. Quiwonkpa knew that his popularity was dangerous to Doe, and he likely feared that Doe would kill him, so he fled in 1983. Then he returned in 1985 and tried to overthrow Doe but was killed. Quiwonkpa's friend Taylor then invaded Liberia in 1989 as head of the NPFL. Their associate Prince Johnson was personally responsible for killing Doe in 1990, but not before venturing out to form his own faction. Other key players in the 1989–2003 war emerged from Doe's patronage network. George Boley led the Liberia Peace Council (LPC) militia after he served as Doe's minister of state. Alhaji G. V. Kromah helped form the United Liberation Movement of Liberia for Democracy (ULIMO) in 1991 after serving as Doe's information minister, and Charles Julue, the former head of the Armed Forces of Liberia, staged his own coup attempt in 1994.

All these people exploited their patronage connections to higher officials for their personal gain and to strengthen their political positions. Unlike earlier presidents, Doe had to struggle much harder to keep them under his control. They had their own connections to illicit and formal commerce in areas where they had supporters, while Doe's sudden rise to power left him without the personal connections or knowledge to reliably determine how they used their resources. As a result, his associates escalated their demands, and new claimants arrived frequently to further strain his resources. Since Doe could not figure out which ones could mount a credible challenge to him if he refused, the result was a proliferation of joint business ventures including many of those people. The deals increasingly took the form of partnerships with foreigners involved in illicit commerce (from the point of view of formal laws and accepted international practice) or who were looking for states like Liberia where they could conceal illicit activities from investigators.[2] The advantage of these arrangements was that they did not depend on the capacity of the state to regulate or promote the economy, and relied instead on the president's authority to grant his partners exemptions from prosecution while pursuing their business rivals for violations of the law.

In this analysis, the overall volume of Doe's corrupt gains, about $300 million during his ten-year rule (Berkeley 1982), was less important than the organization of his patronage network and the degree of influence it gave him with his associates. These associates had no reason to trust Doe, so they sensibly removed as much of their ill-gotten gains from the country as possible. They also were more dangerous to their patron than their predecessors had been, due to their relatively autonomous capacities to go into business on their own behalf. Such a situation creates a special problem for international actors, because some of those people would be seen as "civil society" actors from some perspectives. To the extent that men like George Boley were able to keep their patron at arm's length, they emerged as protectors of their ethnic communities and clans. The same capacity to become warlords also positioned some of these people to become protectors of minority rights and local patrons in their own right as they helped other people survive.

The impact of this structure of patronage appears in the current national legislature, elected in October 2005. Successful candidates included Senator

Jewel Howard-Taylor, former first lady. Her inclusion in a UN travel ban highlights the tension between ceremonial political liberalization and the reality of politics. Other victors included Senator Prince Johnson, Taylor's and Quiwonkpa's earlier ally who broke with Taylor and then played a role in the events that led to Doe's murder. Representative Edwin Snowe, speaker of the House of Representatives until he resigned in early 2007, is also listed in the UN travel ban report, which calls him an "associate of former President Charles Taylor with ongoing ties to him" (UN Security Council 2006a). Snowe allegedly diverted revenues from the state-owned Liberia Petroleum Refining Company for his personal use and that of his followers.[3] Representative Saah Gbollie was a deputy police chief in Taylor's government. Senator Adolphus Saye Dola ("General Peanut Butter") also is subject to the UN travel ban, which labeled him as "aggressive opposition to UNMIL deployment" and a "renegade supporter of former Liberian President Charles Taylor." Militia leaders appear among other victors in the 2005 election. These include Kia ("White Flower") Farley, former commander of the Movement for Democracy in Liberia (MODEL) and a member of the House of Representatives. While in office, his fighters occupied a rubber plantation and maintained contact with fighters in neighbouring Côte d'Ivoire in defiance of UN directives (UN Security Council 2006b, p. 41).

Other aspects of current government operation reveal the decentralized and networked organization of corruption and the influence of wartime actors. Tubman and Tolbert were more watchful of revenue-generating agencies of government, whereas NTGL practice had been to integrate fragmented wartime networks into its capital-based system of rule. Joe Gbala, the former secretary of LURD, was appointed head of the National Port Authority. His chief of security, Ofore Dian, served as Gbalah's chief of staff while with LURD. Samuel Wlue, a senior leader of MODEL, also an armed group, became the minister of finance. These former wartime commanders used their control over parts of the state bureaucracy to provide for their former fighters and arranged for some of them to manage illicit economic activities within Liberia and in other states in West Africa and further afield.

The collapse of a centralized network of control also provides lessons for international actors as they devise ways to tackle corruption in Liberia. Strategies that favor the decentralization of power, often born of the association of decentralization with democracy, might create more disorder in the Liberian setting. Decentralization of the informal structures of Liberian politics in the 1980s and 1990s gave free rein to people who eventually became warlords. Paul Hutchcroft makes a similar point in terms of the organization of corruption. He attributes high growth and managed corruption in China to the "centralization of politics" but warns that formal decentralization can lead to disaster if it also results in a dispersal of control over patronage politics, with Somalia serving as a prime example in his study (Hutchcroft 2001, p. 39).

The decentralized and networked organization of corruption in Liberia highlights the challenges facing "smart aid." Since corruption and informal political networks are integral to the political economy of Liberia, changing this essentially means that Liberia needs a new politics and a new economy, in short, a massive state-building effort. Moreover, the involvement of key elements of the country's incumbent elite in the politics of corruption, including some who are able to call upon fighters to defend their positions and some who enjoy genuine support from former fighters and community members, means that wholesale reform in Liberia risks becoming an exercise in counterinsurgency against people who want to use state office as a platform to continue their informal exercise of power. Thus providing smart aid to Liberia entails significant risks to external actors. It heightens the dilemma for GEMAP and other international actors of having to decide the extent of their financial and political commitment, the subject of the next section.

The Stakes of Intervention for International Actors

Are international actors willing to invest the financial and political capital required to fully remake Liberia? From the point of view of providing security, total UNMIL costs from 2003 to mid-2007 are about $2.9 billion.[4] During the same period, US bilateral aid to Liberia has been about $600 million (Cook 2006). It is estimated that GEMAP implementation over a three-year period will cost about $500 million. That is not much money in comparison to US expenditures for the war in Iraq, but it is enough that politicians in the United States might question whether US taxpayers are receiving good value for their money. GEMAP appears to be producing positive results. For instance, Liberian government revenues have risen sharply from about $80 million in 2004–2005 to an estimated $130 million in 2006–2007 (IMF 2007, p. 6).

A Liberian strongman rooted in the wartime political economy might conclude that GEMAP is effective only because it forces Liberian officials to share their authority with foreign experts. The durability of reforms after GEMAP experts leave remains in doubt. UNMIL is scheduled to depart at the end of 2008 and be replaced by a US-trained Liberian security force. GEMAP was initially scheduled to end in mid-2008 although this schedule is contingent on completing arrangements for debt relief. Under the rubric of the highly indebted poor countries (HIPC) initiative, forgiveness and rescheduling of the country's $3.5 billion external debt was to have been completed at the end of 2006. It was postponed to 2007 when external auditors discovered how difficult it was to ascertain what the government owed. Local actors whose positions are threatened by foreign intervention can simply wait for the scheduled departure of peacekeepers. Even at present, those who use their positions in the state as platforms for personal influence and wealth accumulation appear to have little to fear from Liberia's judicial system. UNMIL investigators in 2006 noted that the "extremely serious problem of corruption in the Liberian judicial system, in particular, remains an enormous challenge to the rule of law and thus to long-term stability" (UNMIL 2006).

Local and international actors thus find themselves in complex and strategic interactions. Local actors strategize to safeguard their fundamental interests, and some retain a capacity to disrupt reform efforts. Contemporary telecommunications and personal links to overseas Liberians help these political actors analyze international developments and coordinate their own strategies.[5] External actors, given the extensive nature of their intervention, are then drawn into very minor disputes. Complaints from workers at Monrovia's port about the GEMAP administrator of the Ports Authority, for example. Some of these protests came from ex-combatants who supported Joe Gbala, the former LURD general secretary, who had become manager of port operations. This dispute eventually required the intervention of the US ambassador once the workers began to press for the removal of the GEMAP ports specialist.[6] UNMIL intervention has been required in several instances in 2006 and 2007 to remove ex-combatants occupying rubber plantations who likewise contested the right of new government-appointed managers to take over these operations.

Faced with tasks of micromanaging a difficult bureaucracy and concerns about the sustainability of the overall reform effort, international actors may reasonably choose to act expeditiously. Transplanting their model of a liberal democratic society in Liberia ultimately may provide leverage to local actors whom the international actors may prefer to exclude. But when faced with the repeated choice between political reform and security, international actors may tolerate the incorporation of elements of patrimonial politics into these arrangements. These choices will become more pressing once UNMIL forces leave the country. The trade-off between local security and reform is well understood by former commanders. More realistically, as resources and political will for intervention decline as the deadline for withdrawal approaches, both sets of actors face substantial incentives to engage in mutual cooptation, provided international actors tolerate what can become a ceremonial practice of political reforms in politically sensitive situations.

The choice between security and reform points to a basic shortcoming in the conceptualization of this version of smart aid. Often outsiders dichotomize state building on the one hand and the actors involved in the political economy inherited from the war on the other hand. However, the two often intermix. Efforts at quick reform often give bureaucrats new opportunities to abuse power (as in the case of judicial and police reform) and provides platforms for elite members of old patronage networks.

One alternative would be to recognize and deal directly with some of the networks of the wartime political economy and try to reincorporate them under the control of the state. Doing so would require recognizing that people often take refuge in their wartime associations to seek protection from the uncertainties of poverty and continued official corruption. Officials whom outsiders or local critics see as corrupt may be viewed as protectors or benefactors by others. Local officialdom and foreigners often see these associations as violent gangs and a continuing problem for the demobilization of ex-combatants. The goals and complaints of some of these people, however, indicate a capacity to take on at least some of the tasks of local governance in a durable fashion that eludes current bureaucratic reform efforts. One example can be found in the Wedjeh Youth Association of Sinoe County, which includes ex-combatants among its members. Its members were targets of UNMIL operations to remove them from rubber plantations, which earned mention of them as security threats in quarterly UNMIL reports.

The complaints of the Wedjeh Youth Association are instructive. They assert that reform programs give license to corrupt outsiders from the capital to take up local appointments. These positions are then used as platforms to exploit local resources, receive foreign aid, and eventually attract foreign investors on their own terms and, in the process, reproduce a more centralized patronage network in the image of Liberia's prewar politics. Local ex-combatants complain that as "sons of the soil," or people who have sacrificed for the benefit of a particular community during the war, they are entitled to exploit local rubber. Their defense of this right does not fit well into contemporary liberal notions of property or of the legal rights of citizenship in Liberia's hastily constructed democratic institutions.[7]

Recognizing and guaranteeing these people some control over local resources would give them a stake in using their influence to see that the state performs well. They would keep an eye on officials, including those from security institutions and the courts. Giving them control would also incorporate some elements of wartime organization into the apparatus of governance. This strategy has been used with positive results in neighboring Sierra Leone, where the Movement of Concerned Kono Youths (MOCKY) was initially seen as a security threat. It was depicted as a renegade militia that contested for control of the country's diamond-mining region at the end of that country's war. MOCKY's main concern, however, was to ensure that Kono youth, including some ex-combatants, were not swept aside in capital-based reform plans. MOCKY eventually became the beneficiary of a USAID project that built on its own institutional structure to monitor local police and government officials. Setting up that project required jettisoning uniform plans for local government reform for that region, as this organization integrated elements of local customary authorities and devised new ways of regulating the local economy and politics.

Is There a Smarter Way to Aid Liberia?

Are direct confrontation and the replacement of incumbent elite groups, including so-called warlords, essential if Liberia's state and economy are to be rebuilt? To do so assumes that the focus of corruption lies in the personal greed and aspirations to power of individuals. But as the organization of corruption in Liberia shows, the relationship of the networks of patronage, personal trust, and insider commercial collusion to the state and to the world economy are determining factors shaping actual policy outcomes. Do examples like the Wedjeh Youth Association, and the many other local associations of landowners, ex-combatants, and others, mean that it is possible to integrate some of these networks into a state-administered economy that serves the interests of citizens?

Charles Tilly explains the importance of what he calls trust networks for managing capital and coercion in the state-building process. Historically, builders of states mix formal and informal networks of authority. If they are to acquire even a minimal capacity to tax them, state builders have to take account of the interests of at least some of these local bosses. Even the strongest states lack the capacity to monitor every transaction that citizens make. State builders need to connect these preexisting networks to official institutions so that bureaucrats can benefit from the detailed market knowledge and social connections of commercial operators and can integrate the networks of trust and loyalty into the realm of state authority (Tilly 2005, p. 33). I do not mean to say that reformers have to accede to the interests of Liberia's most corrupt and violent strongmen. The point, however, is to recognize that some of these people enjoy willing support from followers, have standing in their ethnic communities, and possess connections and business savvy as they link these constituencies to the world economy.

Returning to the organization of corruption, one sees different ways in which this social capital can be integrated into the authority structures of successful states rather than tearing them apart. In the Philippines, Hutchcroft identified oligarchs who colluded with corrupt government officials in decentralized networks to siphon state money into their own pockets as the cause of slow economic growth rates and political instability (Hutchcroft 1998). But David Kang found that "crony capitalists" in South Korea who used informal political connections with officials to exchange bribes for favors actually benefited South Korea's economy. In their words, "money politics can actually reduce transaction costs" (Kang 2002, p. 3). Moreover, even extensive corruption need not produce economic failure. According to Transparency International, China is the 70th least corrupt country in the world, which puts it in the same league as Senegal. Vietnam, rated as the 111th least corrupt, was tied with Zimbabwe in 2005, and found itself partnered with Zambia (Transparency International 2006, pp. 16–17). But

China's per capita income increased by 9.2 percent annually from 2000 to 2005. Senegal's increased by 1.6 percent. Vietnam's income grew 7.4 percent, while its Zimbabwean competition in corruption contracted by 7.6 percent each year (World Bank 2006b, pp. 288–289). Liberia was absent from this list, but surely it would rank as among the most corrupt. It is not just that Liberia's corruption is awful; the *organization of corruption* in Liberia is distinctive, and it plays a major role in the economic contraction associated with violence.

East Asia's international context is very different from Liberia's. Perhaps Liberia is just unlucky. By the early 1980s, Liberia had become marginal to the superpowers, while East Asian countries were central to the US Cold War strategy of containing communism at a critical time in their development. US officials tolerated domestic arrangements in frontline states like South Korea and Taiwan so long as they maintained high rates of economic growth and contributed to burden sharing in military matters. That tolerance extended to opening up the US market to East Asian manufactured goods, regardless of the degree of subsidy or officials' collusion with industrialists (Haggard 1990). Similarly, because China's economy is so huge, and as a major purchaser of US government bonds to cover US deficit spending, Chinese officials have been able to design domestic economic policies without major international interference.

But internal organization of corruption matters too. China's corruption captures local networks and knowledge in ways that benefit the state. Collusion between Chinese Communist Party cadres and entrepreneurs functions alongside formal politics that are designed to promote rapid economic growth (Dittmer 2000). Local cadres acquire the leeway to distribute patronage to their subordinates and expand their circles of clients. From the point of view of high officials, "laxity toward official corruption can be viewed as a side payment to officials to give them a stake in reform" (Shirk 1993, p. 144). This approach works so long as local officials who extract bribes pay their superiors to protect them. Protection from arbitrary enforcement of anticorruption measures is tied to the local cadre's performance in promoting economic growth, thereby increasing the circle of productive supplicants to provide payoffs for officials to kick back to their superiors. Business owners tap into these personal connections among government officials to get preferential access to utilities and lax enforcement of labor and environmental regulations.[8] Since they can identify individuals who enjoy the confidence of higher officials, these businesspeople know whom to bribe and how much to offer. Ironically, their behavior leads to a situation in which the most efficient local cadres can be the most corrupt, and the least corrupt may also receive poor performance evaluations and thus have the worst prospects for promotion and experience the most fear of prosecution.[9]

The form of corruption described above presents a huge political problem for China's rulers and ultimately undermines the regime's legitimacy.

In the more immediate politics of holding together a large state during a period of extremely rapid social change, it permits continued economic growth and the creation of a large indigenous commercial class that is not in conflict with the state. This kind of control privileges close connections to social networks, a difficult element to build into "smart aid" but that Tubman and Tolbert used to manage their political circles when they presided over Africa's fastest-growing state. Even though the Liberian system of patronage was extremely narrow and ultimately helped lay the seeds for Liberia's 1989–2003 war, its maintenance through much of the twentieth century highlights the importance of social networks and knowledge to state authority. Likewise, Latin America's *groupos económicos,* though privileged, bring to state officials the trust and loyalties "normally associated with family or kinship groups . . . characterized by a higher standard of fair dealings and disclosure than that which is generally found in arm's length commerce" (Strachen 1976, p. 3). Pakistan's Twenty-two Families similarly play a big role in recent per capita yearly growth rates of over 5 percent after decades of poor performance. The country's shift to a central position in the US government's war on terror brought US help in integrating its economy into global markets and major debt write-offs.

This is not to suggest that corrupt insider networks are optimal ways to organize business-state relations. Instead, the argument is that rulers in some countries have managed to control and co-opt the types of social relationships and exchanges in the corridors of power that are repressed in foreign plans for state building in Liberia. Some did so because they lacked resources to wage a war against powerful segments of their own societies, such as existing clan, community, and other personal networks. For example, one scholar found "institutionalized patrimonialism" to have been a major factor in the formation of successful business groups in South Korea (Biggart 1990). Businesses often know better than states how to organize efficient network connections to the global economy. Moreover, they are much better at ad hoc arrangements that use family ties and local political networks to manage crises and allocate capital (Grenovetter 1994, p. 469). Even if networks that are often defined in terms of corruption are not ideal paths for development, they can help solve some of the problems of state building. Indeed, successful state builders in Europe and elsewhere dealt with commercial operators who were bandits and warlords too (see, for example, Barkey 1997).

This conclusion does not gloss over the fact that Liberia's networks of corruption incorporate violent people who are responsible for war crimes and other abuses into the inner workings of government. It does, however, point to some of the tradeoffs of state building that do not conform to an ideal blueprint of modern liberal democratic state. Corruption has played an important role in the construction of some states and their economies. In all the successful cases, corruption takes place in contexts where the bureaucratic apparatus of the state was permitted to intervene in a wide array of activities, especially economic. That gives the state the instruments it can use to co-opt local authority structures, including religious organizations, bandit groups, and warlords involved in economic exchanges. All those entities have histories of operating as "states within states" as their leaders sought to control commerce, to survive, and to take care of their followers. These networks and relationships have to be grafted onto the central authority of states if their states are to exercise real authority. Moreover, successful grafting can bring these commercial networks and acumen into the arena where the state can provide support and promote linkages with the international economy.

That leaves us with two basic lessons for smart aid. First, as GEMAP designers and many others understand well, the key to political stability and economic expansion lies in building the capacity of state agencies. The second lesson is more controversial. It proposes that some powerful individuals and networks that featured in Liberia's wartime political economy may have material and social assets that can contribute to a restructured Liberian political economy. Incorporating them would require great flexibility in applying evolving standards of international justice (as perpetrators from the past become beneficiaries of future policies) and a more nuanced application of reforms to capture some of the commercial and political networks that Liberia's new rulers need in order to govern effectively.

Notes

1. Older regimes included Britain (1689), the United States (1789), and Sweden (1812).

2. This is outlined in the personal correspondence between a businessman and his partner, President Doe, in the author's possession.

3. Monbo and Company, "Auditor's Management Letter Resulting from the Audit of the Liberia Petroleum Refining Company for the Years 2004 and 2005," London, April 20, 2006, in author's possession.

4. Calculated from Security Council quarterly reports on UNMIL operations.

5. Interview with a former spokesman for George Boley (LPC chairman), April 22, 2007.

6. "Roar Over NPA's GEMAP Agent," *New Democrat,* March 19, 2007, pp. 1, 14.

7. "Sinoe Youths Want Investors on Rubber Plantation," *Analyst,* February 8, 2007, p. 10; "Land Dispute: Liberia's Next War Trigger," *Analyst,* March 21, 2007, pp. 1, 10.

8. Chengze Simon Fan and Herschel Grossman, "Incentives and Corruption in Chinese Economic Reform," paper presented at Yale University, 2002 [in author's possession].

9. I owe this analysis to Zhu Jiangnan, a PhD student in the Department of Political Science, Northwestern University.

10

Beyond the Political Economy of Corruption: The Kenyan Challenge

Peter Anyang' Nyong'o

Editor's note: This chapter was adapted from a speech delivered by the author to a large audience at the University of Nairobi in March 2006. It presaged the controversial vote counts after the December 2007 elections that triggered widespread violence and political upheaval.[1] Long-standing tensions rose to the surface with disastrous effects, including great loss of life and property destruction, widespread displacement of persons, enflamed ethnic animosities, and political polarization. Although written well before the postelection conflicts of early 2008, the chapter provides an instructive commentary on the roots of the Kenyan political crisis. The author details the exclusionary and exploitative governance that prevailed in Kenya for decades. The 2007 elections and their aftermath can be traced to these practices and failures of domestic and international actors to curtail them.

CORRUPTION HAS ALWAYS BEEN an issue in Kenyan politics. The degree of concern about it and the intensity with which it occupies public discourse have, however, varied since independence. Official records of the National Assembly in the 1960s (the *Hansard*) show very few debates on the issue (see, for example, Gertzel, Goldschmidt, and Rothchild 1969, pp. 91–97). It was not until a minister was engaged in a major scandal concerning the marketing of maize that pressure in parliament forced the president to look into the matter by establishing a commission of enquiry (Kenya 1966). From this report, it became evident that both the Maize Marketing Board and the minister were engaged in conflicts of interest and the use of public office for personal gain.

But the inquiry also revealed that people in public office were very reluctant to discuss issues of corruption even when they were not themselves involved. In response, a writer in the *Sunday Nation* commented that "by and large Kenyans seem to adopt the time-honored philosophy of hearing nothing, seeing nothing and saying nothing about corruption in public life."[2] But with the annual publication of the reports of the watchdog committees in parliament—the Public Accounts Committee and the Public Investments Committee—even within the confines of the one-party state, discussions of corruption in parliament started to increase.

Part of the pressure for democratization in the 1970s and 1980s arose out of increasing concern about corruption and the defiant use of public resources by state officials and politicians for largely personal gain and political aggrandizement. Indeed, if there is any one pillar of support on which the authoritarian regime, particularly under President Daniel arap Moi, relied for sustenance, it was corruption. It has also been a major contributor to Kenya's underdevelopment.

This chapter seeks to trace the roots of corruption in Kenya and the road it has traveled in Kenya's political economy since independence. It notes that one of the key policies in government that institutionalized corruption in the public service was the legalization of the engagement of civil servants in private business. With certain echelons of the public service making substantial use of discretionary powers, the culture of corruption took root, becoming almost acceptable as the norm of "eating where you work."

Attempts to establish institutions to fight corruption have not been very successful, even after the transition to multiparty politics in 1993. Indeed, it was with the advent of multiparty politics that megacorruption in the form of the Goldenberg scandal hit Kenya, which was subsequently followed by the Anglo Leasing scam at the turn of the millennium. Therefore in this chapter I go deeper into analyzing the relationship between megacorruption and the demands of sustaining authoritarian rule threatened by popular pressures for democratization.

I conclude the analysis by drawing lessons from the past to answer the question, "What is to be done?" Battling corruption will depend on progress in three areas: capable anticorruption institutions and legal processes, political leadership and independent and qualified persons staffing the institutions, and a shift in political culture. Democratization and popular pressure can play an important role in achieving these ends.

Corruption: What Is It, and Why Do We Abhor It?

Corruption is akin to cheating, but it goes beyond that. It is cheating in the use of public office so as to achieve personal gain in terms of resources such as money, services, and other goods. Corruption is also akin to bribery: when a public official receives a side payment in any form in exchange of some service rendered to an individual or the public. In short, corruption is the misuse of public office for personal gain. The important word here is *misuse,* or putting to wrongful use.

In democratic systems of government, public affairs are conducted in accordance with the rule of law by both civil servants and elected officials. In both cases, there are laws and regulations that guide public conduct and the delivery of services. When an act of corruption is alleged to have been committed, it must be subjected to and proven in a legal process. As we shall subsequently realize, when the legal process is itself flawed or subject to injunctions that border on filibustering, punishing corruption can at times be a daunting task.

It has been argued quite often that when civil servants and elected officials do not receive sufficient remuneration for the work they do, they may be tempted to supplement their wages through corrupt deals. The logical outcome of such arguments leads to the conclusion that public officials, judicial officers included, should be paid well enough to protect them from the temptations of corruption.

Yet even in situations where very well off people are elected to positions of leadership and public officials are well remunerated, incidents of grand corruption still occur. Thus, to avoid corruption in public offices, more is needed than a good pay package and terms of service. Laws, regulations, and procedures must be both strong and enforceable to ensure that any act of corruption is severely punished to deter public officials from the corrupt use of such offices. But more than that, a political culture and a political leadership that frowns on corruption is necessary to reinforce the legal process.

For example, when civil servants are allowed to engage in private business, they will easily be tempted to use public procurement systems to their advantage by giving their own companies preference in providing goods and services to the state, quite often at inflated prices. Thus the Ndegwa Commission (1972) that allowed Kenyan civil servants to engage in business provided a big loophole for corruption in Kenya. Indeed, after the Ndegwa Commission Report was published, corruption in public offices started to escalate.

When laws are loose and leave too much room for discretion in decision-making and the application of the same laws, public officials may also abuse the discretion for personal gain. In such a context, conflicts of interest multiply. For example, during the days of foreign exchange allocations and import licensing, too much discretion was given to the minister of finance to make such allocations and provide licenses. Obviously, it is such discretionary powers that led to the schemes such as the Goldenberg scandal, and others of equally astounding magnitude before then.[3] Discretionary powers in the judiciary, the tax collection system, the public vehicle inspection system, and many other branches of government have also encouraged corruption.

Substantial public resources have been diverted from the public domain to private hands, crippling government activities, undermining the delivery of services, and deepening underdevelopment in the economy as a whole. Cumulatively, corruption makes the public lose faith in government, and that often leads to—among other things—avoiding paying taxes, encouraging a shadow economy, and flight of capital.

Many professionals whose skills are internationally marketable are also likely to emigrate to other countries where their services are not only better appreciated but often better remunerated. Such professionals often put a premium on the improved governance environment in their new countries of residence. Since the 1980s, Kenya has lost hundreds of doctors, nurses, lawyers, accountants, engineers, surveyors, university dons, and even clergymen to southern African countries and the West, as well as to Australia and New Zealand. In effect, we spend billions of shillings developing rare skills, only to lose them to more developed countries such as the United States and Great Britain. This process of draining our brains is part and parcel of the process of underdevelopment that corruption aids and abets.

But much more ominous is when corruption destroys the productive capacity of our nation and diverts the process of development toward a mercantile economy and pure speculation. Between 1991 and 1994, as a result of the Goldenberg scandal involving the fictitious export of gold and diamonds from Kenya, billions of shillings were paid from the treasury, leaving behind a big hole in the public purse. The treasury was then forced to borrow heavily from the domestic market through treasury bills and bonds, driving interest rates for them to close to 76 percent per year.

Many banks, rather than lend to the productive sector and stimulate economic growth and create jobs, preferred trading in these government monies and hiking up their own interest rates as well, making it very difficult for manufacturers, industrialists, and traders to service their bank loans. Many industries and businesses were foreclosed during this period, and Kenya, to this very day, has not really recovered from the adverse shocks of the Goldenberg scandal on the economy.

Corruption in Colonial Times

Let it not be said that corruption is a uniquely African disease, nor would it be correct to assert that it is an affliction of postindependence Africa. The white settlers in colonial Kenya made their fortunes through corruption. Without cheating in collusion with colonial officials, stealing from the coffers of the colony, appropriating land for which they paid next to nothing, sacking the blood of poor peasants for labor not paid for, and literally getting public transport for free for their farm products, the Blundells and

Delameres of colonial Kenya would not have built their fortunes and "moved to better things" when the nationalists finally took over political power.

In a recent book about the Mau Mau called *Histories of the Hanged,* David Anderson unearths corruption in the then City Hall of Nairobi involving white administrators and Asian contractors during the construction of the Ofafa and Mbotela residential estates for what was then regarded as the African middle class. He says:

> Never had a commission of enquiry been less welcome in Kenya than was that led by Sir Alan Rose. A distinguished barrister of the Inner Temple, and a confirmed bachelor with a reputation for probity, austerity and sternly conservative values, Rose was hardly the kind of man likely to find many kindred spirits among the robust, hard-drinking and womanizing white highlanders. . . . The scale of corruption unearthed by the Rose Commission surprised even Kenya's most cynical observers. The operation of the City Architect's office and its supervision of the Ofafa and Mbotela contracts in particular, came in for savage criticism. . . . On inspection, numerous contraventions of the building specifications came to light—shallow excavation footings, under-strength concreting in floors and lintels, substandard joinery, the use of cheaper, weaker materials throughout, and generally poor standards of workmanship. Yet, throughout the contract this work had apparently been inspected and approved by City Council officers. . . .
>
> The implications of these revelations soon became clear. European officials had accepted "gifts" from building contractors before and during the Ofafa and Mbotela contracts, entering false specifications and logging inspection reports when no inspections had taken place. Malpractice was found to be widespread in every aspect of the tendering and management of the Council's building contracts, and had evidently been so for many years. (Anderson 2004, pp. 226–229)

Sounds very much like today, and it is as if Kenya really never became independent. We decided to inherit from the colonialists the good, the bad, and the ugly in governance, with corruption remaining at the center of what subsequently came to be known as neocolonialism.

But the civil service, though corrupt in colonial times, had its avarice kept to a minimum by the vigilance of the white settler community that it served. It was not as avaricious as its counterpart that emerged after the Ndegwa Commission legalized official corruption. It was a service that was meant for the white society, and to deliver goods and services at the least cost to the master. It had to be small, lean, and efficient, and any corrupt deal was carefully tucked away under some justifiable expenses at the senior levels dominated by the whites and therefore kept to a minimum. If it was discovered that someone was taking advantage of an administrative office for personal gain and hence passing the transaction cost to the master, the punishment was prohibitive at the junior levels, where most of the officials were Africans.

The Civil Service After Independence: Lost Virginity?

The much-spoken-about clean and efficient civil service at independence was therefore not an accident. It had its origin in the political economy of colonial Kenya. After independence, the service became an employment bureau, an arena—quite understandably—of rewarding the boys and girls with jobs and new opportunities. As it expanded, it demanded more wages and more services for itself: houses, clinics, schools, holidays, pension schemes, and so on. These salaries and services were paid for from taxes levied on ordinary Kenyans.

The Kenyatta government opted for the easier, though more sinister, approach to this scenario. Rather than raise taxes to sustain a bloated civil service, the service was allowed to supplement its own wages through private business; that was the essence of the Ndegwa Commission Report, a commission set up to review salaries and terms of service of civil servants in the early 1970s and a commission that, for all intents and purposes, legalized official corruption. From then on, the civil service lost any hope of probity. In the ranks of the police and provincial administration, corruption and the most debilitating forms of rent seeking soon brought the whole administrative edifice to its knees as far as both service delivery and economic growth were concerned.

A Political Culture of Corruption

What the Ndegwa Commission brought to the civil service was already an acceptable practice in the world of politics. Jomo Kenyatta and his courtiers had no qualms about interpreting their ascendancy to state power as also meaning immediate inheritance and usurpation of economic power from the departing colonialists, justified as the Africanization of the economy.

There was, of course, nothing fundamentally wrong with the Africanization of the economy, especially when it meant opening up the frontiers of private property to Africans in terms of agricultural settlement schemes, trading licenses, small and medium-size enterprises supported by the Kenya Industrial Estates, new business empires financed by bank loans from the Industrial Development Bank, housing estates put up through the Housing Finance Company of Kenya, and so on.

When some people used their proximity to state power—particularly the presidency—to access these business opportunities for themselves and their friends to the exclusion of others, quite often disregarding the wider interests of society, that was wrong. They also indulged in corruption when they used their discretionary powers within the state (powers to license, to allocate foreign exchange in the treasury and the Central Bank, to approve and award contracts, to procure goods and services, etc.) to enrich themselves and their friends, to accumulate power and wealth, and to "Africanize" businesses and enterprises to themselves. Many of the economic and political potentates who today stride the streets of Nairobi as successful African businesspeople can retrace their steps to the corrupt deals of this era. It is not surprising that they were averse to any talk of truth and reconciliation and the dismantling of the authoritarian presidency.

Amendments to the independence constitution that heaped more and more powers on the presidency had a lot to do with the material interests of the power elite around the president, who found the authoritarian presidency a ready tool for aiding and abetting their accumulation of power, property, and wealth. This phenomenon was not unique to Kenya: it has been the cause of corruption and underdevelopment in Indonesia, the Phillipines, Mexico, and Nigeria, among many other low-income developing nations.

Very early in the life of the independent parliament, cries of corruption started to be heard. One of the key issues that the Kenya People's Union (KPU) raised in breaking away from the Kenya African National Union (KANU) government was corruption. A substantial section of the Wananchi Declaration, the KPU's manifesto of 1966, is devoted to a discussion of corruption in Kenya, which the party billed as "the biggest drawback to the country's future development." Even the minister of economic planning and development, Tom Mboya, Kenyatta's ablest and perhaps least corrupt minister, decried corruption and nepotism in the following words in a speech at the University of Nairobi: "I find it appalling that some of us in positions of power and authority quite often resort to cheap clanism in making appointments to public positions, and very often this is done to aid and abet corruption."[4]

When Paul Ngei, then minister for marketing and cooperatives, diverted maize meant for food relief to Emma Stores, a shop belonging to his wife, thereby inviting tremendous public disapproval, Kenyatta was quick to change the law and allow him to retain both his parliamentary seat and his position in the cabinet. Kenyatta perhaps saw nothing wrong with what Ngei had done because for Kenyatta, it was a way of Ngei "improving himself," helping himself to something that did not belong to any particular person, something that was not owned by "anybody's mother." Thus when the KPU cited corruption as one of the ways by which KANU misruled Kenya, Kenyatta chided Bildad Kaggia in that famous speech at the rally in Nairobi in 1966 where he accused Kaggia of having failed to build a house for himself while he, Kenyatta, had put up a mansion in rural Gatundu. For Kenyatta corruption was not the issue; it was the inability of some "leaders" to make use of "opportunities" open to them within the state to improve themselves. In this public and dramatized setting, a tradition was set from the highest level of political authority to provide immunity to public officials should they be accused of corruption. When corruption goes unpunished, it soon becomes rooted in a society's political culture. Kenyatta aided and abetted the institutionalization of corruption in Kenya. Moi and Mwai Kibaki followed in this tradition, quite often more than excelling in the art, much to the dismay of ordinary Kenyans.

The Fight Against Megacorruption Under Kenyatta, Moi, and Kibaki

Not all Kenyans have sat by and watched corruption happen without doing something about it. Struggles have been waged, and resistance has been put up, but the forces of corruption have always ignored, removed, pushed aside, or totally eliminated those who have fought against the vice. The student and staff revolts in the public universities, the Saba Saba uprising—a prodemocracy demonstration that rocked Nairobi and outlying towns in July 1990— helped move Kenya to its first mulitparty elections (Mungai 1991 and Amisi 2007).

The Public Accounts Committee, the Public Investments Committee, and many other parliamentary reports and debates have documented corruption during the Kenyatta, Moi, and Kibaki presidencies. The law books are full of laws meant to keep corruption in check, the Anti-Corruption and Economic Crimes Act being the latest addition among the speed bumps created. Many books, treatises, and articles have been written analyzing and drawing attention to the debilitating effects of corruption on economic growth, poverty eradication, and democratic governance. Politicians and other leaders have been detained, imprisoned, killed, and assassinated in Kenya for having spoken about, investigated, and opposed corruption in society and high places. We can remind ourselves of Pio da Gama Pinto, Tom Mboya, J. M. Kariuki, and Robert Ouko, all of whom lost their lives as a consequence of their bold stance.

Lawyers have been killed in broad daylight in the streets of Nairobi while dealing with cases of corruption in the courts, yet arrests have rarely been made that led to conclusive prosecutions. University dons have been thrown into police cells and detained, students butchered while demonstrating, and violence meted out against their parents as they demanded transparent use of national resources in the development of the nation. Recently a policeman, hot on the trail of drug traffickers, was gunned down in his compound. The police do not seem to be making much progress on that case either. Law enforcement agents began operating in fear, and fear leads to conscious omissions in the performance of their duties to apprehend criminals engaged in corruption or complicit in such affairs. An ineffective and compromised law enforcement agency becomes a weak and ineffective check on corruption. If anything, it constrains people intent on fighting corruption; it joins the chorus of those calling for "going slow" in dealing with corruption cases and investigations.

If law enforcement agents had not been ignored, compromised, derailed, or stopped from performing their duties, such megacorruption cases as those of Ken Ren, Molasses Plant, the expansion of Nzoia Sugar Mills Phases I and II, the Turkwell Gorge, and the many botched privatization schemes would not have gone unpunished. We should not be surprised about mega-rip-offs like Goldenberg and Anglo Leasing. A culture became set in the civil service and the high echelons of government that it was normal to make money in this way! And, as John Githongo soon found out, being a law enforcement agent under such circumstances can easily earn you a ticket to the gallows.

When the Hunters Became the Hunted

When the hunters become the hunted, then the fight against corruption in government is hijacked by a mafia of plutocrats who rail against the vice in public but, in private, urge the hunters to go slow in their job or abandon it altogether. Even the judges before whom corruption cases are brought engage in the game of filibustering, adjourning cases endlessly, losing files deliberately, and even excusing themselves from hearing a case after evidence has been given and witnesses grilled for months. The rich and powerful are quick at filing injunctions in courts to delay and even completely obstruct corruption cases against them, while the poor are punished severely for receiving or giving miniscule bribes.

Lawyers seeking witnesses in corruption cases have been bought off or killed. Prosecutors have been threatened. Witnesses have been made to disappear without a trace. The wrong people have been deliberately arrested and brought to court, charged with corruption or drug smuggling, while the law enforcement agencies know exactly what they are doing: pulling the wool over the faces of the Kenyan people in a make-believe exercise of fighting corruption.

The Anglo Leasing Affair

What is now known in Kenya as the Anglo Leasing scam, had it been allowed to persist as long as Goldenberg did, would have had an equally devastating effect on the Kenyan political economy.

Some time in 2000, the government of Daniel arap Moi worked out a scheme of purchasing security-related equipment and services from abroad under "lease financing" contracts with certain companies. One of these companies, called Anglo Leasing Financing Company, provided a home address somewhere in the United Kingdom. When the National Rainbow Coalition came to power in 2003, President Mwai Kibaki appointed John Githongo as his permanent secretary in charge of ethics. The new government decided to implement the scheme and to use it, as Moi had done with Goldenberg, to access money from state coffers under the guise of procuring security goods and services from abroad. Githongo's thorough inquiry revealed that Anglo Leasing was a fictitious company, and billions of shillings had been paid or committed to these contracts by the government. Attempts by Githongo to get to the bottom of this affair put him in great conflict with the president and his men and Githongo had to flee the country in December 2004 for a safe haven at St. Anthony's College in Oxford, England.

Like the Goldenberg scandal, the Anglo Leasing affair involved both public officials and private wheeler-dealers who entered into the affair for two purposes. One was for those in politics to make easy money from the state for the purpose of buying and keeping political power. The other was for the wheeler-dealers to make money for private gain as well as for access to and control of high-level public officials and politicians in the Kibaki government. For both groups, this scam could not have succeeded if the rule of law were respected. In order to execute it in the name of the state, some form of legality had to be devised. Hence, certain public officials with powers to sign documents had to be brought in to provide a veneer of legality, notwithstanding the criminality of the scheme.

Under the previous regime of President Moi, such schemes could be carried out by invoking the name of the president to compel public officials to do what they knew to be illegal. Since the presidential authoritarian regime was still very much in place, few people feared being found out. Even if they were, the president's name was enough to protect them. This is why Kamlesh Paul Pattni moved so easily within the corridors of power, and why he could sit and scheme with vice presidents, ministers of finance, permanent secretaries and customs officials.[5]

Under the regime of President Kibaki, presidential authoritarian powers, though still intact in the constitution, had been substantially eroded in the sphere of politics. Following the December 2002 elections, the voters had asserted their power against the political order: society would no longer simply be ordered around by the politicians. It was now a more open and free society. In addition, parliament had itself become increasingly assertive and independent of the executive since the Inter-Party Parliamentary Group reforms of 1997. The 2002 coalition politics acknowledged this independence by creating counterpart departmental committees in parliament. And finally, a free, independent, and fierce mass media was now a menace to the corrupt.

So a scheme like Anglo Leasing had to be conducted much more carefully and much less ruthlessly with authoritarian politics on the wane. That is what the schemers in the president's office and their civilian underworld contacts in the Anglo Leasing company did not fully appreciate. But they knew that in order to retain political power after breaking power-sharing promises with other ruling party members and usurping power from the coalition by trashing the memorandum of understanding, they needed some muscle to get their way. This muscle, they concluded, would be found in building a financial war chest with which to control the National Rainbow Coalition, the constitutional review process, and votes in parliament. What they did not factor in was an unusual man of integrity as a law enforcement agent who was working in State House as the permanent secretary in charge of ethics: John Githongo.

The men and women who had been involved in wheeling and dealing as politicians and "businessmen" under Moi were still around: Kamlesh Paul Pattni, Deepak Kamani, Merilyn Keterring, Anura Pereira, and their associates abroad. Some had been elected to parliament under the National Rainbow Coalition (NARC) arrangement, whereas others had even financed the National Rainbow Coalition campaigns without revealing their underworld identities. Those who were looking for easy money to buy and control political power did not lack for advisers or partners with whom to do business. In due course, these partners came forward and offered their services, and the new NARC clients were only too eager to play ball.

The Anglo Leasing deals had been started but not consummated under Moi. The wheeler-dealers advised that here was an area where easy money could be made. The NARC officials could actually do so under cover of legal procedure. The wheeler-dealers would make their money by selling fictitious goods and services to the state, while the politicians would raise enough cash to buy and keep power. All that was done under the name of the president.

Unfortunately for both the politicians and the business tycoons, John Githongo discovered the scam and reported it to the president. In no time, monies that had been paid out to the nonexistent Anglo Leasing Company were returned to the treasury and placed in what was called the Miscellaneous Revenue Account.

The ministers and government officials involved claimed that since the money had been returned (close to US$15 million), the matter should end there and no further investigations were necessary. Githongo thought otherwise. Thorough investigations were necessary, and all involved had to be prosecuted in accordance with the Economic Crimes and Anti-Corruption Act. A constellation of these politicians and their counterparts in the business underworld now threatened Githongo to either shut up or face the consequences. By the end of 2004, Githongo decided to quit when the opportune moment presented itself.

Presidential Involvement in Corruption

Many questions have been asked regarding the involvement of the President Kibaki in this scam. Did the president know what was going on? Did he sanction it? If he did not know, was it because information was kept from him? If he did, why didn't he stop it? From Githongo's published diaries, it is clear that the president was informed and he knew what was going on. The question to ask, therefore, is why didn't he stop it and bring the culprits to justice? One possible answer is that he sanctioned the scam. If that is the case, then Kenya has a Watergate-type situation. Another possible answer is that the president knew but was mentally and physically unable to do anything, in which case the responsibility must be put squarely on the cabinet, the chief justice, and the speaker of the National Assembly.

Section 12 of the Constitution of Kenya, "Removal of the President on Grounds of Mental or Physical Incapacity to Hold Office," gives the chief justice the power to appoint a tribunal to look into such matters after an appropriate cabinet resolution requesting him to do so. The report of the tribunal is then handed to the speaker for further action. From Githongo's diary, it was evident that by June 2004 ministers and high officials in government had been involved in procuring security-related services and equipment under the names of fictitious companies, chief among which were Anglo Leasing and Finance and Infotalent. When Githongo pressed the relevant officials about these fake contracts, monies were paid back to the treasury equally mysteriously. Githongo comments in his dossier to the president:

> I found this unsettling. First Euro 956,700, on 17-05-04 and then USD 4.7 million is repaid on 07-06-04, by a company that does not have legal status and no indication from within the government who its owners were. Only Hon. Mwiraria's admission to me on the 14th of June 2004 that J. Oyula, then Financial Secretary, had called up Kamani who had then repaid the money gave an indication as to who Anglo Leasing was. Now another bogus company, Infotalent, had "repaid" Euros 5.2 million.
>
> Your Excellency, I informed you of these developments on this day 16th June, 2004. We agreed that we were talking about the "refund" of almost Kenya shillings 1 billion and no one was celebrating; those making the refunds were not making themselves known; none of the civil servants involved were saying they knew who Anglo Leasing was.
>
> Anglo Leasing refunded USD 4.7 million (Kshs.370 m.) on the Forensic Laboratories project; Anglo Leasing refunded Euros 956,700 (Kshs.95 m.) on the Immigration Security project and Infotalent Ltd refunded Euros 5,287,164 (Kshs.506 m.) on the E-Cops Security project.[6]

Why didn't the president take any action on these anomalous repayments? Why did he continue to say nothing one year later when Githongo finally submitted this report to him?

These questions remain pertinent and will need to be addressed by the relevant organs of government, particularly parliament and its select and departmental committees. No doubt this process is under way and may soon answer questions that bother every Kenyan who desires good, clean, and democratic governance that can deliver on the rule of law, human rights, and development.

Corruption: What Is to Be Done?

"Philosophers have explained the world in various ways; the point, however, is to change it." That was Marx's invocation to the revolutionaries of the nineteenth century when he wrote in 1845 *The German Ideology: Including Thesis on Feuerbach*. Likewise, it does us no good to analyze and describe corruption in all its forms and its historical evolution in Kenya if we do not use this knowledge to do something about it. Kenya has the institutions and laws needed to fight corruption. The Anti-Corruption and Economic Crimes Act was well crafted and gives parliament, the courts, and other law enforcement agencies sufficient powers and institutional leverage to investigate, apprehend, and prosecute corruption. As the Mexican novelist Carlos Fuentes says: "The question is not whether there is corruption, it is whether corruption can be exposed and punished" (Fuentes 2001).

To expose and punish corruption, three interdependent factors, institutions, and processes are necessary: a political leadership with the vision, program, and will to do so; a political culture that encourages, nurtures, and supports exposure and punishment; and law enforcement agencies, particularly the judiciary, that will try and punish corruption. We have seen the weakness of the past and present Kenyan political leadership in the fight against corruption. Since 1992, however, with the tremendous growth of an open society—freer press, political pluralism, aggressive assertion of civil liberties—the fight against corruption has been heightened.

In 2003, soon after National Rainbow Coalition came to power, the minister for justice and constitutional affairs carried out what was seen as a surgery in the judiciary. It was meant to root out compromised, incompetent, and corrupt judges and magistrates. New people were to be recruited to take their places on grounds of merit. As it turned out, the exercise was undermined by favoritism and nepotism, promoting people who did not deserve these positions and victimizing others on fictitious charges or mere suspicion.

Although a tremendous effort was made to turn the judiciary upside down, it has not led to improved performance. It is not simply a question of "fighting the good fight" in trying to bring about changes in the judiciary. It is more important to ensure that this good fight delivers in terms of performance in the administration of justice and the fight against corruption. The same can be said of the Kenya Anti-Corruption Commission (KACC) formed in 2003. Since it was revamped in 2007 during the NARC administration, with a director and a bevy of officials earning large sums of money to justify their "heavy duties" and "to keep them away from temptation," the number of people who have been prosecuted for corruption in high places is not very impressive. A recent advertisement published by the government communication officer in the dailies showed hundreds of Kenyans apprehended for corruption involving embezzling 200 to 20,000 Kenya shillings. Although we would not want to forgive such sins offhand in the fight against corruption, they really cannot be paraded, in good conscience, as major achievements by KACC in three years.

What is the implication of our argument? First, good institutions and laws are not enough in the fight against corruption. Qualified, committed, and *independent* people are needed to work in these institutions and to exercise these laws for the corrupt to be duly apprehended and punished. By independent, we mean independent from undue external influence by the powers that be or any other party interested in subverting the cause of justice. But independence is tough and costly: it requires high resolve and tremendous competence and courage in the Kenyan context, as Githongo's experience has shown.

Second, getting the right individuals into the right institutions is not enough. A society needs to develop a *political culture* that discourages corrupt practices or makes it difficult for the corrupt to parade the proceeds of corruption as signs of success or high social status. With the recent Anglo Leasing revelations and the call for ministers to resign from office following their implication in the scandal, we may have started on the road toward effectively shaming corruption and the corrupt. As long as the corrupt of yesterday are able to pose as the saints of today to get elected and appointed to public offices, nurturing a political culture for fighting corruption will be hampered.

Such a culture will not emerge spontaneously; it has to be cultivated through struggle. And it is a struggle that will not, at the moment, be led from the top. It has to be engineered from below, whether we are talking about government, the religious order, civil society or the business community. At the top of all these institutions in Kenyan society are men and women intertwined by webs of interest and relationships that have been compromised by corrupt practices, knowingly and unknowingly, over many years. Although a few may commit class suicide like Githongo did and fight bare-knuckled against the vice, the majority will compromise themselves through silence. It is the usual middle-class sin: complain and do nothing; partake of the benefits of corruption but blame others for it.

But the realm of the political is always the most visible and the quickest to activate. It concentrates the experiences of society and the aspirations of the people into one act: the vote. If, in that one act, the issue of corruption and how to fight it is condensed—if, in that one act, the true soldiers are selected with the armor and the spirit to fight bereft of the compromises of the past—then a political leadership can take up the fight against corruption. Good, committed, visionary, and truly democratic political leadership is what Kenya needs to successfully keep corruption at bay.

In this regard, civil society organizations that are ready to go beyond the rhetoric of accusation into the realm of constructing a future of zero tolerance for corruption must now take up their crosses and make this history.

The next general election in Kenya in 2008 needs to be fought on the anti-corruption platform. Parties need to qualify and disqualify candidates given their anticorruption credentials: corruption-free ones allowed to run and those blemished by the vice must decline from contesting for any elected office. In this way, we shall change history for the better, and not simply continue to just analyze and discuss causes of our underdevelopment woes, including corruption.

Lessons for the Struggle Against Corruption

1. Any repressive regime prepares a fertile breeding ground for corruption. From colonial rule to the darkest days of the Moi government, corruption and authoritarianism has risen in tandem. In fact, it was during the most repressive time of Moi from the mid-1980s onward that megacorruption became a feature of governance in Kenya.

2. It is the struggle for democracy, and the progress that the popular national forces have made in opening up society, that have provided the means to challenge corruption. A few brave ambassadors like Smith Hempstone, Bernd Mützelburg, and Sir Edward Clay must be congratulated for their contribution, but these laurels cannot be bestowed on the external donor community in general.[7] The victory of the popular national forces in the 2002 elections is what opened the democratic political space for transparency, free debate, an aggressive press, an independent parliament, a vibrant civil society, and now the exposures of the Goldenberg and Anglo Leasing scandals. We still need to know more about the Halal meat factory scandal, the Ken Ren saga, and many other scandals that occurred under the single-party regime but could not be exposed because of the severity of political repression.[8]

3. If it had not been for John Githongo, Anglo Leasing would have gone the way of Ken Ren, with very little exposure and hence very little known. We therefore need public officers of high integrity and patriotism in the fight against corruption—men and women who will implement procurement procedures and laws in the public interest.

4. We need to eliminate the culture of impunity in our political system and government as a whole. Big or small, public officers indulge in corruption because we have set a poor precedent—the corrupt are left to flaunt their wealth and are serenaded as "development-conscious leaders." A competent and homegrown rule of law culture must be nurtured.

5. A politically committed leadership with a clear democratic and national developmental vision for Kenya is a sine qua non for fighting corruption. As Githongo has shown, the fight against corruption must begin at the very top of government and be seen to begin there.

6. Transparency in government expenditures and procurement, including the hitherto sacred defense and security expenditures, is vital.

7. We must, as Kenyans, believe in ourselves and congratulate ourselves when we do something good. Those who have given so much for the democratic struggle in this country must be recognized and encouraged. We often overstate the role of donors in the fight against corruption. It is to be noted that aid to Kenya was at its highest when the country was most repressive and corrupt (1988–1991). It was cut when Kenyans shamed donors by coming out on the streets regarding Saba Saba and several times in the early 1990s. Even with Anglo Leasing, it is the loud and clear voice of Kenyans that have now compelled significant changes in government and will, finally, herald a truly democratic and clean government.

8. As the Anglo Leasing saga has revealed, there are international networks of corruption. To fight corruption effectively, a global approach is needed, with governments in developed countries effectively supporting measures in the developing countries to confront the issue. For example, when substantial evidence has been placed in the public domain regarding public officials who are corrupt, even when their governments are reluctant to prosecute them, foreign governments should constrain such persons from making use of their illicit wealth.

To take a much more proactive stance, we need to look at the relationship between development assistance and the propensity of governments in developing countries to become corrupt. Shantayanan Devarajan, Vinaya Swaroop, and Andrew Sunil Rajkumar (1998) and Vinaya Swaroop, Shikha K. Jha, and Shantayanan Devarajan (2000) argue convincingly that foreign aid often substitutes for already earmarked government spending. The central government spends funds freed by aid on nondevelopment activities, and we dare add, "on corruption." Aid often softens the government's budget constraints and facilitates the ease with which it can devise corrupt ventures to finance politics and other noncore budget activities (see, for example, Njeru 2003). Development partners must therefore seek to provide assistance of a new and smart kind, in which core programs are agreed between partners in the context of the budget as a whole and of commitments to build a capable, democratic, and developmental state.

Notes

1. For a summary of these events by Joel Barkan, Kenya expert and author of Chapter 5 in this volume, see Barkan (2008).

2. *Sunday Nation,* January 20, 1968.

3. As the pressure mounted for multiparty politics in 1992, the one-party government of Daniel arap Moi decided to organize a shady scheme of exporting fictitious gold and diamonds from Kenya, for which the trading company called Gold-

enberg International would receive export compensation from the Treasury of close to 30 percent of the total money "earned" from such exports. Kamlesh Pattni, the regime's operative behind Goldenberg, received monumental sums of money from this deal, which led to an inflationary spiral in the economy lasting several years. The effects of this scam greatly undermined Kenya's economic growth during the last ten years of Moi's rule (1992–2002).

4. Tom Mboya (April 1968), in a panel discussion with Prof. J. J. Okumu and Ceere Cerira, at the Education Lecture Theater No. 2, University of Nairobi, speaking on "African Socialism and Its Application to Planning in Kenya."

5. Pattni is a businessman involved in the 1990 Goldenberg scandal, in which Kenya lost a billion dollars in fictitious operations of gold export and diamonds.

6. John Githongo, *Report on My Findings of Graft in the Government of Kenya,* submitted to President Mwai Kibaki, November 2005, p. 11.

7. Smith Hempstone, journalist and the US ambassador to Kenya in 1989–1993. He was a vocal proponent of democracy, fighting for free elections in Kenya in 1991. Bernd Mützelburg, ambassador from the Federal Republic of Germany to Kenya in 2001. At the same time, he served as permanent representative with the United Nations Environment Programme and UN-Habitat. Sir Edward Clay, former British high commissioner to Kenya, exposed corruption within the Kenyan government.

8. Halal was a major government-linked corruption scandal in 1973, involving funds ostensibly to be used to build a meat-processing factory in which large sums were embezzled by private businessmen and government officials. The Ken Ren saga is a 1978 case in which an American fertilizer company signed an exclusive import deal with the Kenyan government, collected millions, but never did any work in the country.

11

Voters But Not Yet Citizens: Democratization and Development Aid

Michael Bratton and Carolyn Logan

Democracy is ultimately based not on voters, but on *citizens*.
—Guillermo O'Donnell (2007)

Transitions to competitive, multiparty politics in African countries during the 1990s were jubilantly welcomed, both on the continent and internationally. Today, Africans enjoy unprecedented opportunities to vote, and many still revel in greater individual and political freedoms. But the full potential of democracy—including the promise of accountable governance—has yet to be fulfilled. Economic growth is still elusive, corruption remains widespread, and aid dependency continues to frustrate recipients and donors alike. As global leaders contemplate massive increases in international assistance to the continent, questions have therefore been raised about indigenous capacity to absorb an influx of new funds without exacerbating old problems. A smart aid approach would seem to require that African political leaders are held accountable—not only to donor agencies but, more importantly, to their own people—for sound policy choices and the effective use of resources.

But why has democratization so far failed to secure better governance? If elected leaders are supposed to be rewarded for good choices and sanctioned for bad ones, why is policy performance still so poor? Why haven't competitively elected governments in Africa demonstrated a significantly greater degree of accountability to their publics than the authoritarian systems that they replaced? How is it, for example, that multiparty regimes in Kenya, Uganda, Zambia, and Nigeria have received lower scores on Transparency International's Corruption Perceptions Index than much less open societies like Burkina Faso, Gabon, Rwanda, Equatorial Guinea, and Côte d'Ivoire?[1] After nearly two decades of promoting democracy, many donors have joined the chorus asking why democratization has, so far, fallen short of expectations.

One answer concerns how Africans themselves understand the contours of new political regimes and, in particular, their own roles in a democracy. Analysts and practitioners often assume that voting in elections automatically endows individuals with a sense of ownership of their political systems and a will to control leaders. But that may not necessarily be so. Our intention in this chapter is to explore Africans' own understandings of political accountability and their responsibility for securing it. To what extent do they demand answers from their elected leaders? To what extent do they feel they receive satisfactory responses? And what are the implications for donor policy and programs?

Our findings suggest that the road to accountable governance may be a long one. On the one hand, Africans enthusiastically support electoral politics, in principle the most direct means for influencing leaders. They do not, however, believe that elections have been particularly effective at securing political accountability. And when it comes to monitoring leadership performance in the long intervals between elections, a substantial number of Africans do not see any role for themselves. Instead, a majority apparently opts for a broadly *delegative* form of democracy, granting authority to oversee elected representatives either to the president or to other political actors. Only about a third of the Africans we interviewed apparently feel confident in asserting that elected leaders must answer directly to them. Nor do many Africans feel that they receive accountability from leaders; the reported supply of vertical accountability is even lower than the demand for it.

People in African countries may have begun to transform themselves from the "subjects" of past authoritarian systems into active "voters" under the present dispensation. But at the same time, they do not appear to fully grasp their political rights as "citizens," notably to regularly claim accountability from leaders. As such, most African political regimes have yet to meet the minimum requirements of representative democracy. Some indicators point toward these regimes as "delegative democracies," albeit in a somewhat broader form than originally described by O'Donnell (1994). But that description does not necessarily capture the crux of the deficiencies that we observe. In fact, the problem for many new democracies in Africa is not so much that citizens knowingly *delegate* authority to strong presidents but that democracy remains *unclaimed* by mere voters.

In this context, what can international donors do to promote the deepening of democracy via the emergence of fully engaged citizens? One danger of externally provided financial assistance, even when closely monitored, is that it divorces governments from the need to depend on and answer to their own people. The imposition of tight political conditions on development spending can actually exacerbate, rather than overcome, the voter-citizen gap.[2] The challenge for donors is to devise methods to encourage governments to account *to their people*. Make no mistake: the sustainability of effective democracies that can successfully pursue a national development agenda lies in the hands of African citizens and cannot rest solely on the goodwill of leaders or the vigilance of the international community.

Steps in this direction have already been taken. At least on paper, international donors increasingly rely on political partnerships rather than political conditionality. Host government officials are encouraged to share responsibility for selecting and implementing development policies with representatives of civil society (Harrison 2001). The broadly consultative procedures required by the World Bank for developing national Poverty Reduction Strategy Papers (PSRPs) are one example. In addition, the US government's Millennium Challenge Account selects country participants based on present performance of good governance, rather than trying to extract promises of future concessions from reluctant reformers. It is welcome that an indicator of "voice and accountability" is now an integral component of the donor community's principal measurement tool for appraising good governance. But the term is still narrowly interpreted as "the extent to which a country's citizens are able to participate in selecting their government, as well as freedom of expression, freedom of association, and free media" (Kaufmann, Kraay, and Mastruzzi 2006). Little or no account is taken of whether citizens actually make use of available rights between elections to *demand* accountability from their leaders.

In this chapter we reveal that the public's understanding of its role in securing government accountability appears, in part, to be a historical legacy. If unclaimed democracy is a product of previous authoritarian precedents, then it is hardly subject to external manipulation. Moreover, it is not clear that individuals can simply be taught or trained to adopt the attitudes and mindset of a citizen, as compared to those of a voter or mere subject. But over time, political learning does occur. And although it is ultimately up to Africans themselves to lay claim to their rights as citizens, there may, nonetheless, be a number of ways that donors can help to foster a more engaged and demanding public. Among other things, the evidence we present suggests that a popular sense of ownership of government will most readily develop at the local level. In addition, public access to information, including government budgets and expenditures, is a fundamental condition for effective monitoring of officials. Awareness of these factors invites creative responses from donors, and points in particular to strategies of advocating governmental transparency, promoting local control over resources and decisions, and fostering responsiveness among elected representatives, especially at the local level.

Donors can also support a variety of mechanisms for giving greater voice to an emerging citizenry, for example, via public attitude surveys, support for an accessible and independent media, and promotion of public ombudsmen. They can also continue to insist on popular input into public policy processes. Among other things, it is critical to expose leaders' self-serving claims that they alone comprehend popular preferences.

Finally, good-quality elections continue to play a powerful role in engaging the public in the political arena. They can serve as a starting point for publicizing the broader rights and responsibilities of citizenship via civic education; indigenous election monitoring groups may serve as seeds for organizations focused on monitoring postelection performance. Thus, although far from sufficient for creating more effective and responsive governments, continuing to promote and support good-quality election processes remains a critical starting point. In sum, being smarter about aid requires that both donors and Africans themselves take greater advantage of the opportunities presented by democratic openings—however faltering—to foster stronger relationships of accountability between African states and their domestic, rather than international, constituents.

Accountability in Perspective

The obligation of political leaders to answer to the public for their actions and decisions—the obligation of *accountability*—is a cornerstone of a well-functioning democracy. In principle, political accountability serves a dual purpose. It checks the power of the political class, diminishing arbitrary or abusive rule and helping to ensure that governments operate effectively and efficiently. As such, accountability may be as crucial to economic development as it is to political progress. Accountability is also intimately linked to citizen participation, leadership responsiveness, and the rule of law, three other pillars that define the practice of democracy. Particularly in representative systems, the level of accountability of elected leaders to their constituents is a key indicator of the quality of democracy (O'Donnell, Cullel, and Iazetta 2004, p. 33; Diamond and Morlino 2005, p. xiii).

O'Donnell (1994) has coined a useful distinction between two primary types of political accountability. *Horizontal accountability* refers to restraints imposed by the state on itself or, more specifically, by one state institution upon another. It rests on the separation of powers between branches of government and refers to the checks on the executive branch exercised by legislative, judicial, regulatory, and monetary institutions. In O'Donnell's initial statement, *vertical accountability*—the primary focus of the present analysis—was defined in terms of elections, or "making elected officials answerable to the ballot box" (1994, p. 61). By definition, this type of vertical accountability exists in every democracy, as long as the political system provides voting opportunities and real choice.

But the inherent limitations of individual votes in enforcing accountability upon elected leaders are well known. Most obviously, voters enjoy infrequent opportunities to cast a ballot; for president or parliament, this opportunity arises only once every four or five years. As such, elections force voters to compress myriad preferences—of political identity, competing policies, retrospective evaluation, and future expectation—into a single choice. In Africa, where ethnic or regional voting patterns are common and party platforms are weak, elections rarely offer real programmatic alternatives, thus limiting choice itself. Moreover, incumbent leaders can easily break promises and resort to evasion (Maravall 1996). And voting does almost nothing to hold bureaucrats, the judiciary, or security forces to account for their actions. Elections thus constitute a blunt instrument for enforcing accountability.

Analysts increasingly recognize that popular demands for accountability are far more varied and important than those captured by elections alone. Anne Marie Goetz argues that "the new accountability agenda is characterized by an *expansion* of accountability. . . . Accountability-seekers . . . now include more ordinary people seeking to engage directly—rather than relying upon intermediaries—in efforts to make power-holders answer for their actions" (2003, pp. 4–5).[3] In the long intervals *between* elections, there is considerable scope for popular initiative—both individual and collective—through mass mobilization and public protest, advocacy and lobbying campaigns, lawsuits and other "new accountability initiatives" such as participatory budgeting and expenditure monitoring (Anderson 2006; Goetz and Jenkins 2005; Malena et al. 2004). Catalina Smulovitz and Enrique Peruzzotti (2000) argue that these measures can serve as an effective form of control over public servants, potentially destroying their reputations and political capital and activating horizontal mechanisms of accountability. As such, "the linkage between voters and elected representatives sets the tone for all other accountability relationships" (Mainwaring 2003, p. 21), because "the effective operation of vertical accountability, through the electoral process, the news media and concerted civic action, causes governments to take seriously the perils of failing to sustain horizontal accountability" (Schacter 2001, p. 3).

But the current literature on vertical accountability mostly fails to address whether individuals are actually *willing and able* to seek accountability from elected leaders. How do ordinary people in new democracies understand their relationships to political representatives and thus their own political roles in a democracy? It is easy to assume that competitive electoral politics automatically unleash public desires and expectations for answerability (see, e.g., Goetz 2003, p. 3). But it is not at all clear that popular understandings of political rights and obligations can be taken for granted.[4] Ayesha Jalal, for example, argues that "the extension in India of universal adult franchise did not energize the polity with the spirit of citizens' rights as distinct from the formal periodic exercise of voters' rights" (1995, pp. 19–20), and that relations between voters and leaders were thus largely limited to elections.

Yet Gabriela Ippolito-O'Donnell proposes that "democracy entails a particular conception of the human being *cum* citizen as an *agent* . . . an autonomous, reasonable and responsible individual" (2006, pp. 10–11; see also O'Donnell, Cullel, and Iazetta 2004, pp. 24–31). Similarly, Smulovitz and Peruzzotti note that societal mechanisms of civic action tend to be activated by actors "that recognize themselves as legitimate claimants of rights" (2003, p. 310). But immense metamorphoses may be required for individuals to transit from "subjects" under authoritarian rule to "voters" in electoral democracies, and thereafter to rights- and accountability-demanding "citizens." The assertion by individuals of *superior authority* over public officials is no small matter (Mulgan 2000, cited in Malena et al. 2004, p. 2). History matters: democratic citizenship is not built in a day, and a legacy of authoritarianism cannot be wiped out overnight (see North 1990).

In new electoral regimes that lack deep democratic traditions, it is more common for the members of general public to *delegate* rather than claim their legitimate political rights. In Latin America, for example, voters may demand vertical accountability at election time, but they all too readily grant presidents a mandate to rule essentially unilaterally once elected. In O'Donnell's words: "Delegative democracies rest on the premise that whoever wins election to the presidency is thereby entitled to govern as he or she sees fit. . . . After the election, voters/delegators are expected to become a passive but cheering audience of what the president does" (1994, pp. 59–60).

O'Donnell characterizes the key distinction between delegative and representative democracies as an institutional, rather than individual, infirmity (pp. 61–62). But by emphasizing institutional weaknesses, his formulation may overlook the crux of the problem: the failure of the public to *claim* a representative democracy. Although he implicitly conceives of the public in transitional societies as having an underdeveloped desire for accountability, he treats such demand-side failures as secondary to the shortcomings of governmental institutions and to the president's successful efforts to undermine them.

We thus offer an alternative characterization that focuses on whether individuals *demand* vertical accountability, especially between elections. We contend that political accountability remains incomplete in Africa because individuals have a limited appreciation of political rights, of reasonable expectations, and of their own public roles and responsibilities. In other words, the general public's adoption of an ethic of citizenship may lag well behind their enjoyment of the freedom to vote in competitive elections. In effect, the inherent potential of democracy in these societies remains *unclaimed* by the people. Many Africans may be evolving from subjects into voters, but too few of these voters can be regarded as fully formed citizens. As a result, mechanisms of accountability—and the governmental effectiveness they should produce—remain underdeveloped, even in some of Africa's most progressive new democracies. This gap in the accountability dynamic presents one of the greatest challenges to a smart aid approach to providing development assistance.

The Origins of the Data

This analysis draws on the results of 25,397 face-to-face interviews conducted in 2005–2006 during Round 3 of the Afrobarometer. By conducting public attitudinal surveys at regular intervals in a number of African countries, Afrobarometer data offers systematic insights into views of Africans about democracy. The data are pooled from eighteen country surveys, all of which used a standard survey instrument.[5] Each country is represented by a national probability sample in which every adult citizen had an equal and known chance of inclusion. Sample sizes ranged from 1,161 to 2,400 respondents per country, although in the descriptive statistics reported here, the data are weighted to represent each country equally (n = 1,200). The margin of sampling error never exceeds 3 percent at a 95 percent level of confidence.[6] The reader should note, however, that Afrobarometer surveys are concentrated in countries that have undergone at least some degree of political and economic liberalization since the 1990s. As such, the results represent the continent's most open societies and cannot be taken as representative of sub-Saharan Africa as a whole.[7]

Afrobarometer data present novel opportunities to explore Africans' political perceptions. Here we begin by considering popular opinions about the conventional mechanism of vertical accountability: elections. We then turn attention to the primary object of inquiry: individual attitudes toward vertical accountability between elections. Only if people routinely demand accountability from elected leaders can we conclude that average Africans are evolving into democratic citizens. As an indication of the quality of emerging African democracies, and in a quest to find points of leverage for aid policy reform, we will also be interested in knowing whether people think that leaders are supplying accountability.

Vertical Accountability: Are Elections Working in Africa?

Periodic elections are among the only formal occasions on which citizens can punish or reward political representatives for their performance in office.

There is little doubt that Africans welcome the advent of competitive elections. Across eighteen countries in 2005–2006, more than four out of five Afrobarometer respondents (82 percent) agree that "we should choose our leaders in this country through regular, open and honest elections." Fewer than one in four (16 percent) disagree: "Since elections sometimes produce bad results, we should adopt other measures for choosing this country's leaders." Strong majorities favor elections in all eighteen countries surveyed, peaking at 94 percent in Benin. Having voted for turnovers in top leadership, fully nine out of ten Beninois express "very strong" agreement that elections are the best way for ordinary people to select the political elite. Thus, like democracy, free elections have become widely regarded—almost universally in some places—as a desirable public good (Bratton 2006a, p. 2).

But because people easily pay lip service to universal norms, expressions of support for electoral mechanisms may not always reflect deep popular commitments. If they have never experienced free and fair contests, citizens may regard "no party" or "one-party dominant" elections as desirable. Therefore, it is important to know whether Africans endorse the idea of multiparty competition itself. Here the evidence is also positive though less compelling: some 63 percent prefer "many political parties . . . (so people) have real choices," versus 32 percent who regard many political parties as "unnecessary" because they cause "division and confusion." But the proportion supporting multiple parties is rising over time—up 8 points from 55 percent circa 2002 (Afrobarometer Network 2006b, p. 21). In places like Zimbabwe, where a de facto one-party state has used manipulation and violence to dodge accountability, fully three-quarters of all adults now call for "real choice" among multiple political parties.

On the whole, people also express considerable confidence in the quality of African elections. Across all eighteen countries, two-thirds (66 percent) report that their elections were either "completely free and fair" or "free and fair, but with minor problems." Those results obscure the fact, however, that in four countries—Malawi, Nigeria, Zambia, and Zimbabwe—ratings of electoral quality are much lower; an average of just 35 percent. But across the remaining fourteen countries, positive marks are given by an average of 75 percent, peaking at 84 percent in Botswana.

Even so, Africans have yet to be convinced that competitive contests always guarantee the vertical accountability of leaders to the electorate. Asked to consider "how elections work in practice in your country," fewer than half think they work well. Just 47 percent report that elections "enable voters to remove from office leaders who do not do what the people want," and only 46 percent consider that elections "ensure that members of parliament reflect the views of voters." To be sure, these averages conceal considerable cross-national variation: whereas three quarters of Ghanaians (79 percent) see elections as a reliable means of replacing unresponsive political representatives, barely one-quarter of Nigerians (26 percent) share the same conviction. In-evitably, these public views embody popular judgments about whether the last national election—that is, Ghana's model 2004 poll and Nigeria's dis-puted contest of 2003—accurately reflected the will of the voters. Unless well conducted, elections can hardly be expected to serve as mechanisms of vertical accountability.

Most importantly for an inquiry into accountability, Africans insist that political representatives should respond to their needs. By almost six to one (82 percent), they believe that "elected officials should listen to constituents' views and do what they demand." They roundly reject the proposition that "elected leaders should follow their own ideas in deciding what is best for the country" (14 percent). Voters thus do not regard elections as a blank check that permits political representatives to exercise wide discretion. Kenyans are especially insistent on controlling their leaders; a mere 4 per-cent are willing to cede decisionmaking authority between elections exclu-sively to legislators and local government councilors.

It is within the context of these popular views—widespread support for elections, general satisfaction with their quality, mixed feelings about their effectiveness, and strong preferences for responsive governance—that we pose our central research questions. Among Africans, who wants vertical ac-countability? And why don't people think they are getting it?

Vertical Accountability: Who Wants It?

Delving deeper into the demand side of the political process, this section ex-plores forms of vertical accountability other than elections. It asks whether Africans see roles for themselves—beyond voting—as citizens in a repre-sentative democracy. We limit our inquiry to the public's interaction with elected representatives (members of parliament or deputies in the national assembly, and local government councilors), rather than all government of-ficials. We want to know whether ordinary people feel responsible for hold-ing these elected leaders accountable between elections, or whether they would rather delegate the monitoring function to other agents or institutions.

Africans appear divided on whether they prefer a representative or del-egative form of democracy. When asked, "Who should be responsible for making sure that, once elected, members of parliament do their jobs?" they split into two main camps. Across eighteen African countries in 2005–2006, one-third of respondents say that "the voters" should take the lead in holding legislators accountable (34 percent). Countering this view, however, a pro-portion of equal size believes that "the President" (or "the executive branch of government") should supervise the work of legislators (33 percent). The remainder of the survey respondents either say they "don't know" who is responsible for ensuring accountability (10 percent) or that the political parties represented in the parliament should police their own members (23 percent).

One can make a case from these results that Africans *prefer* a broadly *delegative* form of democracy. Adding together all valid responses that do not cite "the voters," we can see that, between elections, more than one-half of all adults (56 percent) apparently stand ready to abdicate their democratic right to discipline their representatives. In lieu of vertical accountability, they seem willing to accept some form of horizontal accountability exercised by either the legislative or executive branches of government. Let us be clear: those are weak substitutes for popular oversight. Accountability of elected representatives to a legislature or party requires leaders to monitor themselves without any form of external check or balance. And accountability to a president constitutes an extreme form of horizontal accountability in which the arrow of sovereignty—which, in a democracy, grants precedence to an elected legislature—is reversed. It proposes that the legislature should be held accountable to an executive branch whose members, save usually the president, are unelected.

Do Africans everywhere spurn vertical accountability between elections? Not necessarily. Figure 11.1 shows the percentage of survey respondents in each country who say that "the voters" are responsible for making sure parliamentary representatives do their work. The Afrobarometer mean score (34 percent) conceals a remarkably wide range of cross-national variation. To be sure, only 6 percent of Namibians say they want legislators to be answerable to voters in a context where almost half the adult population (48 percent) would gladly delegate that task to the executive president. A further 17 percent regards the ruling party, the South-West Africa People's Organization, as a reliable agent of restraint. By contrast, a clear majority of almost three-quarters of Malawians prefer that legislators report directly to voters, in a country where only 12 percent countenance entrusting such authority to the president.

Similar patterns prevail when people consider local government councilors. Once again, Malawians are more insistent than other Africans on the right of popular review (76 percent). They are followed by Malagasy (74 percent), in whose vast country local government is often more visible than central authority, and Ugandans (61 percent), who enjoy a strong recent tradition of participatory local administration. As before, Namibians readily surrender their political rights (just 12 percent demand vertical accountability), but now less so than Cape Verdeans (5 percent), where local government is seen as highly dependent on, and therefore largely indistinguishable from, national government.

Importantly, the Africans we interviewed demand more popular accountability from local government than from central government. Overall, some 40 percent think that local government councilors should be subject to oversight

**Figure 11.1 Popular Demand for Vertical Accountability of
Legislative Representatives to Voters, 2005–2006**

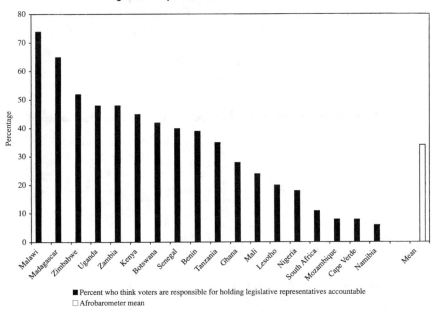

■ Percent who think voters are responsible for holding legislative representatives accountable
□ Afrobarometer mean

from voters, compared to 34 percent for legislators. Moreover, only 19 percent think that the national president should have any role in supervising councilors, some 15 points lower than for legislators. These differences reflect the relative physical proximity of voters to local councilors and, by contrast, the remoteness of the office of the president, other agencies of central government, and even members of the national legislature from the areas where citizens live. The data also suggest that a popular constituency for *representative* democracy (rather than delegative democracy) is likely to emerge first at the local government level, and only later with regard to the national parliament.

Nonetheless, popular attitudes about the accountability of elected representatives at all levels are forged from the same mold. Public opinion about the locus of responsibility for responsive governance is correlated across central and local government levels.[8] At both levels, there are strong delegative and weaker representative tendencies. Because these attitudes are linked, for purposes of further analysis it is possible to combine them into a single item that refers generally to elected representatives, both local and central.[9] This produces a single variable on a 3-point scale that we call "popular demand for vertical accountability."[10] It constitutes the object of explanation in the analysis that follows.

To understand what factors determine an individual's inclination to demand vertical accountability, we use regression analysis. Our main model tests three sets of explanatory factors: social characteristics, political attitudes, and national-level political and institutional legacies (see Table 11.1, Model 1).[11]

We already know that mass demand for vertical accountability varies

Table 11.1 Popular Demand for Vertical Accountability, Explanatory Factors Compared

	Model 1			Model 2		
	B	Beta	Adj. Block R Square	B	Beta	Adj. Block R Square
Constant	1.851[a]			1.340[a]		
Social characteristics			.007			.007
Rural	−.011	−.008		.018	.013	
Female	−.003	−.002		−.007	−.005	
Age	.002[a]	.046		.001[a]	.028	
Employment status	−.026	−.018		.000	.000	
Education	.015[a]	.041		−.005	−.013	
Wealth	.019[a]	.036		.026[a]	.048	
Political attitudes			.060			.060
Know political leaders	.041[a]	.048		.088[a]	.103	
Know term limits	.046[a]	.033		.026	.018	
Reject one-man rule	.023[a]	.035		.028[a]	.043	
Perceive corruption	.028[a]	.032		.016	.018	
Question leaders	.007	.015		.012[a]	.025	
Leaders should listen	.008	.011		.027[a]	.036	
Country contexts			.160			
South Africa	−.429[a]	−.190				
Nigeria	−.349[a]	−.163				
Namibia	−.471[a]	−.154				
Mozambique	−.528[a]	−.150				
Lesotho	−.474[a]	−.128				
Cape Verde	−.592[a]	−.120				
Ghana	−.185[a]	−.056				
Botswana	−.135[a]	−.043				
Mali	−.134[a]	−.043				
Benin	.152[a]	.045				
Madagascar	.361[a]	.116				
Malawi	.450[a]	.128				
Institutional legacies						.085
Years of independence				.009[a]	.156	
Past presidential rule				−.109[a]	−.117	
Liberation movement				−.002[a]	−.070	
Plurality electoral system				.063[a]	.043	
Adjusted R square	*.183*			*.103*		

Notes: For country dummies in Model 1, Tanzania is the excluded category. Only countries for which B is significant at p = <.001 are shown.
  a. p = <.001.

substantially across countries. So it is reasonable to expect that the aggregate-level features of nation-states—whether historical, economic, or institutional—will play a significant role in explaining differences in whether Africans grant voters the leading role in seeking accountability. Before leaping to this conclusion, however, we wish to probe alternative explanations embedded in the social characteristics and political attitudes of individuals. For example, it is reasonable to expect that urban residents would be more politically sophisticated than rural dwellers and thus more likely to think that voters should be responsible for monitoring leaders. We might also expect that those with more education would have a better understanding of the rights and responsibilities of citizens in a democracy. Additionally, it is also plausible to propose that people who possess relevant political knowledge—such as the names of elected representatives or the requirements of presidential term limits—would be more insistent about vertical accountability.

We find, however, that, other things being equal, the effects of standard social indicators are very limited.[12] Rural residence and gender are not significant determinants of the demand for vertical accountability. Age, education, and wealth all have positive and significant—but quite small—effects.[13] It is hardly surprising that people who are better educated and have amassed personal assets will be more active in seeking direct accountability, as they are likely to have both an economic stake in political outcomes and the social status to make effective demands on their representatives. But the effects of these factors are nonetheless very small, so the moving force behind accountability must lie elsewhere, perhaps in the attitudinal realm of mass opinion.

We considered a wide array of attitudinal predictors. For the record, we find that an individual's level of political engagement[14] and sense of personal political efficacy[15] play no role in shaping demand for accountability, nor does a belief that elected leaders should listen to their constituents rather than following their own ideas. Even persons who say they are inclined to "question leaders" rather than to automatically "respect authority" are no more likely than anyone else to want leaders to answer directly to voters.[16] Instead, what matters most is an individual's level of political knowledge. Not surprisingly, people who know the names of their legislative representatives and local government councilors are most likely to demand accountability from them.[17] People who know the constitutional rule about how many terms in office a national president may serve (usually just two) are also more likely to call their representatives to account. People who reject a "strongman" presidential regime in which "elections and parliament are abolished so that the president can decide everything" (i.e., "one-man rule") also want an assertive citizenry. Finally, the more that people perceive that elected representatives are corrupt, the more likely they are to want to hold them to account.[18]

But we must again concede that the overall explanatory power of these attitudinal effects is quite small.[19] This result suggests that, in sub-Saharan Africa, demand for the accountability of elected leaders to voters is nascent at best. In the realm of public opinion, such preferences are barely formed. And the limited demand that does exist is widely dispersed among all classes and categories of people. We can only conclude that, even in new African democracies, most people have yet to make the difficult personal transition to active citizenship.

Where, then, does this prevalent public mindset originate? Our findings confirm that, rather than being an attribute of particular individuals or groups, low demand for accountability is better understood at the country level through the shared experiences of whole populations. In particular, people who live in South Africa, Nigeria, Namibia, and Mozambique, among other countries, are less likely than the average African to demand popular accountability.[20] By contrast, living in Malawi or Madagascar significantly increases such demand.[21]

But attributing demand for vertical accountability simply to "country effects," indicating that characteristics specific to each country are the determining factors, is particularly unhelpful when it comes to either building theory or prescribing policies. The challenge is to replace country names with *common* underlying historical and institutional features. We test several possible alternatives that offer some insight into the factors that underlie country effects (see Table 11.1, Model 2). Nonetheless, the total explanatory power of these alternatives is just over half that of the "country effects" alone, so we must conclude that other, as yet unidentified or unmeasured influences are also at work.[22]

First, African citizens are more likely to demand vertical accountability if their countries have been independent for a long time. That implies that the demand for public accountability is an attribute that people learn gradually and that learning occurs largely through accumulated experience—good or bad—with self-governance. In other words, citizens usually seek to hold leaders to account only after they discover that the latter are not governing in the public interest. This insight helps us to interpret the relatively high levels of demand for vertical accountability in countries like Benin, Madagascar, and Malawi, all of which gained independence in the early 1960s and subsequently suffered indigenous dictatorships. In newly free countries, such as South Africa (1994) and Namibia (1990), insufficient time has yet elapsed for citizens to learn this lesson. Like other Africans did before them, South Africans and Namibians are allowing leaders considerable latitude in the early years of the founding democratic regime.

But the way in which leaders governed after independence was also important, especially the extent to which they concentrated power in the presidency. As a way of differentiating among African countries on this dimension, we calculated the number of years between independence and 1989 that each country spent under personal dictatorship, military rule, or plebiscitary one-party rule as a share of the total years since independence ("past presidential rule"). We think that the relatively low demand for accountability in Nigeria, for example, can be traced in part to eighteen years of highly centralized military dictatorship during this period (Sklar, Onwudiwe, and Kew 2006, p. 102), which counteracts the positive effects of the country's early independence. At a general level, a legacy of past presidential rule is negatively and significantly correlated with demand for accountability. To state the result differently, Africans who were socialized under the rule of strong presidents in the past have limited experience with representative democracy and are likely to default to a delegative form of democracy today. A long period of independence therefore helps all countries, but it helps those who lived under a repressive system much less than those who lived under more open regimes.

Third, the mode of decolonization also matters. National liberation movements led armed struggles in South Africa and Namibia, the latecomer countries mentioned above, plus Cape Verde, Mozambique, and Zimbabwe. This mode of decolonization featured dominant political parties based on revolutionary discipline and democratic centralism. These organizational features were carried over into the postcolonial phase, with leaders like Samora Machel, Sam Nujoma, and Robert Mugabe being resistant to, or even intolerant of, political pluralism and competition. Instead, they sought to indoctrinate their compatriots to follow an official party line. In this way, the legacy of national liberation has discouraged a political culture of bottom-up accountability.

Finally, as an alternative to historical path dependencies, we consider contemporary political institutions, notably the electoral system. Among the countries studied here, eleven possess plurality systems ("first-past-the-post" elections in single-member districts), and five employ proportional systems (like "list proportional representation" with various district magnitudes).[23] We find that plurality systems have a more positive effect than proportional and mixed systems on popular demands for political accountability. That stands to reason since, under plurality systems, citizens can identify and locate a single representative whom they can potentially hold accountable. Under the list PR system, especially as in South Africa where the whole country forms one electoral district for parliamentary elections, citizens do not know whom to approach as "their" representative. A mixed electoral system has been introduced for local government elections in South Africa, in part to address the problem of ambiguous lines of accountability. Thus respondents in the February 2006 Afrobarometer survey in South Africa were somewhat more likely to demand accountability from local councilors (17 percent) than national legislators (11 percent).

Unfortunately, even after replacing vague "country effects" with specific institutional structures and legacies, it is evident that these findings offer little in the way of clear direction for donors or democracy advocates who recognize the need to enhance vertical accountability. Past institutional legacies are not subject to manipulation! Moreover, we must weigh the findings here concerning the accountability benefits of plurality systems against the benefits of proportional systems (representativeness and inclusivity) before taking a position on this matter. As an alternative method of identifying means for improving vertical accountability, we therefore turn to the supply side. We now ask, Who perceives that they get vertical accountability from elected leaders, and what factors influence these perceptions?

Vertical Accountability: Are Africans Getting It?

What do Africans have to say about the delivery of accountable governance? If citizens perceive low levels of vertical accountability (they do), what are the roots of this sentiment? Can citizen discontent with the accountability of leaders again be traced to institutional histories, or, in this case, do we discover more proximate causes embedded in mass opinions about the current behavior (and misbehavior) of political elites? If so, through empirical analysis, we may be able to distinguish specific ways ahead in addressing Africa's accountability deficit.

To measure the supply of vertical accountability, we focus on the perceived credibility of politicians. The Afrobarometer survey asks, "In your opinion, how often do politicians keep their campaign promises after elections?" Like people elsewhere in the world, Africans have skeptical views on this subject. Across eighteen African countries in 2005–2006, an average of just 15 percent consider that elected leaders keep their word "often" or "always." Some 38 percent say they do so "rarely," and a plurality (44 percent) say "never." With only 3 percent who "don't know," almost everyone has an opinion on this hot topic.

Figure 11.2 depicts the extent to which people think campaign promises are believable across African countries. More than one-third of Namibians put faith in the pledges of politicians, whereas just 3 percent do so in Benin. A visual comparison of Figures 11.1 and 11.2 reveals two insights. First, fewer people perceive a supply of vertical accountability than the (already low) proportion who demand it (15 versus 34 percent). And, second, there is a systematic inverse relationship between demand and supply of vertical accountability at the country level.[24] For example, Namibians and Mozambicans are very unlikely to say they *want* accountability, and also much more likely to report that they are *getting* it. In these places, low popular expectations are more easily satisfied. By contrast, Malawians and Zimbabweans insist that they *want* leaders to be beholden to citizens, but they do not report *getting* much responsive service. In these settings, widespread popular demands are routinely frustrated.

Africans also doubt that politicians "do their best to deliver develop-

Figure 11.2 Perceived Supply of Vertical Accountability Credibility of Campaign Promises by Politicians, 2005–2006

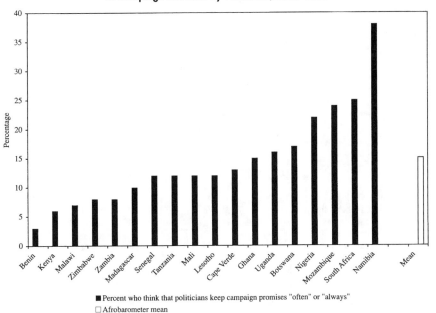

■ Percent who think that politicians keep campaign promises "often" or "always"
□ Afrobarometer mean

ment after elections." Instead, people commonly complain that candidates for office make grandiose guarantees of social and economic investments that are never subsequently fulfilled. The distribution of this attitude closely mirrors opinion about campaign promises.[25] Accordingly, we calculate an average construct of these two items that we call "the perceived supply of vertical accountability" to serve as the object of explanation.

What accounts for the generally low levels of this indicator in sub-Saharan Africa? In particular, why are most Africans getting less accountability than they say they want? We again use regression analysis, this time to test social and contextual predictors, as well as a variety of evaluations of system and leadership performance. Detailed results are shown in Table 11.2.

We note again the almost total absence of a demographic story. When country effects are accounted for (Table 11.2, Model 3), only wealth has a significant—and again very small—effect on assessments of the supply of vertical accountability. Neither gender, education, age, rural residence, nor employment status helps to discern whether people see themselves as supplied with accountability. For all intents and purposes, every segment of society sees itself as supplied—or, more commonly, *under*supplied—to a roughly equal extent.

Table 11.2 Perceived Supply of Vertical Accountability, Explanatory Factors Compared

	Model 3			Model 4		
	B	Beta	Adj. Block R Square	B	Beta	Adj. Block R Square
Constant	.394			(0.920)		
Social Characteristics			.006			.006
Rural	−.005	−.003		−.008	−.005	
Female	.018	.012		.024	.015	
Age	.000	.006		.000	−.009	
Employment status	.016	.010		.042[a]	.027	
Education	.007	.017		.020[a]	.052	
Wealth	.016[a]	.028		.014	.024	
Performance Evaluations			.106			.106
Political leaders do listen	.114[a]	.135		.115[a]	.137	
Think elections work	.075[a]	.118		.070[a]	.110	
Enforcement gap:						
Rule of law	−.043[a]	−.093		−.058[a]	−.125	
Performance gap:						
Legislator service	−.042[a]	−.072		−.057[a]	−.097	
Trust representative						
institutions	.043[a]	.076		.032[a]	.057	
Perceive corruption	−.050[a]	−.054		−.038[a]	−.041	
Country Contexts			.068			
Nigeria	.379[a]	.149				
Namibia	.455[a]	.137				
South Africa	.257[a]	.094				
Mozambique	.336[a]	.083				
Uganda	.130[a]	.056				
Zambia	.166[a]	.047				
Madagascar	.108[a]	.034				
Botswana	−.119[a]	−.035				
Malawi	−.203[a]	−.057				
Institutional Legacies						.016
Years of independence				−.008[a]	−.114	
Past presidential rule				.001[a]	.045	
Liberation movement				.006	.280	
Plurality electoral system				.008	.005	
Adjusted R square	.158			.123		

Notes: For country dummies in Model 3, Kenya is the excluded category. Only countries for which B is significant at $p = < .001$ are shown.

　　a. $p = < .001$.

Instead, performance evaluations now loom large. Even when controlled for country contexts or institutional legacies, these assessments lie at the heart of how people evaluate whether their leaders are accountable.

　　First, from a popular perspective, an accountable leader is seen primarily as one who listens carefully to constituents. The most important determinant of the supply of accountability is the evaluation of political responsiveness, or the extent to which citizens think elected representatives actually "listen." The interviewers asked, "How much of the time do you think MPs try their best to listen to what people like you have to say?" Again, local leaders fare slightly better than national leaders: 62 percent think local councilors listen at least "sometimes," compared to 54 percent for national legislators. But, importantly, only about one-quarter of all adults think that either set of leaders listen "often" or "always."

Confidence in the effectiveness of elections also matters. As reported earlier, less than half of all Afrobarometer respondents think that elections work well at replacing unresponsive leaders and ensuring that popular preferences are aired in parliament.[26] But those who "think elections work" are significantly more likely to believe that they are being supplied with accountable governance. That result helps to confirm the centrality of elections to any popular conception of vertical accountability, including in Africa.

The next most important consideration is whether people think leaders get special treatment under the law. The survey asks, "How likely do you think it would be that the authorities could enforce the law if a top official: a) committed a serious crime; or b) did not pay tax on some of the income they earned?" The same questions were then asked about the likelihood of law enforcement if "a person like you" committed these offenses. The "enforcement gap" is wide. For example, 90 percent think that ordinary citizens would be punished for committing a serious crime, but only 53 percent think that a top official would receive the same treatment.[27] The uneven application of the rule of law is another leading factor that explains the perceived supply of accountability: if citizens think that leaders benefit from a culture of impunity, then they doubt that vertical accountability is being supplied.

Leadership performance between elections is also important. In this case, we probe whether legislative representatives actually perform constituency service with the intensity expected by citizens. The survey asks two related questions: "How much time *should* your MP spend in this constituency?" and "How much time *does* your MP spend?" The "performance gap" between these two estimates is again wide. For example, 33 percent of Africans interviewed want their legislative representative to visit the community at least weekly, whereas only 8 percent report that he or she actually does so.[28] The performance gap on legislator service is a solid, negative predictor: the larger the gap between expectation and delivery, the less the general public thinks it is being supplied with vertical accountability. The clear implication is that leaders must be present and visible in the locality for citizens to consider that they are being served.

Finally, there are two other important considerations, though they pull in opposite directions. On the positive side, citizens who trust representative institutions (the national assembly and local government council) are more likely to perceive accountable governance. But on the negative side, citizens who see corruption among assembly and council representatives are less likely to think they are being supplied with accountability (Githongo 2006). As expected, institutional trust and perceptions of official corruption are inversely related.[29]

Before we settle on a conclusion that political attitudes and performance evaluations are the primary factor explaining the supply of vertical accountability, it is necessary to confirm that these evaluations are not trumped by institutional legacies. We find that "country effects" are again significant (Table 11.2, Model 3). A familiar pattern emerges: Nigerians, along with Namibians, South Africans, and Mozambicans, think they are getting more accountability than the average African, whereas Malawians think they are getting less.[30]

But are these "country effects" really institutional legacies (Table 11.2, Model 4)? In this case, years of independence actually have a negative effect on the perceived supply of vertical accountability. Perhaps, even as demand for accountability goes up over time, the supply goes down. However, we instead interpret that to mean that citizens more readily give elected representatives the benefit of the doubt in newly liberated countries: popular expectations are lower than in other countries, so (relative) evaluations of supply are higher.[31] Consistent with our earlier argument, citizens have not yet learned—either because insufficient time has passed, or because representatives are so far doing a good enough job—that, in the long run, leaders are rarely effective at holding themselves to account. Likewise, years of "past presidential rule" once again partially counteracts the effects of years of independence. The effects of this factor on perceived supply of accountability are positive, suggesting that individuals who spent many years living under systems of centralized, repressive rule are likely to be less critical than those who have lived in more open and competitive societies.

Importantly, however, neither country context nor institutional legacies displace an explanation based mainly on political attitudes and performance evaluations.[32] We get considerably more explanatory mileage from a set of performance evaluations—especially whether citizens think that leaders listen to constituents, think that elections are effective, and subject themselves to a rule of law—than from shared institutional histories. This is just as well for purposes of devising policies to improve vertical accountability. After all, institutional histories can hardly be changed. But elite behaviors (like failing to listen to constituents or attempting to evade the law) are prospectively subject to at least a measure of reengineering. Thus, in the final section below, we make use of the previous analysis to suggest a smart approach to development policy to boost accountability.

Conclusion: Beyond Unclaimed Democracy?

In this chapter we have explored the stance of ordinary Africans in relation to their attitudes toward accountability and the choice between delegative and representative forms of democracy, with a view to assessing the implications for the provision of development assistance to Africa. At first glance, the concept of delegative democracy would seem to travel well: there is an apparent affinity between O'Donnell's image of unrestrained presidential government in Latin America and the continued dominance, even after democratic transitions, of Africa's political big men. We found evidence that a substantial proportion of Africans seem to prefer a delegative model of governance to a representative one: one-third of the electorate wants the *president* to hold legislators accountable.

Yet the evidence also requires that the delegative model be adjusted to African circumstances. First, an equal proportion of the electorate thinks that *voters—not* the president—should be responsible for holding leaders accountable. Second, large majorities in every country firmly oppose the notion of one-man rule in which the president decides everything. And, perhaps most tellingly, two out of three Africans interviewed say that, at least in principle, the legislature and the courts should limit the decisionmaking power of the political chief executive. In this regard, ordinary Africans reject a key tenet of delegative democracy, namely that the president should be unrestrained by horizontal checks.

In reality, however, the legislative and judicial branches of government remain weak in Africa and usually prove ineffective in the face of presidential power. We therefore paid particular attention to vertical accountability, both as a mode of direct popular control of elected leaders and as an essential complement to the strengthening of horizontal agencies of restraint. We expanded the definition of vertical accountability beyond the common references in the literature to periodic elections, or even to the watchdog functions of organized civil society. Putting a spotlight on individual Africans in the periods between elections, we asked instead whether ordinary people demand vertical accountability from elected representatives, and whether they think such accountability is actually supplied.

Across virtually all social and attitudinal groups, we found low effective demand for representatives to do their jobs between elections. In short, we discern a vacuum in African politics in the arena where pressures for representative democracy are expected to originate, that is, at the mass level where individual citizens *claim their right* to monitor leaders. In newly minted democracies, especially in countries without previous experience of indigenous dictatorship, people tend to absolve representatives of the responsibility of reporting back to the grassroots communities, and instead defer to the authority of big men. Moreover, since people broadly agree that the promises of politicians lack credibility, we found even lower perceived levels of a supply of accountability. Which few leaders are deemed accountable? Only those who have developed a reputation for listening to the needs of constituents and of subjecting themselves to equal treatment under the rule of law.

What implications does limited vertical accountability hold for democratization? Africans clearly value open and competitive elections and vote in large numbers. In this role, they undoubtedly help to underpin fragile new electoral democracies in Africa. But elections are hardly inconsistent with delegative democracy; indeed, elections are the very device by which delegation of authority occurs from people to president. A more rigorous test is whether Africans demand—and think they receive—vertical accountability in the long intervals between elections. To do so, Africans would have to assert citizenship rights more regularly and vigorously than the survey evidence so far reveals. In the absence of a popular groundswell in this direction, we cannot describe African political regimes as representative democracies.

Are African regimes therefore best regarded as being delegative democracies? Not necessarily. The term "delegative" suggests a degree of agency on the part of individual members of society that may be misleading. Coming out from under the shadow of authoritarian pasts, Africans may not so much be intentionally delegating power to their governments, as failing to claim it from them. Whether unwilling, unable, or simply unaware, many Africans have hesitated to take advantage of the rights and opportunities—along with the accompanying responsibilities—that are meant to be theirs in a liberalized political world. They have adopted the attitudes of voters who show strong support for the electoral process but have yet to transform themselves into citizens who take on the added responsibility of monitoring and, where possible, sanctioning their leaders in the long intervals between elections. Too many ordinary people instead assume that the head of state (or, to a lesser extent, other arms of the government and the political system) will somehow perform the role of holding elected representatives to account. Thus, to the extent that democracy is supposed to mean "power to the people" and not just "a vote to the people," democracy in Africa remains largely unclaimed. Under such circumstances, government accountability to African publics remains weak, and the effectiveness of government handling of public resources—including donor resources—is likely to continue to disappoint Africans publics and international donors alike.

What, then, is to be done? Like others in this volume, we have argued that accountability to donors is a poor—perhaps even destructive—substitute for the accountability to domestic forces that democracy is supposed to engender. Yet accountability is also critical to the smarter, more effective use of donor resources. Can donors therefore help Africans themselves to become rights-demanding citizens? Despite the residual influence of historical legacies, there remains considerable room for popular political learning. As

Jean Ensminger (1997) has aptly observed, "African social norms and informal institutions are currently a rapidly moving target" (p. 175).

Our analysis in this chapter suggests that in their efforts to foster mechanisms of vertical accountability in support of a smart aid approach, donors might therefore consider the following:

- Start locally. People seek—and secure—accountable representation more readily through local government channels than via the national parliament. Among other things, it suggests support for programs of administrative decentralization that transfer authority over local affairs not only to locally elected officials but to citizens themselves.
- Promote transparency and access to information. Political knowledge, especially about government budgets and expenditures, is a first step in enhancing mechanisms of vertical accountability. Require recipient governments to make information about donor-funded policies and programs public, especially at the local level. Pressure legislators to pass, and administrators to enforce, freedom of information laws. Support processes of public budgeting, which can engage the public while reducing the diversion of public funds.[33]
- Give voice to citizens. Africa's emerging citizenry is still in the process of finding its voice, a process that would benefit from expansion of the venues and opportunities for that voice to be heard. Support public opinion surveys, which offer essential benchmarks for assessing leadership performance, rating the quality of democracy, and measuring progress toward reaching development goals. Publicize their findings and make use of them in planning. Continue to insist on popular input into public policy processes. Promote development of mechanisms for public action and outlets for complaints, such as ombudsmens' offices, recall provisions in electoral laws, and public hearing processes.
- Encourage representatives to engage with their constituents. Another path for citizen voice is through elected representatives, but the relationship between elected representatives and their constituents remains a distant one for most Africans. Consider providing incentives for greater engagement between elected representatives and their constituents, such as by enabling community groups to organize "meet the representative" forums or initiating report cards that track and publicize the constituency service of every elected representative.
- Fight corruption and legal inequality. Popular perceptions about the extent of corruption and legal inequality play an important role in assessments of the supply of accountability. Encourage citizen engagement in the fight against corruption via watchdog groups and public budgeting processes. Support protections for whistleblowers. Support local efforts to track outcomes for official law breakers.

• Build on elections. Since Africans value their rights as voters, use elections as vehicles for publicizing the broader rights and responsibilities of citizenship. Expand voter education campaigns into civic education programs. Support citizen groups to monitor not only elections, but the post-electoral performance of elected representatives.

• Above all, do no harm. Purge aid programs of requirements that cause governments to concentrate more on accountability to foreign agencies than to their own citizens. Donors should employ political conditionalities mainly in conjunction with enhanced efforts to strengthen the capacity of local individuals, groups, and institutions to make such demands for themselves.

For all these recommended actions, the key actors are African citizens. After all, the choice about whether to leave unclaimed one's share of political authority, or to assert one's political rights, is the individual's alone. Ultimately the international community can do more for improving the quality of democracy not by demanding accountability themselves, but by fostering demands for it from within society. Only internal, vertical accountability imposed by an active and engaged citizenry can provide a truly secure foundation for an effective and lasting democracy, and for a sustainable program of social and economic development. In the final analysis, only citizens—and not external agencies—can guarantee representative democracy.

Notes

An earlier version of this chapter can be found on the Afrobarometer website, www.afrobarometer.org.

1. Transparency International, Corruption Perceptions Index 2005, www.transparency.org/policy_research/surveys_indices/cpi/2005.

2. See also Chapter 1 by Alexandra Gillies and Richard Joseph and Chapter 2 by Paolo de Renzio in this volume.

3. Goetz also suggests that the goals of accountability are also expanding, not just to encompass procedural concerns with process integrity but also to incorporate a new outcomes-based objective of social justice as well (p. 5).

4. See, for example, Frederic Schaffer's (1998) excellent analysis of Senegalese society. He highlights the importance of "how local populations understand their own actions" (p. 7) and finds that, in Senegal, people vote for reasons of community solidarity or for personal gain, rather than to influence public policy or ensure accountability. He also argues that the very notion of public accountability must be questioned in Senegalese society, where many people have a weak sense of a "national good" that politicians should be expected to pursue or of themselves as individuals with democratic rights in the national arena.

5. Benin, Botswana, Cape Verde, Ghana, Kenya, Lesotho, Madagascar, Malawi, Mali, Mozambique, Namibia, Nigeria, Senegal, South Africa, Tanzania, Uganda, Zambia, and Zimbabwe.

6. The large size of the pooled sample means that measures of association eas-

ily qualify as statistically significant at conventional levels of 0.05 or even 0.01. We therefore use a more rigorous standard for the pooled data by reporting significance only at p = < 0.001.

7. For more information on the Afrobarometer, visit the website at www.afro barometer.org.

8. Pearson's r = 0.711, p = < 0.001.

9. Cronbach's Alpha = 0.830.

10. 1 = "think president is responsible for holding elected representatives accountable"; 2 = "think elected representatives will hold themselves accountable" (plus "don't know"); 3 = "think voters are responsible."

11. The regression method is ordinary least squares. Only those predictors that are significant at p = <.001 are indicated.

12. With a block R-squared of just 0.007, social characteristics explain less than 1 percent of the variability in demand for vertical accountability.

13. Wealth is measured on an additive scale (0–6) of the number of personal assets owned among a book, radio, television, bicycle, motorcycle, and motor vehicle.

14. A construct of expressed interest in politics and regular discussion of public affairs.

15. This consists of two separate indicators of comprehending government and feeling that others listen to you.

16. Although it should be noted that both "questioning leaders" and believing that "leaders should listen" do become significant at p = <0.001, when country contexts are replaced with institutional legacies in Model 2.

17. "Know political leaders" is a construct of these two related items (Cronbach's Alpha = 0.556).

18. "Perceive corruption" is a construct of items tapping the reputations for corruption of national legislators and local government councilors. Note, however, that the experience of corruption (actually paying a bribe) is not significant (and the sign is negative).

19. All told, attitudinal factors explain just 6 percent of the variability in demand for vertical accountability.

20. Across eighteen countries, the proportion of Tanzanians who demand accountability to voters most closely matches the Afrobarometer mean (31 percent for *both* legislators *and* councilors). Thus, for the purpose of the analysis in Model 1, which is based on country dummy variables, Tanzania is the excluded reference category.

21. Indeed, a model that includes only country effects is very nearly as effective in explaining demand for vertical accountability as a more comprehensive model that also includes social and attitudinal factors. A model with country dummies alone explains 16 percent of the variance. Thus, cumulatively, social and attitudinal variables add just 2 percent to explained variance.

22. The adjusted R square for Model 2 using common historical and institutional factors is just 0.103, compared to 0.183 for the model testing country effects.

23. The remaining two systems—in Lesotho and Senegal—are mixed, but are grouped with the proportional representation systems that they more closely resemble for the purposes of this analysis.

24. With aggregated data (n = 18 countries), wanting accountability and getting it are strongly correlated (r = –0.690). At the individual level, however, the relationship is negative and significant, but it is hardly strong (r = –0.084).

25. Pearson's r = 0.634, p = <0.001, Cronbach's Alpha = 0.776.

26. Because these outcomes are seen to go together (Pearson's r = 0.559, p =

<0.001, Cronbach's Alpha = 0.717), we construct a single indicator of whether people "think elections work."

27. Because expectations for both crimes are correlated, average expectation scores are generated for leaders (Pearson's r = 0.805, Cronbach's Alpha = 0.892) and "person(s) like you" (Pearson's r = 0.646, Cronbach's Alpha = 0.784). The "enforcement gap" is calculated by subtracting the leaders' score from the citizens' score.

28. The "performance gap" is calculated for each respondent by subtracting the "does visit" score from the "should visit" score on a 5-point scale from "never" to "all of the time."

29. Pearson's r = –0.377, p = <0.001.

30. On the supply side, the mean (excluded) reference category is Kenya.

31. See the negative sign on "years of independence." Nigeria is an anomaly in this regard, perhaps reflecting the "fresh" democratic start initiated by the founding elections of 1999.

32. Alone, country contexts and institutional legacies explain just 7 percent and 2 percent of variance, respectively.

33. Lessons can be learned from successful pilot projects in this realm, which have reduced the diversion of public funding from primary education in Uganda (World Bank 2004a) and drawn attention to inappropriate budget priorities and funding mechanisms in South Africa (People's Budget Campaign). See http://www.sangoco.org.za/site/index.php?option=content&task=view&id=48&Itemid=48 for a description of this joint initiative of the South African NGO Coalition, the Congress of South African Trade Unions, and the South African Council of Churches.

12

Democratizing Donor–Civil Society Relations: Evidence from Governance Programs in Nigeria

Darren Kew

THE VITAL ROLE of civil society groups in African political development has been well documented and explained, and the 2005 Commission for Africa report clearly envisions these organizations as integral partners in the development enterprise.[1] Fifteen years into the third wave of democratization on the continent, there is widespread agreement that civil society can help improve African governance capacities and democracy in particular. There is little consensus, however, on strategies for donor support of this vital role.

Donor policies in Africa have tended to focus on how civil society activities can advance democratization by influencing the behavior of political elites. It can be argued, however, that civil society's more important governance contribution is its impact on the relationship between elites and the public. Neopatrimonialism—the so-called godfather syndrome that is widely seen as a central governance problem—requires that supporters perceive an upward dependent relationship with their patron and, to some extent, believe in the rightness of this relationship. Over time, civil society activity can help replace this perception with a democratic social contract, in which supporters believe that elites owe their positions to the mandate given by their constituents. In exchange for power, elites must deliver public goods with the required good governance.

Specific civil society activities can affect policy outcomes and the institutional development of the state, but the *experience* of these activities can inculcate political norms in individuals involved in them. This kind of experiential learning is how political culture changes over time, weakening the dominance of neopatrimonialism in favor of the democratic social contract.

Democratically structured civil society groups can provide this experience and therefore inculcate democratic values most effectively.

Rather than promoting the democratic social contract, however, donor–civil society relationships in Africa are often reminiscent of neopatrimonialism, so donors may inadvertently reinforce neopatrimonial patterns. Donors and their Western "implementing partners" usually play commanding roles in setting the strategic agendas for their African civil society partners, as well as making major programming decisions. Donors need to consider not only the substantive governance issues—such as transparency, accountability, and civil society access—but also the *ways* in which they make decisions and give their support and how those can influence political culture patterns in Africa. Democratizing donor-recipient relationships can therefore support patterns of governance within civil society that facilitate a shift of political culture away from neopatrimonialism.

Civil Society and the Transformation of Neopatrimonial Governance

A leading explanation of why many African governments have resisted broad-based democratization is the persistence of neopatrimonialism. Although some authors argue that neopatrimonialism does not apply to all African cases (Rwanda, for instance), the neopatrimonial pattern is clearly evident across much of the continent.[2] Neopatrimonialism posits that the centralization of political and economic opportunity in Africa creates an environment in which individuals in power develop strong hierarchical loyalty networks fueled by resources and patronage from government coffers:

> The essence of neopatrimonialism is the award by public officials of personal favors, both within the state (notably public sector jobs) and in society (for instance, licenses, contracts, and projects). In return for material rewards, clients mobilize political support and refer all decisions upward as a mark of deference to patrons. (Bratton and van de Walle 1994, p. 458)

These neopatrimonial networks are built on older patterns of political organization, typically in the prebendal fashion in which power holders channel jobs and largesse to people of similar ethnoreligious groups in order to bolster their position and create a support network of loyal clients for the power holder (Joseph 1987).

In countries across Africa, many "big men" who control these networks have expanded them beyond their ethnoreligious bases to include clients from a variety of identity groups. As neopatrimonial networks grow more diverse, money and patronage can rival or eclipse identity factors as the driving forces in their construction, particularly among their elite members.

Power and loyalty then depend increasingly upon "cash and carry" principles of simple clientelism, and the political subcultures of the networks become characterized more by individual cost-benefit calculations and personal greed than by the group logic of ethnoreligious interests.

The neopatrimonial contract between the big man and his supporters is based on a shared understanding of these relationships. In this hierarchical arrangement, legitimacy and power flow from the top down, and both patron and client typically presume that these privileges are inherent and proper. Personal relationships give the neopatrimonial network its structure and delineate the limits of big man authority: their decisions are generally unquestioned within the reach of the network. Big men, in turn, demand absolute loyalty and often require regular demonstrations of trustworthiness from subordinates.

Democratic societies also establish hierarchies, but they are built upon different values and assumptions. Table 12.1 contrasts the basic elements of the neopatrimonial contract between big men and subordinates with the democratic social contract between democratic leaders and supporters.

The political culture of neopatrimonial networks can hollow out newly democratized states by subverting and thwarting the transparent, law-based, and publicly accountable patterns of political behavior that democratic institutions need in order to function well. Social anthropologists and psychologists have long argued that every social "container," or group, has its own culture: the common created and learned experience of a group of individuals (Avruch 1998, pp. 17–18; see also Tajfel and Turner 1986). Culture is the shared memory of a group, disproportionately inculcated into each member,

Table 12.1 Terms of the Neopatrimonial and Democratic Social Contracts

	Neopatrimonialism	Democracy
Legitimacy derives from	Position of power	Voters' mandate via elections
Structure relationships by	Strength of acquaintance, personal trust	Law
Means of decisionmaking	Executive fiat, top-down; secretive process	Votes, or executive authority exercised through consultative process and checks; transparent process
Subordinate is ultimately accountable to	Patron	Public
Superior gives to subordinate	Money, government patronage, personal favors	Broad-based policies, access, and observance of rights
Subordinate gives to superior	Loyalty, services rendered	Votes, selective policy support, obedience to law and system
Political change through	Coup, collapse, or ascendance of a rival network	Vote for alternative candidate/policy, or run for office

amended with new experiences, and passed on to new members over time. Consequently, states, ethnic groups, religious organizations, civil society groups, neopatrimonial networks, and businesses all have their associated cultures, which typically overlap to some extent. As individuals move between different social organizations, they take their cultures with them and are also exposed to new cultures.

Civil society groups, as social organizations, contain their own political cultures and contribute to the marketplace of values that makes up a national political culture. Consequently, the political cultures of civil society groups may compete with those of neopatrimonial networks to gain prevalence within the national political culture. Alternatively, the two profiles may overlap, such that the political cultures of neopatrimonial networks and civil society groups reinforce one another.

In short, what Alexis de Tocqueville taught us long ago (Tocqueville 1956, p. 205) is present in Africa today: civil society groups are the classrooms of democracy, imparting norms of democratic political culture (the democratic social contract) to their members and expanding these norms throughout the polity. Some organizations serve as better classrooms than others. My study (Kew 2008) of over sixty civil society groups in Nigeria indicates that the ones that inculcate democratic values most deeply among their members, and the ones that spread these norms most effectively across the larger polity, are themselves *structured democratically*. The primary gauge of a democratic structure in a civil society group is whether its executive is elected by group members.

Members of democratically structured organizations gain democratic experience when they engage in the group's activities, such as electing officials, debating policy, or reviewing the actions of the organization's elected officers. In addition, the study showed that democratically structured civil society groups form more durable coalitions with other organizations, stay committed to democracy promotion longer, and bridge ethnic divides more effectively than nondemocratic groups. Moreover, democratically structured groups are less inclined to opportunism in seeking donor assistance, because the pressure to deliver on constituent interests keeps elected organizational leaders focused on these concerns and accountable for their results.

Consequently, democratically structured civil society groups help challenge the prevalence of neopatrimonial political culture within a polity and, in time, undermine neopatrimonial networks by raising democratic expectations among subordinates regarding the elites. Undemocratically structured groups, which advocate democracy and democratic values, can also work against neopatrimonial culture, but overall they are less effective in doing so than their democratically structured counterparts. Undemocratically structured groups also tend to see their organizational cultures come to reflect their organizational structures over time, with their cultures growing less democratic both in their internal workings and in their external politics (Kew 2008).

Civil Society on the Donor Agenda

Along with internal structure, the democratic nature of civil society's relations with donors also contributes to their effectiveness in combating neopatrimonialism and building democracy at the national level. Donors have turned to African civil society groups over the last fifteen years out of frustration with the slow pace of change or ambivalent attitudes of African governments toward democratization, and from a belief in the important role that civil society groups can play in the process (Robinson 1994). The persistence of "electoral democracies" (Diamond 1999a, pp. 8–10) across the continent, which exhibit the outer trappings of democracy without deep commitment to its substance, led donors to seek alternatives to direct government assistance. Consequently, donors approached African civil society groups with high expectations of what they could accomplish. With models from Eastern Europe and Latin America in mind, Western government donors set high goals for recipients of their aid: regime change where authoritarian governments remained in power and democratic consolidation where they did not.

During the 1990s, these expectations were largely unmet, and donors grew increasingly ambivalent about the impact of civil society groups on governance. These groups have in fact made progress on a range of governance concerns, but overall donors seem dissatisfied with the results. Donors have set more realistic goals since the late 1990s, but several dilemmas constrain their support for civil society governance work.

Ambivalence Toward Capacity Building and Partnership

The poor capacities of African civil society groups have become a fundamental concern for Western donors, and many groups do indeed lack a range of basic resources, institutional capacity (such as accounting), and professional skills in their areas of work. Nonetheless, in regard to civil society activities to support democracy, governance, and development, Africa now enjoys extensive local capacity, not just in terms of academic analysis or political knowledge, but also technical expertise in advocacy, management, and strategy.

Donors have been reluctant to trust this growing local capacity with full partnerships in which African organizations enjoy relatively equal decision-making powers and joint strategic control over project development and implementation. They have also grown less willing to support African civil society capacity-building needs such as infrastructure and salaries, preferring instead to fund specific projects on a contractual basis. This targeting of aid has shifted strategic control of programming to the donors, who identify priority issues and benchmarks for review, while local groups are responsible for daily operations. Rather than providing general funding for democracy and governance and allowing African civil society groups to decide what the priority issues are, donors may decide that transparency, accountability, and anticorruption are key governance issues and set targets within those areas for civil society groups to achieve.

Fears of Politicization

Civil society can help counter the power of the state, check its abuses, and expose corruption. Donors are usually supportive of these roles in theory— take the US Agency for International Development's (USAID's) "transformational development," for instance.[3] In practice, their support is restrained by concerns about being accused of meddling by African governments. Groups are often encouraged to promote reform but not to rock the boat. Donor government interest in protecting their relations with friendly African governments inhibits their support of civil society political activities that may be at odds with the politics of governing parties.

The Nigerian Labor Congress (NLC), for instance, has since 2000 received assistance for internal reform and skills development from a number of sources, including USAID. Since the NLC has become a leading opposition movement in Nigeria, however, USAID and other donors have grown reluctant to involve unions too centrally in their civil society programming. Donors also find it politically difficult to support civil society activities related to opposition parties, crucial actors in successful democratization processes. Viable opposition movements are in fact the pivotal element that distinguishes Africa's governance success stories from the continent's marginal or failed states (Kew 2005).

Local or National Focus

Donors have struggled with the difficult choice of focusing either on local, smaller, and more rural civil society organizations or the larger national ones that seek to affect national policies. A focus on local civil society can lead to relations with the base of the political pyramid and have an influence on individual lives in a more direct and dramatic way than national initiatives, but it is extremely labor-intensive and financially draining and requires long-term commitment. Support for nationally oriented civil society groups can affect national policy, but such successes can be few and far between. Moreover, national civil society groups are generally larger and stronger, requiring higher levels of assistance and thus making them less amenable to donor priorities. The question of focusing locally or nationally has been particularly problematic in the large African states and where tightening aid budgets have forced difficult policy choices.

Market Forces and Civil Society Opportunism

Donors have long known that they create markets that entrepreneurs will seek to capture, but they have had difficulty preventing such entrepreneurialism from undermining civil society's impact on local political development. The negative impacts of such opportunism include the award of funds to organizations skilled in self-promotion but without adequate specialization or long-term commitment to the issues at hand and the rise of catch-all nongovernmental organizations (NGOs) that promise action in several areas (such as human rights, conflict resolution, the fight against corruption, and HIV/AIDS) but may not have expertise in all of these. These factors work against organizations that are less agile in their marketing but have more expertise in specific issue areas or greater ability to make change in targeted communities.

A Preference for NGOs

Donors have also shown a general preference for working with NGOs—the smaller professional organizations that address issues relating to human rights, conflict resolution, local economic development, or health—as opposed to other sectors of civil society, such as business associations, trade unions, student and academic unions, professional associations, community and ethnic associations, and traditional institutions. NGOs generally speak the same language as donors, are professionally conversant on topical issues, and understand donor policies and practices. Their smaller size often adds to their adaptability and responsiveness to donor concerns.

Other civil society groups are typically larger than NGOs, more bureaucratic, less amenable to donor policy direction, and more steeped in corruption. Yet the larger ones in particular tend to be more representative of constituencies across countries and can deliver greater political leverage and enjoy wider political legitimacy than many NGOs.

Current Donor Strategy for Civil Society Democracy and Governance Activities

Related to the above dilemmas are three recurring themes that structure the relationships between donors and civil society groups in the conduct of democracy promotion in Africa.

- Staffing limits. Governmental and private donors often have limited staff to manage democracy and governance funding in Africa. Given the relative strength of their currencies in comparison to those of Africa in a context of widespread poverty, a small amount of donor funds can go a long way in African civil society. For donors, however, management of small grants can be very labor-intensive.
- Control. Government-based donors typically expect civil society aid recipients to respond to their foreign policy goals and undertake actions to serve those ends upon request. USAID is particularly frank in this regard, but other Western donors also exert leverage over their grantees. Private donors, such as the Ford Foundation, are usually less inclined to control the policies of their grantees, but some private donors do occasionally exercise influence on issues of particular interest.
- Timely results and accounting needs. Donors typically demand regular demonstrations of progress toward the goals for which grants have been provided. Government donors often insist on seeing speedy political returns on their investments in order to demonstrate progress to impatient legislatures. USAID, in particular, faces pressure annually from the US Congress to show tangible results in extending democracy in Africa. Private donors frequently permit longer timelines, but they must also demonstrate results to their boards and other stakeholders. In addition, donors have concerns over the ability of African civil society grantees to meet their accounting requirements.

Donor preferences for staffing, programmatic control, and speedy results can mesh uncomfortably with democracy promotion goals. First and foremost, these concerns lead donors, particularly governmental ones, to be intrusive in dealing with grant recipients. Given their financial strength relative to these recipients in Africa, fundamental decisionmaking functions regarding the strategic direction of projects are at times retained by the donors.

The factors listed above have led governmental donors to delegate management responsibility of in-country programs to implementing partners (IPs)—organizations that implement projects and disburse aid under specific grant programs. USAID in particular turns frequently to Western civil society groups, and businesses in some cases, to serve the IP function. That practice will likely continue because USAID has been particularly impressed with the model's effectiveness in the President's Emergency Plan for AIDS Relief (PEPFAR), which relies heavily on the hierarchical IP model to allocate billions of dollars for HIV/AIDS services and treatment. IPs are often well versed in meeting USAID's accounting needs; they do not usually provoke concerns about capacity as do African partners; and they relieve overstretched democracy and governance offices from making a multitude of small individual grants to African civil society partners. The Western IP typically consumes much of the project budget, since they need new office infrastructure and import expatriate staff that require expensive, Western-standard facilities as well as the time to acclimate to the African political landscape.

The result is a multilevel hierarchical relationship between donors, IPs, and African civil society groups, with donors setting overall strategy and policy direction. Figure 12.1 provides a generic version of this model, in which USAID sits atop a democracy and governance program run by an American IP. The IP then recruits a prominent African NGO to lead the organization and manage NGO coalitions. Coalition members are often trained in such techniques as election monitoring, conflict resolution, policy advocacy and monitoring, and economics and are then tasked to conduct these activities in their respective locales. Coalition members are also asked to support various government lobbying efforts of the lead NGOs.

Figure 12.1 Lead NGO Model

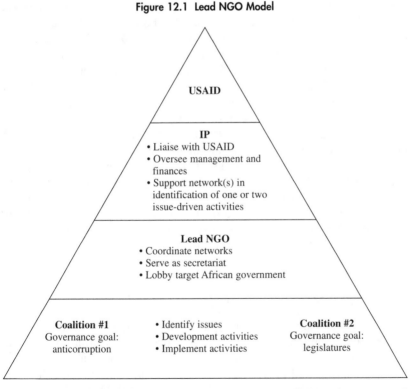

Source: Darren Kew, Jenna Luche, and Dawn Traut, "Nigeria: Civil Society Assessment," USAID report, March 2004.

When donors such as USAID adopt this model, they set the broad policy objectives of the projects and the evaluation criteria by which the coalition(s) and the IP will be judged. The IPs and some civil society groups at times provide input into developing the criteria. Donors retain the right to change the strategic direction of projects midstream, and occasionally do. Coalition partners below the lead NGOs rarely introduce new policy alternatives for consideration by the coalition, and lead NGOs do so only rarely. Once USAID funding expires, IPs often leave the country and coalitions frequently dissolve. Although USAID does not always choose the hierarchical IP model for its democracy and governance programming, it has shown a strong preference for it in recent years. In Nigeria, USAID has chosen to use both IP and non-IP approaches, offering an interesting opportunity for their comparison.

Two Approaches: USAID in Nigeria

USAID undertook an ambitious democracy promotion strategy in Nigeria shortly after the return to civilian rule in 1999. From an initial annual budget of $15 million for democracy and governance in 2000, funding dropped precipitously to roughly $3 million per year by 2004. Consequently, USAID-Nigeria increasingly focused its efforts on priority issues where it could have the most impact. Civil society support emerged as a focus sector as USAID also sought to scale back its direct governmental support in response to increases in Nigerian oil revenues after 2003.

USAID-Nigeria also felt that, relative to other foreign government donors, it had a comparative advantage in this areas thanks to its relationships and experience with Nigerian civil society groups in democracy and governance. USAID had worked with a range of such groups since the time of the Abacha regime (1993–1998), first to help undermine military rule and then to strengthen civil society access after the return to civilian rule in 1999. USAID's Office of Transition Initiatives (OTI) in particular worked closely with Nigerian civil society groups over the 1998–2001 period, funding Nigerian NGOs and other civil society groups directly.

The Transition Monitoring Group

Perhaps the largest and most enduring element of USAID democracy and governance programming in Nigeria is support for election monitoring. Central to this effort has been its support of the Transition Monitoring Group (TMG), a coalition of NGOs originally formed to observe the 1999 elections. Tracing the path of the TMG between the 1999 and 2003 election periods reveals how internal organizational structure and donor-recipient relations can influence civil society's democratic impact.

The formation of TMG was led by Nigeria's top human rights groups from the 1990s, particularly the Civil Liberties Organization, the Constitutional Rights Project (CRP), Community Action for Popular Participation, and others. These NGOs had been prominent in the struggle against military rule and were well-known to USAID at the time. A core group of these leading NGOs formed the TMG as a coalition and then proceeded to recruit partner organizations from across the federation, reaching a total membership of sixty-six by the time of the 1999 elections. The early membership voted that the CRP should house the TMG secretariat, which foisted much of the management and organizing burden on the CRP. USAID-OTI funded the TMG through direct funds to CRP, which then disbursed funds to the rest of the network.

In part because of these heavy management responsibilities, TMG partners decided to create an independent organization in 2001 to house the secretariat. That essentially turned the TMG into an NGO of its own, with the founding organizations sitting on its board of directors and partner groups forming its membership. Problems soon arose as the new executive director charted an independent course for TMG, which included highly publicized attacks on the then chairman of the Independent National Electoral Commission. The board installed a new executive director who oversaw a rise in TMG member groups to over 160, allowing TMG partners to field 15,000 monitors for the 2003 elections. Many TMG affiliates provided vital documentation of the deep flaws in the elections. A number, however, did little on Election Day or, in some cases, were influenced by local political networks (Kew 2004).

Continuing problems with the TMG secretariat and debates over control of funds led its board in effect to end its NGO status and return to its original model of rotating the secretariat among member organizations. It is currently housed with the Lagos-based CLEEN Foundation (Center for Law Enforcement and Education in Nigeria). Control of funds has been a difficult issue from the beginning for the TMG, with partner organizations questioning how lead NGOs or the secretariat have utilized funds.

A number of observations can be made regarding the impact of these organizational changes and USAID's shifting approach. Some TMG members contend that their finances were managed more effectively under the 1999 TMG, with its more democratic structure, which allowed greater discussion and scrutiny of issues than in 2003. They also indicated that TMG policy was subject to greater member participation under the 1999 structure than in 2003.[4]

Another shift took place between 1999 and 2003 as a USAID IP began to assume a greater role in organizing the TMG coalition than did the CRP. The International Human Rights Law Group had initially agreed to implement a transparency and accountability program for USAID, but several months after its launch, USAID requested that the Law Group switch to overseeing the election monitoring work, bogging the IP down in renegotiating the terms of its contract over five months. Once these negotiations were completed, the Law Group was able to secure a trebling of TMG's membership, providing elections and conflict training for most members.

Both USAID's implementing partner and TMG affiliates complained about what they saw as USAID's top-down approach during the 2003 election period. USAID frequently voiced concerns about decisions made by TMG or the Law Group that it felt were too controversial in the eyes of the Nigerian government and at other times would limit communication between itself and its partners. USAID also told its partners to put other work on hold in order to focus on the elections. TMG, for its part, vowed not to accept funding from USAID for the 2007 elections.[5]

The Conflict Resolution Stakeholders Network

While fostering the development of the TMG in 1998–1999, USAID-OTI undertook an additional democracy and governance project to strengthen civil society capacity to advance conflict resolution across Nigeria. Spurred in part by massive religious riots in Kaduna in February 2000, OTI held a conference that month that brought together conflict resolution groups with community-based organizations in order to improve the conflict management capacities of at-risk communities. The assembled groups then decided to form a self-help network.[6]

The result was the formation in 2000 of the Conflict Resolution Stakeholders Network (CRESNET), a network of over 100 Nigerian NGOs engaged in conflict resolution efforts, including both experienced groups and newcomers. Members took the lead in organizing the network, and USAID-OTI was careful not to fund any of the members directly so as to minimize conflicts over finances. OTI instead funded a series of conflict resolution trainings for the network and provided logistics assistance for network meetings. Nonetheless, CRESNET nearly imploded over a dispute among members over regional representation in the leadership of the network. An OTI-brokered compromise enabled CRESNET to resume operations after several months of inaction (Bruton 2002).

As part of an early restructuring, CRESNET developed a zonal structure and democratically elected national leaders, resulting in the election of Kaduna-based SEMA, Ltd. (Strategic Empowerment and Mediation Agency) as its executive director. OTI had insisted on this arrangement, including a CRESNET constitution, in order to prevent any one organization from monopolizing strategic positions. Some of the founding members favored such arrangements. When OTI ceased operating in Nigeria in late 2001, CRESNET had largely succeeded in organizing its network and conducting trainings of its own members, but it had yet to assume any overarching strategic direction as a coalition, much less undertake actual conflict interventions. A number of member groups did pursue a range of local initiatives on their own.

With OTI gone, USAID-Nigeria developed a new conflict resolution grant program that was intended to help address the continuing capacity needs of CRESNET members. The Institute for Democracy in South Africa (IDASA) was invited to oversee the program as IP in late 2001. IDASA, however, had its own priorities for conflict resolution in Nigeria, and it was soon at odds with the CRESNET leadership. CRESNET's leaders complained that IDASA neglected the network and undertook several conflict resolution projects itself, bringing along a number of Nigerian NGOs to provide assistance rather than playing the supporting role that USAID had intended. CRESNET leaders also accused IDASA of approaching CRESNET members directly, bypassing the secretariat and even "badmouthing" its leaders, while engaging with controversial ethnonationalist groups like the Oduduwa People's Congress (OPC) and the Movement for the Survival of the Ogoni People.[7] IDASA was credited with providing some training assistance, but some member groups complained that, despite ambitious promises, IDASA grants were inadequate to cover the grassroots scope of their conflict resolution strategies and that the IP was too slow and bureaucratic in its approach.

IDASA, for its part, was deeply upset with what it perceived as USAID intrusiveness. Much as it did with the Law Group, USAID abruptly told IDASA in mid-2002 to focus on election conflicts, and five months were lost renegotiating terms of the new arrangements. USAID also expressed displeasure, in part prompted by the US embassy, over IDASA's engagement with the OPC and other ethnonationalist groups. It also objected to IDASA efforts to build bridges with potential conflict-generating groups, including Nigerian security agencies.[8]

CRESNET's primary successes appear to have been the development of the network itself and holding occasional training sessions for its members, although by 2004 they were infrequent. CRESNET members grew disillusioned with the network secretariat, which appears not to have held an election since 2001 even though its constitution calls for elections every two years. One member organization complained that when CRESNET held trainings, only one or two network organizations would be invited, monopolizing the available funds, and the participating organizations would then address the media in the name of the entire network. Increasingly, some members saw CRESNET as a function of the organization holding the network chair, SEMA.[9] By 2005, CRESNET as a network appeared to have become dormant, although the secretariat continues to exist through SEMA. CRESNET's decline can in part be attributed to recurring rivalries over control of funds within the network, and between the network and IDASA. CRESNET leaders felt that the network could do little without funding, and consequently the network did little on its own outside USAID programming.

More fundamental to CRESNET's problems, however, were the structure of the network itself and the hierarchical relationship later established with USAID and its IP, IDASA. Initially, CRESNET had a highly democratic and participatory governance structure, featuring an elected executive and zonal representative bodies that proved capable of managing thorny conflicts among members of the network. Over time, however, these democratic processes in CRESNET were allowed to lapse, and the executive's mandate was not renewed. CRESNET leaders blame IDASA for not releasing the funds that members needed to attend conferences and elections, but other NGO networks have managed elections on shoestring budgets, albeit with difficulty. CRESNET increasingly became essentially a program of its national manager, the director of SEMA, and grew hollow without active member participation. Moreover, with IDASA controlling USAID funds and CRESNET dependent upon this funding, IDASA had strategic control of the relationship, which it used to pursue its priority policies. IDASA, for its part, felt that USAID often exercised undue control over key programmatic decisions.

In regard to both the TMG and CRESNET, a decline in the performance of both civil society coalitions occurred with the exit of USAID-OTI in late 2001 and as USAID-Nigeria shifted to the IP-led governance model. OTI released money directly to Nigerian organizations, but, just as importantly, it insisted that civil society coalitions be structured democratically. Both the OTI and the IP models contended with difficult rivalries and funding disputes among coalition members, and OTI partners were able to negotiate solutions that allowed activity to move forward.

As IPs, IDASA and the Law Group were able to get coalition partners to take part in central activities, such as election monitoring and conflict training, and the Law Group oversaw a large increase in TMG membership. Once funding lapsed, however, activities proved unsustainable for CRESNET, and the TMG became dormant. TMG and CRESNET members, who experienced both the OTI and IP models, as well as many other USAID aid recipients, almost universally prefer OTI's methods, both for its democratic ethos and for its direct and speedy disbursal of funds to Nigerian organizations.

Both coalitions were overwhelmingly dominated by NGOs, many of which were not democratically structured themselves. Unions and religious institutions were absent, as were other sectors of civil society. USAID did have a separate IP-managed program with labor unions that played a role in managing 2003 election-related conflicts in some areas and also cooperated with the TMG to some degree in monitoring the elections.. The deep donor dependency of most Nigerian NGOs makes them less likely to act without funding. Consequently, their networks went dormant or disappeared when

USAID funding ended. In addition, NGOs often lacked the extensive local constituencies of other civil society groups, so they do not face the same pressures to demonstrate progress to constituents, who expect action even in the absence of external funding.

The Implications of Donor–Civil Society Relationships

The manner in which donors structure their relationships with civil society recipients determines the efficacy of their democracy and governance work. As shown with regard to USAID in Nigeria, direct USAID-OTI contact and support for democratic structures in civil society produced more vigorous civil society involvement in democracy and governance work and had a greater political impact. The hierarchical IP model appears particularly problematic; it centralizes funding and control in the hands of a foreign organization, creating a power imbalance between the IP and its local partners that resembles business relationships. The IP sets the terms of the contract, the parameters of which are decided by the donor (USAID in this case). The local partners—typically NGOs—provide a short-term service that ends once the specific terms of the contract are met. Little of the sponsored work continues once the funding dries up, and the partners themselves feel little ownership of the project and its objectives. Local partners walk away with experience in service provision, but not in democratic participation and decisionmaking.

Regardless of its potential efficiency, this donor–civil society relationship replicates key features of neopatrimonialism. First, donors seem to prefer undemocratically structured actors—typically NGOs—that can deliver on specific democracy and governance goals. As discussed above, democratically structured civil society groups are far better than their undemocratic counterparts at promoting a democratic political culture among their members and are more effective at achieving a variety of other democracy promotion goals. Nonetheless, donors presume that these NGOs can "get the job done" fairly quickly and without the slow, cumbersome democratic processes of membership-based groups like trade unions and professional and community associations. Although the Nigerian case suggests otherwise, authoritarian-structured groups are often seen as able to respond directly to donor needs and adapt quickly as these needs change because they do not require the consent of members for specific initiatives. Authoritarian-structured groups can be directly accountable to their funders, since they typically have few active constituents. They are also usually politically weak in comparison to other civil society groups and are thus less capable of seriously scrutinizing or disagreeing with the fundamental goals that donors advocate. Donors generally prefer such groups not because they are weak per se, but because powerful civil society groups can be seen as posing political risks.

USAID support for the powerful Nigerian Labor Congress, a federation of twenty-nine unions across the country, counters these assumptions. The program, run with the American Federation of Labor–Congress of Industrial Organizations Solidarity Center as its IP, emerged only after a long period of relationship building and negotiation. The NLC insisted on being treated as an equal and on deciding the strategic parameters of the programming itself. Interestingly, however, once this relationship was established, the NLC was able to respond quickly to changes that USAID requested. USAID in 2002 asked the NLC to join in election monitoring, much as it did the Law Group and IDASA civil society networks. The NLC negotiated and approved the changes within a week, rather than the five months taken by the Law Group and IDASA.[10]

In addition to preferring to work with undemocratically structured African partner groups, donors also have organized some of their own relationships with African civil society in an undemocratic fashion. Table 12.2 demonstrates how the hierarchical IP model resembles the neopatrimonial contract. Most striking in this regard is that the locus of strategic decisionmaking in this model resides with the donors. Donors solicit partner comments during the strategy development process, but neopatrimonial "big men" also give subordinates some consultation roles. Neither donors nor big men allow their partners to make the final strategic decision. In addition, just as clients are ultimately accountable to their patrons under neopatrimonialism, civil society groups under the hierarchical IP model are primarily

Table 12.2 Neopatrimonial and Hierarchical IP Approaches

	Neopatrimonialism	Donor–Civil Society Relationships Through Hierarchical IP Model
Legitimacy derives from	Position of power	Funding
Structure relationships within the network by	Strength of acquaintance, personal trust	Contracts, but varying role of personal acquaintance in choice of contract partner
Means of decisionmaking	Executive fiat, top-down, secretive process	Donor and IP make primary strategic decisions, with some consultation from African civil society partners; NGO partners themselves often have undemocratic organizational structures
Subordinate is ultimately accountable to	Patron	Funder
Superior gives to subordinate	Money, government patronage, personal favors	Money, some global access, promise of future work for good services rendered
Subordinate gives to superior	Loyalty, services rendered	Services, loyalty
Political change for subordinates through	Coup, collapse, or start a rival network	Some feedback permitted; find another donor or raise local funds (though rarely possible)

accountable to the donors, who give money in exchange for services. What gives the donor the legitimacy to have such a commanding role in this relationship is its control of funds. Deriving authority from financial power in this way is reminiscent of how big man legitimacy depends on their downward distribution of resources.

The parallels between the hierarchical IP model and neopatrimonialism also extend to loyalty. Donors in this arrangement typically demand loyalty from their partners, although not to the same extent as African big men. But disloyal activities on the part of donor partners can often end the relationship. USAID officers in Nigeria often spoke of "our NGOs," and IDASA saw its relationship with USAID nearly terminated in part because of its unwillingness to cease working with ethnic associations that the US embassy felt would offend the Nigerian government.

Donors structure their relationships via contracts, which reflect the democratic ethos of the rule of law. In arranging those contracts, however, they often show preferences for African civil society groups with which they have personal relationships. A number of USAID civil society partners in Nigeria complained that USAID and its IPs "favored friends" in their choices of which organizations were to receive democracy and governance funding, an accusation frequently leveled at other donors, both in Nigeria and across Africa.[11]

Donors often show a willingness to exert their commanding roles in the hierarchical IP relationships by withholding funds and changing the terms of contract as political priorities change. Moreover, the focus on business-style service provision encourages profit motives in partners rather than democratic motives. The flow of cash in the relationship follows the same direction as in neopatrimonial arrangements, although the sources of donor funds are naturally legitimate and the process is more transparent, whereas the big man's funds may have been captured through state rents and both legitimate and illegitimate businesses. Donors occasionally request constructive feedback from African civil society partners. However, in light of the power disparities, providing that feedback can often prove difficult, and criticism may not result in a change of donor strategy.

A Strategy to Support Civil Society

Donors' apparent preferences for hierarchically structured or business-style relationships may have some advantages in terms of service delivery and economic development. The delivery of specific services, however, may in fact strengthen neopatrimonial patterns that plague African governance. Using the hierarchical IP model, donors can finance programs, policies, and training but not necessarily achieve democratic learning. What would a better strategy entail?

Civil society support strategies are typically constructed to impact specific elite behaviors, such as exposing corrupt practices or monitoring elections. If, however, we consider that elite behavior is structured by *relationships* between elites and their broader publics, then assistance for civil society must consider influencing these relationships over time, transforming neopatrimonial contracts into democratic social contracts.

As argued above, the central vehicle for promoting the democratic social contract, and thus democratic political culture, is individual participation in democratic experiences. In order to promote this experience, two general principles should guide donor–civil society practices:

1. Civil society groups that are themselves democratic advance democratic culture and teach the social contract to members far better than their undemocratic counterparts; and
2. Donor–civil society relationships that are democratic offer more democratic experiences to civil society groups (and to donors).

With these principles in mind, donor strategy should first consider whether their civil society partners are themselves democratic. Although some undemocratically structured groups can contribute to political development, those with democratic structures can advance a democratic political culture and help undermine neopatrimonialism. Thus donors should consider encouraging the democratization of their partner organizations and civil society coalitions. The process of coalition building itself can be a vehicle for advancing democratic norms within civil society and the polity at large.

Donors should also consider that civil society extends beyond the NGO sector, which tends to feature undemocratic organizational structures. Democratic structures predominate in a number of other sectors, such as trade unions, academic and student unions, professional associations, community associations, and business associations. Some religious and traditional institutions are also democratically structured and should also be considered in this light.

Beyond their impact on democratic political culture, these sectors of civil society are better able to challenge government actors and build pressure for greater inclusion of public interests on the elite agenda. If civil society is to counter the power of the state and check its abuses, and in so doing help reconnect the African state with its citizens, then donors must turn to the organizations capable of performing this role. The large democratic institutions of the trade unions (which in Nigeria alone claim 5 million members), national women's associations and federations, professional groups like the bar association, and religious institutions and organizations have important roles to play in checking the power of the state. I do not mean to say that NGOs deserve less aid. Rather, civil society should be considered in its entirety, so that a broader array of energies and resources can be brought to the effort to improve governance.

Second, donors can also encourage a democratic political culture and undermine neopatrimonialism by thinking more about the structure of their own relationships with African civil society groups. The more these groups can be included in making decisions about priorities and how aid is spent, the more the aid process will assist in establishing patterns that promote democratic development.

Experience in Nigeria and elsewhere suggests that the hierarchical implementing partner model is particularly problematic. IPs are not, of course, antidemocratic, and they have much to contribute to the struggle for good governance in Africa. The problem resides in the structuring of relationships among USAID, IPs, and African civil society groups in a hierarchical manner that leaves African groups without substantive strategic impact. Without such empowering roles, civil society groups—and donors—gain less democratic experience.

One solution is to remove IPs from the relationship altogether and to fund African civil society groups directly and in a manner that places strategic responsibility for the programming in the hands of African partners. The British Department for International Development has done exactly that, opting to do away with most IPs in their in-country democracy assistance programming. USAID-OTI in Nigeria went further, encouraging civil society partners to develop constitutions for their networks, hold elections for leadership positions, and make strategic decisions for the networks.

Figure 12.2 suggests a second, hybrid alternative to the hierarchical IP approach, an alternative that better reflects the direct assistance approach that USAID-OTI utilized in Nigeria. In this governing council model, the IP is present but has an advisory and administrative role. The IP can be a Western organization if the donor prefers, but an effort should then be made to place it physically within an African democracy think-tank, university, or similar institution with strong political analysis skills. Both the Western IP and the African institution will gain from each other's knowledge, and the African institution will have stronger incentives to remain active even after the IP leaves and the funding ceases.

The Governing Council consists of several civil society groups elected by all the participant civil society groups, and it assumes the primary decisionmaking role. If necessary, the Governing Council could elect a lead organization to act as the secretariat to oversee daily activities, implement Governing Council decisions, and facilitate the work of the network. The IP sits on the Governing Council, votes, and represents the interests of the donor but does not control the process once the network has been established. IPs may play a lead role initially in organizing the network but should relinquish control as soon as democratic structures are put in place. Note that this model

Figure 12.2 Governing Council Model

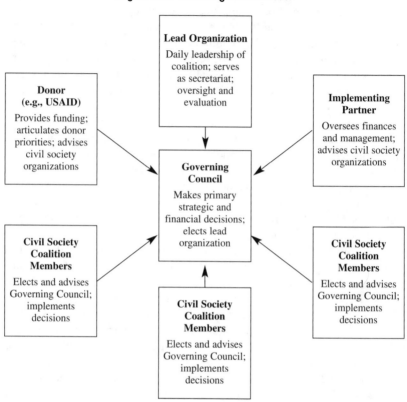

Source: Darren Kew, Jenna Luche, and Dawn Traut, "Nigeria: Civil Society Assessment," USAID report, March 2004.

encourages the involvement of civil society groups beyond NGOs, particularly the large federations of trade unions, women's groups, professional associations, and others.

This model provides democratic experiences for all participants, thus better inculcating democratic values more than the hierarchical IP model, and should achieve greater overall results in civil society democracy promotion. In addition, a growing body of evidence is casting doubt on whether the hierarchical IP model is more efficient in providing services and fulfilling accounting needs than its alternatives. A recent study of PEPFAR funding, for instance, found that nearly half its funds remain in the hands of the IPs themselves (IRIN 2007a); and USAID-Nigeria's democracy and governance IPs consumed similar portions of the available funds. Illustrating the point, member groups of both CRESNET and the TMG felt that coalitions worked more efficiently during the period when USAID-OTI insisted on democratic governing structures without an IP or direct OTI engagement. CRESNET all but disintegrated under the hierarchical IP model, and TMG became largely dormant until donor funds returned in election years.

Donors also need to reconsider their fears of politicization and identify tactics that protect their relationships with African governments while supporting civil society's ability to challenge the state. One avenue that may allow donors to pursue both goals is to channel assistance directly to democratically structured civil society coalitions or indirectly through hybrid models like the Governing Council, in which decisionmaking authority rests with the coalition partners. With civil society groups in the lead, or at least as equal partners, responsibility will also shift to these groups, insulating donors from the ire of African governments to some degree when partner groups try to check the state.

Infusing greater democracy into donor relationships with African civil society groups, and within these groups themselves, can help undermine neopatrimonialism on the continent and improve the democratic impact of civil society overall. African civil society groups, more than donors, should be the correct owners of the African democratic agenda. If donors "walk the talk" of democracy and governance, it will improve the sustainability of the democracy agenda and avoid replicating relationships reminiscent of neopatrimonial networks.

Notes

1. See, for example, Ndegwa (1996); Gyimah-Boadi (2004), chapter 4 ; Diamond (1999a), chapter 6.
2. Peter Uvin, comments on "The State in Africa," Conference on Innovative Approaches, Fletcher School of Law and Diplomacy, Tufts University, April 14, 2006. Cited with permission.
3. See http://www.usaid.gov/our_work/global_partnerships/gda/report2006.html.
4. Interviews with TMG member organizations, January 19–21, 2004.
5. Interview with Innocent Chukwuma, TMG executive director, August 2006.
6. For a review of CRESNET's early years, see Bruton (2002).
7. Interview with CRESNET leaders, Abuja, January 21, 2004.
8. Interview with IDASA leaders, Abuja, January 13, 2004.
9. Interview with a CRESNET member organization, Kaduna, January 21, 2004.
10. Interview with the Solidarity Center, Abuja, January 14, 2004.
11. Interviews with USAID democracy and governance aid recipients, January 19, 2004.

13

Africa After Gleneagles: Overcoming Misrule and Stalled Development

Richard Joseph

B Y 1980 IT WAS RECOGNIZED that development in sub-Saharan Africa had stalled. Despite multiple reforms backed by considerable financial aid, per capita incomes continued to decline. Edward (Kim) Jaycox, World Bank vice president, warned in 1990 that Africa faced further marginalization from the global economy ("Africa" 1990, p. 2). His warning was prescient as Africa registered a 16 percent decline in per capita income between 1980 and 2000 (USAID 2004, p. 4).[1] While world trade and foreign direct investments soared globally, Africa's share continued slumping, amounting to approximately 1.5 percent in both categories by 2003 (Lancaster 2005). Today most Africans are not only poor relative to citizens of other developing areas; they are also poor relative to Africans of earlier decades. Real per capita income in sub-Saharan Africa was 9 percent lower in 1998 than in 1970 (USAID 2004, p. 6). According to one commentator: "Africans are getting poorer not richer. They are living shorter, hungrier lives" (Rice 2005, p. 1). It is estimated that Africans living in poverty could increase from 300 million in 2005 to 400 million by 2015 (Lancaster 2005). To avert such a calamity, the renewed growth of African economies at the start of the new millennium must be sustained and deepened in the face of many internal and external constraints (see Joseph 2008).

Exactly two decades ago, starting in 1988, I was given the opportunity to organize a program at the Carter Center in Atlanta, Georgia, that would address what I believed was the principal reason for Africa's stalled development and persistent poverty: a mode of governance that treated public (and also private) institutions as reservoirs of capital to be extracted and diverted to satisfy the needs of individual officeholders, their kinfolk, and cronies (see Joseph 1987). A document prepared for the inaugural conference of the African Governance Program of the Carter Center in February 1989 expressed hope that an agenda for collaborative research and practical recommendations for policymakers would emerge from our deliberations.[2] The underlying premise of the conference was that "a considerable store of knowledge about the African predicament circulated within the academic community" and that it should be made more widely available. Today, an understanding of the critical link between misrule and stalled development has moved beyond the academic community and is regularly reflected in official policy pronouncements. Mo Ibrahim, who personally funds the African Leadership Prize awarded to African leaders who govern fairly and cede power gracefully to an elected successor, has expressed this consensus: "Unless you rule properly, you cannot move forward. Everything else is second" (Wallis 2008). In gripping detail, Peter Anyang' Nyong'o shows how misrule and corruption have hobbled Kenya. He could have been writing about most African countries.

Despite the wide agreement about the link between misrule and stalled development, we still lack convincing strategies for transforming them. It can be explained in great detail how government and politics in Africa continue to undermine national cohesion, state legitimacy, and economic productivity. Experts and media commentators can identify poorly built roads, crumbling prestige projects, decayed universities and hospitals, and declining food reserves and connect them to the misuse of financial resources and other institutional failings. Yet there are no compelling strategies for generating modes of governance in Africa that would build and sustain key public and private institutions rather than erode them.[3] As Carol Lancaster states in her chapter in this book: "The most complex and difficult problems are those at the heart of the development process in Africa—the functioning (or nonfunctioning) of African institutions." Unless answers are found to this central dilemma—pervasive misrule and weak institutions—sub-Saharan economies will not grow at the rate and in the sustained way needed to lift African peoples out of dire poverty.

An indigenous developmental dynamic in Africa has eluded investigations by many international agencies and academic scholars, not to mention numerous exercises by African governments themselves. Every country in the world that has left the ranks of the underdeveloped in recent decades has fashioned a dynamic that combines the virtues of local institutions and imported technologies. Nowhere has sustainable development occurred simply as a consequence of massive external aid flows. Since colonial rule ended, a few acknowledged developmental states have emerged in Africa, notably Botswana and Mauritius. After the collapse of apartheid in the early 1990s, South Africa experienced improved growth, though not yet at the level needed to dent its high poverty and unemployment rates. During this period, other African countries such as Ghana, Mozambique, Namibia, and

Tanzania also showed signs of recovery. For most of the forty-eight countries of sub-Saharan Africa, however, it has been a tale of slow growth and stagnation interrupted by calamities of one kind or another. Economic growth levels have increased since the turn of the new century, closely associated with the boom in commodity prices. However, productivity increases linked to expanding employment will require the emergence of a more robust institutional culture and law-based governance in both public and private institutions.

Today's global economy rewards agility and predictability. The strength of countries ultimately resides in the strength of their institutions—the capacity to produce public goods, whether to generate profits, serve the public, or both, and to do so predictably and reliably. At the most basic level, governments must be able to build and maintain transportation systems and public utilities, establish capable judiciaries and police services, and efficiently manage monetary and other economic policies. These goals, for the most part, have eluded many African countries. Given the speed of change in the global economy, the reliability and adaptability of a country's public and private institutions have become critical attributes. Despite their abundant natural resources, African countries such as Cameroon, Nigeria, and Kenya cannot join the ranks of middle-income countries without a revolutionary transformation in the governance of their public and private institutions. Cameroon has been caught for a quarter-century in the clutches of a predatory system led by its president, Paul Biya. The promised transformation of governance in Nigeria under Olusegun Obasanjo (1999–2007) fizzled as he undermined the very democratic and economic advances that his government was espousing (see Joseph and Kew 2008). In the case of Kenya, international financial agencies and bilateral donors are deeply implicated in the dramatic failure of that richly endowed country to break the vise of predatory governance: "For too long," it has been argued, "Kenya's foreign donors and strategic allies ignored the corruption, inequities and flawed democracy that together proved such an explosive mix."[4]

Misrule and Stalled Development

Since the late 1980s, several major studies have analyzed the connections between misrule and stalled development and have advanced similar recommendations. A path-setting World Bank report declared:

> Sub-Saharan Africa as a whole has now witnessed almost a decade of falling per capita incomes, increasing hunger, and accelerating ecological degradation. . . . Major efforts are needed to build African capacities. . . . they must go hand-in-hand with good governance. . . . Weak public sector management has resulted in loss-making public enterprises, poor investment

> choices, costly and unreliable infrastructure, price distortions . . . and hence inefficient resource allocation. . . . Even more fundamental in many countries is the deteriorating quality of government, epitomized by bureaucratic obstruction, pervasive rent seeking, weak judicial systems, and arbitrary decision making. (1989, pp. xxi, 1, 3)

The preparation of this report "involved African researchers, private businessmen, and public officials as well as a broad spectrum of the representatives of the donor community" (World Bank 1989, p. xi). Fifteen years later, the British government launched a similar exercise: the Commission for Africa. As Vivian Lowery Derryck discussed in Chapter 4, the commission's key argument is that substantial increases in financial assistance were needed to "jump-start" development in sub-Saharan Africa. In a close study of the commission's report, Africa scholar Nelson Kasfir identified a theoretical gap at the center of its argumentation.[5] The report stated that "governance is at the core" of successful development and identified "the central cause" of Africa's problems to be "weakness in governance and capacity." Nevertheless, the commissioners went on to propose major increases in development assistance without showing how such assistance would avoid reinforcing the very practices responsible for economic stagnation and decline. "They need to explain," Kasfir argued, "why these larger investments will escape the same fate as weak governance in the past" (see Moss and Subramanian 2005; Mistry 2005, p. 667).

Three years before this UK-led initiative, the U.S. government issued an important study, *Foreign Aid in the National Interest,* commissioned by Andrew Natsios, then administrator of the US Agency for International Development. The Natsios report received much less attention than it deserved. It boldly stated:

> No amount of resources transferred or infrastructure built can compensate for—or survive—bad governance. Predatory, corrupt, wasteful, abusive, tyrannical, incompetent governance is the bane of development. Where governance is endemically bad, rulers do not use resources effectively to generate public goods and thus improve productivity and well-being of their society. . . . Unless we improve governance, we cannot foster development. (USAID 2004)[6]

Any "aid" program to Africa that fails, simultaneously, to address this central issue should be challenged on substantive as well as ethical grounds. Two months prior to the July 2005 Gleneagles summit, the Northwestern University conference on "Aid, Governance, and Development in Africa" brought together forty leading African and Africanist researchers. They shared misgivings about the heavy emphasis on massively increasing the volume of aid rather than improving its quality and effectiveness.[7] They criticized the inadequate attention paid to Africa's profound governance and institutional weaknesses and worried that increased inflows of overseas aid, without attention to significant delivery and absorption constraints, would exacerbate these weaknesses. In a study published shortly before the conference, one of the participants, Nicolas van de Walle, expressed skepticism that "a massive infusion of yet more aid will bring about a transformation of these economies" (van de Walle 2005, p. 36). Such arguments have fallen largely on deaf ears in the policy world. On the whole, the participants disagreed with economist Jeffrey Sachs, who regularly minimized, to understandable applause from African leaders, governance deficiencies in his prescriptions for ending African poverty.[8]

Despite these reservations, the G8 summit in Gleneagles, Scotland, capped a remarkable and historic upswing in global attention to Africa. This growing interest was also reflected in the deliberations and recommendations of the previous four G8 summits. The 2001 Genoa summit produced a Plan for Africa that was expanded by subsequent summits in Kananaskis, Canada; Evian, France; and Sea Island, Georgia, United States. Prior to the Kananaskis meeting in June 2002, a series of high-level meetings in Africa had put together a comprehensive reform program and requested $64 billion in financing from rich countries. What initially seemed to be very ambitious proposals, linked to the creation of the New Partnership for Africa's Development (NEPAD) and advanced by global campaigns for debt relief such as Jubilee 2000, have now achieved substantial international acceptance. Even Nigeria, which earned well over $300 billion from oil exports since 1970 and has benefited handsomely from the recent surge in petroleum prices, obtained significant debt cancellation in 2005 (see Chapter 6 of this volume).

As Paolo de Renzio and Vivian Lowery Derryck explained in Chapters 2 and 4, respectively, the Gleneagles summit agreed to double global official development assistance by 2010, an increase of about $50 billion annually. Half of this increase, or $25 billion per year, would go to sub-Saharan Africa. It should not be overlooked that such an increase will follow the doubling in official aid that took place between 1999 and 2003, from $12.7 billion to $23.2 billion annually (Lancaster 2005). When added to the large sums provided for the prevention and treatment of HIV/AIDS and other significant forms of humanitarian assistance such as emergency relief and food aid, sub-Saharan Africa has been promised substantial financial assistance during the first decades of the twenty-first century. Will significantly increased aid improve the environment for development in Africa? Three years after Gleneagles, not only have the rich countries failed to provide the increases in promised aid, but also there is perhaps less confidence that the promise of increased aid will significantly affect the way most African countries are governed. (See the Appendix to this chapter for detailed information on official development assistance by OECD countries in 2007 and projections to 2010; see also Figure 2.1 in Chapter 2.)

Reinforcing those concerns is the post-Gleneagles increases in the size of the loans and credits China is now making available to sub-Saharan Africa, wholly outside the framework of the G8 and other international frameworks. A further complication concerns how much of the aid flows actually stay in Africa. Little progress has been made in stemming the seepage of African public capital overseas. It is believed that 40 percent of Africa's capital wealth is now lodged outside the continent (Lancaster 2005). The World Bank estimates that $90 billion went "out the back door" from Nigeria and Kenya during the 1990s. In the case of Angola, $2 billion a year was quietly disappearing from oil export earnings until an international nongovernmental organization (NGO), Global Witness, raised the alarm (Reed 2005). The African Union puts the loss to Africa from corruption as equaling a quarter of its gross domestic product annually (Rice 2005).[9] Whatever the exact figures, Africa's capital wealth continues to be siphoned from the continent as fast as it can be restored by overseas donors. Larry Diamond, Michael Bratton, Carolyn Logan, and Darren Kew make, in different ways, a strong case for the donor community devoting even more support to strengthening African civil societies so that they can hold governments accountable. Aid, as Paul Collier has argued, is essentially a form of rent similar to earnings from exported petroleum. If the external countries and international agencies are willing to provide such rents to poor countries, they surely have an obligation to make sure that the people themselves, and their representatives, have an effective say in how they are utilized. One of the major recommendations to emerge from this project is the need to strengthen the mechanisms by which African societies, via institutions of vertical and horizontal accountability, can ensure that aid is used for the creation of public goods rather diverted to private uses or to strengthen the instruments of misrule.[10] Larry Diamond has coined an apt way of describing this process: "aid must be smartened."

After Gleneagles

Reflecting over the past thirty years and looking ahead to the coming decades, we can see that an unprecedented transfer of public resources will be made from one area of the world to another. Even if the most ambitious Gleneagles promises are not met, these transfers would still dwarf US transfers to Western Europe after World War II. Seldom included in discussions of aid and development are the extensive contributions of philanthropic entities and the tens of billions in remittances sent annually to families and communities by Africans living overseas. Even before the post-2000 "big push," several hundred billion dollars had already been transferred to sub-Saharan Africa since the 1970s. "By the early 1990s," according to van de Walle,

"Africa's relationship with the international economy was almost entirely mediated by public aid flows" (van de Walle 2001, p. 189). The consequence is that many sub-Saharan African governments now rely on overseas aid to cover more than 40 percent of their annual budgets. Even a "strong-performing" country such as Uganda currently receives over 50 percent of government expenditures in foreign aid. The average for Africa could exceed 70 percent if some of the aid projections are realized (Moss and Subramanian 2005, table 2, p. 6).

Limited absorptive capacities and the harmful impact of massive aid flows on government accountability and incentive structures cannot be wished away. Transforming African governments into aid-administering entities, even more than they are today, raises fundamental issues of dependency and the sustainability of externally financed projects. Also eclipsed is the process of building institutions through problem solving and mobilizing local tax and other revenues.

To ensure the proper use of aid funds, donors relied heavily in the 1980s on conditionalities (governments' receipt of aid was subject to meeting detailed conditions). These conditionalities became discredited, however, because they were often easily evaded. Even when adhered to, they were generally viewed as counterproductive (see van de Walle 2005; Gordon 1993). In place of conditionalities, there is an increasing tendency to channel funds to countries considered to be strong performers according to various governance benchmarks. In 2004 the administration of US president George W. Bush introduced what was touted as an improved approach to development assistance based on the demonstrated performance of potential beneficiaries. However, its implementation was slow, leading to the sudden resignation in June 2005 of its first director, Paul Applegarth. It still remains to be seen how the mandate of the Millennium Challenge Corporation (MCC) will evolve to complement the broader mission of USAID. Countries declared eligible for MCC grants at the end of 2005 included such exemplars of pseudo-democracy as the Gambia. And donors still have difficulty curbing the misuse of governmental power in high aid recipients such as Ethiopia, Kenya, and Uganda.

Among a welter of policy recommendations, the Gleneagles communiqué identified three areas requiring urgent global action: increased aid flows, debt cancellation, and fairer trade. There have been commendable responses to the first two. Rich countries have been most resistant to the third agenda item because it requires confronting their own powerful agricultural lobbies and farming communities. Implicit in the commission's report is a fourth challenge for which there is as yet no credible strategy, namely, reducing bad governance in Africa. The Gleneagles communiqué includes a long list of desired improvements in the conduct of African governments. In an important breakthrough, it also addressed the contributions of citizens and institutions in rich countries to the fostering of corrupt practices and proposed concrete action against persons at home and abroad who engage in bribery (see Jackson 2005, p. 660). But we are left unenlightened about how to act upon the commission's warning that until "good governance and capacity building" are in place, "Africa will be doomed to continue its economic stagnation." That is a mantra whose repetition, in report after report, only accentuates the mystery about how progress will occur.[11]

Perhaps the most important work on this topic is being done by teams at the World Bank Institute under the leadership of Daniel Kaufmann. They have created statistical systems to demonstrate the linkage between improved governance and development (see Kaufman, Kraay, and Mastruzzi 2005). The US Council on Foreign Relations also joined this global inquiry. For several months in 2005, a high-level independent task force examined how the United States should reshape its Africa policies.[12] Its report repeats the central argument of its predecessors—namely, that improved governance, capable legal systems, and open democracies will ultimately determine the success of efforts to alleviate African poverty. I concur with task force member Chester Crocker that this incisive report did not pay sufficient attention to "the cardinal importance of strengthening African state capacity and institution-building. . . . Weak states need more than democracy promotion" (Council on Foreign Relations 2005, p. 126). After Gleneagles, as before, the primary challenges for Africa are reducing its huge governance and institution-building deficits and breaking the tragic bond between misrule and stalled development. Instead of retreating from this challenge because of frustration with the tragic course of events in several African countries, the time has come to redouble the search for the varying mix of strategies and policies that put improved governance at the center of donor relationships. Their determination can draw on the insights and information provided in this book, including the lessons from in-country experiences in Chapter 7 by Ian Hopwood on Senegal, Chapter 8 by John Ohiorhenuan on Liberia, Chapter 10 by Anyang' Nyong'o on Kenya, and Chapter 12 by Darren Kew on Nigeria.

Toward a Dynamic Model of Development Cooperation

Most African governments have failed to make effective use of the considerable financial resources they have received since the 1960s to shift their countries onto different development trajectories. This point should be very clear from the extensive research we have distilled. Special efforts are now needed to bring more countries in the continent fully into the mainstream of global development. Either sub-Saharan Africa becomes much better governed—which means conduct by officials that builds institutional capacity and social trust and helps expand the supply of public goods—or it will remain largely marginalized from the dynamic trends in the global system. An Africa that experiences significant gains in productivity in its agricultural and industrial sectors, and therefore the expanded employment that the export of minerals customarily do not provide, is the only one that can ultimately overcome stalled development.

In seeking to understand what is preventing African countries from taking greater advantage of the abundant opportunities afforded by the rapidly expanding global economy and the unprecedented levels of development assistance from multilateral and bilateral agencies, it is necessary to take account of both behavioral and institutional impediments. Bruce Berman contends that centuries of contact with the industrializing areas of the world, and over a century of colonialism and postcolonialism, have yielded "the very restricted introduction of capitalist forms of production and exchange in Ghana." Millions of Ghanaians, he claims, are still trapped in modes of production—whether in agricultural or informal sectors of the economy—that are "technologically backward and stagnant," while locally owned firms are "limited technologically" (Berman 2003, p. 31). Ghanaian entrepreneurs, Berman concludes, contend with "a low level of trust in business relations" and in dealings with the state because of the "lack of enforcement of clear rules of the game."

From the 1970s to the turn of the century, many scholars have written about the "economy of affection," "neopatrimonial practices," "prebendalist behaviors," and "the politics of the belly" and coined other formulations for the social and political logics that determine resource allocation and utilization in Africa and that steadily undermine the building of strong modern institutions. David Brooks, a US columnist, pertinently wrote: "You can't just urge someone to be disciplined; you have to build a structure of behavior and attitude. Behavior shapes thought. . . . it's easiest to change the mind by changing behavior" (Brooks 2008, p. A23). Brooks contends that this principle is probably as true of the behavior of workers in an office as of athletes on a sports field.

Seeking to change minds through exhortation has repeatedly failed in Africa. Minds will only change when behaviors must, and the latter will only occur if there are institutions that require such practices and have the incentive and enforcement structures to uphold them. The vicious cycle in Africa of bad leadership, poor governance, weak institutions, and low outcomes must be broken. The most likely point of entry are the institutions, in government and society, whose strength can be influenced by the material and other incentives that are abundantly available to external actors and agencies to reinforce the efforts of in-country reformers in both public and private sectors.

In his inaugural address in February 2005 as professor of political science of the University of Ghana, E. Gyimah-Boadi discussed the behavioral and institutional impediments to development in Ghana in a trenchant paragraph:

> Institutional renewal has continued to lag behind. Bureaucracies remain bloated, inefficient, and corrupt; legal infrastructure in most states is also still too weak to adequately supervise state business of resource extraction and allocation as well as safeguard property rights and manage the new challenges facing transforming economies; and privatization of state-owned enterprises is not yielding expected dividends and has largely served only to entrench avenues for rent-seeking. Above all, official corruption and neo-patrimonialism persist, in spite of liberalization.[13]

Bear in mind that Gyimah-Boadi is writing about one of the better-performing states, politically and economically, in contemporary Africa. If state quality, to use an important concept of Larry Diamond, is still deficient in Ghana, what can be said in this regard about Cameroon or Nigeria or Uganda? (see Diamond 2008a).

International agencies are adjusting to the reality that the central Gleneagles promise of doubling aid to Africa between 2005 and 2010, even if fulfilled, will not overcome these institutional and behavioral challenges. President Meles Zenawi of Ethiopia was a member of the Commission for Africa and therefore sanctioned its report. That did not stop his regime from brutally suppressing protests at the outcome of his country's 2005 elections. Close attention was paid to elections in Rwanda in 2003, Uganda in 2006, and Nigeria and Kenya in 2007, and Zimbabwe in 2008, and yet the regimes in power behaved as if the pledges to uphold greater accountability, transparency, and fairness in their political systems had never existed (despite lofty commitments made under NEPAD and the African Peer Review Mechanism). Complicating the landscape for improved governance and institutional growth in Africa is the impact of the new wave of booming economies in East Asia, especially China, India, and Vietnam (Daneshkhu and Guha 2007). As the train bombing in London on the final day of the Gleneagles conference symbolized, global insecurities today can trump well-meaning initiatives. There are multiple vectors of influence on the behavior of African governments. That of Western countries and international agencies seeking to advance good governance is only one of them and may increasingly be less influential or determinative of behaviors.

An important part of the answer, I believe, lies in identifying forms of international cooperation with Africa that go beyond anything previously attempted. Three decades of development assistance that rely on capital transfers, through direct grants to governments and soft loans, have not yielded the desired results. The emergence of "breakthrough nations" in Africa that can compete in the global economy will require wide, deep, and sustained partnerships between them and countries with established or fast-growing economies. And these relationships will include external actors who care about fostering good governance and those who do not. Hence the need to bring local civil societies more prominently into the equation so that governments are not left to make promises to external actors, most of which they do intend to uphold. Instead, as abundant evidence right up to the present shows, they will seek the maximum freedom of action and end up doing as they have done for decades: serving those in power and making minimal transfers outside the circles of power wielders and their clients. As Darren Kew and others argue in this book, those recurrent patterns can only be altered through strategic alliances in which the organizations of civil society are as important partners as the governments of the day (see Chapter 12).

Critical and innovative thinking is needed to help build bridges between Africa's weak governance and institutional capacities and a future terrain on which African countries can compete effectively in the global economy. Central to smart aid is overcoming the false but still widespread assumption that Africa's developmental failures are mainly attributable to the insufficiency of international aid. Doubling or tripling these flows without transforming the capacity to use them efficiently and productively will just add to the already monstrous waste of public capital. It can amount, as Larry Diamond contends, to little more that "the care and feeding of the massive network of career professionals, nonprofit organizations, and private sector companies that constitute the global aid industry" (Daneshkhu and Guha 2007, p. 47). Moreover, using his terminology, there is the moral hazard of further strengthening "predatory" forms of governance.

Even when African countries succeed in getting their political and economic systems into reasonable order, as Ghana has done, expecting them to quickly overcome the deficits in operational performance is tantamount to asking someone to rush up a ladder from which several rungs have been removed. The steady drain of personnel means that professionals in health and education, even with the greatest determination, cannot reinvent what took decades to build.[14] We are therefore challenged today to discover how countries that have experienced high out-migration of trained persons in response to better job opportunities overseas, can turn this trend to their advantage. Anyang' Nyong'o highlighted this issue in the case of Kenya. In confronting Africa's development challenges, there is a need to transcend some of the rigidities of country and place and begin thinking of institutional capacities in transnational ways.

Well over a million people currently in the United States were born in Africa. Many of them remain actively engaged in economic and social networks that crisscross the Atlantic. They represent a bridgehead on which an international strategy of "migration and development" can be based. As increasing numbers of Africans flee the continent or postpone returning after completing their studies, the balance is shifting in the standard of life, professional satisfaction, and disposable income between those who emigrate and those who remain at home. For African countries to overcome the growth and development hurdles, they must identify ways to benefit from the financial, as well as the human, capital represented by their many emigrants. The discretionary financial resources of these emigrants are urgently needed, but so also are their resources in knowledge and professional behaviors. The latter includes the knowledge acquired overseas about how to build and sustain fundamental institutions of today's dynamic societies: schools, hospitals, banks, transportation systems, corporations, and universities. Rapidly developing countries in Asia and Europe gain enormously from enterprising members of their diasporas who transmit valuable technologies, basic as well as sophisticated. Africa must ramp up what is being done in this area.

What are the factors and forces, it may be asked, that would make it possible for stable and democratic African countries to overcome the behavioral and institutional deficits identified by Berman, Gyimah-Boadi, and many others? How can development cooperation help to mobilize the resources of overseas Africans more effectively to meet the challenges at home? How can incentives for an inside-outside strategy of building healthy institutions be fostered? In seeking answers to these questions, I have selected key components of a new transformative model of development cooperation. The list can readily be expanded and refined based on insights provided throughout this book and others that will be solicited. Smart aid is not a one-time exercise in view of the vast scope of the "aid business" today and the tens of millions of lives that are affected adversely or positively. Smartening aid should become a collaborative international project that supersedes the unhelpful dueling between aid optimists and pessimists.

Toward a Smart Aid Agenda

Building on African Successes

A number of institutions in the formal state, parastatal, and private sectors of African societies have successfully developed reliable systems of governance and strengthened their capacities despite huge constraints. After the transition to more democratic systems in the 1990s, a number of such institutions, such as Ghana's Election Commission, now deliver reliable public service. It is important to understand the nature of, and reasons for, such successes and to examine how they can be deepened and replicated. Drawing on this information, more appropriate training and other projects could be devised.

Establishing Partnerships to Build Capacity

There is a tendency to look mainly to governments and international financial institutions to provide assistance for Africa. In fact, much greater resources are available in educational, health, business, and other sectors in the industrialized and rapidly developing world. Long-term partnerships can lead to the transfer of significant technical knowledge, including governance and institution-building practices, from strong external institutions. At present, such efforts are limited to the work of individuals overseas who create such partnerships based on personal contacts with institutions in particular African countries. More comprehensive approaches are needed (see Joseph 2002, 2003). New models of cooperation must be devised, especially on a South-South basis, to facilitate the transfusion to Africa of the institution-building capacities of fast-developing nations. Cooperation agreements between African countries and such nations as Japan, China, India, Brazil, and Korea should involve more than trade and infrastructural projects. Along with transferring skills and expertise, international actors, using their own networks, can expand incentives to build stronger institutional capacity in Africa.

Strengthening Higher Education in Africa

In 2000, four US foundations—Carnegie, Ford, MacArthur, and Rockefeller—established the Partnership for Higher Education. They were later joined by the Mellon and Packard Foundations, and additional multiyear funding was provided. This partnership has helped rebuild operations in several African universities. However, the need is enormous.[15] Enrollments are usually high, classes are greatly overcrowded, retention of faculty is weak, opportunities for productive research are limited, and facilities are strained and inadequate. Substantial resources will be needed over many years to bring the African university system closer to international standards. Many established African professionals, at home and abroad, attended better schools than are available for greatly expanded student bodies today. Higher education institutions in developed countries should commit to train more African students, researchers, and faculty over a designated period. No such comprehensive and consistent program currently exists.[16] An African scholars program would help meet the commitments made at the Gleneagles summit for the creation of networks of excellence between institutions of higher education and science and technology in Africa and other countries. Africa cannot advance within the global economy while its systems of higher education stagnate or deteriorate.

Involving Corporations and Training Executives

Greater attention is being devoted to private sector development in Africa, both multinational and African-owned. Corporations are also recognizing the need to be more socially responsible. In Africa this commitment requires international and local businesses to improve the environment in which they operate and advance the education and health of their workers. Such initiatives should be facilitated by appropriate government policy instruments. Also, executive training programs should be created by international business schools to prepare cadres of skilled African entrepreneurs to meet the opportunities generated by liberalized economies experiencing renewed growth. To supplement formal training programs, many retired executives can participate in hands-on skills training in Africa. According to the Natsios report, investments should be made to create "a class of entrepreneurs who can build businesses" (USAID 2004, p. 9). In fact, a new wave of entrepreneurs, adept at taking advantage of communication technologies, is already emerging in many countries. The challenge is to equip them to function at increasing levels of organization, reliability, and efficiency and overcome the normative and societal constraints Bruce Berman and others have identified.

Expanding Incentives for Good Governance

The distortion and corruption of financial systems in Africa continue to benefit small elite groups in each country. In such contexts, virtue seldom pays. It is necessary to provide expanded incentives and greater recognition to individuals who exemplify good governance and institution-building practices. What prizes are currently awarded for good governance and institution building in Africa? Sudanese businessman Mo Ibrahim has taken a worthy step forward with the creation of the Mo Ibrahim Prize for Achievement in African Leadership in 2006.[17] Yet where is the range of programs that encourage innovative approaches to tackling the continent's crippling governance and operational deficiencies? Incentive structures in Africa have been grossly distorted by the vast material benefits acquired by malefactors. They must be countered by initiatives to alter public perceptions in the direction of honoring and empowering honest institution builders. And those perceptions must be able to inform appropriate institutions of advocacy, representation, and restraint. Such initiatives must also be well-financed based on multiyear commitments as there are no short-term solutions to the key aspects of misrule and stalled development identified in this book and elsewhere.

Taking Vigorous Action to Curb Corruption

There are a number of international initiatives now aimed at curbing the illicit financial inducements by overseas firms to African government officials. Developed countries need to expand these supply-side efforts, including legislation, prosecutions, and repatriation of funds, to discourage bribery and the trafficking in stolen public resources. It is important that both sides of these nefarious practices be tackled simultaneously. On the demand side, the many anticorruption agencies and codes of conduct established in African countries have not had a great impact. The Economic and Financial Crimes Commission (EFCC) of Nigeria, under the leadership of Nuhu Ribadu, despite the stringent criticisms to which it has been subjected as an instrument of the Olusegun Obasanjo government, had systematically tackled the main vectors of institutionalized corruption—from the 419 scams that were so destructive of Nigerian international economic relations to the skimming of public revenues by governors, ministers, and other public officials. Nigeria still has to demonstrate that this plague can be significantly reduced, especially after Ribadu was removed in December 2007 from his position by Obasanjo's successor, Umaru Yar'Adua. Nevertheless, the EFCC has shown what can be done in a country perennially listed as among the most corrupt in the world (Smith 2007). It has also provided a model that can be improved upon in Nigeria and can be adapted to the circumstances of other countries. Of increasing importance, in this regard, is the Extractive Industries Transparency Initiative (EITI) launched by the British and Norwegian governments and taking root in some African countries.

Securing the Rights of Women

Women, already discriminated against in many areas, have been tragically impacted by the erosion of health care systems. They are already more vulnerable than men to HIV infection. The decline of pre- and postnatal care has led to increases in maternal and infant deaths and local epidemics of gynecological disorders. In conflict zones, including camps for refugees and displaced persons, the rape of women and girls is often a systemic practice. Poverty forces many young women to engage in "transactional" sex for money and other material benefits. Nothing short of a revolutionary transformation in the condition of women is needed in sub-Saharan Africa. Much is already being done in this area. There are few areas that provide value for money, and that have such transformative potential, as enhancing the status, training, and employment of women in Africa.

Rescuing Youths

Millions of African youths today have little stake in the prevailing political and economic systems that have served them so poorly. The schools, job opportunities, and civic amenities that should have expanded since the end of colonial rule are usually unavailable. Many of these undereducated youths become ready recruits for violent criminal gangs and the shock troops of politicians, as seen in Côte d'Ivoire, Democratic Republic of Congo, Liberia, Nigeria, Sierra Leone, and Zimbabwe. The postelection violence and mayhem in Kenya in early 2008 demonstrated how quickly the anger and distress of unemployed youths can exacerbate political conflicts. Thousands of such individuals seek to escape lives of despair through criminal and antisocial pursuits or perilous attempts to escape the continent by land and sea. Urgent public and private initiatives should be introduced to provide African youths with training and public service jobs while longer-term development measures are being planned.

Engaging the New African Diasporas

Many African countries have proposed mobilizing their diasporas for development. None have done so on the scale of countries with rapidly growing economies, such as India, China, and Ireland. Africans constitute one of the fastest-growing diasporas in many countries, and their communities often consist of highly motivated individuals who rapidly acquire professional skills and capital resources. A World Bank report states that 47 percent of Ghana's college graduates live overseas. Celia Dugger (2005) describes the brain drain from Africa appropriately as "the loss of institution builders—hospital managers, university department heads, and political reformers, among others." Innovative measures must be designed to facilitate their reengagement beyond sending remittances to their families and communities. Already organizations are emerging within these communities to assist development associations at home. More comprehensive strategies should be designed by concerned governments, private sector agencies, and NGOs to accelerate and deepen these linkages.[18]

Forging a New Pan-Africanism

In an interview with a Nigerian magazine in 2004, I stated: "It is time that all African people, all people of African descent, to start saying, 'This is not what we fought for,' and find ways to change it" (*The News* 2004). A new paradigm in African development must be backed by a new pan-Africanism that directly confronts, not excuses or disregards, misrule and stalled development in Africa and the special contributions that must be made by African people worldwide to overcome them. Discussions about poverty, development, and governance must begin in earnest in forums outside the halls of governments, international financial institutions, and NGOs. Africans, and people of African descent, must play a much more significant role worldwide in addressing the crushing failure of African leaders and elites to deliver on their promises over five decades. They should use the many institutions available to them—civic, professional, political, media, and religious—to push for greater action to reduce misrule and corruption in Africa.

Strengthening Democracy and the Rule of Law

Several countries worldwide have followed an undemocratic path to jump-start development. As their economies expand and a sizable middle class emerges, demands increase for greater political openness, participation, and the rule of law. Such sequencing has not occurred in Africa. Autocratic rule reinforces the patrimonial nature of African economic, social, and political systems and has accentuated governance deficiencies. This pattern is repeated cyclically, and cynically, whatever the promises made by new leaders. The legitimizing of opposition political parties; greater freedoms of the press, movement, and association; and progress toward constitutionalism and the rule of law are indispensable for creating the framework for limiting abuses, exposing governance deficiencies, and facilitating action to change them. Daniel Kaufmann and his colleagues (2005) contend that there is a 300 percent development dividend from good governance and that sharply reducing corruption can dramatically improve per capita incomes. Of particular note is that their governance indicators incorporate democratic prescriptions: political, civil, and human rights and the rule of law. On the basis of Africa's postcolonial record, it can be affirmed: no true democracy—no sustainable development.

Forging Public-Private International Partnerships

Although we live in an era of global economic expansion, we are also witness to deepening misery in many countries, especially in Africa. With just a handful of exceptions—Botswana, Mauritius, Namibia, and South Africa—most sub-Saharan countries cannot compete effectively in sectors of the new global economy. It is now widely recognized that the path to accelerated growth and poverty reduction must include a dynamic and expanding private sector assisted by a capable state. By 2010, most African countries will have experienced a half-century of postcolonial rule. We can predict that most of their populations will remain poor into the following decades and that many of their trained professionals will continue to emigrate abroad.

The time has come rethink international collaboration and the challenge of ensuring that many more sub-Saharan Africans can enjoy the fruits of modern political and economic systems. At the heart of such relationships must be new strategies to accelerate capital investments in Africa. Because such strategies will require major attention being paid to Africa's deficits in infrastructure, legal systems, education, health care, and environmental protection, they must involve public-private partnerships of a different order than anything attempted so far. There are now enhanced inflows of international private capital into Africa, and major funds are being provided by China, India, and Japan. However, it should not be assumed that the governance and institutional deficits mentioned throughout this book will simply be eclipsed by inflows of private capital to complement the international public capital on which Africa has relied for so long.

Big Aid to Smart Aid

"If sheer volume of official development assistance were the answer" to Africa's problems, wrote Nicholas Eberstadt, they "would be solved already." The postcolonial era, he contends, has already consumed the equivalent (adjusted for inflation) of "over six Marshall Plans" with precious little to show for it (Council on Foreign Relations 2005, p. 126). In a similar vein, Percy Mistry argued that in the next twenty years aid to sub-Saharan Africa could exceed the trillion dollars disbursed to the continent in the previous forty years (see Mistry 2005, p. 666). International donors have essentially been replenishing the drainage of African financial and human capital with their own inputs. The fundamental premise of the "big push" campaign is that scaling up direct financial transfers will boost economic productivity and growth since Africa is too poor to do so unaided.

Drawing on the work of many scholars and development practitioners, I have emphasized the insufficiency of this argument. Poverty has been increasing in much of Africa for more than three decades because of structural imbalances between Africa and the external world, but also because African financial, human, and institutional resources have been so badly used. Misrule, institutional decay, economic stagnation, and poverty constitute a vicious and ever-tightening cycle. The big push has already lost much momentum. The starting point of a revised post-Gleneagles international effort, emphasizing smart rather than big aid, would be a willingness to deal frankly with Africa's severe governance and institutional deficiencies.[19] Special attention must also be devoted to examining how increased inflows of private capital can help to reduce the destitution of most of the continent's people. Scholars have identified an ever-widening demographic-economic gap in Africa, reflected in the increasing youthfulness of its population and the insufficient number of jobs that will be created based on projected rates of economic growth (Sandell, Sorroza, and Olivié 2007). The Gleneagles summit represented an important milestone in boosting international awareness of persistent poverty in Africa and the need to expand and sustain financial assistance. However, a more comprehensive strategy would also address the governance, institutional, and human capital deficits identified in this chapter and by others in this book. Although we do not pretend to have arrived at all the answers to meet this multifaceted challenge, helping international aid become a more transformative force is an issue on which wider agreement can be reached, within Africa and in the international donor community.

Appendix

Table 13.1 Net Official Development Assistance, 2007

	2007		2006		2007[a]	
	ODA (US$ millions)	ODA/GNI (%)	ODA (US$ millions)	ODA/GNI (%)	ODA (US$ millions)[b]	Percent Change (2006 to 2007)[b]
Australia	2,471	0.30	2,123	0.30	2,145	1.0
Austria	1,798	0.49	1,498	0.47	1,613	7.6
Belgium	1,953	0.43	1,978	0.50	1,756	−11.2
Canada	3,922	0.28	3,684	0.29	3,585	−2.7
Denmark	2,563	0.81	2,236	0.80	2,302	2.9
Finland	973	0.40	834	0.40	880	5.5
France	9,940	0.39	10,601	0.47	8,918	−15.9
Germany	12,267	0.37	10,435	0.36	11,048	5.9
Greece	501	0.16	424	0.17	446	5.3
Ireland	1,190	0.54	1,022	0.54	1,068	4.6
Italy	3,929	0.19	3,641	0.20	3,509	−3.6
Japan	7,691	0.17	11,187	0.25	7,824	−30.1
Luxembourg	365	0.90	291	0.84	325	11.7
Netherlands	6,215	0.81	5,452	0.81	5,621	3.1
New Zealand	315	0.27	259	0.27	268	3.7
Norway	3,727	0.95	2,954	0.89	3,349	13.4
Portugal	403	0.19	396	0.21	359	−9.4
Spain	5,744	0.41	3,814	0.32	5,103	33.8
Sweden	4,334	0.93	3,955	1.02	3,853	−2.6
Switzerland	1,680	0.37	1,646	0.39	1,596	−3.0
United Kingdom	9,921	0.36	12,459	0.51	8,839	−29.1
United States	21,753	0.16	23,532	0.18	21,197	−9.9
Total DAC	103,655	0.28	104,421	0.31	95,605	−8.4
Average country effort		0.45		0.46		
Memo items						
EC	11,771		10,245		10,556	3.0
DAC-EU countries	62,095	0.40	59,035	0.43	55,639	−5.8
G7 countries	69,422	0.23	75,539	0.27	64,919	−14.1
Non-G7 countries	34,232	0.52	28,882	0.51	30,685	6.2
Non-DAC economies						
Chinese Taipei	514	0.13	513	0.14	474	−7.6
Czech Republic	179	0.11	161	0.12	155	−3.6
Hungary	91	0.07	149	0.13	75	−49.9
Iceland	45	0.25	41	0.27	39	−6.5
Korea	672	0.07	455	0.05	650	42.8
Latvia	16	0.06	12	0.06	15	23.4
Lithuania	47	0.11	25	0.08	44	74.8
Poland	356	0.09	297	0.09	306	3.2
Slovak Republic	68	0.09	55	0.10	55	0.6

Source: OECD, 4 April 2008.

Notes: The data for 2007 are preliminary pending detailed final data to be published in December 2008. The data are standardised on a calendar year basis for all donors, and so may differ from fiscal year data available in countries' budget documents.

a. At 2006 prices and exchange rates.

b. Taking account of both inflation and exchange rate movements.

Table 13.2 Share of Debt Relief Grants in Net Official Development Assistance, 2007

	2007		2006		Percent Change Without Debt Relief Grants 2006 to 2007[a]
	ODA (US$ millions)	of which: Debt Relief Grants	ODA (US$ millions)	of which: Debt Relief Grants	
Australia	2,471	12	2,123	277	15.6
Austria	1,798	919	1,498	757	6.3
Belgium	1,953	185	1,978	396	0.6
Canada	3,922	15	3,684	260	4.3
Denmark	2,563	123	2,236	113	3.2
Finland	973	—	834	—	5.5
France	9,940	1,505	10,601	3,433	5.6
Germany	12,267	2,868	10,435	2,722	9.8
Greece	501	—	424	—	5.3
Ireland	1,190	—	1,022	—	4.6
Italy	3,929	570	3,641	1,596	46.7
Japan	7,691	1,576	11,187	3,003	−24.0
Luxembourg	365	—	291	—	11.7
Netherlands	6,215	392	5,452	312	2.5
New Zealand	315	—	259	0	3.7
Norway	3,727	61	2,954	23	12.4
Portugal	403	1	396	0	−9.4
Spain	5,744	243	3,814	503	47.6
Sweden	4,334	75	3,955	292	3.4
Switzerland	1,680	59	1,646	98	−0.5
United Kingdom	9,921	70	12,459	3,503	−2.0
United States	21,753	29	23,532	1,585	−3.5
Total DAC	103,655	8,701	104,421	18,874	2.4
Memo items					
EC	11,771	—	10,245	—	3.0
DAC-EU countries	62,095	6,949	59,035	13,629	8.8
G7 countries	69,422	6,632	75,539	16,102	−1.1
Non-G7 countries	34,232	2,069	28,882	2,772	10.4

Source: OECD, 4 April 2008.
Note: a. Taking account of both inflation and exchange rate movements.

Table 13.3 Gross Official Development Assistance, 2007

	2007	2006	2007	
	ODA (US$ millions)	ODA (US$ millions)	ODA[a] (US$ millions[b])	Percent Change (2006 to 2007[b])
Australia	2,471	2,123	2,145	1.0
Austria	1,813	1,510	1,627	7.7
Belgium	2,012	2,047	1,809	−11.6
Canada	3,959	3,730	3,619	−3.0
Denmark	2,667	2,315	2,395	3.5
Finland	973	838	880	5.1
France	11,556	12,764	10,367	−18.8
Germany	13,807	12,049	12,434	3.2
Greece	501	424	446	5.3
Ireland	1,190	1,022	1,068	4.6
Italy	4,231	4,003	3,779	−5.6
Japan	13,578	17,115	13,813	−19.3
Luxembourg	365	291	325	11.7
Netherlands	6,607	5,889	5,975	1.5
New Zealand	315	259	268	3.7
Norway	3,727	2,954	3,349	13.4
Portugal	396	402	353	−12.2
Spain	5,947	4,160	5,283	27.0
Sweden	4,334	3,955	3,853	−2.6
Switzerland	1,687	1,657	1,603	−3.3
United Kingdom	11,759	13,075	10,476	−19.9
United States	22,634	24,532	22,056	−10.1
Total DAC	116,528	117,112	107,924	−7.8
Memo items included in the above				
EC	12,182	10,678	10,924	2.3
DAC-EU countries	68,157	64,743	61,071	−5.7
G7 countries	81,523	87,267	76,545	−12.3
Non-G7 countries	35,004	29,845	31,379	5.1

Source: OECD, 4 April 2008.
Notes: a. At 2006 prices and exchange rates.
b. Taking account of both inflation and exchange rate movements.

Figure 13.1 Net Official Development Assistance, 2007

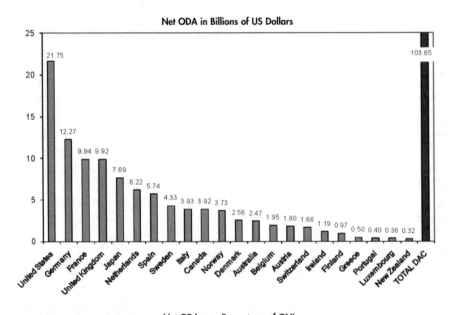

Net ODA in Billions of US Dollars

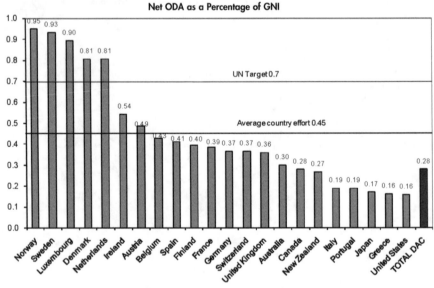

Net ODA as a Percentage of GNI

Source: OECD, Development Assistance Committee, 2008, http://www.oecd.org/dac/stats.

Figure 13.2 Performance Against 2005 Gleneagles ODA Projection

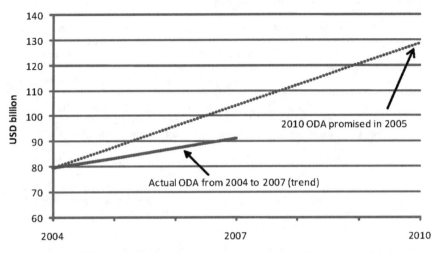

Source: OECD, Development Assistance Committee, 2008, http://www.oecd.org/dac/stats.
Note: This figure does not show actual ODA figures for 2005 and 2006, which were affected by exceptional debt relief.

Notes

1. For an excellent overview of African development issues with many helpful tables and charts, see Moss (2007).

2. "Perestroika Without Glasnost in Africa," 1989, Carter Center, *Conference Report Series* 2 (1), Atlanta, GA.

3. Every few years a new book appears exploring what has gone wrong in Africa. For the period discussed here, see Whitaker (1988) and van de Walle (1999).

4. Editorial, *Financial Times,* March 3, 2008.

5. Nelson Kasfir, "Does the Blair Report Help or Hinder Governance in Africa?" www.northwestern.edu/african-studies/Pdfs/May2005Conference/kasfir.pdf.

6. The views of Larry Diamond, as reflected in the Foreword of this book, and also cited in our conclusion, are clearly reflected in these comments.

7. For the conference papers and report, see www.northwestern.edu/african-studies/AGD.html.

8. For a characteristic critical response to Jeffrey Sachs's positions, see Rice (2005).

9. Mistry (2005, p. 666) claims that a conservative estimate of capital flight from Africa is $50 billion annually.

10. See Chapters 11 and 12 in this volume, Collier (2007), and Diamond (2008).

11. In the sources cited in footnote 10 above, and in Chapter 8 in this volume, specific recommendations are made for more innovative approaches by the international community.

12. I was a member of the task force.

13. It is interesting to compare this 2005 statement by Gyimah-Boadi with the quotation from the 1989 World Bank report in the section, "Misrule and Stalled Development."

14. See the discussion on overcoming the sustained decline in higher education in Nigeria in "Nigeria 2007: Political, Social and Economic Transitions," report of an international conference, Northwestern University, November 2–4, 2006: www .northwestern.edu/african-studies/publications_conf.html.

15. For a report on the extent of the problems at the University of Makerere, Uganda, one of Africa's better universities, see Wax (2005).

16. In fact, as Wall (2005) argues persuasively, the rich countries have been systematically draining professionals from the poorer countries.

17. For more information on the prize, see http://www.moibrahimfoundation .org/the-prize.html.

18. See the report of the UN Global Commission on International Migration (October 2005), www.gcim.org/en/.

19. In December 2005, on the eve of a major conference in Nigeria on AIDS in Africa, the Global Fund to Fight AIDS, Tuberculosis, and Malaria announced its suspension of ongoing grants to Nigeria because of the mismanagement (and slow utilization) of funds already disbursed.

PART 4

Conclusion

14

Aid, Transformation, and Growth in Africa

Richard Joseph and Alexandra Gillies

THE POLITICAL ECONOMIES of sub-Saharan Africa are virtually unique in the preponderant role that development aid has played in sustaining and shaping them for over three decades. Nicolas van de Walle stated the central paradox that is at the heart of this project: "By the early 1990s, Africa's relationship with the international economy was almost entirely mediated by public aid flows" (van de Walle 1999, p. 189). Such assistance began in many cases even before African countries gained independence from colonial rule. Outgoing colonial powers and philanthropic foundations hastily threw together programs to prepare incoming governments to assume their new responsibilities. What were meant to be transitional operations, however, have expanded over time, sometimes ebbing but more often growing, as African economies became distorted, stagnated, or contracted.

Today, aid to sub-Saharan Africa amounts to billions annually and often accounts for half or more of the income of a number of governments. Meanwhile, prominent advocates of African development insistently call on the richer countries to provide significantly greater amounts of aid. For the citizens of the recipient countries, as well as donors, the time has come to deal frankly, fearlessly, yet humanely with the paradox of abundant aid that too often deepens dependency, sustains corrupt governance, warps the incentive structures of recipient societies, and inadequately substitutes for the private capital that many Africans, not to mention foreign entrepreneurs, have been reluctant to invest.

By bringing together scholars and practitioners with many years of experience studying and witnessing the evolution of African political economies, this book has provided its readers with an opportunity to increase their knowledge both of the global "aid business" and of its frequent, deleterious consequences. The contributors accepted the challenge to report accurately and incisively what has occurred in Africa and also, under the general rubric of "smart aid," to suggest improvements that can be made by different categories of participants. They provided a range of responses to this challenge. Although we never aimed for unanimity, we were surprised by the level of consensus that emerged from this collaborative exercise.

Aid was never intended to be a hodgepodge of balms and bandages applied to over forty countries with great diversities of culture, language, society, and natural endowments. Outside of, but not excluding humanitarian assistance, we believe that the central purpose of external aid should be to contribute to transforming those aspects of African political economies that hinder steady, sustainable, and equitable growth. This book has identified many of the hurdles and also the opportunities. If aid does not help generate higher levels of economic production and income, it is essentially an international welfare system. With regard to this ultimate goal, the citizens of donor and recipient countries are agreed: neither group wants to play indefinitely the roles of humanitarian rescuers and rescued. No matter which euphemisms (e.g. "partnerships") are used, aid is essentially the transfer of part of the earnings of one people to another. National self-respect and sovereignty require that the aid business, as it has evolved, will only succeed when it can put itself out of business.

Yet, this is not remotely what is happening in Africa four to five decades after the end of colonial rule. Advocates for "big aid" propose that aid commitments to Africa must be made at ever higher levels far into the future. In contrast, we believe that more attention should be devoted to how aid can be better designed and implemented and how its objectives and operations can better correspond to Africa's highly varied physical, political, and economic landscape. As this project was nearing completion, Paul Collier's pathbreaking book, *The Bottom Billion,* appeared. In addition to his core argument that one-sixth of the world's population is not benefiting from the current expansion of the global economy, Collier identifies the structural impediments to development in the various "Africas." One half of the "Bottom Billion," he contends, are sub-Saharan Africans. His approach is consonant with many of the themes and arguments of this book.

Smarter aid would be a more nuanced, flexible, and adaptable system. In addition to shoring up Africa's weak safety nets, aid must target the potential drivers of economic growth. External assistance must adjust to the structural impediments of a continent that was carved up by competing imperialists to yield a territorial grid that still complicates development more than a century later. Aid must be calibrated to tackle the special needs of Africa's failed states, as well as those that are still viable but faltering and those that are gaining coherence and competence.

We have devoted attention to the critical issue of the impact of large and prolonged aid allocations on local economic and political incentive structures. It stands to reason that if 90 percent of a country's export earnings derive from petroleum, as has been the case for decades in Nigeria, Gabon, and Congo-Brazzaville, then oil revenues will skew the pursuit of economic advancement of much of the society unless bold countervailing actions are taken. Aid can also distort political dynamics, as public offices become disproportionately vehicles for rent distribution rather than the provision of public goods. Similarly, as aid becomes a steady financial resource for African governments, it can overwhelm and even marginalize other major forms of revenue generation and inhibit institutional maturation and the emergence of entrepreneurial classes in recipient countries (Birdsall 2007, p. 10).

Aid and governance are inevitably twinned concepts. Governance essentially concerns how countries make use of available public resources in the pursuit of public goals. Although corruption is present in all societies, its prevalence and significance can be exacerbated or minimized by the nature of leadership, legal structures and instruments, and public attitudes. As a report about corruption during the Daniel arap Moi regime in Kenya demonstrates, the theft and diversion of government revenues can be "breathtaking" in their scale and arrogance, even to seasoned students of African political economies (see Kennedy 2007). Even recently reforming economies such as Uganda's can sink back into a pit of corruption, nepotism, and political repression with little effective and collective response from the donor community (Mwenda 2007).

Whatever the level of aid, the experiences of Africa have shown, over and over again, that governance is a key link between aid and development. Bad governance yields poor development results. Moreover, multilateral and bilateral donors have painfully learned that *democratic* governance is an imperative for the smarter use of aid to Africa. Governments must increasingly be held accountable to their societies, acting through institutions of vertical and horizontal accountability, and not just to their external benefactors. Citizens of African countries need to know what funds are given from abroad in their name, for which purposes, and how much is actually used as intended. Several of the book's authors, especially Peter Anyang' Nyong'o in Chapter 10, emphasize the degree to which an effective anticorruption effort depends on democratization. Openness, participation, and transparency must characterize to an ever-increasing degree the planning and implementing of aid.

Aid donors are challenged, perhaps more than other deliverers of financial resources to Africa, to demonstrate how much their transfers contribute to achieving their stated purposes. The increasing emphasis on budget support and the locally driven, consultative decisionmaking processes of the Poverty Reduction Strategy Papers and Millennium Challenge Account reflect the convergence of two sets of attitudes: the persistent demand for greater ownership of aid-funded programs by African governments and the discomfort felt by granting agencies as they perennially oversee the public policies of sovereign African nations. The consequence is that some African aid recipients now enjoy greater freedom to determine the uses to which these external flows are put. Leakage to security forces, the need to lubricate domestic patronage networks, and the appropriation of aid for personal gain are risks that accompany this otherwise desirable loosening of the purse strings.

Demands for greater transparency, accountability, and democratic empowerment are inexorably components of the effort to curb elite misappropriation of aid resources. The formal institutions renewed or introduced during Africa's democratic transitions of the 1990s—opposition parties and independent media, competitive elections, legislative and judicial bodies, and diverse agencies to enhance accountability—have been shown to be necessary but not sufficient for the efficient and honest use of external aid. Although periodic elections have again become a defining aspect of Africa's political landscape, the capacity of citizens to "claim democracy," as Michael Bratton and Carolyn Logan argue in Chapter 11, and make their elected representatives accountable to them, is still generally weak. A resurgent civil society can serve as an important counterweight to the abuse of power, as has already been demonstrated in re-democratized countries such as Zambia.

However, the scales are still largely tilted against popular masses desiring basic public services and in favor of elites who appropriate public revenues with impunity. "Rentier systems" was a term often used to describe postcolonial African political economies, as agricultural earnings were taxed by government agencies and potential rural incomes and savings transferred to urban dwellers and elites. Highly aid-dependent societies today are rentier economies par excellence. In these cases, aid can be considered as unearned income that external countries provide on the basis of their perceived national security interests, to facilitate favorable treatment of their business investors, and to satisfy the humanitarian impulses of their citizens. What happens on the side of the recipient countries, as has been demonstrated in several chapters, essentially depends on the developmental intentions of their leaders, the capacities of government agencies, the effectiveness of institutions of accountability, and the strength and vigilance of civil society organizations.

Internal organizational factors and weak coordination by donors impair the emergence of transformative, effective aid. In Chapters 3 and 4, Carol Lancaster and Vivian Lowery Derryck identify some of these challenges. As amply demonstrated in this book, aid that promotes transformation and growth depends, to a significant degree, on donor interventions that privilege positive internal dynamics over negative ones. The record suggests, unfortunately, that the opposite has often been the case. By acquiring nuanced understandings of local dynamics and refusing to underwrite corrupt systems and practices, donors can increase the likelihood that their assistance will strengthen domestic forces and institutions essential to accomplishing this task. Hopwood makes a compelling case in Chapter 7, based on the Senegalese experience, for allowing space in aid programs for local actors to adjust program guidelines to the specifics of country contexts and to take advantage of opportunities for learning that occur during the course of implementation. At the same time, donors should be ready to recognize when their aid reinforces negative dynamics, as Joel Barkan argues in the case of Uganda (see Chapter 5), and as Thomas Callaghy (Chapter 6) shows in the decades of on-again off-again donor support of the former Moi government in Kenya (van de Walle 2005). By frankly and publicly exposing the hurdles they encounter and facilitating their exposure by independent groups and media, donors can encourage local civil and political processes to advance the search for effective institutional remedies.

Larry Diamond has called attention to how much the scales are being tipped globally in favor of autocratic rule after the post-1989 democratic upsurge (Diamond 2008c). Although he was not an initial contributor to this project, his strong advocacy for the smarter use of international aid made him the most appropriate person to be invited to write the book's foreword. His writings on democracy bolster understandings that are implicitly or explicitly present throughout this book. Diamond contends that the dominant pattern of governance in Africa—neopatrimonialism—favors the production of private goods by those in power over public goods that can benefit the greater majority of the people. Sustainable development has therefore "been stymied by the same factor that has undermined democracy itself: bad governance" (Diamond 2008b, p. 147). He concludes a recent essay with a strong message to the international aid community that articulates central concerns and arguments of smart aid:

> In the circumstances of predatory rule in Africa, aid functions like the revenue that gushes from oil exports—it is just another source of external rents that enables rulers to float on a cushion above their societies, controlling the state without having to answer to their own people. . . . Most of all, principled pressure is needed from international actors, tying substantial flows of development assistance to concrete institutional improvements in governance. Donors can also provide generous financial and technical assistance to the institutions of governance—legislatures, judiciaries, counter-corruption commissions, and other agencies of horizontal accountability—that must work well if the balance is to tip from autocracy to democracy. . . . We know that the continent is not condemned to perpetual misrule. The challenge now is for the international donors to join with Africans in demanding that their governments be truly accountable. (Diamond 2008b, p. 148)

In Africa, many societies that have been stripped of their best over the centuries for the development of other regions—in human capital, agricultural crops, and minerals—have not yet figured out how to alter their relative positions in the global economy. The data that confirm this observation are readily available in a mountain of scholarly books, articles, and reports of international agencies and special commissions. A half-century ago, it was expected that growth and development would accompany freedom from colonial rule in sub-Saharan Africa. Instead, boom and bust, slow growth and stagnation, elite affluence and mass poverty, better describe what has ensued. Several African countries have recently experienced renewed growth, but it still remains to be seen if such expansion reflects real productivity and income gains beyond the boom in commodity prices, increased aid income, and the inflow of remittances from overseas migrants.

Smart aid must be based on genuine partnerships but not in the way that has been usually advocated by African government leaders. The core message of the latter usually goes as follows: "Send us more money but do not impose too many conditions as we know best what the development needs of our societies are." Instead, it is argued here, smart aid would emphasize long-term partnerships between *citizens* of prosperous countries and those of poorer ones, mediated by their governments and international agencies. Smart aid would be, quite deliberately, democratic in its aims and instruments. The evolution of the contemporary global system generates winners and losers, and many countries are in the hunt to capture larger shares of the expansion of global wealth and prosperity. Longtime economic losers are figuring out ways to join the winners, notably India, China, and increasingly Vietnam. Others, for example countries of southern and Eastern Europe, have benefited fortuitously from what, after the creation of the United States, is perhaps the greatest development framework of states, namely the European Union.

The ultimate aim of smart aid is to facilitate transformation and growth in Africa that would yield "breakthrough nations" comparable to those that have emerged in waves in Asia since the 1960s. Those nations have broken free of the political and social traps that constrain development. In seeking to smarten aid, the donor community should devote more attention to helping the people of Africa get smart about these processes, which means insisting that aid and its core implementing institutions work for the population's advantage. An appropriate sequel to this book, therefore, would be one that seeks to operationalize our findings and recommendations. It should be possible to compare and contrast countries on the basis of how smart has been the aid partnerships they have forged, with a focus on evaluating the transformative potential of new aid mechanisms and strategies.[1] Moreover, an international smart aid project can become a continuous one because the Internet can be used to highlight examples of "dumb aid" and "smart aid" from multiple localities. Such a project can help break the nexus between big aid and bad governance as Africans, and their advocates worldwide, can post concrete examples of their occurrence and contrast them with smart aid and good governance. As Derryck argues in Chapter 4, the recognition by the Commission for Africa of the need for continuous dissemination and monitoring has not been fully met. This book carries such a commitment forward and also recognizes how much more remains to be done.

Another important companion project would study the impact of the accelerating penetration of Africa by Chinese state and private firms, small traders, and laborers. The modus operandi of the rapidly growing Chinese presence in Africa involves the provision of loans and lines of credit, often to finance projects that Chinese firms then undertake. Issues of governance, debt levels, transparency, and environmental impact are some of the considerations given short shrift in China's drive to sew up access to a wide gamut of natural resources in Africa and open new markets for its consumer exports. On the basis of the large credits that China, followed by India, is making available to African governments with few strings attached, Western nations and international agencies are coming under increasing pressure to dilute their insistence on improved governance, democracy, human rights, and environmental and labor standards. One important way of tackling this quandary is to empower African civil societies so they can pursue even more vigorously, in association with international advocacy organizations, the genuine developmental interests of their countries. Via instruments of vertical and horizontal accountability, they can hold not just their government officials accountable but also Chinese, Russian, and other entities that are bringing mega-investment projects to Africa that will significantly alter the continent's economic and political landscape.

We end this book on a hopeful but, unfortunately, not confident note. Persistent poverty in Africa is today a matter of high global concern. It is understood that grave human suffering as a consequence of wars, epidemics, environmental decay, an iniquitous international trading system, and predatory and corrupt governance cannot be contained within national and continental borders. Just as European nations continue to benefit from generous intra-European aid that has lifted formerly distressed countries, such as Spain and Ireland, to high levels of growth and prosperity, so also the substantial aid flowing to Africa from West and East can be turned to Africa's advantage. But we should not minimize the scope of this challenge. Success in generating sustainable growth and equitable development in Africa would mean drastically changing the course of African history, going back to the colonial era. The transformation of Africa along paths of democratic development will require new formulas of aid, growth, and political organization. Diamond calls this "reinventing" aid. We hope that such formulas will be further distilled from the chapters of this book by individuals and organizations involved in the vast and unprecedented global enterprise to lift three-quarters of a billion people out of the numbing predicament of misrule, conflict, and poverty. Whether this transformation eventually occurs, we conclude, will depend on the extent to which these hard-earned lessons actually inform the practices of institutions within African countries and their external partners.

Note

1. For an insightful study of the interactions of donors, Tanzanian government officials, and civil society activists that demonstrates key aspects of smart aid in practice, see Holtom (2007).

ACRONYMS

AfDB	African Development Bank
AGOA	African Growth and Opportunity Act (United States)
APRM	African Peer Review Mechanism
AU	African Union
BCE	Bureau of Customs and Excise (Liberia)
BMA	Bureau of Maritime Affairs (Liberia)
CAPP	Community Action for Popular Participation
CBL	Central Bank of Liberia
CCM	Chama cha Mapinduzi
CDP	Consortium for Development Partnerships
CGD	Center for Global Development
CLEEN	Centre for Law Enforcement and Education in Nigeria
CLO	civil liberties organization
CMC	Contract and Monopolies Commission
CODESRIA	Council for the Development of Social Science Research in Africa
COMESA	Common Market for Eastern and Southern Africa
CRP	Constitutional Rights Project (Nigeria)
DAC	Development Assistance Committee
DDRR	disarmament, demobilization, rehabilitation, and reintegration
DFID	Department for International Development (UK)
DOD	United States Department of Defense
DOS	United States Department of State
DRC	Democratic Republic of Congo
ECOWAS	Economic Community of West African States
EFCC	Economic and Financial Crimes Commission (Nigeria)
EGSC	Economic Governance Steering Committee
EITI	Extractive Industries Transparency Initiative

ESF	Economic Support Fund
EU	European Union
FDA	Forestry Development Agency (Liberia)
G8	Group of Eight
GBS	general budget support
GEMAP	Governance and Economic Management Assistance Programme
GDP	gross domestic product
GNI	gross national income
GOL	government of Liberia
GRC	Governance Reform Commission
HIPC	heavily indebted poor countries
HIV/AIDS	human immunodeficiency virus/acquired immune deficiency syndrome
IBRD	International Bank for Reconstruction and Development
ICGL	International Contact Group on Liberia
IDA	International Development Association
IDASA	Institute for Democracy in South Africa
IFC	International Finance Corporation
IFIs	international financial institutions
IMF	International Monetary Fund
INEC	Independent National Electoral Commission
IOM	International Organization for Migration
IPs	implementing partners
I-PRSP	interim poverty reduction strategy paper
ISP	Institutional Support Program
IT	information technology
KACC	Kenya Anti-Corruption Commission
KANU	Kenya African National Union
KPCS	Kimberley Process Certification Scheme
KPU	Kenya People's Union
LPC	Liberia Peace Council
LPRC	Liberia Petroleum Refining Corporation
LURD	Liberians United for Reconciliation and Democracy
MCC	Millennium Challenge Corporation
MDRI	Multilateral Debt Relief Initiative
MDGs	Millennium Development Goals
MLME	Ministry of Lands, Mines, and Energy (Liberia)
MOCKY	Movement of Concerned Kono Youths (Sierra Leone)
MODEL	Movement for Democracy in Liberia
MOF	Ministry of Finance (Liberia)
MP	member of Parliament
NEEDS	National Economic Empowerment Development Strategy

NARC	National Rainbow Coalition
NEPAD	New Partnership for Africa's Development
NGO	nongovernmental organization
NIEO	new international economic order
NLC	Nigerian Labor Congress
NPA	National Port Authority (Liberia)
NPA	nonproject assistance
NPFL	National Patriotic Front of Liberia
NRA	National Resistance Army
NRM	National Resistance Movement
NTGL	National Transitional Government of Liberia
NPA	nonproject assistance
ODA	official development assistance
ODI	Overseas Development Institute
OECD	Organization for Economic Cooperation and Development
OPC	Oduduwa People's Congress
OPEC	Organization of the Petroleum Exporting Countries
OTI	Office of Transition Initiatives (USAID)
PEPFAR	President's Emergency Plan for AIDS Relief
PFM	public financial management
PGB	Presidential Guard Brigade
PRSC	Poverty Reduction Strategy Credit
PRSPs	Poverty Reduction Strategy Papers
PSI	policy support instrument
RFTF	Results-Focused Transitional Framework
RIA	Roberts International Airport (Liberia)
SAIs	supreme audit institutions
SAPs	structural adjustment programs
SEMA	Strategic Empowerment and Mediation Agency
SES	Senior Executive Service (Liberia)
SOE	state-owned enterprise
SPA	Strategic Partnership with Africa
SWAPO	South-West Africa People's Organization
TMG	Transition Monitoring Group (Nigeria)
ULIMO	United Liberation Movement of Liberia for Democracy
UNAIDS	Joint United Nations Program on AIDS
UNCTAD	United Nations Conference on Trade and Development
UNDP	United Nations Development Programme
UNMIL	United Nations Mission in Liberia
UPDF	Uganda People's Defence Force
USAID	United States Agency for International Development
WTO	World Trade Organization

REFERENCES

"Africa: A Turning Point." 1990. *Africa News,* October 22.

Afrobarometer Network. 2006a. "Citizens and the State in Africa: New Results from Afrobarometer Round 3." Afrobarometer Working Paper No. 61, http://www.afrobarometer.org.

———. 2006b. "Where Is Africa Going? Views from Below." Afrobarometer Working Paper No. 60, http://www.afrobarometer.org.

Ake, Claude. 2000. *The Feasibility of Democracy in Africa.* Dakar: CODESRIA.

Amisi, Otieno. 2007. "Amisi's New Book of Poetry Reviewed." Creative Ventures, http://otienoamisi.wordpress.com/2007/08/.

Amnesty International. 2003. "Liberia: International Contact Group Must Focus on Ending Human Rights Abuses," May 12. http://asiapacific.amnesty.org/library/Index/ENGAFR340092003?open&of=ENG-LBR.

Amnesty International USA. 2006. "Kimberley Process: An Amnesty International Position Paper." http://www.amnestyusa.org/diamonds/document.do?id=ENG-POL300572006 (accessed March 8, 2007).

Anderson, David. 2004. *Histories of the Hanged.* New York: W. W. Norton.

Anderson, Leslie E. 2006. "The Authoritarian Executive? Horizontal and Vertical Accountability in Nicaragua." *Latin American Politics and Society* 48 (2): 141–169.

Avruch, Kevin. 1998. *Culture and Conflict Resolution.* Washington, DC: USIP Press

Azeem, V., P. de Renzio, and V. Ramkumar. 2006. *Budget Monitoring as an Advocacy Tool: Uganda Debt Network Case Study.* Washington, DC: International Budget Project.

Balls, Andrew. 2004. "Foreign Aid Threatened by Anti-terrorism, Says Oxfam." *Financial Times,* December 6.

Barkan, Joel D. 2005. "Uganda: An African Success Past Its Prime." In Woodrow Wilson International Center, *Challenges and Change in Uganda.* Washington, DC.

———. 2008. *Breaking the Stalemate in Kenya.* Washington, DC: Center for Strategic and International Studies. http://www.csis.org/component/option,com_csis_pubs/task,view/id,4267/type,1/.

Barkan, Joel D., L. Adamolekum, and Y. Zhou, with M. Laleye, and N. Ng'ethe. 2005. "Emerging Legislatures: Institutions of Horizontal Accountability." In B.

Levy and S. Kpundeh, eds., *Building State Capacity in Africa: New Approaches, Emerging Lessons.* Washington, DC: World Bank.

Barkey, Karen. 1997. *Bandits and Bureaucrats: The Ottoman Route to State Centralization.* Ithaca: Cornell University Press.

Bayart, Jean-Francois. 1993. *The State in Africa: The Politics of the Belly.* London: Longman.

Becker, Elizabeth. 2004. "Guess Who's Invited to Dinner." *New York Times,* September 23.

Berg, Elliot. 2000. "Why Aren't Aid Organisations Better Learners?" Paper for Expert Group on Development Issues Seminar, "What do Aid Agencies and their Co-operating Partners Learn from their Experiences?", August.

Berkeley, Bill. 1982. "Liberia: Between Repression and Slaughter." *Atlantic Monthly* (October): 64.

Berman, Bruce J. 2003. "Capitalism Incomplete: State Culture and the Politics of Industrialization." In Wisdom J. Tettey, Korbla P. Puplampu, and Bruce J. Berman, eds., *Critical Perspectives on Politics and Socio-Economic Development in Ghana,* 21–44. Leiden, UK: Brill.

Biggart, Nicole Woolsey. 1990. "Institutionalized Patrimonialism in Korean Business." In Craig Calhoun, ed., *Business Institutions,* vol. 12 of *Comparative Social Research.* Greenwich, CT: JAI Press, 114–133.

Binnedijk, Annette. 2000. *Results Based Management in the Development Co-operation Agencies: A Review of Experience,* Background Report, Development Assistance Committee (DAC) Working Party on Aid Evaluation.

Birdsall, Nancy. 2007. "Do No Harm: Aid, Weak Institutions, and the Missing Middle in Africa." Center for Global Development Working Paper No. 113, Washington, DC.

Birdsall, Nancy, and John Williamson. 2002. *Delivering on Debt Relief: From IMF Gold to a New Aid Architecture.* Washington, DC: Center for Global Development, Institute for International Economics.

Booth, D., D. Cammack, J. Harrigan, E. Kanyongolo, M. Mataure, and N. Ngwira. 2006. "Drivers of Change and Development in Malawi." Working Paper 261, Overseas Development Institute, London.

Bratton, Michael. 2006a. "How Africans View Elections." In Richard Soudriette and Juliana Geran Pilon, eds., *Tyranny Busters: How Elections Advance Freedom.* Washington, DC: International Foundation for Electoral Systems.

———. 2006b. "Poor People and Democratic Citizenship in Africa." *Afrique Contemporaine* (December).

Bratton, Michael, and Nicolas van de Walle. 1994. "Neopatrimonial Regimes and Political Transitions in Africa." *World Politics,* July 4.

Brautigam, D. 2004. "The People's Budget? Politics, Participation and Pro-poor Policy." *Development Policy Review* 22 (6): 653–668.

Brooks, David. 2008. "Pitching with Purpose." *New York Times,* April 1, p. A23.

Brown, David. 1982. "On the Category 'Civilised' in Liberia and Elsewhere." *Journal of Modern African Studies* 20 (2): 287–303.

Bruton, Bronwyn. 2002. "The Conflict Resolution Stakeholders Network." Los Angeles: UCLA School of Public Policy and Social Research, March. http://www.spa.ucla.edu/ps/research/bruton.pdf (accessed January 22, 2007).

Callaghy, Thomas. 1984. *The State-Society Struggle: Zaire in Comparative Perspective.* New York: Columbia University Press.

———. 2003. "The Paris Club and International Economic Governance: Double

Crisis and Debt." In Vinod K. Aggarwal and Brigitte Granville, eds., *Sovereign Debt: Origins, Crises and Restructuring,* 201–228. London: Royal Institute of International Studies.

———. 2004. "Innovation in the Sovereign Debt Regime: From the Paris Club to Enhanced HIPC and Beyond." Operations Evaluation Department Working Paper, World Bank, Washington, DC.

Callaghy, Thomas, Ronald Kassimir, and Robert Latham. 2001. "Networks and Governance in Africa: Innovation in the Debt Regime." In Thomas Callaghy, Ronald Kassimir, and Robert Latham, eds., *Intervention and Transnationalism in Africa: Global-Local Networks of Power.* Cambridge: Cambridge University Press, 115–149.

Callaghy, Thomas M., and John Ravenhill, eds. 1993. *Hemmed In: Responses to Africa's Economic Decline.* New York: Columbia University Press.

CARE and Action Aid International. 2006. *Where to Now? Implications of Changing Relations Between DFID, Recipient Governments, and NGOs in Malawi, Tanzania, and Uganda.* London.

Cho, Wonbin. 2007. "Ethnic Fractionalization, Electoral Institutions, and Africans' Political Attitudes." Afrobarometer Working Paper No. 66, http://www.afrobarometer.org.

Clapham, Christopher. 1996. *African and the International System: The Politics of State Survival.* Cambridge: Cambridge University Press.

Clower, Robert, George Dalton, Mitchell Harwitz, and A. A. Walters. 1966. *Growth Without Development: An Economic Survey of Liberia.* Evanston, IL: Northwestern University Press.

CMI (Christian Michelsen Institute). 2005. "Should Corrupt Countries Receive Budget Support?" CMI Brief, Bergen.

Collier, Paul. 2007. *The Bottom Billion: Why the Poorest Countries are Failing and What Can Be Done About It.* Oxford: Oxford University Press.

Commission for Africa. 2005. *Our Common Interest: Report of the Commission for Africa.* London.

Cook, Nicolas. 2006. "Liberia's Postwar Recovery, Key Issues and Developments." Report RL 33185, Congressional Research Service, Washington, DC, March 12.

Council on Foreign Relations. 2005. "More than Humanitarianism: A Strategic U.S. Approach Toward Africa." Report of an Independent Task Force, December. http://www.cfr.org/content/publications/attachments/Africa%20Task%20Force%2012_12_05.pdf.

Daneshkhu, S., and K. Guha. 2007. "Aid Agencies to Begin Helping 'Fragile' States." *Financial Times,* April 14–15.

de Renzio, P. 2005a. "CSOs and Budgets: Linking Evidence and Pro-poor Policies." CSPP Paper, Overseas Development Institute, London.

———. 2005b. "Increased Aid vs. Absorptive Capacity: Challenges and Opportunities Towards 2015." *IDS Bulletin* 36 (3): 20–27.

———. 2006. "Aid, Budgets, and Accountability: A Survey Article." *Development Policy Review* 24 (6): 627–645.

———. 2007. "Briefing: Paved with Good Intentions? The Role of Aid in Reaching the Millennium Development Goals." *African Affairs* 106 (422): 133–140.

de Renzio, P., and J. Hanlon. 2007. "Contested Sovereignty in Mozambique: The Dilemmas of Aid Dependence." Working Paper 2007/25, Global Economic Governance Programme, Oxford.

De Renzio, Paolo, with David Booth, Andrew Rogerson, and Zara Curran, 2005. "Incentives for Harmonization and Alignment in Aid Agencies," Working Paper 248, Overseas Development Institute, London.

De Souza, C. 2001. "Participatory Budgeting in Brazilian Cities: Limits and Possibilities in Building Democratic Institutions." Working Paper No. 28, International Development Department, University of Birmingham.

Devarajan, Shantayanan, Vinaya Swaroop, and Andrew Sunil Rajkumar. 1998. "What Does Aid to Africa Finance?" AERC/ODC Project on Managing a Smooth Transition from Aid Dependence in Africa. Washington, DC.

DFID (Department for International Development). 2004a. "Historical Overview of UK DBS" [Direct Budget Support]. London.

———. 2004b. "Political Governance and Supporting National Poverty Reduction Strategies with Budget Support." Department for International Development, London, May.

———. 2005. "Characteristics of Different External Audit Systems." Briefing, Policy Division, UK Department for International Development, London.

Diamond, Larry. 1996. "Is the Third Wave Over?" *Journal of Democracy* 7 (July): 20–37.

———. 1999a. *Developing Democracy.* Baltimore: Johns Hopkins University Press.

———. 1999b. "Institutions of Accountability." *Hoover Digest,* no. 3, http://www .hooverdigest.org.

———. 2008a. "The Democratic Rollback: The Resurgence of the Predatory State." *Foreign Affairs* 87 (2): 36–48.

———. 2008b. "The Rule of Law Versus the Big Man." *Journal of Democracy* 19 (2): 138–149.

———. 2008c. *The Spirit of Democracy: The Struggle to Build Free Societies Throughout the World.* New York: Henry Holt.

Diamond, Larry, and Leonardo Morlino. 2005. "Introduction." In Diamond and Morlino, eds., *Assessing the Quality of Democracy.* Baltimore: Johns Hopkins University Press, ix–xliii.

Dittmer, Lowell. 2000. "Informal Politics Among the Chinese Communist Party Elites." In Lowell Dittmer, Haruhiro Fukui, and Peter Lee, eds., *Informal Politics in East Asia.* New York: Cambridge University Press, pp. 106–140.

Dollar, David, et al. 1998. *Assessing Aid: What Works, What Doesn't, and Why.* Washington, DC: World Bank.

Dollar, David, and Jakob Svensson. 2000. "What Explains the Success or Failure of Structural Adjustment Programmes?" *Economic Journal* 110 (October).

Dorotinsky, William, and Robert Floyd. 2004. "Public Expenditure Accountability in Africa: Progress, Lessons and Challenges." In B. Levy and S. Kpundeh, eds., *Building State Capacity in Africa: New Approaches, Emerging Lessons.* Washington, DC: World Bank.

Driscoll, Ruth, with Alison Evans. 2005. "Second-Generation Poverty Reduction Strategies: New Opportunities and Emerging Issues," *Development Policy Review* 23 (1): 5–25.

Dugger, Celia W. 2005. "Study Finds Small Developing Lands Hit Hardest by 'Brain Drain.'" *New York Times,* October 24.

Dwan, Renata, and Laura Bailey. 2006. *Liberia's Governance and Economic Management Assistance Programme (GEMAP).* Washington, DC, LICUS Initiative, May.

Easterly, William. 2001a. *The Elusive Quest for Growth.* Cambridge: MIT Press.

———. 2001b. "Study Finds Small Developing Lands Hit Hardest by 'Brain Drain.'" *New York Times,* October 24.

————. 2006. *The White Man's Burden: Why the West's Efforts to Aid the Rest Have Done So Much Ill and So Little Good.* New York: Penguin Press.

Edwards, Michael. 2004. *Future Positive: International Co-operation in the 21st Century,* Earthscan, London.

Elliot, Larry. 2004. "U.S. Softens Line on Debt Relief." *Guardian,* April 26.

Ellis, Stephen Ellis. 2006. "Liberia." In Andreas Mehler, Henning Melber, and Klaus van Walraven, eds., *Africa Yearbook, 2005.* Leiden: Brill.

Ensminger, Jean. 1997. "Changing Property Rights: Reconciling Formal and Informal Rights to Land in Africa." In John Nye and John Droback, eds., *Frontiers of the New Institutional Economics.* New York: Academic Press, 165–196.

European Commission. 2006a. "Institutional Support Program." European Commission's Delegation to Liberia website, http://www.dellbr.cec.eu.int/en/eu_and_country/institutional_support.htm (accessed January 2, 2007).

————. 2006b. "What's New Section." European Commission's Delegation to Liberia website, http://www.europa-eu-un.org/articles/en/article_5031_en.htm (accessed January 1, 2007).

Evans, Peter. 2004. "Development as Institutional Change: The Pitfalls of Monocropping and the Potentials of Deliberation," *Studies in Comparative International Development* 38 (4) (Winter): 30–52.

Farah, Douglas. 2004. *Blood from Stones: The Secret Financial Network of Terror.* New York: Broadway.

Foster, Mick, and Tony Killick. 2006. "What Would Doubling Aid do for Macroeconomic Management in Africa?" ODI Working Paper 264. London: Overseas Development Institute.

Fuentes, Carlos. 2001. *The Years with Laura Diaz.* New York: Farrar, Straus, and Giroux.Gallup Poll. *Public Opinion, 1935–1971.* Vol. 2, *1949–1958.* New York: Random House.Galvin, Dennis C. 2004. *The State Must Be Our Master of Fire.* Berkeley: University of California Press.

GEMAP. 2005. http://www.gemapliberia.org/pages/Gemap_docs?PHPSESSID=4819e135b79e81023afd9ccf9da7e387.

Gertzel, C. J., Maure Goldschmidt, and Donald Rothchild, eds. 1969. *Government and Politics in Kenya: A Nation Building Text.* Nairobi: East African Publishing House.

Githongo, John. 2006. "Africa: A Culture of Accountability." *Africa Focus Bulletin,* June 13, http://www.africafocus@igc.org.

Global Witness/International Transport Workers Federation. 2001. *Taylor-Made: The Pivotal Role of Liberia's Forests and Flag of Convenience in Regional Conflict.*

Goetz, Anne Marie. 2003. "Reinventing Accountability—Making Democracy Work for the Poor." Presentation to the Community of Practice on Social Accountability Launch, World Bank, Washington, DC, November 12.

Goetz, Anne Marie, and Rob Jenkins. 2005. *Reinventing Accountability: Making Democracy Work for Human Development.* New York: Palgrave Macmillan.

Goldwater, Barry. 1960. *The Conscience of a Conservative.* Shepardsville, KY: Victor Publishing.

Gomez, P., J. Friedman, and I. Shapiro. 2005. "Opening Budgets to Public Understanding and Debate: Results from 36 Countries," *OECD Journal of Budgeting* 5 (1): 7–36.

Gordon, David F. 1993. "Debt, Conditionality, and Reform: The International Relations of Economic Restructuring in Sub-Saharan Africa." In Thomas M. Callaghy and John Ravenhill, eds., *Hemmed In: Responses to Africa's Economic Decline.* New York: Columbia University Press.

Grenovetter, Mark. 1994. "Business Groups." In Neil Smelser and Richard Swedberg, eds., *The Handbook of Economic Sociology.* Princeton: Russell Sage Foundation.

GTZ (German Agency for Technical Cooperation). 2004. "Needs Assessment in Post-Conflict Situations: Case Study, Liberia." Working Paper No. 9.

Gunning, Jan William. 2004. "Why Give Aid?" Paper presented at the 2nd AFD-EUDN Conference, "Development Aid: Why and How?" Paris, November 25.

Gupta, Sanjeev, Robert Powell, and Yongzheng Yang. 2005. "The Macroeconomic Challenges of Scaling Up Aid to Africa," IMF Working Paper WP/05/179. Washington DC: International Monetary Fund.

Gyimah-Boadi, Legon E. 2004. *Democratic Reform in Africa: The Quality of Progress.* Boulder: Lynne Rienner.

Haggard, Stephen. 1990. *Pathways from the Periphery: The Politics of Growth in Newly Industrialized Countries.* Ithaca: Cornell University Press.

————. 2004. "Institutions and Growth in East Asia." *Studies in Comparative International Development* 38, no. 4: 53–81.

Hanson, Kara. 1998. *Health Sector Reforms in Africa: A Review of Eight Country Experiences,* Evaluation Working Paper Series, UNICEF, New York.

Harrison, Graham. 2001. "'Post-Conditionality Politics and Administrative Reform': Reflections on the Cases of Uganda and Tanzania." *Development and Change* 32: 657–679.

————. 2004. *The World Bank and Africa: The Construction of Governance States.* London: Routledge.

Heller, P. S. 2005. "'Pity the Finance Minister': Issues in Managing a Substantial Scaling Up of Aid Flows." Working Paper WP/05/180, International Monetary Fund, Washington, DC.

Helmke, Gretchen, and Steven Levitsky, eds. 2006. *Informal Institutions and Democracy: Lessons from Latin America.* Baltimore: Johns Hopkins University Press.

Hodges, A. and R. J. Tibana. 2004. *Political Economy of the Budget in Mozambique.* Oxford: Oxford Policy Management (later published in Portuguese as *A Economia Política do Orçamento em Moçambique.* Maputo: Princípios).

Holtom, Duncan. 2007. "The Challenge of Consensus Building: Tanzania's PRSP, 1998–2001." *Journal of Modern African Studies,* 45, 2: 233–251.

Hutchcroft, Paul. 1998. *Booty Capitalism: The Politics of Banking in the Philippines.* Ithaca: Cornell University Press.

————. 2001. "Centralization and Decentralization in Administration and Politics: Assessing Territorial Dimensions of Authority and Power." *Governance* 14 (1) (January): 23–53.

Ibrahim, Jibrin. 2007. "Nigeria's 2007 Elections: The Fitful Path to Democratic Citizenship." Special Report No. 182, US Institute of Peace, January.

IDA (International Development Association) and IMF. 2006. "Review of Low-Income Country Debt Sustainability Framework and Implications of the MDRI." Washington, DC, March 27.

IDD (International Development Department) and Associates. 2006. *Evaluation of General Budget Support: Synthesis Report.* University of Birmingham.

IMF (International Monetary Fund). 2001. "Conditionality in Fund Supported Programmes—Policy Issues." Washington, DC, February.

————. 2007. *Liberia: Second Review of Performance Under the Staff-Monitored Program and New Program for 2007.* Washington, DC, January 18.

IMF, Liberia. 2005a. *Liberia: 2005 Article IV Consultation.* Country Report No. 05/166.

————. 2005b. *Liberia: Selected Issues and Statistical Appendix.* Country Report No. 05/167.

————. 2006a. *First Review of Performance Under the Staff-Monitored Program.* Country Report No. 06/412.

————. 2006b. *Liberia: 2006 Article IV Consultation and Staff-Monitored Program.* Country Report No. 06/166.

————. 2007. *Second Review of Performance Under the Staff-Monitored Program.* Country Report No. 07/49.

IMF and World Bank. 2004. "Debt Sustainability in Low-Income Countries: Further Considerations on an Operational Framework and Policy Implications." Working Paper, September 10.

International Budget Project. 2001. *A Guide to Budget Work for NGOs.* Washington, DC.

International Campaign to Ban Landmines. 2006. *Landmine Monitor Report 2006* (Canada).

International Crisis Group. 2004. *Liberia and Sierra Leone: Rebuilding Failed States,* Africa Report No. 87, December 8.

————. 2006. *Liberia: Resurrecting the Justice System.* Africa Report No. 107, April 6.

Ippolito-O'Donnell, Gabriela. 2006. "Political Clientelism and the Quality of Democracy." Paper presented at the Twentieth World Congress of the International Political Science Association, Fukuoka, Japan, July 9–13.

IRIN (Integrated Regional Information Networks). 2007a. "Africa: Donors Call the Shots in HIV/AIDS Sector." February 21. http://www.plusnews.org/AIDSreport.asp?ReportID=6711 (accessed March 21).

————. 2007b. "Liberia: Refugee Returns Creating Ethnic 'Time Bomb.'" http://www.irinnews.org/Report.aspx?ReportId=70055 (accessed February 2007).

Jackson, Penny. 2005. "Briefing: The Commission for Africa, Gleneagles, Brussels, and Beyond." *African Affairs* 104 (417) (October): 657–664.

Jalal, Ayesha. 1995. *Democracy and Authoritarianism in South Asia: A Comparative and Historical Perspective.* Cambridge: Cambridge University Press.

Jenkins, R., and A. M. Goetz. 1999. "Accounts and Accountability: Theoretical Implications of the Right-to-Information Movement in India." *Third World Quarterly* 20 (3): 603–622.

Johnson-Sirleaf, Ellen. 2006. Speech to the US Congress, delivered March 15, 2006.

Joseph, Richard. 1987. *Democracy and Prebendal Politics in Nigeria: The Rise and Fall of the Second Republic.* New York: Cambridge University Press.

————. 1998. "Africa, 1990–1997: From Abertura to Closure." *Journal of Democracy* 9 (2): 3–17.

————. 2002. "Smart Partnerships and African Development: A New Strategic Framework." Special Report, US Institute of Peace, May.

————. 2003. "Africa's Predicament and the Academy." *Chronicle of Higher Education,* March 7.

————. 2008. "Progress and Retreat in Africa: Challenges of a 'Frontier Region.'" *Journal of Democracy* 19 (2): 94–108.

Joseph, Richard, and Darren Kew. 2008. "Nigeria Confronts Obasanjo's Legacy." *Current History* 107 (708): 167–173.

Kang, David. 2002. *Crony Capitalism: Corruption and Development in South Korea and the Philippines.* New York: Cambridge University Press.

Kaufmann, Daniel, et al. 2005. "Nigeria in Numbers—The Governance Dimension: Moving in the Right Direction, Opportunity over the Next Year." Washington, DC: World Bank. http://worldbank.org/wbi/governance/.

Kaufmann, Daniel, Aart Kraay, and Massimo Mastruzzi. 2005. "Governance Mat-

ters IV: New Data, New Challenges." Washington, DC: World Bank. http://
www.worldbank.org/wbi/governance.

———. 2006. "Governance Matters V: Aggregate and Individual Governance Indicators for 1996–2005." Washington, DC: World Bank. http://siteresources
.worldbank.org/INTWBIGOVANTCOR/Resources/1740479-1150402582357/
2661829-1158008871017/gov_matters_5_no_annex.pdf.

Kennedy, Elizabeth A. 2007. "Ex-President Hit with Graft Claims." http://www
.forbes.com/feeds/ap/2007/08/31/ap4072647.html.

Kenya, Republic of. 1966. *Report of the Maize Commission of Enquiry.* Nairobi:
Government Printers.

Kew, Darren. 2004. "The 2003 Elections in Nigeria: Not Credible, but Acceptable."
In Robert I. Rotberg, ed., *Crafting the New Nigeria: Strengthening the Nation.*
Boulder: Lynne Rienner.

———. 2005. "Building Democracy in Twenty-First-Century Africa: Two Africas,
One Solution." *Seton Hall Journal of Diplomacy and International Relations*
(Winter–Spring): 149–161.

———. 2008. *Classrooms of Democracy: Civil Society Groups, Conflict Resolution,
and Building Democracy in Nigeria.*

Kew, Darren, Jenna Luche, and Dawn Traut. 2004. "Nigeria: Civil Society Assessment." USAID Report, March.

Killick, Tony. 1998. *Aid and the Political Economy of Policy Change.* London:
Routledge and Overseas Development Institute.

———. 2004. "Politics, Evidence, and the New Aid Agenda," *Development Policy
Review* 22 (1): 5–29.

———. 2005. "The Politics of Ghana's Budgetary System." Policy Brief No. 2, Centre for Democratic Development and Overseas Development Institute, Accra.

Koeberle, Stefan, Zoran Stavreski, and Jan Wallise, eds. 2006. *Budget Support as
More Effective Aid? Recent Experiences and Emerging Lessons.* Washington
DC: World Bank.

Kull, Steven. 1995. *Americans and Foreign Aid.* College Park: PIPA, School of
Public Affairs, University of Maryland.

Lancaster, Carol. 2005. "Development in Africa 2005: The Good, the Bad, the
Ugly." *Current History* 104 (May): 222–227.

———. 2006. *Foreign Aid: Diplomacy, Development, Domestic Politics.* Chicago:
University of Chicago Press.

Lawson, A., and D. Booth. 2004. *Evaluation Framework for General Budget Support.* London: Overseas Development Institute.

Lawson, A., D. Booth, M. Msuya, S. Wangwe, and T. Williamson. 2005. *Does General Budget Support Work? Evidence from Tanzania.* London: Overseas Development Institute.

Lawson, A., and L. Rakner. 2005. *Understanding Patterns of Accountability in Tanzania: Final Synthesis Report.* Oxford and Bergen: Oxford Policy Management
and Christian Michelsen Institute.

Leonard, David K., and Scott Straus. 2003. *Africa's Stalled Development: International Causes and Cures.* Boulder: Lynne Rienner.

Liberia, Government of. 2006a. *Governance and Economic Management Assistance
Program (GEMAP) Status Report: Year 1.*

———. 2006b. *150-Day Action Plan: A Working Document for a New Liberia.*

———. 2007a. *Civil Service Reform in Liberia: An Overview.* Liberia Partners
Forum, Washington, DC, February 13–14.

————. 2007b. *Peace and Security—Reaching a "Steady State."* Liberia Partners Forum, Washington, DC, February 13–14.

Liberia, Government of, Liberians United for Reconciliation and Democracy, Movement for Democracy in Liberia, and Political Parties. 2003. *Comprehensive Peace Agreement.* Accra, Ghana, August 18.

Liberia, Government of, United Nations, World Bank, and International Monetary Fund. 2006. *Interim Poverty Reduction Strategy (Final Draft),* Monrovia, January.

Liberia, Government of, and United Nations Development Programme. 2006. *National Human Development Report, Liberia 2006: Mobilizing Capacity for Reconstruction and Development.*

Liberia, Republic of. 2004. *Millennium Development Goals Report.* MDG Report, Monrovia, September. http://www.lr.undp.org/Liberia%20MDGR%202004.pdf.

Liebenow, J. Gus. 1987. *Liberia: The Quest for Democracy.* Bloomington: Indiana University Press.

Lockwood, M. 2005. *The State They're In: An Agenda for International Action on Poverty in Africa.* Rugby: ITDG Publishing.

Mackay, Keith. 2006."Institutionalization of Monitoring and Evaluation Systems to Improve Public Sector Management." *ECD Working Paper Series No. 15.* Washington DC: World Bank.

Mainwaring, Scott. 2003. "Introduction: Democratic Accountability in Latin America." In Scott Mainwaring and Christopher Welna, eds., *Democratic Accountability in Latin America,* Oxford: Oxford University Press, 3–33.

Malena, Carmen, with Reiner Forster and Janmejay Singh. 2004. "Social Accountability: An Introduction to the Concept and Emerging Practice." World Bank Social Development Papers, Participation and Engagement Paper No. 76, Washington, DC, December.

Manning, Nick, and Rick Stapenhurst. 2002. *Strengthening Oversight by Legislatures.* PREM Note 74, World Bank, Washington, DC.

Maravall, José María. 1996. "Accountability and Manipulation." Working Paper No. 92, Instituto Juan March de Estudios e Investigaciones, Madrid.

Mendelson-Forman, Johanna. 2002. "Achieving Socio-Economic Well-Being in Post-Conflict Settings." *Washington Quarterly* 25 (2): 127.

Mintzberg, Henry. 2006. "Developing leaders? Developing Countries?" *Development in Practice* 16, no. 1: 4–14.

Mistry, Percy S. 2005. "Reasons for Sub-Saharan Africa's Development Deficit That the Commission for Africa Did Not Consider." *African Affairs* 104 (417) (October): 665–678.

Moore, Mick. 2004. "Revenues, State Formation, and the Quality of Governance in Developing Countries." *International Political Science Review* 25 (3): 297–319.

Moss, Todd J. 2007. *African Development: Making Sense of the Issues and Actors.* Boulder: Lynne Rienner.

Moss, Todd J., and Arvind Subramanian. 2005. "After the Big Push? Fiscal and Institutional Implications of Large Aid Increases." Working Paper No. 71, Center for Global Development, October.

Moss, Todd, G. Pettersson, and Nicolas van de Walle. 2006. "An Aid-Institutions Paradox? A Review Essay on Aid Dependency and State Building in Sub-Saharan Africa." Working Paper 74, Center for Global Development, Washington, DC.

Moss, Todd, Scott Standley, and Nancy Birdsall. 2004. "Double-Standards, Debt

Treatment, and the World Bank Country Classification: the Case of Nigeria," Working Paper Number 45, Center for Global Development, Washington, DC. http://www.cgdev.org/content/publications/detail/2741/.

Mulgan, Richard. 2000. "'Accountability': An Ever-Expanding Concept?" Australian National University Graduate Program in Public Policy, Discussion Paper No. 72.

Mungai, Ndungi Wa. 1991. "Kenya; One Year After the Saba Saba Uprising." *Green Left Online,* 21 August. Available from *Green Left Weekly,* http://www.green-left.org.au/1991/24/783.

Mwenda, Andrew W. 2007. "Personalizing Power in Uganda." *Journal of Democracy* 18 (3): 23–37.

Ndegwa, Stephen. 1996. *The Two Faces of Civil Society: NGOs and Politics in Africa.* West Hartford: Kumarian.

Njeru, James. 2003. "The Impact of Foreign Aid on Public Expenditure: The Case of Kenya." AERC Research Paper no. 135, Nairobi.

NORAD (Norwegian Agency for Development). 2005. Direct Budget Support, Disbursement Mechanisms and Predictability. Oslo.

North, Douglass C. 1990. *Institutions, Institutional Change, and Economic Performance.* Cambridge: Cambridge University Press.

NTGL (National Transitional Government of Liberia) and United Nations. 2004. *Millennium Development Goals Report 2004.*

NTGL (National Transitional Government of Liberia), United Nations, European Union, Economic Community of West African States, African Union, United States, International Monetary Fund, and World Bank. 2005. *Governance and Economic Management Assistance Program (GEMAP).*

NTGL, UN, and WB (National Transitional Government of Liberia, United Nations, and World Bank). 2004. *Joint Needs Assessment.*

―――. 2005. *Results-Focused Transitional Framework Revision.*

Oddone, F. 2005. "Still Missing the Point: Unpacking the New World Bank/IMF Debt Sustainability Framework," Eurodad, September.

O'Donnell, Guillermo. 1994. "Delegative Democracy." *Journal of Democracy* 5 (1): 55–69.

―――. 2005. "Why the Rule of Law Matters." In Larry Diamond and Leonardo Morlino, eds., *Assessing the Quality of Democracy.* Baltimore: Johns Hopkins University Press, 3–17.

―――. 2007. "The Perpetual Crises of Democracy." *Journal of Democracy* 18 (1): 5–11.

O'Donnell, Guillermo, Jorge Vargas Cullel, and Osvaldo Iazetta, eds. 2004. *The Quality of Democracy: Theory and Applications.* South Bend: University of Notre Dame Press.

OECD (Organization for Economic Cooperation and Development). 2007. "Development Aid from OECD Countries Fell 5.1% in 2006." https://www.oecd.org/document/17/0,3343,en_2649_201185_38341265_1_1_1_1,00.html (accessed September 30, 2007).

OECD/DAC. 2001. *Evaluation Feedback for Effective Learning and Accountability.* Paris: Organization for Economic Cooperation and Development.

―――. 2007. *Working Party on Aid Effectiveness and Donor Practices: Evaluation Follow-up to the Paris Declaration,* Briefing Note for WP-EFF, 9th Meeting, March 8–9 (DCD/DAC/EFF(2007)12). Paris: Organization for Economic Cooperation and Development.

Okonjo-Iweala, Ngozi, Charles C. Soludo, and Mansur Muhtar. 2003. *The Debt*

Trap in Nigeria: Towards a Sustainable Debt Strategy. Trenton: Africa World Press.

Olivier de Sardan, J. P. 1999. "A Moral Economy of Corruption in Africa?" *Journal of Modern African Studies* 37 (1): 25–52.

Olukoshi, Adebayo. 1999. "State, Conflict and Democracy in Africa: The Complex Process of Renewal." In Richard Joseph, ed., *State, Conflict, and Democracy in Africa.* Boulder: Lynne Rienner, 451–466.

Ostrom, Elinor, Clark Gibson, Sujai Shivakumar, and Krister Andersson. 2001. *Aid Incentives and Sustainability: An Institutional Analysis of Development Cooperation,* SIDA Studies in Evaluation 02/01. Stockholm: SIDA.

Ottaway, Marina. 2003. *Democracy Challenged: The Rise of Semi-Authoritarianism.* Washington, DC: Carnegie Endowment.

Peruzzotti, Enrique. 2002. "Towards a New Politics: Citizenship and Rights in Contemporary Argentina." *Citizenship Studies* 6 (1): 77–93.

Pomerantz, Phyllis R. 2004. *Aid Effectiveness in Africa: Developing Trust between Donors and Governments.* Lanham, MD: Lexington Books.

Pugel, James. 2006. *Key Findings from the Nation Wide Survey of Ex-combatants in Liberia: Reintegration and Reconciliation.* February–March. New York: UNDP. http://unddr.org/docs/nation_wide_survey_of_excombatants_in_Liberia_Reintegration_and_Reconciliation.pdf.

Quartey, P. 2005. "Innovative Ways of Making Aid Effective in Ghana: Tied Aid Versus Direct Budgetary Support." *Journal of International Development* 17: 1077–1092.

Rakner, Lise, Luke Mukubvu, Naomi Ngwira, Kimberly Smiddy, and Aaron Schneider. 2004. *The Budget as Theatre: The Formal and Informal Institutional Makings of the Budget Process in Malawi.* Bergen: Christian Michelsen Institute.

Reed, John. 2005. "Angola Plans to Join Fight Against Corruption." *Financial Times,* October 27.

Rice, Andrew. 2005. "Why Is Africa Still Poor?" *Nation,* October 24. http://www.thenation.com/doc/20051024/rice.

Robinson, Pearl T. 1994. "The National Conference Phenomenon in Francophone Africa." *Comparative Studies in Society and History* 36 (3): 575–610.

Rogerson, Andrew. 2005."Aid Harmonization and Alignment: Bridging the Gaps Between Reality and the Paris Reform Agenda," *Development Policy Review* 23 (5): 531–552.

Rogerson, Andrew, and Paolo De Renzio. 2005. "The Seven Habits of Effective Aid: Best Practices, Challenges and Open Questions," Opinions No. 36. London: Overseas Development Institute.

Roth, Guenther. 1968. "Personal Rulership: Patrimonialism and Empire-Building in the New States." *World Politics* 20 (2): 194–206.

Ruggie, John Gerard. 1982. "International Regimes, Transactions, and Change: Embedded Liberalism in the Postwar Economic Order." *International Organization* 36 (2): 379–415.

Sachs, Jeffrey. 2005. *The End of Poverty: Economic Possibilities for Our Times.* New York: Penguin Press.

Sandell, R., A. Sorroza, and Iliana Olivié. 2007. "Immigration: A Challenge Offering Opportunities?" Atlantic Conference of the Chicago Center for Global Affairs, Seville, Spain, March 22–24.

Santiso, Carlos. 2004. "Legislatures and Budget Oversight in Latin America: Strengthening Public Finance Accountability in Emerging Economies." *OECD Journal of Budgeting* 4 (2): 47–76.

Sayeh, Antoinette, Liberian Minister of Finance. 2007. Lecture, "Rebuilding an Economy: Restoring Confidence," Wilton Park conference center, UK. In *Africa: Business, Growth and Poverty Reduction*.

Schacter, Mark. 2001. "When Accountability Fails: A Framework for Diagnosis and Action." *ISUMA* 2 (Summer): 1–9. http://www.isuma.net/v02n02/schacter/schacter _e.shtml.

Schaffer, Frederic C. 1998. *Democracy in Translation: Understanding Politics in an Unfamiliar Culture*. Ithaca: Cornell University Press.

Schedler, Andreas. 1999. "Conceptualizing Accountability." In Andreas Schedler, Larry Diamond, and Marc F. Plattner, eds., *The Self-Restraining State: Power and Accountability in New Democracies*. Boulder: Lynne Rienner, 13–28.

Schick, Allen. 2002. "Can National Legislatures Regain an Effective Voice in Budget Policy?" *OECD Journal of Budgeting* 2 (1): 15–42.

Schmitter, Philippe C. 2005. "The Ambiguous Virtues of Accountability." In Larry Diamond and Leonardo Morlino, eds., *Assessing the Quality of Democracy*. Baltimore: Johns Hopkins University Press, 18–31.

Shirk, Susan. 1993. *The Political Logic of Economic Reform in China*. Berkeley: University of California Press.

Sklar, Richard. 1987. "Developmental Democracy." *Comparative Studies in Society and History,* 29 (4): 686–714.

Sklar, Richard, Ebere Onwudiwe, and Darren Kew. 2006. "Nigeria: Completing Obasanjo's Legacy." *Journal of Democracy* 17 (3): 100–115.

Sleh, Aaron. 2005. "Tumult at Assembly." *New Democrat* (Monrovia), March 16.

Smith, Daniel Jordan. 2007. *A Culture of Corruption: Everyday Deception and Popular Discontent in Nigeria*. Princeton: Princeton University Press.

Smulovitz, Catalina, and Enrique Peruzzotti. 2000. "Societal Accountability in Latin America." *Journal of Democracy* 11 (4): 147–158.

———. 2003. "Societal and Horizontal Controls: Two Cases of a Fruitful Relationship." In Scott Mainwaring and Christopher Welna, eds., *Democratic Accountability in Latin America*. Oxford: Oxford University Press, 309–331.

SPA (Strategic Partnership with Africa). 2006. *Survey of Budget Support 2005*. Washington, DC: World Bank.

Stapenhurst, Rick, and Jack Titsworth. 2001. *Features and Functions of Supreme Audit Institutions*. PREM Note 59, World Bank, Washington, DC.

Steadman, J. Stephen. 1997. "Spoiler Problems in Peace Processes." *International Security* 22 (2): 5–53.

Stern, Marc. 1998. *Development Aid: What the Public Thinks*. United Nations Development Program, New York. http://www.undp.org/ods/pub-working.html.

Strachen, Harry. 1976. *Family and Other Business Groups in Economic Development: The Case of Nicaragua*. New York: Praeger.

Swann, Christopher, and Ed Crooks. 2004. "World Bank: Low Levels of Aid for Poor 'Unacceptable.'" *Financial Times,* April 26.

Swaroop, Vinaya, Shikha K. Jha, and Shantayanan Devarajan. 2000. "Fiscal Effects of Foreign Aid in a Federal System of Governance: The Case of India." *Journal of Public Economics* 77 (2000): 3007–3030.

Tajfel, H., and J. C. Turner. 1986. "The Social Identity Theory of Inter-group Behavior." In S. Worchel and L. W. Austin, eds., *Psychology of Intergroup Relations*. Chicago: Nelson-Hall, 1986.

Takahashi, Chie. 2006. "Partnerships, Learning, and Development: A Case Study from Ghana," *Development in Practice* 16, no. 1: 4–14.

Thakur, Ramesh, Andrew F. Cooper, and John English, eds. 2005. *International*

Commissions and the Power of Ideas. Tokyo: United Nations University Press.

The News (Lagos). 2004. "Article title." March.

Tilly, Charles. 2005. *Trust and Rule.* New York: Cambridge University Press.

Tocqueville, Alexis de. 1956. *Democracy in America.* New York: Mentor.

Transparency International. 2005. *Corruptions Perceptions Index.* www.transparency.org/policy_research/surveys_indeces/cpi/2005.

———. 2006. *Annual Report 2006.* Berlin: Transparency International.

Uganda, Republic of. 2002a. *Judicial Commission of Inquiry into Allegations of Illegal Exploitation of Natural Resources and Other Forms of Wealth in the Democratic Republic of Congo 2000 (May 2001–November 2002).* Legal Notice No 5/2001 as amended. Final Report, November 2002.

———. 2002b. *Government White Paper on the Report of the Judicial Commission of Inquiry into the Purchase of Military Helicopters.* Entebbe: Uganda Printing and Publishing Corporation.

———. 2003. *Report of the Commission of Inquiry into the Ghost Soldiers and Other Malpractices in the UPDF.* Entebbe: Uganda Printing and Publishing Corporation.

UNDPKO (United Nations Department of Peacekeeping Operations) and World Bank. 2005. *UN Peacekeeping and the World Bank: Perceptions of Senior Managers in the Field.*

UNDPKO Peacekeeping Best Practices Section, and World Bank's Fragile States Group. 2006. *Liberia's Governance and Economic Management Assistance Program (GEMAP).*

UNICEF (United Nations Children's Fund). 1999. *Master Plan of Operations.* New York.

United Nations Development Group and World Bank. 2004. *Practical Guide to Multilateral Needs Assessments in Post-Conflict Situations.*

———. 2006. *PCNA Review: Phase One Liberia Needs Assessment Case Study.*

UNDP (United Nations Development Programme). 2005. "Sustaining Post-Conflict Economic Recovery: Lessons and Challenges." BCPR Occasional Paper 1, October.

———. 2006. *Liberian National Human Development Report 2006.* New York: UNDP, 2006.

UNDP and World Bank. 2006. *Peace Processes and State-building: Economic and Institutional Provisions of Peace Agreements.* July.

UNMIL (United Nations Mission in Liberia). 2006. Human Rights Protection Section. "Quarterly Report." New York: United Nations.

UN Millennium Project. 2005. *Investing in Development: A Practical Plan to Achieve the MDGs.* New York.

UN Security Council. 2002. *Report of the Panel of Experts Appointed Pursuant to Security Council Resolution 1395 (2002), Paragraph 4, in Relation to Liberia.* New York, April 11.

———. 2003a. *Resolution on Establishment of the UN Mission in Liberia (UNMIL).* S/RES/1509(2003).

———. 2003b. *Security Council Resolution 1497 on the Situation in Liberia.* S/RES/1497.

———. 2004a. *Report of the Panel of Experts Pursuant to Paragraph 2 of Security Council Resolution 1549 Concerning Liberia.* S/RES/2004/752.

———. 2004b. *Report of the Panel of Experts Pursuant to Paragraph 2 of Security Council Resolution 1549 Concerning Liberia.* S/2004/955.

———. 2006a. "List of Individuals Subject to the Measures Imposed by Paragraph

4 of Security Council Resolution 1521 (2003) Concerning Liberia." New York: United Nations, 15 December.

———. 2006b. *Report of the Panel of Experts Submitted Pursuant to Paragraph 5 of Security Council Resolution 1689 (2006) Concerning Liberia.* New York: United Nations, December 15.

UN, World Bank, and United States. 2004. "Proceedings of the International Reconstruction Conference for Liberia."

Unwin, Tim. 2004. "Beyond Budgetary Support: Pro-poor Development Agendas for Africa." *Third World Quarterly* 25 (8): 1501–1523.

USAID (US Agency for International Development). 2002. "Foreign Aid in the National Interest." Washington, DC. http://www.usaid.gov/fani/ (accessed September 30, 2007).

———. 2004. *Foreign Aid in the National Interest: Promoting Freedom, Security, and Opportunity.* Washington, DC.

———. 2005a. *Democracy and Governance Assessment: Republic of Uganda, 2005.* Washington, DC.

———. 2005b. *Fragile States Strategy.* Washington, DC. http://www.usaid.gov/policy/2005_fragile_states_strategy.pdf (accessed June 2006).

van de Walle, Nicolas. 1999. *African Economies and the Politics of Permanent Crisis, 1979–1999.* New York: Cambridge University Press.

———. 2001. *African Economies and the Politics of Permanent Crisis, 1979–1999.* Cambridge: Cambridge University Press.

———. 2005. *Overcoming Stagnation in Aid-Dependent Countries.* Washington, DC: Center for Global Development.

Waldman, Peter. 2004."Evangelicals Give US Foreign Policy an Activist Tinge." Associated Press, MSNBC, http://msnbc.msn.com/id/5068634/.

Wall, Norman W. 2005. "Stealing from the Poor to Care for the Rich." *New York Times,* December 14.

Wallensteen, Peter, Mikael Eriksson, and Daniel Strandow. 2006. *Sanctions for Conflict Prevention and Peace Building: Lessons Learned from Côte d'Ivoire and Liberia.* Uppsala, Sweden: Uppsala University.

Wallis, William. 2008. "The Bounty of Africa." *Financial Times,* February 16–17.

Wang, V., and L. Rakner. 2005. *The Accountability Functions of Supreme Audit Institutions in Malawi, Uganda and Tanzania.* CMI Report. Bergen: Christian Michelsen Institute.

Wax, Emily. 2005. "Underfunded and Overrun, 'Harvard of Africa' Struggles to Teach." *Washington Post,* October 29.

Wehner, J. 2004. "Back from the Sidelines: Redefining the Contribution of Legislatures to the Budget Cycle." Working Paper, World Bank, Washington, DC.

Whitaker, Jennifer Seymour. 1988. *How Can Africa Survive?* New York: Harper and Row.

White House. 2002. "The National Security Strategy of the United States." http://www.whitehouse.gov/nsc/nss.pdf (accessed September 30, 2007).

Willame, Jean Claude. 1972. *Patrimonialism and Political Change in the Congo.* Stanford: Stanford University Press.

Williamson, T. 2006. "General Budget Support and Public Financial Management Reform: Emerging Lessons from Tanzania and Uganda." In S. Koeberle, Z. Stavreski, and J. Walliser, eds., *Budget Support as More Effective Aid? Recent Experiences and Emerging Lessons.* Washington, DC: World Bank.

World Bank. 1989. *Sub-Saharan Africa: From Crisis to Sustainable Growth.* Washington, DC: World Bank.

————. 2003. *Annual Review of Development Effectiveness: The Effectiveness of Bank Support for Policy Reform.* Washington, DC: World Bank.

————. 2004a. *World Development Report, 2004: Making Services Work for Poor People.* Washington DC.

World Bank. 2004b. *Annual Review of Development Effectiveness: The World Bank's Contributions to Poverty Reduction.* Washington, DC.

————. 2005a. *Capacity Building in Africa: An OED Evaluation of World Bank Support.* Washington, DC: World Bank Operations Evaluations Department.

————. 2005b. "Good Practice Note for Development Policy Lending: Budget Support Groups and Joint Financing Arrangements." Washington, DC. June.

————. 2005c. "The Political Economy of Uganda: The Art of Managing a Donor-Financed Neo Patrimonial State." Washington, DC. November 20.

————. 2006a. *Annual Review of Development Effectiveness.* Washington, DC: Independent Evaluation Group. http://www.worldbank.org/ieg/arde2006?intcmp=5308777.

————. 2006b. *World Development Report 2007: Development and the Next Generation.* Washington, DC.

World Bank and UNDP (United Nations Development Programme). 2006. *Phase II: WB/UNDP Study on State-building and Peace Agreements: Case Study Liberia.* Washington, DC, and New York.

Wreh, Tuan. 1976. *The Love of Liberty: The Rule of President William V. S. Tubman in Liberia, 1944–1971.* London: C. Hurst.

Yancy, Ernest Jerome. 1954. *Historical Lights of Liberia's Yesterday and Today.* New York: Herman Jaffe.

Young, Crawford. 1996. "Africa: An Interim Balance Sheet." *Journal of Democracy* 7 (3): 53–68.

Zakaria, Fareed. 1997. "The Rise of Illiberal Democracy." *Foreign Affairs* 76 (November): 22–42.

THE CONTRIBUTORS

Joel Barkan is professor emeritus of political science at the University of Iowa and a senior associate at the Center for Strategic and International Studies. A specialist on democratization and governance across Anglophone Africa, he served as the first regional democracy and governance adviser for eastern and southern Africa at USAID. His most recent book is *Beyond Capitalism Versus Socialism in Kenya and Tanzania.*

Michael Bratton is distinguished professor of political science and African studies at Michigan State University and also a founder and the current executive director of Afrobarometer, a cross-national survey research project on public opinion in Africa. His numerous publications include *Public Opinion, Democracy, and Markets in Africa* (with Robert Mattes and E. Gyimah-Boadi).

Thomas M. Callaghy is professor of political science at the University of Pennsylvania. His current research focuses on the politics of debt. His recent publications include "Innovation in the Sovereign Debt Regime: From the Paris Club to Enhanced HIPC and Beyond" and "The Paris Club and International Economic Governance: Double Crisis and Debt" in Vinod K. Aggarwal and Brigitte Granville, eds., *Sovereign Debt: Origins, Crises, and Restructuring.*

Paolo de Renzio is pursuing doctoral studies in the Department of Politics and International Relations at the University of Oxford. His research focuses on the interplay between aid policies and public-finance management systems in developing countries. He served for six years as an economist and policy adviser in Papua New Guinea's Ministry of Finance and earlier as a UNDP public-sector specialist.

Vivian Lowery Derryck is senior vice president and director of public-private partnerships at the Academy for Educational Development. She previously served as the assistant administrator for Africa at USAID, where she was the senior government official directing foreign assistance to Africa.

Larry Diamond is senior fellow at the Hoover Institution, coeditor of the *Journal of Democracy*, and codirector of the International Forum for Democratic Studies of the National Endowment for Democracy. He is also a professor of political science and sociology (by courtesy) and coordinator of the Democracy Program of the Center on Democracy, Development, and the Rule of Law at Stanford University. His latest books are *The Spirit of Democracy: The Struggle to Build Free Societies Throughout the World* and *Squandered Victory: The American Occupation and the Bungled Effort to Bring Democracy to Iraq*.

Alexandra Gillies is based at the Centre of International Studies at the University of Cambridge, where she is conducting doctoral research on African government participation in oil-sector governance reform (with a focus on Nigeria). Previously, she was assistant director of Northwestern University's Program of African Studies.

Ian Hopwood has worked with UNICEF since 1972 in a variety of field positions in Africa and Asia and is currently the UNICEF representative in Senegal. He headed the UNICEF Headquarters Evaluation Office in 1996–2000 and has a long-standing interest in policy reform and aid effectiveness, with a special emphasis on health and education.

Richard Joseph is John Evans Professor of International History and Politics at Northwestern University and a senior fellow (nonresident) at the Brookings Institution. Formerly, he was professor of political science at Emory University and director of the African Governance Program at the Carter Center. His publications include *Radical Nationalism in Cameroon; Democracy and Prebendal Politics in Nigeria; State, Conflict, and Democracy in Africa;* and the Africa Demos series produced by the Carter Center.

Darren Kew is assistant professor in the Dispute Resolution Program at the University of Massachusetts, Boston. Kew studies the connection between democratic institution building in Africa and the development of political cultures that support democracy, with a special focus on the role of civil society groups. He has worked with the Council on Foreign Relations Center for Preventative Action and consulted for the United Nations, USAID, the US State Department, and several NGOs.

Carol Lancaster is associate professor of government and director of the Mortara Center for International Studies at Georgetown University. She has served as deputy administrator of USAID and deputy assistant secretary of state for African affairs and is a member of the UN Secretary-General's Panel on International Support for NEPAD. Her publications include *Organizing US Aid; Aid to Africa; Transforming Foreign Aid;* and *Foreign Aid: Diplomacy, Development, Domestic Politics.*

Carolyn Logan is associate director of Afrobarometer and assistant professor in the Department of Political Science and in the African Studies Center at Michigan State University. Her research focuses on political development in Africa, especially in East Africa and the Horn, and the role of traditional leaders.

Peter Anyang' Nyong'o, secretary-general of Kenya's reformist Orange Democratic Movement, was appointed minister of medical services in the coalition government formed in April 2008. Previously, he has been associate professor of political science at the University of Nairobi, a member of the Kenyan Parliament, and minister of development and national planning. He has written numerous books and articles, including the forthcoming *A Leap Into the Future: The Political Economy of Change in Kenya.*

John F. E. Ohiorhenuan is deputy assistant administrator and senior deputy director of the Bureau for Crisis Prevention and Recovery at UNDP. Previously, he served as UN resident coordinator in South Africa, where he produced the *South Africa Human Development Report* for 2003. Prior to joining UNDP, he was a professor of economics at the University of Ibadan in Nigeria.

William Reno is associate professor of political science at Northwestern University. His publications include *Corruption and State Politics in Sierra Leone, Warlord Politics and African States,* and the forthcoming *Evolution of Warfare in Independent Africa.* Currently, he is conducting research on the local organization of militias and other armed groups in the context of wider conflicts, with a focus on Sierra Leone, Nigeria's Niger Delta, Somalia, and the Caucasus region of the former Soviet Union.

INDEX

19–23; emergence and importance of, 7–8; general budget support, 20, 29(n9); potential benefits and actual results, 74–78; PRSP funding, 108; smart versus dumb, 83–84; Tanzania and Uganda, 29(n6), 78–83, 85(n11); as vehicle for donor-client partnerships, 72–74; World Bank "country portfolio," 68(tab.)
Bureaucratic Caesarism, 151, 152
Burkina Faso: budget support figures, 68(tab.); debt burdens before and after HIPC and MDRI debt relief, 94(tab.)
Bush, Mary, 62
Bush administration, 28, 89, 95, 235
Business Action for Africa, 56
Business registrations, Liberia, 141(n2)

Cameroon: stalled development linked to governance, 231
Canada: debt relief to Iraq, 90; gross ODA, 2007, 249(tab.); net ODA, share of debt relief grants, 2007, 248(tab.); net ODA as percentage of GNI, 250(fig.); net ODA by country, 2007, 247(tab.); net ODA in billions of US dollars, 250(fig.)
Capacity building: budget reforms and domestic accountability, 23–24; civil society's role in budget oversight, 27; Commission for Africa priorities, 52, 53–54; donor ambivalence toward civil society partnerships and, 211–212; establishing partnerships for, 240–241; Liberia's corruption damaging, 151; reconstituting Liberia's social and human capital, 133–134; supreme audit institutions, 25–26
Capacity Building in Africa (World Bank report), 23–24
Cape Verde: budget support figures, 68(tab.); vertical accountability, 190
Capital flight: aid seepage, 234; Liberia, 123, 154
CARE, 29(n9)
Carnegie Commission on Preventing Deadly Conflict, 50
Carnegie Foundation, 241

Carter Center (Atlanta, Georgia), 229–230
Center for Global Development (CGD), 95, 98
Chama cha Mapinduzi (CCM; Tanzania), 81, 85(n8)
Cheating, corruption as, 164
Child Survival/Global Health and Development Assistance, 40, 41
China: accelerating penetration of Africa, 261; donors ignoring governance deficiencies, 234; increasing interest in aid involvement, 7, 17; net ODA by country, 2007, 247(tab.); as obstacle to Blair Commission implementation, 58–59; organization of corruption, 159–160
Chirac, Jacques, 90
Christian Right, 7, 46–47, 48(n5)
Citizens: accountability transcending elections, 184–187; confidence levels in elections, 187–189; delivery of vertical accountability, 196–200; making government accountable to, 12; nonelection venues of vertical accountability, 189–196; understanding of accountability, 182–183
Civil service: defining corruption, 165; Kenya's colonial corruption, 167–168
Civil society: budget policies role, 26–27, 29(n10); countering corruption, 212; demanding service delivery, 29(n11); donor agendas, 211–213; donor–civil society relations in Nigeria, 207–227; donor-IP-civil society hierarchy, 215–216, 215(fig.); implications of donor–civil society relationships, 221–223; increasing government accountability, 234; Liberia's social decay, 123–124; market forces and civil society opportunism, 213; neopatrimonial and hierarchical IP approaches, 222(tab.); neopatrimonialism in donor–civil society relationships, 221–223; PRSP involvement, 109; reconstituting Liberia's social and human capital, 133–134; strategies for democratic donor–civil society relationships, 213–216, 223–227;

ABOUT THE BOOK

DESPITE HUNDREDS of billions of dollars spent on foreign aid to sub-Saharan Africa, a sure path to growth and development has not yet been found—and each new heralded approach has crumbled amid regrets and recriminations. The authors of *Smart Aid for African Development* provide critical assessments of the main components of foreign assistance and examine how smarter use can be made of available resources to advance growth and democracy, rebuild war-torn societies, and reduce the crippling poverty that underlies the continent's fierce conflicts.

Richard Joseph is John Evans Professor of International History and Politics at Northwestern University. **Alexandra Gillies** is based at the University of Cambridge, where she is conducting research on oil-sector governance reform in Africa.